Virginia S...

SEEKING LOVE AND ACCEPTANCE ON A PATH OF ADVERSITY

Susan Kelly

authorHOUSE®

AuthorHouse™
1663 Liberty Drive
Bloomington, IN 47403
www.authorhouse.com
Phone: 1-800-839-8640

©2010 Susan Kelly. All rights reserved.

No part of this book may be reproduced, stored in a retrieval system, or transmitted by any means without the written permission of the author.

First published by AuthorHouse 1/13/2010

ISBN: 978-1-4490-5077-1 (e)
ISBN: 978-1-4490-5076-4 (sc)

Printed in the United States of America
Bloomington, Indiana

This book is printed on acid-free paper.

Introduction

Mary Sullivan was born illegitimate, and partially blind. She was adopted from a Catholic orphanage by a fanatical, middle aged couple with no children of their own. Because of Mrs. Sullivan's health problems, and inexperience with small children, Mary was volleyed back and forth between the infant home, and her adopted home. She had bonded with one of the nuns, and preferred the infant home to the Sullivan home. This caused a lot of anger and resentment; which resulted in years of physical, verbal, and psychological abuse. Mary was set along a path of institutions, and more abuse.

When she was twelve Mary was diagnosed as semi autistic. Because of this and her compulsion to run away, she wound up in a very controversial treatment center up North.

Then at age seventeen Mary received her big break, when she was enrolled in the Perkins School for the blind in Massachusetts. She fell in love with the school, and did well, but her emotional scars from her past got in the way frequently. After two years she reluctantly graduated, and stumbled head long in to the adult world, not knowing what she was doing.

It wasn't until she was in her forties that Mary was able to summon the courage to locate her biological family. Her real mother had already died, but her family acknowledged, and accepted her. Although Mary continued to struggle with emotional issues, learning about her roots, and being accepted in to her family helped her to feel whole. She had found her way home. This book is for people who have been beaten down by the system, but not beaten.

The author would like to thank her siblings, and her friends for their support.

Chapter One

Expulsion

Mary stood staring out the living room window. It was a cold February morning in 1968. She wore her snow suit and boots. She was eagerly waiting for the school bus. Her mother informed her that morning that she would not be returning to school. "You managed to get yourself expelled from this school too!" she told her in an angry hiss. Mary's father was sleeping late because he was tired from working over time. For once Mary's mother was more concerned about being quiet, then with punishing her daughter.

Mary couldn't believe that she had been expelled from first grade. She wouldn't believe it! She stubbornly waited for the bus to pick her up and take her to Meeting St School, where she had been going for the last five months. Her school was for children with disabilities. Mary had been visually impaired since birth. Some of the students in her class had problems with their sight. Others were in wheel chairs. In the beginning Mary did well in her class. She liked Miss Cameron, her teacher and she liked her class mates. She was learning to read and do simple math problems. Then as in the past, her hyper activity, and aversion to rules and boundaries caught up with her. Soon she was throwing tantrums in class, and going to visit the younger students during recess, when she was supposed to stay in the school yard. She became obsessed with a bus driver, named Mr. Tully. He was a jolly, older man who drove some of the preschool students. Mary liked him so much that she followed him and helped him unload the afternoon students and then get the morning students ready to go home. She hoped that Mr. Tully would like her enough to take her home with him. She developed a fantasy in which he became her adopted father. One of his passengers, a blonde, three year old girl, named Alice became her adopted sister; the three of them lived happily ever after. When Mr. Tully didn't return her feelings, or contradict her teacher when she stopped Mary from hanging out with him, Mary gradually began to turn against him. The last straw was when the kindergarten teacher, who sat with Miss Cameron during lunch, went outside and snatched Mary and ran in the building as soon as Mr. Tully's bus arrived. Mary was enraged! She struggled in the teacher's arms and managed to punch her in the mouth, loosening her tooth in the process. When told of the teacher's loose tooth, Mary felt no remorse. Instead she was gleefully triumphant.

Mary was average height for a six year old. She was thin and had long medium blonde hair. Unlike other little girls, Mary wore dresses and skirts that came down to her knees. She didn't like her clothes, and was jealous of the girls in preschool because they often wore pants to school. She was tired of being expected to look like a little lady. So after her fight with the kindergarten teacher, Mary asked Billy, her best friend in first grade, to cut her hair. Billy, a cheerful boy with a crew cut happily grabbed the scissors and chopped away Mary's blonde locks. A few minutes later Miss Cameron returned from accompanying the kindergarten teacher to the bathroom.. She took one look at Billy's work, and screamed! Her purse fell to the floor as she ran to grab the scissors away from him. Mary went home with her hair in various lengths; the longest of her hair barely reached her collar. Her devastated mother had to cut it more in order to even it out. When she was finished, Mary's now brown hair was in a pixie style which came to just below her ears. She felt liberated. If only she could get rid of her clothes and go live somewhere else!

The following day Mary came down with the flu. She was ill for several days. She could hear her father when he called the school to tell them that she was still sick. She hadn't yet recovered when she noticed that he stopped calling the school.

Mary waited a long time by the window. Then she sadly turned away, and removed her snow suit. She felt bad about being expelled this time. For the most part, she had really been trying at this school.

Young as she was, Mary already had quite a history. She was born in April of 1961. She was given up for adoption and placed in St. Vincent's infant home, in Providence. Although Mary was given to a middle aged couple by a social worker who was impressed with their money and their strong Catholic beliefs, she spent the first five years of her life being carted back and forth between the Catholic orphanage and her new home. Every time Mary had a problem, minor or major, or whenever her new mother didn't feel well, she was sent back to the orphanage for a week or sometimes a month or more. She was very close to one of the nuns there. Sister Jane Frances had been at St Vincent's infant home for three years when Mary was placed there. When it was discovered that Mary couldn't see well as an infant, she was placed in the care of this particular nun. She was a young, fun loving woman, who had a mischievous side to her. She and some of the other nuns sometimes sneaked out in the evenings, often taking Mary with them. Sister Jane doted on Mary, and the little girl adored her! They took to each other right away. They were like mother and daughter. Sister Jane taught Mary a dance, called the mashed potato when she was two. She also taught her to say things like "See ya later alligator" and "After awhile crocodile". When Mary was three she was at St Vincent's for several months. Mrs. Sullivan had under gone surgery, and she was suffering from complications. During that time Mary experienced things she never experienced at home. She happily ran through the corridors at top speed, she played, unsupervised on the elevator, until she got stuck in it and wouldn't go near it...unless someone held her. She sneaked down to the kitchen and helped herself to bananas, her favorite snack. In an attempt to keep Mary on the straight and narrow, Sister Jane often said "Don't get in to mischief Mary. Remember, I am everywhere" Sometimes Mary sat on the mother superior's lap in the dining room where the nuns ate, and played with the dinner bell. She went to the office to visit the secretaries who worked at the home. But what meant the most to the little girl was being held and carried by Sister Jane. Her parents hugged her, but they didn't carry her or hold her on their laps. They wanted her to be a big girl...at least as far as physical contact was concerned. In other ways they seemed to want her to be helpless. They wouldn't let her run anywhere. She couldn't play outside. And when they went anywhere, she always had to walk in between them, holding both of their hands. Even in the car, she couldn't have any independence. She had to sit up front, between them. They dressed her in old fashioned longish dresses and made her hold a prayer book in church even though she was too young to read. They had her reciting lengthy Catholic prayers by the age of two. Most of her baby, and toddler photos showed her kneeling with her hands folded in prayer. Often a pair of rosary beads was draped over them. It was when she was three that she learned that she was adopted. One of the nuns, or child care workers explained the situation to her. She had been asking a lot of questions; comparing herself to the orphans. Since she was adopted, most of the nuns treated her like a visitor, and doted on her. She loved this.

Once back at home; Mary was no longer the manageable toddler she had been. She begged, cried, and demanded to be sent back to St Vincent's. She not only missed the freedom there, she missed Sister Jane and the love she received from her. She hated her parents for not letting her be where she was happy. When her demands weren't met, Mary began to inform the Sullivans that they weren't her parents and therefore didn't have to do what they said. Her mother responded by being violent with the defiant Mary. She shouted at her, smacked her around, shook her and harnessed her to her cot where she proceeded to spatter her with holy water. She told her she was an evil child, as she waved a crucifix in her face. She was very jealous of the bond that existed between her daughter and the young nun. In spite of the anger Mary's mother had toward her and Sister Jane, who she felt had turned Mary against her, by winning her love at an early age; Mary was sent back to St Vincent's when she was four and again when she was five. This final visit was very brief, only a little over a week. Mary was aware of this and it filled her with a mixture of sadness and panic! She was aware that life at St. Vincent's wasn't perfect. Although the nuns were kind to her, especially Sister Jane, some of the child care workers were abusive with the children there. Mary's first memory of her time at the orphanage was of being in the tub. A thin, angry looking nurse was pushing her head under the water and bathing her in a rough way. Mary was screaming in rage! The nurse didn't holler at her. Instead, she hauled the toddler out of the tub and put her in a dark room without drying her off or dressing her. Eventually Sister Jane found and comforted her.

One of the child care workers resented the special attention that Mary was receiving from Sister Jane She tried to convince her that she was spoiling the child. Fortunately Sister Jane often ignored the feelings of guilt that were being instilled in her, and continued to dote on Mary anyway. So, the child care worker punished Mary whenever she had the chance. Once or twice Mary had accidents. When this happened, the child care worker would tie her to the potty, and make her sit in the middle of the play room. She frequently spanked her for being fresh, and willful.

In spite of this, Mary desperately didn't want to go home. What could she do? She had to think of something. Not realizing that telling the truth about her home life would have been sufficient, Mary concocted an outrageous story. One night Sister Jane entered her room and found Mary curled up in her bed crying. Because Mary used to keep the other children awake at night her crib was moved in to the nun's bedroom.(The children at St. Vincent's were kept in tall, white iron cribs up through the age of five) When asked what was wrong, Mary said that her adoptive parents locked her in the cellar and tied her up in the playpen and placed a net over the top of it. This information was related to the priest who ran the orphanage. Father McGovern was a tall man with dark hair, and a ruddy complexion. He was very strict, but had a fun, caring side to him. Alarmed, he promptly met with the Sullivans who denied everything, and threatened to take him to court if Mary wasn't given to them immediately. He tried to make them see that they weren't offering their little girl a stable, secure home life. They promised to change. Mary was reluctantly given back to them.

The only thing that changed was that Mary no longer had the occasional visits to St Vincent's to look forward to. Still clinging to hope, Mary told her mother that Sister Jane would be taking her to school on her first day. Mrs. Sullivan became indignant and insisted that she or her husband would take Mary to school. "But she promised!" cried Mary. "I was scared of starting kindergarten and Sister Jane told me that I shouldn't be scared. She said don't worry Mary; when its time for you to start school; I'll take you there myself." Mrs. Sullivan called St. Vincent's and talked to the Mother Superior. When Sister Jane was put on the phone she seemed shocked. Mary eagerly grasped the big, black receiver and pressed it to her mouth. But when she reminded her friend of her promise Sister Jane denied ever making it. "Mary I never said that!" She laughed and teased Mary, jokingly referring to her as crazy. Mary felt shocked and betrayed. Why was Sister Jane behaving like this? Could Mary have misunderstood her? She was so sure that Sister Jane had promised. Mrs. Sullivan had no doubts about the situation. "Face it kiddo, your girl friend is a liar!" (She often referred to

Sister Jane as Mary's girl friend when she was angry) "She lied to avoid being reprimanded." pointed out Mrs. Sullivan righteously. Before long she had Mary believing her. She promised to take Mary back to St. Vincent's so that she could confront Sister Jane face to face. But this confrontation never came to pass. Mrs. Sullivan could break promises, but Heaven help Mary if she did.

Mr. Sullivan was at work most of the time. He was a tall thin man in his mid fifties who wore black framed glasses and had dark grey hair. He was an insurance adjuster. Besides office work, his job often took him on the road as he interviewed clients about their accidents. At home he was a passive man who never contradicted his wife, whom he adored. He expected Mary to give her the unconditional devotion that he bestowed upon her. Aside from this, he let Mrs. Sullivan be in charge of Mary's up bringing. He only interfered when she was out of control and hitting the child. On Fridays he would stop by the house to pick up his wife and daughter. They would wait in the car while he interviewed clients in their homes. Mrs. Sullivan carried red lollipops in her big Black Hand bag because she knew that red was her daughter's favorite. She sometimes gave Mary a lollipop to enjoy while they waited. When he was finished for the day, he would take his family out for fish and chips. They always ate them in the car, with newspaper spread across their laps to protect their clothing from the heavy grease.

Mrs. Sullivan was a plump woman of medium height. She was in her early fifties. She wore her wavy, grey, shoulder length hair parted on the side. She touched up her cheeks with blush and was fond of red lip stick. She loved to sew, play the piano, organ, and sing. She had an affectionate, sunny disposition with a touch of assertiveness. However, all too often she would become melancholy and begin sadly to reminisce about the good old days when she worked. One afternoon when Mary was four her mother told her that she now had a baby cousin. Mrs. Sullivan's nephew had married a young teacher. They moved to East Providence. They had a baby girl, named Caroline. Mrs. Sullivan became sad and sentimental as she told Mary that her baby furniture was being given to Caroline. She told her to go with her to the front hallway where the furniture, in big brown boxes was leaning against the walls. Mary was made to kiss each box Goodbye. At other times Mrs. Sullivan would become hostile. Anything could set her off, a look, an innocent remark, or a topic such as death, bathrooms, an adult's age…and as Mary was discovering, any talk of Sister Jane and St. Vincent's.

Along with the Friday evening fish and chips, the Sullivans thought it was fun to stop at various churches to say the Stations of the Cross and light candles and pray. (Back in the sixties churches were still left unlocked all week.) Mary followed her parents as they stopped at each stained glass window to recite a prayer, genuflect and then move to the next window. One day when they were kneeling at the front of the church after lighting candles, Mary spotted a statue of a woman who appeared to be a nun. She pointed and cried out "Look its Saint Sister Jane!" Mrs. Sullivan became livid! She shook Mary and scolded her. She was still angry that Mary had been allowed to carry a small statue of Saint Rita around at St. Vincent's and call it Saint Sister Jane.(Saint Rita was a nun.) After shaking her trembling daughter Mrs. Sullivan told her in an angry hiss that the statue was of Saint Rita, not Sister Jane.

Mary spent most week days cooped up in the house. She played with her numerous toys. The Sullivans were generous. Mary had more clothes and toys then most children did. In the mornings she watched all the kids' shows and sitcoms. In the afternoon Mrs. Sullivan watched the soap operas. Mary had a favorite doll, named Wendy. She was big, with blonde bangs and wore a red suit with a hood that came to a point in back. She was Mary's best friend. She played with Wendy while her mother involved herself in TV drama. One afternoon Mary mimicked one of the women on a soap opera. Her mother took her out to the kitchen and slammed the door in her face! Mrs. Sullivan couldn't let go of the resentment she felt for Sister Jane and Mary. She frequently blew up at her daughter and smacked her. Then she would launch in to an hour long tirade where she brought up all the trouble Mary had caused since she was three. She blamed the nun for spoiling her. Mary still clung to the hope that she might return to the infant home. She started doing things around the house to provoke her mother in to sending her back, but all this got her were more smacks and Holy Water spattered in her tear stained face.

In public Mary frequently became attached to acquaintances, or even strangers, who spoke kindly to her. She would latch on to them and beg them to take her home with them. She was especially found of the receptionist who worked for Dr. Early, the Sullivans family physician. She was a young woman with straight brown hair, who smiled all the time. One day Mary couldn't contain herself. She struck up a conversation with the woman. She told her how much she liked her. "Well I like you too Mary" At this Mary proceeded to beg the woman to take her home with her. The woman smiled her charming smile and gestured toward Mary's parents. Mrs. Sullivan was smiling, but Mary knew that she was angry and would punish her afterward. "I can't take you home. You have nice parents who love you very much" "No- No they don't! I'll be good for you I promise" but it was useless. Mary was dragged from the doctor's office. After they ate their fish one Friday evening Mrs. Sullivan took Mary to a public restroom. Two old women entered and exclaimed over what a cute little girl Mary was. She begged them to stop and talk to her. Mrs. Sullivan dragged her from the restroom. "Wait, hey lady wait! I want to talk to you!" Mrs. Sullivan angrily deposited her yelling daughter in the car and returned to the restroom. Mr. Sullivan, usually so passive, berated Mary for her performance. Several times Mary ran away from her parents in public. One day after being told by her exasperated mother that she could leave if she wanted to,

Mary started walking up the highway trying to hitch a ride. When her father forced her in to the car, Mary was screaming more from fear than anger. Mrs. Sullivan sat glaring at her, her mouth was shut tight, her red lip stick making her mouth look like an angry knife slash. Mary knew that reprisals would soon come.

Despite her rebellion, there were times when Mary was hurting inside to such an extent that she reached out to her mother for comfort. Once in a while Mrs. Sullivan would be in a receptive mood, but usually she saw her daughter's sudden vulnerability as a chance to get even with her. "Get away from me!" she would say venomously. "You don't want me. You want that receptionist from Dr. Early's office. I saw the drawing you did of her. Go cry to that!" Mary did turn to the drawing. Soon she was doing this a lot.

Right after her final visit to St. Vincent's Mary became a patient of Dr. Denton. He was known for his work with children who had Down syndrome, but he also worked with children who had emotional problems like Mary. She was so hyperactive and emotional that she was placed on medication immediately. However it didn't seem to affect her much. Dr. Denton didn't know about the slap-happy woman who was raising Mary, or about the exorcisms she performed on her. He only knew that he had for a patient, a very imaginative and nervous five year old, who was prone to temper tantrums and had already been expelled from nursery school because of them.

The summer when Mary was five the Sullivans bought a small cottage out in Coventry. It was on Iyoho road, and was near a lake. They lived out there until Labor Day weekend. The cottage smelled musty and Mary still had to share a room with her mother, but she was allowed to attend a day camp. Camp Iyoho was just five minutes from the cottage, and was run by an older couple named, Mr. and Mrs. Mantis. On her first day Mary, who had been sitting in the middle up front in the car as usual, ignored Mr. Mc'mantis as he chatted with her parents. She scrambled across her mother's lap and ran toward the play ground. Mr. Mc'mantis called her back to say Goodbye to the Sullivans. Later in the afternoon Mrs. Mc'mantis said that she would be driving Mary home every day. Mary saw this as an opportunity to delay getting home. She pretended not to know where she lived. Mrs. Mc'mantis spent half an hour driving down one dirt road after another. Finally she stopped at her house to call Mrs. Sullivan for directions. She gave Mary a glass of water. Mrs. Sullivan was furious with her daughter. She ranted and raved at her for close to an hour. Oddly enough, one of the things that upset her the most was that Mary didn't ask for a paper cup when the water was offered.

Mary became attached to a young girl named Evelyn. She was fifteen and was a counselor at the camp. She was kind to Mary and knew how to talk to her. Mary was assigned to her as a way to ensure that she wouldn't be disruptive. Mary had a good time at the camp because of Evelyn.

Mr. and Mrs. Sullivan didn't socialize with the neighbors much. In the evenings they sat on the screened in porch and talked. Sometimes Mr. Sullivan went out and bought ice cream for the three of them. Mary had a sweet tooth and loved ice cream. Unfortunately her parents wouldn't let her eat the cone because they were afraid that she would make a mess. As soon as her ice cream was level with the cone one of her parents would say "Alright Mary that's enough" Mary was already learning to hold in her disappointment around them. Still Mary didn't go without sugar. Her parents put sugar on her potatoes and vegetables in order to make her eat them. They also put sugar in her orange juice.

In the fall Mary started attending kindergarten at Gilbert Stuart School in Providence. Gilbert Stuart covered kindergarten through eighth grade. Mary's social worker from State Services for the blind got her enrolled there. The kindergarten was in the basement. Before the enrollment became official Mary and her parents were given a tour of the building. Mary was in awe of the seventh and eighth graders. They seemed almost like adults to her. But what really fascinated Mary was the three story building. The ceilings were high and the corridors were long and caused people's voices and foot steps to echo. The dark floors were shiny and looked good for sliding on. Mary was determined to leave her classroom frequently to explore this marvelous place!

Mary's first day of kindergarten was easy. She participated in all the activities and befriended two little girls. Cheryl was a pretty African American girl who always carried Bazooka bubble gum. She shared some of it with Mary. Debby was Cheryl's friend. She had blonde hair and liked to share her lunch with Mary. They both became good friends of Mary's, but school didn't go smoothly after the first day. Mary grew impatient with all the rules and organized activities. Besides, she had a building to explore. Miss Web was a nice teacher, but she was no push over. Before long she had to stop Mary from excusing herself to use the bathroom so much. Mary had been seen running up and down the stairs and wandering the corridors. She even walked in on a sixth grade class one day. When Miss Web put her foot down with Mary the tantrums began. Cheryl and Debby continued to like her but her behavior shocked them.

One day a substitute came in because Miss Web was sick. She was a crotchety old woman, who irritated Mary to no end. Every time the woman opened her mouth Mary responded by flapping her hand at her in disgust. Before the morning was over Mary and Cheryl were chasing each other around the building, giggling and sliding in their stocking feet down the long corridors. When they returned to the basement Cheryl went back in to the classroom, but Mary sat on the floor and refused. The substitute picked her up and carried her, kicking and screaming, back in to the room. Mary glanced down at her classmates. They were all lined up by the door, and were staring at her open mouthed. Mary didn't like the way they looked at her. She felt like a monstrous villain. As soon as she was set upon her feet, Mary jumped on a table and started dancing. This had been one of her favorite things to do at St. Vincent's. Some of the nuns thought it was cute. Mary hoped her classmates would think her dancing was cute, but they continued to stare at her open mouthed. Mr. Sullivan walked in and found his daughter pink cheeked with disheveled hair dancing on a large table. "Mary what are you doing?" he asked in a shocked, disappointed voice. This was Mr. Sullivan's usual approach to his daughter's misbehaving. It made Mary feel some degree of remorse.

Mary was expelled after only a month. Once again she found herself cloistered in the house with her mother who now had another reason to be angry.

Despite the abuse there were times that Mary wasn't entirely unhappy to be at home. She was allowed to bring a favorite doll in the car. Occasionally she was able to talk her parents in to letting her stay up until seven thirty to watch TV. Her regular bed time was seven o'clock. On Christmas morning she received a bunch of new toys to amuse her. But aside from the Friday evening fish and chips and Sunday morning Mass, Mary spent days on end in the house with a moody woman, and it was often unpleasant for her.

By the time Mary turned six she learned the hard way never to mention her desire to go back to St. Vincent's. One warm sunny Saturday Mary was sitting in the kitchen with her mother. Her father was mowing the lawn and Mary could smell the freshly mowed grass, along with the flowers that were starting to bloom. A nice breeze was blowing through the kitchen. Mary thought that on such a nice day any wish she had would be granted. Informing her mother that she had something to tell her, she climbed on her Yogi Bear hassock and whispered "I want to go back to St. Vincent's" in her mother's ear. Mrs. Sullivan turned and glared at Mary, her red lips sealed tightly. She drew her hand back and delivered such a smack that Mary and the hassock flew backward several feet. Mrs. Sullivan pulled her crying daughter from the floor and put her in her cot. After harnessing her in; she delivered two more smacks to her face than returned to the kitchen.

Mrs. Sullivan's elderly, sick parents lived downstairs. She often stopped down to see them. Mary knew how close Mrs. Sullivan was to her mother. In anger and resentment, she sometimes stomped around over head, knowing that the room she shared with her mother was directly over her Grandmother's room. When Mrs. Sullivan's mother was rushed to the hospital Mrs. Sullivan broke down completely, screaming, and wailing. "Mama!" she yelled repeatedly through her tears. Mary, lying on her cot felt scared, and guilty. She was sure that it was her fault that her Grandmother's condition had worsened. A week later they all attended her funeral. Mrs. Sullivan's step father died days later. Afterward both funerals the Sullivans began looking for another house. They couldn't stand the idea of strangers living beneath them when they had always had family living there.

In the beginning of May Mary's social worker from Services for the blind found another kindergarten to put her in. The small school was called Jack & Jill. It was in the home of a stern, unsmiling woman named Miss. Burns. Three teachers worked for her. One of them, a shrill woman in her forties took a dislike to Mary on her second day. Mary was affected by the woman's intolerant attitude and began to act up. A week later she was expelled because she tripped one of the other teachers.

In the summer the Sullivans once again lived out in Coventry, at the little brown cottage on Iyoho road. Mary was able to return to Camp Iyoho. Mr. McMantis and his wife welcomed her back, but things weren't the same. Mary had been looking forward to being with Evelyn again. Much to her dismay, she hardly saw Evelyn. She was given a different counselor, an irresponsible girl, who flirted with the male counselors and didn't care about Mary. Not one to give up easily, Mary often went searching for Evelyn. It was during one of these searches that she made a new friend. A trailer stood at the edge of the camp. Ann, who was a counselor and her mother, lived in it. Ann's mother's name was Betty. She was an older woman with short, wavy grey hair. When she saw Mary wandering on the dirt road she invited her in to the trailer. Betty's mobile home was compact and left little room for clutter. There was a small dinning area, a bedroom with two sets of bunk beds, and a very small bathroom. In spite of its smallness, Betty's home was cozy. Betty herself was very friendly. She offered Mary cookies and lemonade. When Mary chattered away to her she listened intently and nodded agreeably. Mary took an immediate liking to her hostess. She returned to visit her every day. Betty must have liked Mary as well because she began to play a game with her. She started saying things like "If you lived with me, you would sleep on this bunk" and "If you lived with me we would eat all kinds of fun meals and go out for ice cream every night". Mary was all set to move in with Betty, and not just because of the fun life they would have. Betty really seemed to care about what she felt and thought about things. She even gave Mary a giant rag doll that her daughter, Ann had out grown. One day Mary asked Betty what kind of powder she was wearing. "Oh I couldn't tell you that unless you were my baby girl" Betty said teasingly. Mary spent a good five minutes trying to convince Betty that she was her baby girl. Someone told Mrs. Sullivan what was going on and she abruptly put a stop to it. Mary found herself sitting at the kitchen table in the little brown cottage, wondering when she would escape the Sullivans and get to be with better people. Mary felt helpless and angry as her mother hollered at her and accused her of stealing Ann's doll. Then she did what she often did when they stayed at the cottage. She locked Mary out on the screened in porch and wouldn't let her back in until she had cried and begged enough to be allowed back in.

Two months before Mary was expelled from first grade they left the apartment house in South Providence and moved in to a large blue two story house in the Washington park section of Providence. The first thought that entered Mary's mind was that she wondered where her mother's angry drawn out ranting sessions with her would occur. The last time her mother had a session with her was when a drawing of Mr. Tully, the bus driver had been found by Mrs. Sullivan. She accused Mary of taking the picture to bed and bouncing on it. Mary had been baffled! Why would anyone bounce on a picture? The sessions mostly occurred in Mary's new room. Finally after all these years she no longer had to share a bedroom with her mother. (Mary's parents though loving toward each other slept in separate bedrooms since before her birth.) Mary was so happy to be rid of the cot with railings; and the harness that trapped her there, that she over looked the fact that her new bed was a couch.

After Mary's expulsion from Meeting St. School Dr. Denton recommended that the Sullivans send Mary to Bradley Hospital. Bradley was a psychiatric hospital for children, located in Riverside, RI. A month after Mary eagerly waited for the school bus that never came; she and her parents spent the day at Bradley, being showed around and meeting with doctors and social workers. Bradley Hospital was on a large expanse of property. In front was the main building, a three story red brick structure which contained doctors and secretaries offices an infirmary, and a play room for the youngest boys. Upstairs were the dorms, referred to as units. There were seven units because the patients were divided in to seven groups; only two of which were for girls. All the groups had names. The youngest girls were the Pixies. They ranged from ages seven-nine. The Debs were between the ages of nine-fourteen. The youngest boys were called the cubs. They, like the Pixies ranged from ages seven-nine. The Black Hawks were boys of nine-ten. The Eagles, Rangers, and the Riders all were boys ten-fourteen. The school department was in the other wing of the building. The third floor consisted of doctors offices. Behind the main building was a two story white building which contained a gymnasium, a kitchen, an office, and upstairs was the arts & crafts department, referred to as Hobby Lobby. Across from the art room was a carpentry shop. Beyond the two buildings was a play ground. Beyond this was a dirt path that led down hill toward another red brick building. This structure was called the service building. It was used for preschoolers. They were out patients. At the bottom of the hill were another play ground and an Olympic sized swimming pool. The property was surrounded by woods.

Mary was introduced to a young, petite, soft spoken Thai woman, named Dr. Pat. She greeted Mary warmly and asked her to follow her. She slid open a black door with small windows in it. Mary entered and found herself in an entry way. As she started to open the identical looking door across from the one they entered, Dr. Pat pushed one of the buttons on the wall. To Mary's complete horror, bars rattled across both doors, and the floor began moving beneath her feet! Mary leapt in to Dr. Pat's arms and wrapped her arms around her neck in a strangle hold. The small woman gaped in silent terror as Mary hung on and screamed all the way to the third floor. Mary's fear of elevators had come back to haunt her. She hadn't been on one in two years, and only when Sister Jane carried her. The elevators at Bradley were slightly more modern then the old one at St. Vincent's that required someone to pull a wooden gate across the door before pushing the button. When Dr. Pat left Mary with Dr. Laughy, a dark haired man with a mustache and beard, it was time to say what she could make of pictures of ink blobs. She did puzzles for him and drew a few pictures. Mary became bored after a while and when Dr. Laughy turned his back she slipped out of the room. She ran all over the building until she found the play room on the second floor that belonged to the Pixies. When Dr. Laughy found Mary she was happily pulling toys out of the toy box that sat in the corner of the room.

There were several visits to Bradley before Mary was admitted. She was eager to go live there. On one visit when she found out that she wasn't yet going to be admitted, she started screaming and crying. Her father abruptly ordered her to sit on the bench in the hallway. Mary obeyed, but continued to bawl. She felt some degree of shame when the friendly social worker reassured her that she would be living at Bradley soon. In the mean time Mary stayed at home with her mother. When spring came Mary was allowed to do something she never was allowed to do back at the old house. Mrs. Sullivan allowed her to play in the yard. She started attracting the attention of the neighborhood kids. They stopped by to talk to her. Mary was excited about this. She became friends with a girl around her age, named Arleen. However this was short lived. One afternoon Mrs. Sullivan over heard the little girls talking about how their grandfathers had died, and how sad it was. After Arleen left Mary was called inside. Her mother scolded her for talking about death. "You're a strange child, Mary" she said in a disappointed, pensive manner. Mary wasn't allowed to see Arleen after this. More often then not she was told to remain inside. Mrs. Sullivan continued to go outside though, because there was an addition to the family. When Mary turned seven in April the Sullivans got a puppy. He was a blonde, cocker spaniel, named Sandy. He had a happy friendly personality and suffered from epilepsy. He had seizures as a result. The Sullivans always chased Mary from the room when Sandy had one of his "spells" as they were called. Sandy ran around the house with Mary. She tried to get him to watch TV with her. He slept in a wicker basket with a red cushion. Unfortunately Sandy had weak kidneys. Soon he was imprisoned in the corner of the kitchen behind a screen with newspapers on the floor. The Sullivans continued to take him to the yard to do his business in spite of his not being allowed to roam the house anymore.

One day on a weekend old friends of the Sullivans pulled up in front of the big, blue house. Forgetting about Mary, her parents went outside to talk to the couple. Mary was seized with an over whelming desire to do all the things she was forbidden to do. She raided the sugar bowl, ran up and down the winding stairs, turned the radio and the TV on and off, and sneaked a few drinks of Holy Water (something she had taken to doing lately because she thought it would transform her in to a good girl). Then she grabbed Sandy's leash and ran upstairs with him. She looped the end of the leash on a door knob and gave the puppy the opportunity to watch her run in circles in the hallway. She ran faster and faster like a toy that had been wound too tightly. Sandy barked excitedly as he watched the child run round and round, faster and faster. Mrs. Sullivan was livid when she found child and puppy in the forbidden part of the house. She shouted at Mary as she led the nervous puppy down the stairs. "You know you're not supposed to go up the stairs. Only you're father sleeps up here. There's no need for you to come up here!" She smacked Mary and put her to bed.

Right before Mary was admitted to Bradley Hospital, her mother became enraged with her for breaking a curtain rod. She gave her daughter the chance to leave the house for good. When Mary happily started up the street, she was ordered to return. As she climbed the stairs near the back door, Mrs. Sullivan tripped her! She was so angry at Mary for leaving willingly that she chased her to her room and smacked her to the floor. She not only became violent, she accused Mary of causing her Grandmother's death. Later when Mary stopped crying her mother predicted that she would go to Bradley, make new friends, and together they would poke fun at poor Mrs. Sullivan hanging around the house in her bathrobe, and pajamas. Mary couldn't see the sense in this. It sounded totally ludicrous, even to her.

Chapter Two

Bradley Hospital

Mary spent three productive, happy years at Bradley Hospital. She was placed in the Pixie unit with four other little girls her age. Sally was the tallest. She had wavy long dark blonde hair and a scratchy voice. She stood half a head taller then the other pixies. Carol was a cheerful, plump little girl with a mischievous grin. She wore her brown straight hair short with bangs. Dinah was the smallest pixie. She had short dark hair and big dark eyes. By day she was comical and out going. At night she suffered from bad dreams and needed a night light. Charlene was the only orphan at Bradley. At almost seven, she had been there for three years. Because of her violent tantrums and foul language, foster homes were out of the question for Charlene. She had cerebral palsy, which affected her speech and hands. She could walk and run, if a little clumsily. Her brown hair was cut short and she usually wore jeans and white T shirts. Mary took to this troubled girl for some unexplainable reason. Soon they were best friends. Everyone began saying "Where are Charlene and Mary?" They seldom asked for just one or the other. Charlene and Mary were the only disabled patients at Bradley. It seemed ironic that two little girls, one with poor eye sight, and one with poor hand coordination were so in love with arts & crafts, but this was how it was with them. Charlene wasn't always a good friend. Sometimes she played mean tricks on Mary. One day she asked her if she wanted some koolade. Mary, who had a sweet tooth, eagerly accepted the cup. It contained urine, not koolade! Sickened, Mary spat it out as Charlene giggled with glee. Soon after this she ripped the covers off Mary's bed. When told by the angry unit leader to fix it, Charlene planted her feet apart and urinated on the floor. Charlene was in isolation one afternoon with the door locked. Mary saw an opportunity to get even. She turned off the light and grinned when she heard Charlene cry out on the other side of the door. But Miss Tyler, the unit leader in charge, saw Mary. She put her in the other isolation room with no light on for several minutes. Because Mary had spent so much time in front of the TV at home she was familiar with all the advertisements. She frequently went around singing, and reciting many commercials. She also yelled "Bare naked!!" repeatedly, knowing how shocked her mother would be if she heard her, but Mary was free of her parents now. And this was what made saying it so much fun. Soon the other little girls in her unit were reciting commercials, and yelling "Bare naked!" right along with her. The unit leaders, perhaps understanding Mary's need to do this, tolerated it briefly. Then they put a stop to it. Mary was an exuberant child, with limitless energy, who had a knack for unwittingly saying things that made everyone laugh. The fact that she didn't usually understand why her remarks were funny made her all the more amusing.

It was at Bradley that Mary was exposed to the youth culture. She was allowed to listen to rock and soul music, and watch the TV shows that her peers liked. Although her clothes were old fashioned and too large, she was sometimes given clothes that the other girls had out grown. They were modern, comfortable clothes which pleased Mary. She learned how to share with other kids, and participate in group activities. She settled down enough to learn in school. Her favorite teacher was Miss Murray. She was a plump, elderly woman with a warm disposition. Mary had her during her first year at Bradley.

At meal times she was constantly urged to stop day dreaming, and finish her food. Nobody at Bradley put sugar on her potatoes or vegetables like the Sullivans used to. She had to get used to eating food as it was. Nightly baths was a new concept for her. At home she was never given baths. She just washed up at the sink. Her parents never ran the bath water or used the shower. Mary had never given it any thought. Now she had to over come her fear of water, which resulted from the harsh treatment given to her by a few of the child care workers at St. Vincent's. She was made to slow down enough to follow orders instead of simply running wild. Like most of the other patients, Mary had anger issues that caused her to have frequent tantrums. She needed to learn how to control herself. The learning process wasn't easy for Mary. She frequently found herself in time-out or not being allowed to have dessert. She wasn't alone in this. All the patients were disciplined often. Many of the boys and some of the older girls were locked in the isolation room when they acted up. Even with the discipline Mary preferred Bradley to being at home. Most of the unit leaders were patient, and didn't hold past offenses against her. Saturday was visiting day. From one to four everyone's parents came to see them. Charlene was visited by a young college student, named Meg. Charlene liked Meg a lot, but she desperately longed for parents. The Sullivans always showed up with candy and a doll for Mary. It went without saying that she presented them with a gift that she had made in Hobby Lobby. One Saturday Mary dared to go downstairs empty handed. Mrs. Sullivan demanded an explanation. On the verge of panic, Mary lied and claimed that she made them a gift, but forgot it. She ran upstairs and quickly drew a picture. Five minutes later she handed over a hastily colored picture of her mother and father with "I love you" printed at the bottom. Mrs. Sullivan wasn't fooled. She guessed what Mary did, and wouldn't let her off easy. The visit was spoiled by her yelling and berating Mary for her thoughtlessness. Mr. Sullivan sat quietly beside his wife throughout the visit, and did nothing to diffuse the situation.

Every year the patients, unit leaders, doctors, and parents got together in the gymnasium for a lavish Christmas party. Patients from each unit had the chance to go up on stage and sing a few carols. The Pixie unit was no exception. They're turn came right after the Debs, the older girls unit performed. Together with Dinah, Charlene, Carol, and Sally, Mary sang three songs. Afterward sandwiches, chips, punch, and cake with ice cream was served. The patients ate and talked with their families. Everything was fine with Mary at first. Then her mother's mood turned grim. She remarked on how happy Mary seemed at Bradley. Mary foolishly chattered about the outings, the swimming pool they spent summer days in, and the Big Brother/Big Sister program, where students from Brown University were assigned to each patient. Mary saw an eighteen year old girl, named Carol every Thursday. Mrs. Sullivan had heard enough. "You don't miss us" she said testily. "You were damned glad to get out of the house, weren't you?" Mary anxiously denied this, but her mother wouldn't listen. After yelling at Mary for ten minutes or so, she told her husband to take her home. Mary looked at her father through her tear filled eyes.. He stared at her, his face unreadable. Then he escorted his wife out of the building. Despite the unhappy visit, Mary received many toys for Christmas, just like the other patients did. She managed to forget her mother's attitude for a while, as she played with new dolls, stuffed animals and a doll carriage.

By the time Mary was nine she had learned some self control. She was getting better at cooperating with others. She still got in to trouble for day dreaming at the dinner table though. She often day dreamed wherever she was. Mary hadn't latched on to anyone in almost three years. She got along with the unit leaders, who took turns supervising the Pixies, but she wasn't close to any of them. She played with a few of the girls, but she avoided most of the boys. They frequently made fun of her eyes. Not only did Mary have trouble seeing at a distance; she also had pupils that were oddly shaped. This made her a target for teasing. Mary had imaginary friends, who she turned to for comfort and entertainment. They always took on the form of parental figures. Mary not only pretended to have doting adults accompanying her everywhere she went, she also pretended to be other people. During her first two years at Bradley she pretended to be some of the pre-school students she knew from Meeting St. School. Three year old Alice, a passenger from Mr. Tully's bus was the one Mary imitated the most. Now that she was nine, Mary was starting to look forward to growing up. Recently she swapped Alice for Dorothy from The Wizard of Oz. Mary wore her hair in pig tails and wore skirts with suspenders, or jumpers with full skirts. She sang all the songs from the movie. Her favorite song was "Over the rainbow" Before long the unit leaders decided that she was obsessed, and restricted her from trying to look and act like Dorothy. Without the pig tails and dresses Mary found that she could still pretend to be her favorite character. When not near the unit leaders she sang the songs from the movie, and skipped along just like Dorothy did.

In June Mary finally learned to swim. She had a special goal to work toward. Throughout the summer she became a skilled swimmer. She practiced swimming the back stroke, side stroke, and floating.. In August Bradley held its annual water carnival. Mary was ready for it. Now she would be able to participate.. All the doctors, unit leaders, teachers, administrators, and parents came to observe the various contests that the patients took part in. Mary not only practiced her swimming, she also practiced going down the slide on her stomach, on her back, feet first, and head first. She practiced doing Cannon Balls off the diving board, but she couldn't get the knack of diving. Mary wasn't concerned. She could "wow" them all with her back stroke, front stroke, and side stroke.

Everyone was organized in to teams. Some of the girls in her age group were on a team called The Swimming Beauties. Mary was envious, how she wished that she could be on a team with a name like that. Instead she was put on a team with three boys, who were rather quiet, and timid. The team was called The Fantastic Four. This was some what disappointing, but it didn't matter much. Mary knew that she could play at being a swimming beauty on her own time. She had a vivid imagination that helped her through many disappointments, from not getting the desired part in a play, to not having nice, normal parents. Mary was well known for her fantasies. Once when she was fidgeting while waiting to go in the pool during practice, one of the life guards yelled "Hey Yellow brick road! Pay attention".

Finally that special Saturday in August arrived. Mary, wearing a pink swim suit, and her hair in a pony tail, stood with her team mates. The fenced in pool area, with its row of changing rooms, and concrete walkway, was filled with many people, some standing, some sitting on chairs. Mary, with her limited eye sight, couldn't tell if her parents were there. Her father must have realized this, because he came over, and told her that he and her mother would be sitting in front of the third of the seven changing rooms. He took a picture of Mary, and then went to sit down. When the whistle blew, Mary was ready. She jumped in with her team mates, and began to swim toward the thick, blue rope in the center of the pool, that was the finish line. She glanced to her right, to see how her team mates were doing. Steve, who was two years older then her, was doing the dog paddle, and was right behind her. Timmy, the smallest was ready to give up, and was being pushed to go on. Dana was struggling along, not far behind Steve. Suddenly Mr. Sullivan was beside the pool, and began loudly encouraging her. "Come on, Mary you can do it!!" He ran along side the pool, in a crouched position, beckoning her toward the finish line. As she struggled along, she looked up at her father in his Sunday suit, and horn rimmed glasses, and realized just how much her winning meant to him. If she had been tired, or distracted before, she no longer was. As her father danced along eagerly calling out encouraging words to her, Mary swam like she never swam before! She wanted to win for her father more then she wanted to win for herself. She was so surprised by his enthusiasm. He was usually over shadowed by his boisterous wife. Fleetingly Mary wondered why her mother wasn't beside her father, cheering her on. However her need to win was so great that she forgot about her mother for the time being. Keeping her fingers together, as her father had previously instructed her, she pushed on with her strokes until she reached the finish line. When she heard the cheers, and applause, Mary knew that she had won the race!

By the end of the afternoon, Mary had participated in many events. However she only won in the first race, but that was okay. She had her moment in the sun, and was happy. For one moment Mary was a winner, not a wool gatherer. When she received her trophy, both of her parents were there to congratulate her. Mary didn't ask her mother why she sat on the side line during the events. She didn't want to sound like she was trying to challenge her. This was a definite no no. So Mary just smiled, and enjoyed her special day.

When Mary was nine and a half she met her parent's new social worker. She had been assigned to them when Ms. Sandburg left Bradley in September. The new social worker was named Mrs. Biro. She was a soft spoken, calm woman in her late thirties with glasses and long straight brown hair parted on the side. Mary liked this social worker better then the previous one. In fact, she found that she was becoming very fond of her. Soon she was drawing pictures of Mrs. Biro and pretending that she was with her all the time. She wished that Mrs. Biro was her mother. Mary saw Dr. Pat several times a week. She often talked excitedly about the new social worker, and asked Dr. Pat questions about her. Sometimes Dr. Pat took Mary up to the third floor to visit Mrs. Biro. Then one day in April one of Mary's friends drew a picture of Mrs. Biro in the nude, and showed it to Mary. They both laughed about it. Because of this Mary was no longer allowed to talk to, or about Mrs. Biro. As a result she couldn't invite her to her tenth birthday party. Mary cried her eyes out, but the decision was final.

At the end of April it was decided that Mary would be leaving Bradley in June. The doctors wanted to find a residential school some where in New England to send Mary to. In the mean time she would have to go home. Mary was at first pleased that she was ready to leave Bradley, but as the days passed she became anxious and unhappy. She felt like her world was coming to an end. And her world as she had come to know it had come to an end. No longer would she get to be around other kids her age and enjoy the music and TV shows they liked. No longer would she have companions to play with, act silly with or share secrets with. She would miss having pleasant, young people taking care of her, People who didn't hit her or call her names or rant and rave about God or expect her to act like a helpless, old fashioned, imbecile. She would miss being outside too. At home she was kept inside unless her parents took her out in the car, and that was only on weekends. So when Mary realized that in only a few weeks, the three wonderful years she had spent at Bradley would be over, it did something to her. She became temperamental and was quick to burst in to tears, often accusing someone who had mildly teased or insulted her of being mean. She knew that she was acting too babyish for a ten year old, but she couldn't help it. Within the confines of Bradley, Mary had found it easy to become a some what loving, and faithful daughter, but now that she was leaving, her true feelings were coming to the surface. She blamed Mrs. Biro for the decision to discharge her. Mrs. Biro, who had rejected her and was now sending her back to the lions den!

The day before being discharged Mary, her parents, and Dr. Pat drove to Lancaster, Massachusetts to look at a school for psychiatrically and developmentally disabled children. It was called the Dr. Franklin Perkins School. It was situated on a spacious, beautiful campus. There were a number of buildings, some contained dorms, and some contained class rooms. As they were shown around Mary frequently inquired about her friend Charlene, who had been sent there a year earlier. When the tour ended Mary impulsively broke free of her parents, and ran upstairs to greet Charlene. Her old friend was just getting out of the bath tub. Two women were watching her as she struggled to button her robe. Charlene had made a lot of progress at this school. She was learning to read and write. Her craft work was more recognizable, but more importantly, a couple, who already had a son were adopting Charlene in a few weeks. She was so excited that she rushed past Mary and greeted her parents. After she told them the good news she turned her attention back to Mary. They talked for five or ten minutes before Dr. Pat said that they had to head back to Rhode Island.

The next day was dreadful for Mary. It was June 17th, 1971. School was out and all the other kids were down in the giant swimming pool enjoying the hot summer day. Not Mary however, she was in the older girls' dorm hiding under one of the beds, crying. She didn't want to go home! Why couldn't she be one of the carefree kids down at the pool, looking forward to a whole summer of fun, friends, lime flavored Kool-Aid and young staff members taking care of them? Suddenly Miss McCoy entered the room out of breath. "Mary I've been looking everywhere for you. I know you're in here, so come out" Falling for the oldest trick in the book, Mary crawled out from under the bed. Miss McCoy had always been fond of the girl and today was no exception. She took Mary on her lap and gave her an uplifting pep talk about being brave and looking on the bright side of things. Mary could not see a bright side but she didn't want to argue with this kind, energetic, young woman. Taking the girl by the hand, Miss McCoy led the way downstairs. Mary found her parents standing with Dr Pat. She looked very concerned by Mary's red, tear streaked face." Mary, I've been talking to your parents here." Mary stiffened involuntarily. Her parents were going to be very upset with her for crying so much. They wanted her to be happy about going home. "We've decided that you may spend every Wednesday here at Bradley for the summer" said Dr Pat. So, there was a ray of hope after all.

Mary and her mother sat in the living room at home. It was just the two of them because her father had to return to work, having used his lunch hour to take his wife and collect their daughter from Bradley. Now Mary sat on the couch and cried as she told her mother just how much she was going to miss life at the place she had come to think of as her second home. Her mother shook her head in despair ."I just don't understand you." she complained." We try to give you everything, a nice home, a dog, clothes, toys. What more do you expect?" Mary, who was leaning forward, crying in to her hands, said "it's just that I have no brothers or sisters!! At Bradley I felt like I did" There was more of coarse but she didn't dare complain about the lack of freedom or having to once again go to church on a regular basis and not being looked after by adults who were younger and more modern then her ancient, adoptive parents. And would her mother go back to hitting her like she used to? "Why can't you be like your friend Carol? I'm sure her father is proud of her. She wanted to go home. And she didn't cry, did she?" Mary gazed at her mother sitting dejectedly in her arm chair. She realized that the woman was not going to offer her any comfort. How she longed for her mother to kneel in front of her and embrace her. But that was not to be. Instead, Mary would have to smooth things over by pretending that she was beginning to think that being home was not going to be so bad after all. By the time her father got home from work, he found both Mary and her mother cheerfully talking about how it was so much better that Mary was willing to give up her bed at Bradley to a more needy child.

It was a week later that Mary woke up in the middle of the night. Although her room was dark, she could sense something off to her right. Colors were taking shape. Mary watched with a mixture of fear and amazement as the colors sorted themselves out. She found herself staring at a transparent image of Miss Cooley, a staff member at Bradley hospital who had always been kind to her. She was kneeling beside the bed with her arms were out on each side as if she would stop Mary from getting up. She looked the same as ever. Her long blonde hair was worn loose and parted down the middle. She was dressed nicely in a blouse and mini skirt. But what was she doing in Mary's room? She wouldn't answer Mary's queries; she just knelt there, looking solemn. Finally Mary turned and hid her face in her pillow. A minute later she sneaked a peek. Miss Cooley was still there. However, she had turned away from the bed, her head uplifted, her hands folded in prayer. This was too much for Mary! She buried her face in the pillow and burst in to tears. After a few minutes she dared to look up…The room was bright with morning light and Miss Cooley was gone

Later that day when Mary was visiting Bradley she tried to tell Miss Cooley about her strange experience. But with five or six other girls trying to talk to her, it was impossible for Mary to make her understand just how strange it was and that it wasn't merely a dream.

Aside from the Wednesday visits to Bradley, which were the highlight of the week for Mary, the rest of the summer crept by predictably, but not always pleasantly. Every morning she woke up around seven. She could hear the radio in the kitchen playing the pop music that she had come to love during her three years at Bradley. She would hurriedly dress and proceed to the breakfast table, where her mother, who didn't like the music her daughter liked but was resigned to playing it, served Mary Fruit loops cereal raisin toast and tang in place of orange juice. While the radio played songs like" Spirit in the sky", "We're so sorry, Uncle Albert" and "Dragging the line" Mary ate, sweet talked her mother in to continuing to be in a good mood, and waved to and called out to Sandy, the family's cocker spaniel. The small, sandy colored, dog was three years old. He still was kept penned up in the kitchen. But now he had the back stairs to run up and down on. In front of him was a small patch of floor, covered with newspapers, food bowl, water bowl, and a few toys. A screen separated Sandy from the kitchen and the rest of the house. In spite of this, He was a happy energetic dog who loved his family and was full of fun. When Mary's father was home he petted Sandy, fed him, tossed toys to him, and called him "Mr. Mc'Gillicutty". He would sing and Sandy would dance and twirl round and round.

After breakfast Mary petted the cheerful dog, and then went to the living room to play records for a few hours. Her mother abruptly snapped off the radio. Sometimes when Mary was listening to her records she would pretend that she had two friends from the neighborhood, a tall, thin, dark haired boy with glasses and a shorter boy who looked very much like Charlie Brown! As she imagined them looking at her, she wondered if they would like her if they were real. After all, she spent each week day(except Wednesdays) inside the house with the shades drawn against the summer heat with a middle aged, old fashioned, woman who was sometimes loud and volatile, and lived in the past.

After lunch Mary was allowed to watch TV. She was partial to comedies, and westerns." I love Lucy" and a nature show for kids called "Hodge Podge Lodge "were also on her list of favorites. Later when supper was finished, her parents liked to watch cop shows or comedies, Mary liked these also.

On Saturdays Mary and her parents spent the day at a small cottage out in Coventry which over looked a lake. It was on Yoho road. Her parents had owned the small, brown, musty smelling cottage since Mary was five. They enjoyed getting away from their home in Providence once or twice a week. Mary could remember the summers when she was five and six. They had lived out at the cottage until Labor Day Weekend. She was allowed to attend a nearby day camp which she loved! Even though she had enjoyed those summers, she wasn't eager to live there again. So she didn't ask her parents why they only went there on weekends now.

Sunday morning's Mary woke up to find her mother in her bedroom, ready to give her a wash down with rubbing alcohol. (This was the extent of the bathing Mary received at home. Like before, the tub and shower was never used. Mary had to assume that her mother and father washed up at the bathroom sink. Their laundry was sent out to a local Laundromat weekly.) After this, she was made to go sit in the kitchen with her father in her slip, stockings and shoes. Her mother didn't want her to get a speck of food on her dress. What was so special about the dress? Every Sunday she had three different dresses to choose from. They all looked like they were right out of the 1920s. They each had short, puffed sleeves, and full skirts that started below the hip. Along with this, Mary had to wear a hat with a round brim, and long streamers in the back of it. As her parents led her between them to the church, Mary felt self conscience. She knew that she didn't look like other modern ten year olds. The church they attended was St. Paul, which was just over the Providence/Cranston line. After church they sometimes returned to their cottage out in Coventry. Mary wasn't enthused, but kept quiet about it. By now she knew enough to keep negative feelings to herself when she was around her parents.

Throughout the summer, Mary's mother's moods went up and down like a yo-yo. Mary, who had anticipated this, having been through it when she was very small, put a sign up on the inside of the front door that said "THIS IS THE HOUSE OF PEACE" For a week or two the sign worked like a charm. Then one evening when her mother was ranting and raving, she suddenly turned toward the sign and laughed at it, saying "House of peace, hu?" She pointed at Mary and yelled "Ever since she put up that sign she has been acting like a little stinker!!" Mary, feeling stricken, wondered what she had done to bring her mother's wrath down on her once again. Did it have anything to do with the fact that the Dr. Franklin Perkins School wouldn't be taking her after all? No explanation had been given to Mary for this, but Mrs. Sullivan blamed it on Mary's rude behavior at the end of the tour. "Why would any school want a child who goes running upstairs without permission, and bursts in on someone who is just getting out of the tub?" she demanded angrily. "You're too impetuous. It's very unbecoming!" Mary's father, as usual, said very little except to agree with his wife. Clearly her mother was in charge in this family. He only intervened when his wife became violent and attacked Mary.

As summer turned to fall, Mary continued to visit Bradley, but no longer on a weekly basis, which was too bad because as her mother became moodier and quicker to shout and talk endlessly about the past, Mary began to change. With no one to turn to, she listened to stories of what a difficult, troublesome, mean spirited, baby, and evil, conniving little girl she had been. According to her mother, everyone saw her this way except Sister Jane, who was so loaded with character flaws that her opinion of Mary wasn't supposed to count at all. Every day Mary was not only told that she was sick in the head on a regular basis, she was told that she was bad as well. Mary often wondered why she had been discharged from Bradley. "Did you know that you used to bang your head on the wall as an infant and as a toddler?" inquired her mother a number of times. "Every time we sent you back to St Vincent's, you would start that head banging nonsense!" She paced back and forth, gesturing wildly. "Only that nun liked you, and she was the one who made you the way you are! You used to scream, and whack your fists in the air. You weren't a sweet little infant!" Mary began to feel such overwhelming guilt about the things her mother was dredging up, that She wished she could have a chance to be reborn so that she could be different the next time around.

At times Mary's father was around during these scenes. He had retired at the end of August. More often then not, he was there when his wife blew up at Mary for no apparent reason. One time she hollered at the girl, informed her that she would be a terrible mother someday, then fled from the room exclaiming that she couldn't stand to be in the same room with her anymore. As Mary sat at the kitchen table wondering what she had done this time to offend her mother, she heard her father in the next room, gently coaxing his wife to return to the kitchen. Why was it that all of his sympathy was directed toward his wife and not her?

By early December Mary had invented a fantasy world which consisted of friends, places, and second chances. She started trying to sneak out of the house in the middle of the night, with her belongings packed in a large bag. But her mother was such a light sleeper, that she always caught her before she got outside. Because Mary's social worker from State services for the blind hadn't found her a suitable school to attend, and because Mary was starting to show signs of regression, she was put in the out patient program at Bradley Hospital. She was eagerly looking forward to returning to Bradley, even if she would only get to be there six hours a day. She was also looking forward to the bus rides that she would be taking with some of the other kids in the out patient program. However, this last bit was not to be.

On Monday morning Mary woke up and hurried in to her new dress, a plaid, woolen, jumper that covered her knees. It was when her mother was braiding her hair that she found out that she had been allowed to sleep past seven because her parents didn't want her riding the bus with the other kids. "Your father will be taking you in each morning and picking you up in the afternoons" explained her mother in a matter of fact way. No reason was given for this change of plan, and Mary knew better then to show how disappointed she was.

For the first four days everything went perfectly for Mary. She enjoyed her classes, she not only continued being friends with some of the girls she had known before, she discovered that some of the Boys in the out patient program wanted to be friends with her also. She loved the freedom too. But at home things were still just as turbulent as ever. Mary had been trying to run away at night, but her mother was such a light sleeper that she always caught her.

On Friday morning Mary realized that running away from home was going to be impossible. She was going to have to run away from Bradley. This was something she dreaded doing, since she loved it there. But there was no way that she was going home at the end of the day. She was going to head out west and live and work on a ranch. When she had enough money she would live in a small house in a valley and keep horses and maybe some cows and chickens. If anyone showed up and told her to go back to her parents she would come out on her front porch with her loaded rifle and tell them to get off her property immediately!!

Before leaving the house, Mary was stopped by her mother, who searched her and uncovered a map, some slices of bread, candy, some loose change and a pair of pajamas. Also, she found a note that Mary had written as a result of her mother's constant complaints about the girl's babyhood." You should have killed that baby then" it said. Mary wouldn't give a straight answer to her mother's questions and her father was waiting in the car, so she escaped any interrogation.

Later during recess Mary put her plan in to action. She decided that she was going to run through the woods and come out by the bay. Then she would simply follow the railroad tracks until she reached one of those states out west. As she was heading in to the woods, one of the older boys called out to her to come back. "Don't worry about me!" yelled Mary "I can take care of myself!" Eagerly she ran through the woods, enjoying the feeling of absolute freedom. However, she soon realized that she was being followed. Her happiness was replaced by disappointment and frustration. Why couldn't people leave her alone? She heard one of the boys, Randy, calling to her. She quickened her pace. "Mary stop where do you think your going?" demanded Randy "Leave me alone!!" yelled Mary over her shoulder "I don't need anybody!" She was running as fast as she could, when she suddenly found that there was no longer any ground beneath her feet. She was falling! When she hit the ground the breath was knocked out of her, but she wasn't really hurt, probably because the ground was covered with a thick layer of leaves. Mary looked up and saw that she had fallen off a small cliff, maybe ten or twelve feet high. But to her it looked to be about twenty feet high. Randy, her pursuer, started down the cliff. In a few minutes he was beside her. But Mary tried to run from him once again, and when he grabbed her, she hit him over the head with a chunk of marble she found on the ground nearby. She wasn't going back to Bradley, because that would mean going home afterward. Home where her mother splattered her with holy water, where her parents said the rosary every day and made her join in, where they blessed each other with holy water and a crucifix before going to bed each night. Mary made it through the woods and was happily walking on the railroad tracks, eager to begin her new life when she was suddenly surrounded by five older boys, Randy was with them. As they forced Mary to return to Bradley, she stomped along and swore loudly at them, threatened them, and wished each one of them dead!

Once back at Bradley, she was put in to time-out and informed that she would always have to be accompanied by a staff member where ever she went from then on. All the kids knew that she had run away and hit Randy over the head. Clearly, they were no longer her friends because they all called her names and laughed at her. Mary, still in time-out, not only yelled and swore at her tormentors, she also began hitting the back of her head against the wall. She was remembering what her mother told her. She didn't really know why she felt a desire to act like a toddler again, but she did. In fact, she was becoming much more preoccupied with her baby days then she was with looking forward to growing up.

At three o'clock Mary was informed that she would be spending the weekend at Bradley. She was so excited! However, before she was able to be happy about this, she and Dr Pat had to meet with her parents to try to sort things out. Just seeing them made Mary want to choke! When Dr Pat stepped away to talk to someone else, they began making Mary feel guilty for running away. They wanted her to tell Dr Pat that she wished to go home with them. Feeling pressured, she told Dr Pat that she was fine now and wanted to go home. The doctor became puzzled by the girl. "But Mary, when you were home you didn't want to be home." "Oh but I do now!" Mary cried, glancing quickly at her parents. She hoped that her doctor would refuse to let her go home… she did. Trying to hide her relief, Mary said goodbye to the Sullivans and ran upstairs.

It snowed a lot that weekend. Mary, who didn't know what was going to happen to her on Monday, still wanted to run away. Feeling frustrated, she stared out the window at the falling snow. It would surely hamper her attempts to get away, and how could she survive out in the snow and cold? Of course, she probably wouldn't have been able to get far anyway. On Friday evening, during supper a doctor came to the dinning room and told her that she would be on some medication that would make her feel better. All it seemed to be doing though was making Mary very tired. Every time she sat down she dozed off! What were they giving her?

On Monday Mary was taken to the IMH out in Cranston. This was a psychiatric hospital for adults and adolescents. Mary was given another dose of the mystery drug, allowed to say goodbye to her best friend, Regina, and put in a car with Mr. Meyers. He was a middle aged, balding man with a pleasant, considerate personality. He was head of the school department at Bradley. As they rode to Cranston, Mr. Meyers put on the radio station that he knew all the kids liked. But instead of being able to enjoy it like she usually did, Mary found that it made her feel worse! For instance, when "Precious and few" by Climax came on, Mary stared out the window and quietly cried her eyes out! Mr. Meyers asked her what was wrong, but she couldn't tell him. It would have been embarrassing to try to describe the deep sadness she felt.

Mary found her parents, her doctor, and her social worker waiting for her when she arrived at the IMH. After the in-take process was completed, Mary said goodbye, and was taken to the ward reserved for troubled teenaged girls.

She remained there for a month. And what amazed her was that she wasn't even put off by the dreary and often upsetting environment there. In a strange sort of way, she welcomed it. It seemed like years since that sad day in June when she was discharged from Bradley Hospital. In actually, it had only been six months. Mary wasn't the same person she had been back then. And the sad part was that she didn't even care anymore! Would she ever care again, or had she lost touch with everything when she left Bradley?

Chapter Three

Meeting other legally blind children

Mary was shaken awake early on a Monday morning late in January of 1972. The hand that was shaking and prodding her belonged to a middle-aged woman with, black hair and a Portuguese accent." Wake up Mary! You go to Boston today". The woman was a nurse who worked on the psychiatric ward where Mary had been staying for the past month. The ward was on the second floor of the Adolph Meyer building. This was one of the many buildings which made up the RI medical center.

As Mary got up, she noticed the other girls, all older then her, rushing to dress, wash up, and brush their hair. They were all eager to be first in line at the door. Every meal was enjoyed, or not enjoyed, as the case may be, in the cafeteria, which was right outside of the ward. Under the watchful eyes of the nurses, the girls would file out of ward-9, accompanied by the boys from ward-12. The boys were supervised by large, male attendants, who were more effective in maintaining discipline since some of the boys though under eighteen, were quite big and often out of control.

Along with being hungry, the girls were eager to enter the cafeteria so that they could socialize with the boys. They saw them during school as well, but they couldn't talk to each other much there. The school department was in the basement of the Adolph Meyer building. Classes were held five days a week, for a few hours a day. Mary, being only ten and a half, wasn't yet interested in boys. Besides, she was so consumed by a father need that there was no room for boys. Her current fixation was Sergeant Schultz from a TV show called Hogan's Heroes. Her mother upon discovering this had refused to let Mary watch this show anymore. However, on the ward she was allowed to watch what she liked.

When Mary's parents arrived a little after nine, she was ready. Her long, light brown hair was center parted and held back with red barrettes. She put on her green jacket and red hat and mittens that her mother gave her for Christmas. Although the holidays were over, she liked the red and green combo. Only the nurses were there, to wish Mary good luck at her new school.

During the ride up to Boston Mrs. Sullivan talked about the new school, preparing Mary for what she thought she would find there. "You'll find that some of the students will see about as well as you do, some will see a little better or a little worse. Some won't be able to see at all." Mary nodded in response. Having spent a month in a psychiatric hospital, Mary had grown used to the grim surroundings, the smell of disinfectant the frequent disturbances that occurred on a ward occupied by teens with emotional problems. A few times Mary witnessed a riot in progress. She found that she enjoyed it and was sorry when the nurses were able to bring it under control. She had become comfortable with the idea of being sick. She was beginning to believe she really was .She also liked the lack of responsibility. Nobody on the ward expected much of her. This was partly because of her poor vision, and because she was the youngest. She frequently heard the nurses call her the baby on the ward. She liked this and never contradicted them.

Now as her mother described the new school and its students, Mary pictured them all sitting around in a big day room. In spite of her reluctance to put life at the medical center behind her, Mary was a little interested and perhaps even excited about this new school.

Soon the Boston sky line came in to view. Mary watched it eagerly as her father's car drew nearer and nearer. "Where in Boston is this school any way?" asked Mrs. Sullivan. "It's in Jamaica Plains" answered her husband quietly, before going back to concentrating on his driving.

The Boston Center for blind children was across the street from the VA hospital. It was in between a modern looking nursing home, situated on the right. To the left was the Home for little wanderers. The two buildings that made up the Boston Center were not side by side. They stood, one behind the other. The front building was a white, modern two story structure that stood at the top of the hill. In back of this was a much older structure. It was a Victorian three story house. Besides the new building was a playground. It could be seen by motorists passing by. The playground which was in front of the Victorian structure was in the back of the property, and therefore could not be seen from the street.

Holding Mary by her hands, her parents led her to the front building. They proceeded down the hill and rang the door bell. Inside and down three steps was a small lobby. A young woman with long, blonde hair, wearing a turtle neck top and a short skirt greeted them. "Hi, my name is Pat. I work in the office over there". She pointed to a room that was across the lobby and to the left. Mary noticed that Pat's office was at the beginning of a long hallway, lined with doors on either side. "Those are all offices too". Pat said. "We will be turning right, since I will be taking you on a tour of our school and introducing you to everyone". They went through a heavy, grey door. Mary saw a shorter hallway ahead of her. There were two large classrooms on each side. They stopped at the first classroom on the right. Inside were two people. One was a tall, well built woman with long, straight blonde hair, wearing a blouse and a mini skirt. The boy with her was heavy set with black hair, very light complexion, and some freckles. He looked to be about eleven. "Hi Janice I'm showing a new student, and her parents around, and since she will be in your class, I thought we'd start here". Janice smiled and introduced the boy. "This is Richard. He needed a little extra help today, so I'm keeping him during recess". Seeing that he had an audience, Richard jumped to his feet and brought a watch out of his pocket. "I can do a magic trick for you". He hid the watch in his hand and transferred it to his other pocket. "You see? I'm smart!" Mary didn't see anything magic about what he did, but she smiled and said nothing. "Don't mind Richard" said Janice with a laugh. "He likes to show off".

The other classrooms were empty. Turning left at the end of the hallway, they encountered a small foyer with two bathrooms and a coat rack. Above each hook was the name of the student who was to hang their coat there. At the far left was a hook with a label above it that said "Visiting child" "That will be where you will hang your coat, Mary" announced Pat. "We hope that after your ten day evaluation you will be staying with us". Mary noticed that several women and a man were helping kids of various ages in to coats, hats, mittens and scarves. Minutes later a girl of about ten came rushing inside crying loudly. Her red, tear stained face was framed by long, curly blonde hair. "My foot my foot!" she exclaimed. "I hurt my foot when I jumped off the swing!" A woman with long, brown hair, center parted, wearing big, round glasses and a thick sweater with jeans looked at the girl's foot. "It seems okay to me, Beth. But you shouldn't be jumping off the swing until it stops". She sent the girl back outside. Pat introduced the woman as Jeanette She is one of the staff members here. She works with the Nine to fourteen year olds". Jeanette smiled and greeted Mary and her parents. "Luke here also works with the older kids." Pat gestured toward a young man wearing a plaid, flannel shirt and a pair of jeans. His light brown hair reached the collar of his shirt, and he had a faint mustache. He shook hands with the Sullivans, then Mary. An older woman heavy set, with short black hair was Miss Bow. She took care of some of the youngest students. "There are seven staff members on duty during the day explained Pat, as they made their way past the bathrooms and down a long corridor. Mary noticed a big, old fashioned kitchen on the right. On the left was a long room, lined with shelves, filled with fat, hard cover books. At the far wall was a small organ. "This is our library. Some of the books are in Braille, others are large print. We also use this room for music appreciation classes". Mrs. Sullivan was impressed with the organ. She told Pat about how she enjoyed playing the organ at home. Pat responded with polite enthusiasm. She showed them the huge play room, which was next to the library. A smaller room adjoined the play room. "This is the younger students dinning room. You only eat here if you're eight or under" announced Pat cheerfully. "So you won't be eating here, will you, Mary?" Mary saw a small area, occupied by four round tables, about three feet high. Each had about five little chairs surrounding it. Pat took the family across a big foyer, occupied by only one piece of furniture. It was an up right piano, painted entirely orange! Even the bench was orange! Mrs. Sullivan looked at it with disgust. Beside this monstrosity was the older students dinning room. Mary saw a room with French doors and two long tables. On the walls were old fashioned light fixtures. "Beyond this room is the staff dinning room." Pat led them out in to the foyer, past the orange piano and bench. They went up an old winding staircase. The old wing of the building consisted of three playrooms, an elegant living room, for visitors, and a very spacious staff lounge. Just before reaching the big metal door which divided the old wing from the new wing, Pat stopped to point out two more rooms. One was an arts and crafts room,, the other was the nurse's office.

Once through the metal door, Pat said "These are the dorms" The first room on the left was filled with large, white iron cribs. Mary had a flash back. She was once again five years old. A fat woman in a nurse's uniform was spanking her for climbing out of a white, iron crib. Furious, Mary yelled "I'll tell Sister Jane on you!" Pat noticed Mary gazing at the cribs. "These are for the under sized children that can't walk. We sometimes get them for the ten day evaluation, but they seldom stay" As they all walked down the long corridor lined with bedrooms some with two beds, some with only one. One room had three beds in it. Pat stopped at a room that had one bed. "This will be your room while you're with us, Mary. It's always reserved for the visiting child." The small room was nice enough but like all the other windows in the school, this window was covered by criss cross bars! Between this, the numerous play rooms, and the alphabet and numbers that were painted up and down the corridor in the dorm, this school was looking more and more like a pediatric prison! Mary wasn't sure she was going to like it here.

Mary ate lunch with the older students. Her mother was meeting with one of the social workers. Her father however, stayed in the dinning room with her. Because she knew that he was watching her, Mary made a show of making the sign of the cross on her self and folding her hands in prayer before eating. Mr. Sullivan looked at her but didn't smile or nod.

By four thirty it was decided that Mrs. Sullivan would be staying in one of the guest rooms on the third floor while her husband went home. He would be coming up to visit periodically during Mary's evaluation. Mary was able to observe a lot during her ten day stay. Everyone rose at Seven O'clock, washed, dressed and made their beds. She noticed that the only students who were able to do this without help were Beth, the girl who had cried about her foot, Richard, the boy who tried to do magic tricks with his watch, a loud mouthed boy with a gruff voice named Donald, a deaf girl named Judy and a quiet boy,

named Stan who had a room all to himself. Everyone else needed some degree of assistance. The youngest ones couldn't care for themselves at all, and they were five and six years old!

Everyone was shepherded down stairs to breakfast by the staff members, by eight O'clock. Mary noticed that the eighteen or so students were divided up in to small groups, with a staff member supervising each group. The students under the age of nine turned left, in to the small dinning room that adjoined the play room. Mary was herded in to the larger room with the French doors. Luke, the man with the shaggy hair and thin beard was in charge of two nine year old boys who were totally blind. Peter was bratty, and liked to tease everyone, when he wasn't talking nonsense and making himself laugh up roariously about it. It was the other boy under Luke's care that everyone had to be careful of. Although Steve was paralyzed on one side and as a result, walked with an awkward gait, he had an explosive temper. If he couldn't get his way about something, he would lash out at other people. He often reached out, and grabbed someone's hair and yanked it viciously! This happened to Mary her second day there. Because her hair was long, Steve's grubby hand got snagged in it after he yanked it, causing her to scream in frustration! Jeanette, the woman with the long brown hair and big round glasses was in charge of Donald and Richard. A big boned woman with medium length straight dark hair named Elaine looked after Judy and Stan. Mary and Beth were under the authority of a slim, young woman with medium length black hair and very light complexion. Her name was Mary Ann. Across the foyer the little kids could be heard crying, shouting, babbling like infants, or scraping chairs around as they sat down to eat.

Classes began at 9: O'clock. The older kids started off with arts and crafts in a small classroom on the second floor. At 9:45 they were herded downstairs to the new wing of the building, and dropped off at Janice's classroom. Mary wasn't sure if she liked Janice or not. The teacher gave the other students their tasks, and then sat down with Mary to find out how far she was in reading and math. Mary did fairly well in reading, but she barely knew her multiplication tables. Janice placed a paper with five or six problems on it for her to work on. Mary tried to do the work, but she soon became frustrated. "Keep trying" urged Janice. Mary tried for another few minutes. Then she started making exasperated noises. "Now Mary!" shouted Janice "Don't give me that attitude. Just do the work!" Mary glowered at her teacher. It was then that she knew that she didn't like this impatient, brusque woman, and probably never would.

After an hour and a half of class time they had recess. It lasted for half an hour. Sometimes they were all kept in the large play room on the first floor. Three speakers were hooked up on the walls in this room. They were connected to the stereo that was in the closet in the older kids dinning room. Sometimes the staff played WRKO. This station played the top 40 music. At other times they played records. They were partial to the Beatles, the Fifth Dimension, and Laura Nyro. This last one was a particular favorite of the staff. Mary, who loved music, soon became tired of Laura Nyro. Why did they have to play her music so much?

It was on her first full day at the school that Mary got to meet everyone. She already knew all the older kids. However, there were a number of younger kids, and staff members who took care of them. There was a middle aged woman with short dark hair named Miss Bow (She refused to be on a first name basis with the students). She was no nonsense, nanny-type, who looked after an eight year old boy named Vincent and a six year old girl named Kate. Kate was totally blind, having no eyes at all. Vincent was partially sighted. Both children were unable to speak or use the toilet, though Miss Bow was trying to potty train them. Kate seemed totally clueless. Vincent however was a mystery. He dressed himself, made his bed, and even tidied up his room. He suffered from epilepsy. Then there was a tall, well built woman named Alice who took care of John who was six. He was a happy, active little boy. He was partially sighted and continually waved his right hand in front of his face, because he liked to see the shadow of his hand in motion. He couldn't talk and wasn't even in the process of being potty trained yet. Jimmy, a little black haired boy of five or six had no sight and was also in diapers. He was usually a passive boy, but when he was hungry he screwed up his face like a grumpy old man and whined incessantly. He was also known to pinch people sometimes. The third one in Alice's group was an eight year old girl named Tillie. She suffered from asthma. She had a glass eye. She was able to talk and use the toilet independently. She was known for throwing tantrums when no rain was forecasted. She loved the sound of rain hitting the window pane. When this didn't happen Tillie would kick the walls angrily and scream "Rain! Rain! Rain! Sue was in charge of three boys. seven year old Fritz had no eyes, and couldn't talk or use the toilet yet. He also suffered from epilepsy. Scott was eight, with very short blonde hair. He was a quiet boy who liked to be by himself. However, he could talk and was toilet trained. Louie, a partially sighted boy of eight, who had a hearing aid, was a real thorn in Sue's side. It wasn't because he couldn't talk or use the toilet, but because of what he did after he had a bowel movement. He took delight in pulling down his pants and proceeding to smear himself with his feces! "Louie, I'm going to kill you!" Sue would exclaim as she took him upstairs for a bath.

On the morning of Mary's first full day everyone was sent out to the Play ground in the rear of the building. Mary had already picked Beth, Donald and Richard as her friends. They were loud, and feisty, but were followers as well. They often did what Mary wanted them to do. Now she encouraged Richard to climb the fence with her. She found out that the kids from the Home for little Wonderers next door were curious about their blind neighbors. She thought it would be nice to meet them and tour their school. She also hoped it would give her the opportunity to run away, something that was still a priority to her. She and Richard were half way up the fence when Luke, Steve and Peter's staff member, ordered them to come down at once. Mary became defiant. "You're not our staff member, you can't tell us what to do!" Richard came down, but when Mary continued to climb. Luke threatened to come up and yank her down. Reluctantly she obeyed, saying "Oh Brother! You're such a bully. You look like Tarzan. I'll bet that when you go home you swing from trees!"

After recess Mary had to go see the school's psychiatrist. It had nothing to do with the incident outside. It turned out that all the older kids had to see him once or twice a week. His name was Dr Sachet. He was a tall, dark haired man with glasses. Mary guessed that he was in his thirties. He wanted to know about her back ground and how she got along with her parents. She willingly told him about her early years with Sister Jane at St Vincent's. She also admitted to being afraid of her parents; feeling secure that he would see no reason to tell them this, she asked Dr Sachet about his family. He told her that he was married and, had a Three year old daughter. This sparked Mary's interest. She wanted to know if he and his daughter were close. He said that he believed they were. When she left his office, Mary thought that Dr Sachet was a nice man. She happily went to lunch. Judy, Stan, Beth and all the others were there, eating roast beef and mashed potatoes. Mary wrinkled her nose. Mary Ann, her staff member was reluctant to let her have anything else, but Jeanette went to the kitchen and had a sandwich made for her.

After lunch everyone was taken up to the dorm for rest period, even the older kids. Mary noticed that some of the little kids were taken to sit on the toilet for five or ten minutes. Whether they went or not she didn't know. Afterward everyone eight and under were left with their shirts, diapers and rubber pants on. Their pants, socks and shoes were removed. They were expected to remain in their rooms for the hour and a half of the rest period. Mary stayed in her visitor's room and played with dolls for a while. Then she decided to go exploring. She looked at the garishly painted corridor. The alphabet was painted on the walls in bright colors.

Mary noticed that Miss Bow was the most diligent of the staff. She frequently took first Vincent, then Kate to the bathroom to try to make them use the toilet. There was another staff member on duty up there, but most of them were out somewhere enjoying their lunch break.

At One thirty everyone returned to class for an hour and a half. Then they played outside in the front play ground until they became too cold. After this they hung around the play room until supper which was at Five O'clock. For a while the students were allowed to hang around downstairs since the staff had to clean everything up. At Six O'clock the students were back in the dorm taking, or being given bathes. Once in their pajamas, they were free to watch TV or wander the corridor and visit each other in their rooms. But at eight all this had to stop because it was bed time. There were of course the usual battles over this. A few Students were picked up and carried to bed, while one or two were actually dragged, screaming all the way.

By the end of her second day in this place, Mary decided that she had had enough. So she waited until eleven which was when all the staff went home for the night. After fifteen minutes or so she crept from her room, suit case in hand. She quickly buttoned her coat and put on her hat. Sitting slumped in a chair facing the TV was the night woman. She was old with bushy, grey hair. She was fast asleep, snoring softly. Mary tip toed around the arm chair and reached up to grab the key that she knew hung on a hook, beside one of the exits. She was just tall enough to reach it. But as she was going out the door that would take her downstairs, and hopefully to a door that opened on to the street, the old woman woke up and confronted her. Mary was so taken aback that she couldn't give an intelligible response. The woman made her return to her room. Mary tried to wait for another opportunity to escape, but as time went by she became exhausted and fell asleep.

The following day the Sullivans were allowed to take Mary out for an hour or so. They seemed pleased with the school, but they weren't happy with some of the things that Mary had been doing. Her two attempts to escape upset them, seeing her in Janice's class chewing gum, and swinging her feet didn't make them very happy. However, what really bothered them was finding out that she told the doctor that she was afraid of them. They were both incensed about this, especially her mother. "HOW DARE YOU TELL SOME ONE THAT YOU'RE SCARED OF US!!" Even Mr. Sullivan was joining in with his wife, though not as loudly. "You're a very ungrateful little girl" he informed her. "Did you tell him that we want you to become a nun too?" asked his wife. "You told this to one of the doctors at the Medical school. We found out about that too". Mary was quivering by now. "I- I thought you did want me to become a nun. You used to say that you and Dad prayed that I would become one." "After all we've done for you. Look what trouble you cause us!". She paused, then said "We said that because we thought it was what you wanted!. BUT HOW DARE YOU TELL THAT DOCTOR THAT WE SCARE YOU!!". By this time Mr. Sullivan was trying to calm his irate wife down.

When Mary returned to school she had decided one thing. She was never going to confide in Dr Sachet ever again. He couldn't be trusted. She didn't want to see him!

The weekends were more relaxed for everyone at the school. A few of the students went home late on Friday afternoons and returned on Sunday afternoons. Most of them had to stay because they came from Connecticut or New Jersey. Mary learned that even these students went home on special occasions though. They were allowed to stay home for a week or two. Beth who came from another part of Massachusetts was allowed to go home every other weekend. Although the students had to get up and go to bed at the same time as they did during the week, they played, watched TV, or listened to records upstairs in the Children's lounge in the morning. In the afternoon they were all taken on outings. Mary loved going for rides on the trolleys and subways. The staff took them to movies, the museums, out to eat and to the John Hancock Tower. They rode the elevator right to the top! Mary, who was a little afraid of heights, nevertheless enjoyed the amazing view of Boston. The partially sighted students like her enjoyed it too. The blind students like Tillie, Peter, Steve, had to be content with having it all described to them. Louie and Judy, who were hearing impaired, had to rely on whatever vision they had in order to appreciate it. Sundays were spent pretty much the same way as Saturdays

Finally the ten day evaluation period for Mary was over. Late one afternoon Jeanette sat her down in the older students dinning room and told her that she would be staying. Mary, who had been expecting to be told the opposite, expressed her disappointment. Jeanette was cheerfully firm. "Don't worry Mary, you'll get used to our school quickly, and want to stay." Mary wasn't convinced, but she reluctantly followed Jeanette across the foyer to the play room where everyone else was. A few of the little kids were sitting at the tables in the younger student's dinning room. They didn't know how to play. Instead, they rocked back and forth to the music, or swung their heads from side to side. Kate, the little girl, who had no eyes, was among them. She went home every weekend. This made Mary happy because she had already discovered that Kate was very attached to her father. Mary once saw them heartily embracing each other in the lobby when he brought her back to school. Having already established friendships with Beth, Donald, and Richard, Mary ran off to play with them. She noticed Scott, the quiet, blonde boy of eight doing the only other thing he did besides sitting in the club house that was in the rear of the play room. He was standing beneath one of the speakers and doing the twist, his hands clasped firmly in front of him and a look of deep concentration on his up turned face. He waved shyly at her and said "Hi Buddy…Hi Buddy" in a voice that was barely more then a whisper. He always did this. It was his way of greeting people. Although he was able to talk and had some eye sight, he remained quiet most of the time and entertained himself without complaint. Mary saw Tillie hovering by one of the windows, waiting for rain.

The next morning Mary began to get a real taste of what life at the school was going to be like. First of all, she was smacked in the face at breakfast by Judy, who was having a tantrum. Beth, who liked to be the staff's little helper, jumped up and restrained the older girl. "Sorry Mary!" she cried breathlessly. "Friday is always a bad day for Judy!" She gave Judy the milk and sugar for her cereal, and the girl settled down. Beth sat back down with an air of importance.

During art & craft period Steve had another one of his tantrums. As Mary entered the room she was nearly knocked down by him as he angrily stumbled by her, dragging his paralyzed leg with him. With his good hand he reached out blindly and caught a fist full of her hair! After she was freed from him, she sat down to an art project that she didn't like. Mary Ann had been established as her permanent staff member from Seven-Three. Beth was under her authority as well. Although Mary Ann was sometimes funny and kind of cool, she was usually a little antagonistic with Mary and Beth. Often she seemed more like a resentful fifteen year old taking care of her little sisters, instead of a woman in her twenties who was employed as a staff member. As Mary complained about the unwelcome art project, Mary Ann said"Uh Oh, Mary's bitching!" This was to become a regular observation on Mary Ann's part, because even though Mary loved art, she usually chose to work on her own projects, and the students didn't have this option during class time.

At rest period Mary was told that she would be changing rooms. "But I like having my own room." insisted Mary. "You can't have it anymore" said Luke reasonably. "You're not the visiting child now. Soon another student will need this room for their evaluation". Grumbling, Mary moved her things down the hall. She would be rooming with Judy and Beth. Mary was glad to have Beth as her room mate, but not Judy. Because she was partially deaf and didn't yet know sign language, she became frustrated and had tantrums. Also, she liked to lie on her bed and masturbate. She didn't even try to conceal this, even when Luke or one of the boys entered the room. When Beth saw her doing this, she always rushed right over and grabbed Judy's hand. "No Judy!" she would yell. "That's bad, stop it!" Judy would holler and punch the wall, but she had enough respect for Beth to stop it temporarily.

Less then a week later a new visiting child took Mary's place in her old room. Mary had just finished having a exam by the doctor, when a young mulotto woman with long, wavy black hair entered, carrying a little African American girl of about a year and a half. She was placed on the examination table. Mary couldn't hear what the woman said, but the doctor began looking at the baby's vagina. As

Mary was led from the room she thought Better you then me, Kiddo. This procedure had been

done to her twice recently, and with no explanation.

It turned out that the baby she saw in the doctor's office was the new "Visiting Child". Mary was surprised to learn that she was Three years old! She was partially sighted, couldn't yet talk, and couldn't walk. Her name was Tina. She had a very sweet disposition, and didn't like to be alone. According to her mother, she was like this at home too. A crib was placed in the visiting child's room for her. Mary could hear her crying sadly, rather then shrilly when she was alone in there.

Everyone liked Tina. The only time Mary heard anyone speak unkindly to her was when Donald, who was being restrained in a forced time-out shouted a racial insult at her, as she crawled past him. Fortunately, she was oblivious to his words. After the ten days were up, Tina left. No one knew where she went afterward.

Mary found that she was growing extremely tired of listening to Laura Nyro's record. One day when it wasn't being played, she sneaked in to the closet where the stereo was kept. She grabbed the record and hid it behind the refrigerator in the kitchen. For a week and a half nobody heard Laura Nyro. One day when Mary and some of the other students were returning from a walk, Jeanette commented to Elaine and Mary Ann about the record's disappearance. Mary, who was walking in back of them, couldn't hold back a giggle. All three staff members pounced on her, and demanded an explanation. After they got a confession out of her, she was made to retrieve the record from behind the refrigerator. "Your going to listen to it until you learn to like it!" announced an out raged Mary Ann. It actually did work too. She eventually did come to like Laura Nyro as much as the staff did.

Unfortunately, most disagreements between Mary and the staff weren't resolved so easily. Many times she found herself in time-out, yelling and swearing at whoever put her there. Sometimes she had to be restrained in a forced time-out, like her friend, Donald. Some of this wasn't her fault. Mary Ann, who dealt with her the most, liked to antagonize Mary. She teased her and snapped at her unnecessarily. She also liked to play Mary and Beth against each other. When she was angry at Beth, she would be very sweet to Mary and give her things in front of Beth. When she was angry at Mary, she would be extra nice to Beth. Once she offered Mary a drag from her cigarette. When Beth asked for one, she received a big "NO!" from Mary Ann. When she was upset with Mary she yelled at her and encouraged Beth to join in.

One day a little boy with light blonde hair, of about five came to the school. Mary saw Luke holding him. At first she thought it was John, the little boy who waved his hand in front of his face because he could only see shadows. When she saw him close up, she discovered that they had another visiting child on their hands. His name was David. He was going on six, and couldn't talk. He was a cute little boy with a chubby face and full lips and large blue eyes. He was very active and had a bad temper. Most of the staff said he was spoiled. A few said that he just belonged home with his mother. David was a biter, scratcher, pincher, and a hair puller. The only thing that really soothed him was music. When he wasn't running or twirling around and giggling to the music, he liked to be held and lightly bounced to the rhythm of the song. David was placed in Miss Bow's group, along with Vincent, and Kate. She decided to potty train him. It was obvious though that he wasn't **really** being trained. Miss Bow, with her diligence, and observation, worked out a schedule of **when** to take him to "sit". As a result, he almost always went for her. He didn't like it for some **reason**. Mary noticed that he always screamed and cried when being made to use the toilet. **Miss Bow** took a no nonsense attitude with him. She accused him of putting on a performance and even called him a fake. She took a hard approach to his tantrums too. It was a battle!

Because of David's eye condition, He had to receive eye drops throughout the day. He was given them right after breakfast, at morning recess, after lunch, during afternoon recess, and before bed time. He hated it, and always put up a fight. It took two people to hold him down, while the third person applied the drops. It all resulted in Mary liking and feeling extremely sorry for David. Every chance she got, she carried him around, held him on her lap when she used the swing, and sneaked him toys and snacks. She angrily defended him when some one criticized him. For some reason she desperately wanted an adult to feel bad for him and love him. She was very glad that he went home every weekend. At least he was happy then. He wasn't happy on Monday mornings when he returned to school though. He would scream and cry for two hours before settling down. It was the music in the play room that had the calming effect. Soon he would be twirling, giggling, and running happily, in no particular direction. Mary always watched him closely, even when she and Beth were standing under one of the speakers, singing to their favorite songs. At these times Mary and Beth couldn't count on Donald and Richard's company. Every morning during the half hour break they both helped out the janitor, Russ. He was a good natured, African American in his early Sixties, who had a lot of patience with his young helpers. When they were with him, Beth and Mary weren't wanted. It was Donald's and Richard's time to act like men. Mary didn't mind. She had Beth's company, and was busy looking out for David.

As tough as Miss Bow liked to think of herself, she was no match for some of the big kids. Stan, a partially sighted, fourteen years old, who was obsessed with records, liked to keep to himself. This meant that he didn't usually want people in his room. One day Miss Bow refused to leave his room because she wasn't finished scolding him. With an enraged scream, Stan hurled his stereo at her. It missed her head by an inch!

Mary turned eleven in April. Her parents were allowed to visit and take her out for a few hours. She proudly showed them a letter that she had just received from her former doctor at Bradley Hospital. Dr Pat was a devoted doctor, who liked to keep in touch with her former patients. Mary was impressed. She had recently given birth to a daughter. Her name was Leila. Mary eagerly told her parents about the baby. Mrs. Sullivan became suspicious, then jealous, then angry. First of all, she didn't like adults taking a personal interest in her daughter. Second of all she didn't like Mary discussing women giving birth. Mary should have remembered this. It was a cardinal rule, just as discussing death, or asking adults how old they were was. Mrs. Sullivan hollered at Mary for a while. Then she locked herself in a public restroom. Mr. Sullivan, who had been quiet up until now, turned to his daughter." Mary, you're only a little girl. You shouldn't be talking about such things". She hung her head in embarrassment. Later

Mary apologized repeatedly and claimed that she didn't even want the letter. She disposed of it in front of her parents. After this they managed to have some sort of celebration. Mary received a doll, which she liked very much, and some clothes that she didn't like very much. This was what led to the day of the clothes fiasco, and what a day that was!

Mary was tired of all the dowdy, out dated clothes her mother made her wear. In the era of short dresses, skirts, and bell bottomed pants, which were all the rage in 72, she was expected to wear long, straight, plaid skirts that came to just below the knee. With these, she had to wear blouses with ruffles down the front. Sometimes she wore jumpers over the blouses to cover the ruffles, but the jumpers were usually plaid or grey, and often made of wool. These, like the skirts, came just below the knee. She was allowed a few turtle neck shirts and a few sweaters, but the sweaters were the kind that old women wore. They were thick cable knit, and they buttoned down the front. Although her mother occasionally included bell bottoms in Mary's wardrobe nowadays, they were too big. This made them baggy, and too long. Her mother didn't hem them from the inside. She simply cuffed them up, and sewed them that way. It didn't look right. None of her clothes looked right. They were all a size too large. If the other students at the school didn't notice Mary's odd clothes, the staff certainly did. Yet no body said anything about it. They didn't even try to get her some nicer clothes. Once when Mary suggested taking up the hem of one of her skirts, Mary Ann shook her head disapprovingly. "Uh Uh, Mama wouldn't like that." Mary stomped her foot in frustration. Why couldn't some of her clothes be altered? It wasn't as if her parents came up to Boston every week to see her. Surely the altered clothes could be put aside during the visit. She could wear her 1940's get up while her parents were there. Then she could change after they left.

The only time Mary had a chance to look like other Eleven year olds was when Beth loaned her some of her out fits. It was a lucky coincidence that she was able to fit in to Beth's clothes since Beth was six months younger then she was.

One morning Mary came up with a plan. Her parents were coming up to Boston. They were being permitted to take her out for the day. Mary decided that this would be an excellent opportunity to get rid of all her bother some clothes. She told Mary Ann that most of her clothes were too small for her now, and that she wanted to get rid of them. With any luck she would get her parents to take her shopping for some hip looking clothes… Well maybe slightly hip. However, Mary Ann had other ideas. "We shouldn't just get rid of all these clothes without informing your parents." She told a pouting Mary." Let's let your mother be the judge." Mary groaned loudly and was scolded.

When the Sullivans arrived Mary Ann carried the large garbage bag down stairs. She was followed by a nervous Mary. Mr. and Mrs. Sullivan were waiting in the lobby. When confronted by the bag of clothes, Mrs. Sullivan proceeded to go through it and hold up every piece of clothing. "This isn't too small for you!" she said each time she held a skirt or dress against her daughter. "None of these clothes are too small for you. What is the meaning of this?" demanded an irate Mrs. Sullivan. Mary cringed as she always did when confronted by her mother. "Well, I- I Th-thought they were." mumbled Mary lamely Meanwhile, Mr. Sullivan did what he always did in situations like this. He stood near by and said nothing. Mary Ann leaned against the counter with her arms folded across her chest, looking angry. "She told me they were all too small" she remarked defensively. She gave Mary a dirty look and said that she would see her when she got back. Then she hauled the bag of clothes back upstairs.

After a very tense and unpleasant visit, in which Mrs. Sullivan hollered at her daughter, and Mr. Sullivan said very little, except to agree with his wife, Mary sadly returned to the school. She went upstairs to her room and saw all her ugly clothes back in her wardrobe. Suddenly Mary Ann entered the room. "So, the liar returns!" She threw herself down on Beth's bed and proceeded to tell Mary what she now thought of her. Mary had to hear a whole speech about what a deceitful, hypocrite she was. "Just last week you were showing me a dress of yours, and saying this is my church dress. What a laugh! You obviously haven't gotten anything out of going, have you?" Mary, who hardly ever got along with Mary Ann, would be yelling and swearing at her by now. However, this was one of those times where she just didn't have the heart to defend herself. She felt as bad and as unworthy as Mary Ann thought she was. "You made me look like such an Ass down in that lobby. Now I know what a liar you truly are, and I'll never believe you again!" With that, Mary Ann got up and stomped out of the room. Mary started to cry. She went over to hang up her sweater. When she closed the wardrobe door she struck her head against it in frustration. In doing so, she accidentally chipped her front tooth slightly

Later she went to look at a picture of a man in a magazine advertisement. She had found him intriguing. Normally she carried his picture with her, but she had decided to keep it in her room today. Mary searched every inch of her room. There was no sign of it. Did Mary Ann find it and dispose of it? It wouldn't surprise Mary if she did. It was the kind of thing she would do if she was angry at someone,

especially Mary. Her room mates, Beth and Judy would have no reason to take her picture away. They never touched her things. So it had to be Mary Ann. This was a final blow to a very bad day. Did Mary Ann really think she had suffered just because she felt embarrassed down in the lobby? She didn't

know what suffering was!

The bulletin board was just out side of the entrance to the first floor play room, the one that the students were kept in most of the time. All sorts of notices were tacked upon that bulletin board. Tillie must have her vaporizer on at night. Be sure to give Vinny, Fritz, Richard their seizure meds. No students are allowed in the staff dining room. Be sure to replace batteries in Judy's and Louie's hearing aids. David needs his eye drops five times a day. There was also a detailed schedule of when to take David to the bathroom, with an assurance that the person would have success. Right after Mary's birthday she discovered a notice up there that she didn't like at all. It said Mary Sullivan is no longer allowed to watch Hogan's Heroes. She grabbed the paper off the board and threw it away. Unfortunately

Pat from the front office caught her and made her replace it. Mary was furious! So what if she got carried away and acted silly when she saw Sergeant Schultz? He was her make believe father. Why did people always take things away from her?

In spite of her feelings toward Dr Sachet, she was required to see him for an hour once a week He had to come looking for her because she wasn't about to go to his office volunteerarily Her first visit with him after he told her parents that she was scared of them, Mary sat down and told him that she wasn't really scared of her parents at all. She had promised them that she would do this. "I don't know why I said that to you Dr Sachet. I guess I was just bored and wanted to joke around a little." She giggled nervously as she said this. From then on Mary wasted the hourly sessions by acting silly or belligerent. Let him tell her parents about this. They already knew that she was capable of being both. What could you do or say around someone you couldn't even trust? Dr Sachet came to believe that Mary was an instigator who liked to upset people. Mary decided to let him think what he wanted. Beth seemed to like Dr Sachet. On nice days he let her sit in his car and play with the controls while they talked. She used to start up his car, and shut it off. He let her start up the wind shield wipers and the radio. Sometimes the students were playing in the front play ground when Beth was having one of her sessions with Dr Sachet. Mary would go to the swing set that was nearest to the parking lot. She, Richard, and Donald would sing loudly, toss playful insults at each other and with a little enticement from Mary; hold loud swearing contests. To the boys, it was boisterous fun. To Mary it was all intended for Dr Sachet's ears. For some reason that she couldn't quite explain, she wanted him to hear just how loud, obscene, and nasty she could be. From time to time, as the three of them swung and tried to out swear each other, Mary would glance over her shoulder. But the doctor seemed absorbed in talking to Beth. Still, he must be able to hear us, thought Mary. She laughed and loudly told the boys that she was planning to run away.

One day in May a new boy came to the school. His name was Jimmy, and he was from RI. Mary was delighted about this. "I'm no longer the only kid here from RI" She kept saying. Jimmy was going on nine. He was almost totally blind. He was a cute little boy with straight brown hair. He had a round face and large brown eyes framed by long lashes. He could not only walk and dress himself, he also could talk and use the toilet independently, he could also play the piano and organ. He was rather shy about it though. He had his mother with him much of the time. She was a pleasant, patient woman. She quietly urged him to play a few songs for everyone. Unlike some of the other students, Jimmy was quite passive. He didn't throw tantrums. Once when Mary was sitting beside him during lunch she noticed that his head was lowered and he wasn't eating. Jeanette leaned over him and asked what was wrong. His response was inaudible to Mary. "Well Jimmy if you don't like the milk, you don't have to drink it. There's no need to cry about it though." Mary didn't even realize that he had been crying, that was how quiet he was! He didn't stay after his ten days were up. Once again Mary was the only student at the school who came from RI.

A few days after Jimmy left there was a birthday party in the older student's dining room. Mary, who had been having a bad day mouthed off at Elaine, Judy's and Stan's staff member. Elaine ordered her from the room. Mary refused to leave. Elaine wasn't her staff member. Besides, the cake and ice cream had just been carried in to the room. It looked delicious! Mary Ann backed Elaine up. "GO!" she ordered. Mary sat on the floor in the foyer, where the orange piano was. She was fuming! She was going to have to miss out on Peter's birthday celebration and it wasn't fair! If only Elaine wasn't so abrasive toward her, Mary would get along with her better. She heard the kids sing Happy Birthday to Peter. She wouldn't get to enjoy any of it. Mary turned and put her fist through one of the windows that framed the door that opened on to the back play ground.(The windows by the door in the foyer, and in the older student's dining room were among the few that weren't covered by metal bars) Mary Ann heard the glass smashing. She ran out and took Mary in to the library. She had her in a restrained time-out when she saw Mary's bloody arm. They took a cab to The Boston Children's Hospital. The doctor who stitched up Mary's arm was very friendly and funny. He totally put her at ease. Mary Ann stood in the doorway and gave her angry, murderous looks. Mary was grateful for the doctor's presence in the room.

Tillie was very well known at The Boston Children's Hospital. In spite of her vaporizer, she had frequent asthma attacks. Often she had to be rushed to the hospital late at night. The attacks scared Tillie, and she often screamed and cried as she gasped for breath. People would try to calm her down because her frightened tantrums only made things worse. Another regular visitor at the children's Hospital was Fritz. He was in Sue's group, along with Louie and Scott. Fritz was a quiet, easy going little boy who had no eyes, and was very close to Sue. He was Seven, and couldn't talk yet. He also had epilepsy. One morning he had a seizure, and was rushed to the hospital. Everyone later found out that he died there. Mary wasn't close to Fritz, like she was to David, but his death did effect her. She kept asking how and why it happened. "They just couldn't revive him" someone said. Mary remembered how Fritz had returned to school after spending two weeks with his family. He was quietly sobbing because his father had just left. Sue took him in her arms and held him, soothing him with words of sympathy. As Mary watched she realized that this little boy brought out the best in a woman who was often abrupt and judgmental with some of the other students, Mary included. Of everyone, Sue must have missed Fritz most. If things had been different between her and Sue, Mary might have dared to offer her some words of comfort. However, this was never easy for Mary in the best of situations.

The Fourth of July picnic was on a Saturday. It included everyone. Parents came, secretaries, doctors, staff, students, even Miss Kendal was there. Mary didn't like her. She saw her as a sarcastic, condescending, sour puss. Miss Kendal didn't like Mary either. It was well known that the school's director saw her as a Sarah Bernhardt (old time actress from the 1930's.) Mary retaliated by referring to Miss Kendal as "The Prima Donna." To Mary's complete surprise, her parents found this amusing. Sometimes they joked with her about Miss Kendal being a Prima Donna.

Dr. and Mrs. Waterhouse were at the picnic. Dr. Waterhouse was the director at Perkins school for the Blind. His wife, who was blind, was a teacher there. Mary didn't know Dr. Waterhouse, but she knew his wife. Every week Mrs. Waterhouse came to the school. She liked to spend a half hour or so counseling some of the older students. When it was Mary's turn, she eagerly ran up to the Arts & Craft room for her session. She enjoyed this time. Mrs. Waterhouse was old, but she had a pleasant, humorous, personality which put the often defensive Mary at ease. Along with talking about life at the school, Mary liked to ask Mrs. Waterhouse about the students she taught at Perkins. The one thing she dared not discuss with this woman was her relationship with her parents. She learned the hard way to keep her mouth shut about this.

Mary sat between her parents and watched people arriving. The picnic was at an open field, on the out skirts of Boston. Because most of the parents didn't know how to get there, it was decided that the students who didn't have parents visiting, would ride in the school van. The parents, who did come, would take their son or daughter with them, and follow the van. The students who went home on weekends received directions in advance, and were able to meet everyone there at the field, with their parents. . After Mary and the other kids, who were lucky enough to have their parents come for the picnic, were seated,, the kids who spent weekends at home began showing up. Mary saw Beth, Kate, and Judy arrive with their families. But where was David? She kept looking around, this way and that, wondering aloud about him. Her parents, who were in a good mood that day, assured her that he would be there soon, and sure enough, he was! Little David walked hurriedly along, clutching the hand of an older brother, who had darker hair then David, and looked to be about twelve. A middle aged couple was with them. David suddenly let go of his brother's hand and did what he normally did. He ran around aimlessly, as if he felt trapped. His straight, light blonde hair shone brightly in the hot sun, and he wore red shorts, and a red sweater Richard, Donald, John, Jimmy, Steve, were there with staff. A few of the students who lived in New Jersey were home for a two week vacation.

A big tent was set up with picnic tables and a grill for cooking. For those who didn't mind the sun and heat, chairs were set up outside of the tent. Most people chose to remain under the tent throughout the afternoon. The smell of hot dogs and hamburgers soon drew everyone to the picnic tables. Everyone was hungry, even David, who was fussing a lot that day. Mary saw him sitting on the ground, beside one of the tables. He cried continually, stopping long enough to chew a bite of the hot dog, before going back to bawling loudly. Mary wondered what was wrong. Her mother claimed that he liked an audience. She called him a "little attention getter". Mary shrugged uncertainly at this. She was interrupted by another out burst of crying. At the next table, one of Kate's twin sisters, a little blonde, girl of about five, wearing glasses, bit the side of her mouth while chewing. Her father, who was sitting next to her, comforted her until she calmed down. This confirmed what Mary already thought of Kate's father, he was a very loving, affectionate, man. This made her smile. Kate, despite having no eyes, had a wonderful father. Her mother, who was being attentive to the three girls, seemed nice too.

Some of the people moved out to the lawn chairs after lunch. Beth played with her sister and brothers, while her parents talked to other parents. David curled up on the lap of his plump mother for almost half an hour. Then he was off and running again, throwing tantrums when one of the staff carried him back to the picnic area. Mary introduced Beth, Donald, and Richard to her parents, as her best friends. Several of the staff talked with her parents as well. Luke actually sat down and visited with them, sometimes including Mary in the conversation. Over all it was a very good event Mary decided. Especially since Dr. Sachet, who was on vacation with his family, couldn't attend..

A few days after the picnic, Mary was told to go to the office across the hall from Dr. Sachet's office. Puzzled, she went, without argument. She found a young, woman with shoulder length, brown hair, who looked to be in her early thirties. She wore a white doctor's coat over a blouse and skirt. "Hello, I'm Dr. Bergmann." She had a calm, quiet voice. She gestured for Mary to take a seat across from her. Mary sat and looked at the woman expectantly. Dr. Bergmann told her that she had been brought in to talk to some of the older students, and find out if anything was bothering them, and how she could help. At first Mary had been ready to just play head games, and be obnoxious like she was with Dr. Sachet. But there was something different about this doctor. Mary detected no arrogance or sarcasm in her.

She looked at Mary intently, and seemed to be not only listening, but taking her seriously, even when she was asking Dr. Bergmann if some babies were bad. "I mean like really bad, unlikable…and mean?" She clasped her hands together anxiously, as she waited for a response. Dr. Bergmann appeared bewildered by her question. "Well, no Mary, I don't think there is such a thing as a mean baby." Mary sat forward. "You don't?" Dr. Bergmann shook her head. "Not even if they cry a lot, or wave their fists in the air?" asked an amazed Mary. "It usually means they need attention of some sort, that's all." replied the doctor matter of factly. That's all? Mary, still uncertain, began to fidget and clasp and unclasp her hands. "But-but some grown ups hate crying babies, and they think there is such a thing as a mean toddler too… Do you think so?" Dr. Bergmann remained calm, and very attentive to Mary and her worries. She reassured her that she didn't believe in mean babies or toddlers. There was something about this woman that made Mary want to trust her. It was on the tip of her tongue to tell her all about her mother's angry shouting sessions. She wanted to tell the doctor about all those baby and toddler photos that showed Mary wearing old fashioned dresses, posed in a kneeling position, with a pair of rosary beads. She wanted to tell her about the exorcisms that her mother performed on her when she was living at home, or about the times when she was Seven, and tried drinking Holy Water on a couple of occasions, because she thought it would turn her in to a nice child. In spite of Dr. Bergmann's obvious goodness Mary couldn't take the risk. Suppose her parents found out? Besides, this doctor was only here on a temporary basis, just to analyze the oldest students. So, Mary eventually just laughed nervously, and said "Well, I was just curious, that's all."

Mary tried to forget about Dr. Bergmann. Soon she was stuffing things down the laundry chute with her friends. Toys, books, chairs, everything except laundry went flying down to the basement, much to the extreme frustration of the laundry lady who was employed there. Mary, who discovered that the bars that covered the windows in the dorm, were held closed, not by a lock, but by a thick shoe lace, revealed this discovery to her friends. One day they were caught emptying a bed room of all of its contents. Donald, who set himself up as the boss, even though it was Mary's idea, ordered Richard, Beth, and Mary to throw all the clothes in the wardrobes out the window. Next all the toys were tossed out. Then the sheets, blankets, and pillows from the three beds went sailing out the window. Donald, who was happily jumping on the bed as he gave out the orders, decided that the mattresses would go next. They were grabbing the first mattress when Linda, one of the afternoon staff walked in and had a screaming fit! Not only did they have to bring everything upstairs, they were grounded, with no TV or snacks for the whole weekend.

Even though it was summer, they still had classes at the school. They wouldn't receive vacation time until August. Mary hated this, and she suspected that her classmates did too. It might have been easier if Janice, their teacher, was nicer and made the work more interesting, but she didn't. She either gave hard assignments that caused quiet Stan, who sat right behind Mary to explode in to tantrums, where he screamed, swore, and deliberately banged his head repeatedly against the cabinet in back of him. Mary and Beth would burst in to giggles, followed by Richard and Donald. Janice screamed at them all. At other times she treated them like babies. She would make them listen to Sesame Street, or the sound track to Mary Poppins Sometimes she would make them all lay on the floor and form the shape of a square, or a rectangle. Soon the frustration became too much, and Mary would encourage the others to act up with her. This infuriated Janice! She would punish the others, but it was Mary she especially went after. Often Mary found herself flat on her back, with the teacher sitting on top of her. Every time she moved, Janice would slam her knees against Mary's temples! Sometimes she saw stars.

After school Mary and her friends sometimes pretended to get drunk. The four of them would run to the kitchen, fill their glasses with water, and sugar, then run to the foyer, where the orange piano was. One of them would play fast paced, meaningless songs on the piano, while everyone else danced then ran wildly around the room, bumping in to each other, running in to walls, and twirling until they fell, laughing to the floor. Then they would get up, drink more sugar water, and do the whole routine all over again. Since Richard had epilepsy, he was usually the one banging away at the piano.

They did other things too. Sometimes the staff took them down to the basement. There was a play room, and there were a few classrooms for the day students to attend. Mary and the other residential students didn't see much of them. There was also a gym. When the day students went home, Mary and the others were taken down there to do exercises on the mats, or jump on the trampoline. They loved this best. One evening Stan, the oldest of them was having his turn when the phone rang. Marion, who was watching them, told Stan to sit on the trampoline. As soon as she left Donald did what he always did with Stan. "Hey Stan" he said, in his gruff little voice. "Get up and jump, go on, do it." Stan shook his head. "Nooo!" he whined. "Marion told me not to". Donald kept prompting him. Mary, Beth, and Richard joined in. Minutes later Stan got up and started jumping. He hadn't jumped more then four times when Marion entered the room and yelled at him. She didn't care that the others had told him to do it. He lost his turn, and Donald went next! Although Mary thought it was funny, she wondered why Stan obeyed Donald. He showed no desire to be friends with any of them. Yet every time he was urged to do something he knew was wrong, he always gave in and did it. It was entertainment for Mary and the others, and he became known as the boy who couldn't say "No".

It soon became noticeable that Stan was becoming stranger and stranger, not only because he was doing things like throwing glasses of water at the wall, at Donald's urging, he was also having more head banging episodes in the classroom. He constantly carried an empty record cover around with him, and had to be told to get it out of his face. He sometimes refused. Then one night Mary entered the bathroom and found Stan standing completely naked, in the toilet. He had his back to her and wouldn't respond when she asked him what he was doing. She ran to get a staff member to deal with him.

It was right after this that it was decided that Stan would be leaving the school. No one would tell Mary or her friends where he was going. All the staff would say was that Stan was going to a school where he could learn how to become a man Why all the secrecy? Everyone knew that Judy went to Perkins School for the blind. The staff arranged a birthday party for her right before she left. What was the deal with Stan?

Mary wasn't affected by Judy's or Stan's departure. She still had little David to be a doting big sister to. She had her friends too. While Vinnie was a mystery to the staff because he still wasn't potty trained after two years, Richard was even more of a mystery. After five or six years of schooling, he still couldn't read, write, or spell! He wanted to learn. He actually thought he could spell. Once after a seizure, he went up to a staff member and with a very serious look on his face, he said" I had a e-z-o-p-l-k. It was awful" He looked so earnest about his misspelling that Mary had to turn away and laugh quietly in to her hand

The thing that amazed everyone was that Richard knew the entire subway system in Boston by heart! During rest period, and sometimes at bed time, he would lie on his bed, put his feet on the wall, and pound out the rhythm of the trains. He would pause to call out a stop then resume his pounding. If allowed, he would work his way right through the red line, then go on to the green line, followed by the orange line, then the blue line. Rarely did he get past more then two of the lines. Mary found this amusing, and Richard's room mate, John had no problem with it. The staff however, could only take it for so long. When they asked him to stop, he refused. When they reprimanded him, he would only stop long enough to yell "Get out of my room you fucking frigate!" Mary once over heard a staff member laughingly telling another that Richard didn't realize that frigate was a name for a large ship, not a swear word. So every day the dorm echoed with pounding, accompanied by shouts of "PARK STREET!" And then "DOWNTOWN CROSSING!" and "SOUTH STATION!" etc. This was Richard's passion, and no one was going to interfere with it. It was like the new boy, a sixteen year old with a high voice whose name was Stewart. His passion was sitting in front of the window at the end of the hallway during rest period, leaning forward, with his elbows on his knees, waiting eagerly for a trolley to go by. They rode by the school every ten minutes. For the visiting child, this was better then TV.

Mary loved going on outings in Boston. She loved riding the trolleys and subways too. But she wasn't obsessed with them. She could usually be found running up and down the hallway with Beth, Donald, and Richard, when he was tired of playing conductor. Or she could be found painting pictures on her bed room wall, something she was stopped from doing. She couldn't understand this. The entire hallway was painted with the alphabet for Pete's sake!

In the fall another visiting child arrived. His name was Danny. He was partially sighted, and wore a hearing aid. He was Six years old, and very temperamental. He, like Stewart, stayed on when their evaluation period ended. Then another visiting child arrived for ten days. His name was Elliot. He was Three years old, but looked about a year old. He couldn't walk. His scalp was covered with huge bald spots. The hair that he did have was light brown, and wavy. He wore a cast on his left arm to keep him from pulling out any more of his hair. He didn't stay at the school.

Vinnie, the curly, black haired, toilet warrior was getting out of hand. He had always been a mischief maker, hiding on the staff, turning on the garden hose and aiming it at people. Eventually he took to throwing building blocks at people. His aim was often right on the mark. He found it amusing when his victim cried. When other punishments failed, the staff harnessed him to the old fashioned radiator in the corner of the play room. He usually stayed there for ten to fifteen minutes. He clearly didn't like it, and seemed bewildered as well as upset. The staff hoped this would tame him down.

Along with the potty training, the staff were trying to get David to stomp his feet when he was angry, instead of banging his head. They began putting him in time- out when he misbehaved. Mary noticed that his mother no longer sent him back to school with cute little boy out fits. He now wore turtle necks, sweaters, sweat shirts, and bell bottoms. Miss Bow had obviously been talking to his mother. The staff and teachers were trying to coax him to say the few words he knew. One day when Mary was poking around in one of the basement classrooms, she came across a note on a table that said DAVID CAN SIT Still FOR UP TO FIFTEEN MINUTES. HE CAN SAY YES AND GO FOR PEANUTS. What is he, wondered Mary, an elephant? Unlike David's slow, hesitant, sometimes unwilling steps toward progress, John, who was the same age as David, suddenly began to blossom! He began to speak a few words, and happily took to potty training. He was in the early stages of learning to dress himself and enjoyed it. Perhaps the staff noticed that when Richard wasn't acting out, he was teaching his younger room mate how to talk a little. He also carried John with him when he had to go to the bathroom. He probably started showing him how to dress himself. The staff decided to take it from there. Linda, the afternoon staff member who worked with John, knew that his mother couldn't afford to send him any clothes. She somehow managed to obtain the money to buy him four or five pairs of pants and just as many shirts, plus some training pants. She even tried to get him to stop waving his hand in front of his face as much.

One of the boys from the day school became a residential student. His name was Tommy. He was Eight, but wasn't yet potty trained. He talked like a parrot, repeating back everything that was said to him. Mary Ann, one of the mean staff members, used to like to say "Tommy is an asshole" He would echo her then whimper because he knew that she was making fun of him. Mary wondered if Mary Ann would ever leave. She and Beth still didn't like her anymore then she liked them. Tommy was very lazy. He laid on the floor every chance he got. He was well fed, but remained thin as a rail.

Mary went home on weekends a few times during her time at the school, mainly because her parents pressured her in to asking to go. A couple of the visits went smoothly enough. But the one in September was terrible! It started out nicely enough. She sneaked a picture of her latest heart throb in to her bag.(He was an anchorman from Channel Five. Before him, she was head over heels about another anchor man from the Boston area.) Friday and Saturday went by without incident. Then on Sunday morning when Mrs. Sullivan was cleaning the bathroom, Mary tried to avoid brushing against her as she was passing. Mrs. Sullivan took offense to this. She accused her daughter of insulting her. Mary denied it then apologized repeatedly for it. Her mother wouldn't listen. She yelled instead. Mr. Sullivan stayed out of it. Later when her parents were saying the rosary, Mary tearfully joined them. She looked over at her mother several times to show how repentant she was, but Mrs. Sullivan held her head high, and refused to look at her crying daughter. In the afternoon Mary left a note in the living room for her mother to find. It said I want to go back to the center. Her mother found it a few minutes later. She lost her temper, and had to be restrained by Mr. Sullivan. "I'll send you to the center!!" she screamed. "I'll send you back to the Medical center!" Mr. Sullivan calmed her down. As a result, Mary was stuck at home until the following day. If it hadn't been for Labor Day Weekend, she would have returned to Boston on Sunday, like she wanted.

They weren't taken out trick or treating on Halloween. Instead, they had a party right there at the school. Janice was actually able to organize her unruly class in to putting on a production of Cinderella. Mary played the Fairy God Mother. It went off with hardly any hitches. Afterward there were games and party food for everyone.

In November two visiting children arrived for the ten day evaluation. They were a boy and a girl, both Nine years old, and both in wheel chairs. The boy's name was Ben. He could talk. The girl's name was Sherri, she couldn't talk. However, unlike Ben, she had a devoted, loving family with her. The mother seemed like any mother, asking questions about the school, and what her daughter might get out of being there. Sherri's father was more easy going and fun loving. He and his Three year old daughter talked to, and played with Sherri a lot. In the end either Ben or Sherri stayed at the school.

One more visitor arrived for the ten day evaluation before Mary left the school. The visitor was a Three year old African American girl named Brenda. She was quite independent. She put the Six year olds to shame! She could walk, talk, dress herself, and go to the bathroom on her own. She was legally blind though. She was out going and funny, but she had an annoying way of picking up other people's habits. She swung her head from side to side, and demanded cookies for being good, just like Steve. She threw blocks because she saw Vinnie doing it. Mary didn't know that Brenda had been paying much attention to Richard's habits until one day when Brenda got upset with her for not sharing the crayons. In frustration, Brenda hit the back of her head against the wall several times and yelled "FUCKING MARY!" Mary angrily scolded her for this. Brenda went on to Perkins when the ten days were over.

On Mary's last day at the school everything went the same way it usually did, until the evening. Because the heat in the play room wasn't working, the staff had everyone confined in the foyer where the orange piano was. It was tight quarters for them. David hadn't been taken to the bathroom in awhile. As a result, he smelled terrible, and no one wanted to be near him. This didn't seem to bother him. He rocked slightly, and hummed to himself. Jimmy sat near his staff person, and whined continually. His little face was screwed up like an old man's. Mary didn't give him a second glance. He was like this so often that it didn't surprise her anymore. Tillie was hovering by the window, pleased because it was raining. She kept her ear pressed against the glass. Mary and her friends started getting too rowdy, and silly. When it was time to go upstairs, Linda spoke quite harshly to Mary about it. The fact that Linda said nothing to the others infuriated Mary. She and Linda got in to a shouting match. Then Mary ran upstairs. But instead of heading for the dorm, Mary ran through one the doors that led down to the basement. Then she tore up a flight of stairs where there was a door that led outside. To her surprise, it was unlocked! Only thinking about how angry she was, she ran out in to the rainy, November evening. At the top of the driveway she stopped and looked back. For one fleeting second she wanted to turn back. However, her anger toward Linda, and the unfairness of how she was treated, still burned in her. She walked away.

For almost four hours Mary wandered around Jamaica Plains in the rain. It felt good to be walking along sidewalks, and crossing streets independently. She craved this. After awhile the thrill began to ware off. She had no money on her, no coat, and she was getting very cold. She was almost relieved when the cop brought her back to the school.

When the security guard brought her upstairs it was Ten O'clock. Peter was yelling in his room because he wanted a glass of water. Sara was the only staff member still on duty. She was changing David, who was in a silly, giggly mood. She greeted Mary warmly enough, in spite of the fact that Mary had run away. She asked her to come with her. "Mary I have something to show you." They stopped at Donald's bed room door. Sara brushed her long blonde hair back from her forehead and sighed. "This wasn't my idea, believe me. It's Miss Kendal who decided on this." Mary noticed that the window that Donald had smashed a week ago was now covered by a thick mesh screen. Sara opened the door to reveal a room completely empty, except for a mattress on the floor, with a pillow, and a blanket. "Donald's in another room for now. I'm afraid I'm gonna have to lock you in here, but if you need anything just holler. I'll be right around the corner, Okay?" Mary nodded. Sara was so obviously sorry about what she was being made to do. Mary bore no hard feelings toward her. It seemed just the sort of thing Miss Kendal would want to do to her. They had never liked each other.

The next day Mary was allowed out of her cell, but the fun wasn't over yet. She had to spend the day with her wrist tied to the wrist of whoever was watching her at the moment. During rest period she was tied to Miss Bow. As a result she had to watch David go to the bathroom. Then she had to watch Kate and Vinnie try to go. Beth wanted to come out of her room and help Miss Bow with the little kids. When Miss Bow told her she couldn't, Beth let out an ear piercing scream! Miss Bow rushed back in to her room, pulling Mary with her. As she gave Beth an angry lecture, Mary wished she could change places with Beth, who was sitting on the floor pouting. Even with the tantrum, she was innocent, compared to Mary.

Late in the afternoon Mary's parents arrived for a long conference with Miss Kendal and the doctors. Mary was let off her leash when the staff informed her that she was going home. She whooped with pleasure, and ran around saying goodbye to everyone.

Once in the lobby, Mr. Sullivan, to prove that he trusted his daughter, told Mary to go out and sit in the car. He handed her the keys, and told her that he and her mother would be out in a minute. Miss Kendal and the doctors urged him not to do this. "She won't run." He told them emphatically. Not wanting to let her father down, Mary did as she was told. She sat in the car for five minutes before her parents appeared, carrying her luggage. She grinned at them. However, when they got in on either side of her, and her father started the engine, Mary didn't feel like grinning anymore. She was scared. What would happen now?

Chapter Four

God made you drop that knife

Mary and her parents left the school after four thirty. It was already beginning to get dark outside. Although Mary had whooped with pleasure and ran to pack her things upon hearing that she was expelled, the reality of her situation was sinking in. She was no longer very happy about leaving the Boston Center for Blind children. In fact, going home to live with the old couple she was riding with seemed pretty grim. She could feel her stomach tying itself in knots. Would she be sick? She really didn't want to do anything to provoke her mother right now. Mrs. Sullivan was already a loose cannon, though at the moment the cannon appeared somewhat calm.

Why had Mary run away? Things hadn't been that bad at the school, not bad enough to do something to get herself expelled. If only she had stopped and thought about what she was doing, maybe she wouldn't have run out of the building. If only someone hadn't left a door unlocked.. She wouldn't have been able to get out. Why did someone get careless, was Mary supposed to get out, run away, and get expelled; If so, why?

They were about halfway back to RI when Mrs. Sullivan blew her top. She had been talking to her husband and her daughter about the predicament they were in when suddenly she exclaimed "You're a bum! a shameful, disgusting bum! Look at your hair. You look like a boy!" She gestured at Mary'sShort, unevenly cut bob, which she had done herself a few nights ago "Do you know what that policeman must have thought of you, picking you off the streets of Boston at ten at night, with that hair?

He must have thanked God that he doesn't have a delinquent, bum of a daughter!" When Mary told her about the cell she slept in the previous night, and being tied to the wrist of whoever was watching her at the time, her mother angrily informed her that Miss Kendal was making an example of her. No child had ever run away from that school before, and no one ever would again. She went on to catalogue all of Mary's faults, there were many. Mary cringed as she always did when her mother shouted at her. She knew what was coming .Mrs. Sullivan proceeded to yell at her for all the things she had done wrong over the years, paying special attention to the year that Mary was three. This was apparently the year that Mary officially turned corrupt in her mother's eyes. As his wife ranted on, Mr. Sullivan, in his gray, hat and Sunday suit quietly drove on. At a red light he stopped to clean his dark framed glasses. His clean shaven face was gaunt and worried looking.

They stopped at a McDonalds, ten or twelve miles from home. As was their custom, Mrs. Sullivan stayed in the car and waited while Mr. Sullivan went to get the food. Mary asked for her usual order of two fish filets and a coffee milk shake. "ONE!" shouted Mrs. Sullivan."Ah, yes one" Mary eagerly agreed, hoping to get back on her mother's good side. As she stole cautious glances at her mother, she could tell that it was going to take a lot of hard work to win the woman's approval back. Was she up for the challenge?

All Mary wanted to do was curl up in the lap of her imaginary father's lap and forget about everything .Mrs. Sullivan sat with her head held high, her chin thrust out self righteously. Her wavy, gray hair was parted on the side and partially covered by a black velvet hat. Her full cheeks were made up with blush and she wore red lip stick. Mary was glad she couldn't see her mother from the front. She didn't like the way she looked with lip stick when she was angry. Her closed mouth looked like a angry, red slash! This used to scare Mary when she was small, especially when it was followed by a hard smack across her face!

Not only was Mary feeling regret about running away from the school, she was now faced with the knowledge that "home" was no longer in Providence. Five days earlier the Sullivan had moved out to Coventry. It was hard to believe that only a year earlier Mary was fantasizing about escaping to the country to live on a ranch. Now she would do anything to remain in the city. Before going to the house, they stopped at a small white house with a white picket fence. It was right at the top of their street. Not street, Mary thought gloomily, lane…They lived on a lane now. Her parents took her in to the white house with the picket fence. It turned out to be Dr Early's office. He no longer lived in or had a practice in the city. He's a traitor too thought Mary. Along with this office, he also had some property out in rural Coventry. He lived out there and loved it.

After exchanging cheerful greetings and congratulating each other for getting away from the noisy, crime ridden city, the Sullivan took their sullen, but passive daughter home. It was dark, but Mary could see a small, one story house with a car port. She was able to glimpse a back yard and a hill beyond, before being led up a narrow, concrete walkway. Upon entering, the lights were turned on. Mary found herself in a kitchen. To the right was a tiny bedroom. "That's my room" her father said. To the left was the living room. Before going in there, Mary greeted Sandy, their cocker spaniel. He was being kept in the utility room, which was at the back of the kitchen, near the back door. The floor was covered with urine and feces soaked newspapers. Scattered among this were Sandy's toys. The poor dog's living conditions were obviously going to be the same as they were in the old house. Little Sandy was paying for being born with epilepsy and a weak bladder. Mary secretly suspected that her parents picked out Sandy so that they would have a handicapped dog to go with their handicapped daughter. She liked Sandy though. He remained cheerful in spite of his illness and terrible odor. (The Sullivans didn't seem to realize that pets needed to be bathed regularly).

Beyond the dim, cluttered living room was a long carpeted hallway. On the first left was the bathroom. On the second left was Mrs. Sullivan's room. Beyond this was another, more formal looking living room. Where was Mary to sleep?

The house was over two hundred years old. The property had originally been a small farm. Before moving in, the Sullivans had the hallway, bathroom, bedroom and back living room added on. The original house had only one bedroom, a kitchen and utility room. Mary wasn't impressed. She kept this to herself though as she kept most of her feelings to herself when she was with her parents. Timidly she sat on the couch across from her parents, who sat in the arm chairs. Now she would really begin to pay for running away from school. Not only was her mother angry at her for running away, she was also furious with her for being a tomboy. "Look at your hair and those awful clothes!!" She noticed a book that Mary brought home with her from school. It was about a noisy, obnoxious, boy who craved attention. His name was Gregory. Mrs. Sullivan picked up the hard cover book and looked at it with utter contempt. "Well there is to be no more such nonsense, because it's goodbye book, GOODBYE BOOK!!" And at that she jumped to her feet, lunged forward and hurled the offending book at Mary' head. She wouldn't have missed but for the fact that her husband jumped up and grabbed at her arm, causing her aim to be slightly off. As a result, the book hit the wall beside Mary's head.

After some more screaming, during which Mary cringed and gave what she hoped were appropriate answers, she found out about her sleeping arrangements. She was to sleep on a cot in the middle of the front living room. During the day the cot would be folded up and used as a seat.

Two days later the Sullivan's celebrated Thanksgiving. Although they had all the traditional foods, everyone was subdued. There were no visits from family members, and there were relatives who could have been there. Mary remembered the holidays when she was four, five and six years old.

Relatives had often stopped by on the holidays. Mr. Sullivan had some nieces, nephews, and cousins. But they lived in upstate New York. His parents, who moved to RI with him when he was a boy of eight, were both dead. He had no siblings.

Mrs. Sullivan was born in Belmont, MA. Her parents moved to RI when she was two and her older brother was seven. Her father died in the influenza epidemic of 1918. Several years later the two children found themselves with a very kind, mild mannered stepfather. Mary' Uncle George, Mrs. Sullivan' brother was married and had two grown children, who were married and had two children each. One of these couples had moved out to Wisconsin when Mary was seven. The other couple only lived in East Providence, and could surely have visited. Her Uncle George and Aunt Agnes lived close by in West Warwick, in a fancy trailer park for senior citizens. Mary didn't particularly care for any of these people, but having them there would have eased the tension between her parents and herself. "Dad, will we be seeing Kenny and his wife and the kids?" asked Mary cautiously. She knew that it was risky asking questions in her parent's home. Mr. Sullivan was fixing the thanksgiving dinner while his wife, who wasn't feeling well took a nap. "No, they're going over to your Cousin Kenny's mother in-law's house" He looked up at Mary. "The least you could do is set the table. After all we've done for you, you could kiss our asses a little bit!" Mary was surprised to hear her father swear. In fact, she was surprised to hear him complaining. Her mother usually did enough of it for two people.

The next day the Sullivans went back to Providence to get the last of their belongings from the Perry's, who now occupied the old house, the house that Mary wished they still lived in. Why did her parents have to be afraid of the city?

They took both cars. Mrs. Sullivan drove one car and her husband drove the other. Mary was relieved to be allowed to ride with her father. They rode in silence for the most part, with the radio taking up the slack, playing the pop tunes which Mary loved, and her parents had finally come to accept. When they reached Roger Williams Park her parents had a quick conversation before getting back in to their cars. It was decided to Mary's surprise and disappointment, that she and her father would wait in the car right there in the park while Mrs. Sullivan drove the last half mile to the house to get everything. When she asked about this, her father told her not to worry about it. "Why don't you think instead of the trouble you caused when you ran away from that school?" He told Mary that one day she would be begging God's forgiveness for her meanness. Then, after a few minutes of uncomfortable silence, Mr. Sullivan pulled out some string and asked her if she wanted to learn how to make a sailor's knot.

A half hour later Mrs. Sullivan returned with a car of household paraphernalia. They took up all the back seat. Some of it was even tied to the roof of the car. Mr. Sullivan took the lead, with his wife following, as they left the park and headed back to Coventry. Mary had wanted to see her house on Alabama avenue one last time. But this was not to be. And she had learned years ago not to be argumentative with her parents. So she sat there and listened to Elton John's Crocodile Rock and smiled to herself at how the car her mother was driving looked.

As the days went by Mary fell in to a routine at home that was to remain pretty much unchanged until spring. Each morning she got up around nine thirty, stripped the sheets and pillow from her roll away bed, folded it up, and went in to the kitchen to have breakfast. The radio which was put on by eight was playing the local top 40 station. Sometimes Mrs. Sullivan was in a fairly decent mood. (She was never completely jolly). Sometimes she was in a calm, but melancholy mood. Other times she was in an angry, aggressive mood, and could be heard slamming the carpet sweeper in to chair and table legs, or slamming cabinet doors and pots and pans, as she sang in a harsh voice. Mary liked her mother' almost happy mood the best, of coarse. She kind of liked her melancholy mood too, only because her mother reminisced about her childhood and her days as a career woman back in the thirties and forties. "I grew up in providence with my mother and my big brother, your uncle George" she would begin sometimes." Our father died when we were small. But I was close to our mother. I was the kind of child who would come running to her when she called. George did too, but he was off with the boys playing ball when he wasn't in school" "Did you have a lot of toys?" Mary would ask between bites of raisin toast. "Oh yes I had dolls and carriages to push them around in. I had a tricycle to ride on too." She paused and looked sad. "I remember playing with some other little girls one day. One of them, a very mean little girl started throwing dirt in my eyes "What did you do?" asked an astonished Mary. "I ran home and cried on my mother's lap" She couldn't explain why the girl had been so mean to her. She talked about having good, but very strict school teachers, who marched them to and from the classroom. She made no complaints about this. She seemed to admire them. They taught her many things including how to dot her I s and cross her T s.

She was surrounded by an affectionate, French speaking family. They refrained from speaking French at the table, when they had guests. "I had a few good friends in school that enjoyed home Economics just like I did. And they were good Catholic girls like I was" Later when she grew up and married Mr. Sullivan, who was a state trooper, they both thought it was a good idea for her to work. He was away sleeping at the barracks during the week, and Mrs. Sullivan loved working at the Boston store, which was located in downtown Providence. She was a floor walker. She made a lot of friends there. In the early 1950s when Mr. Sullivan retired from the state police and decided to become an insurance adjuster, Mrs. Sullivan retired too, in order to become a house wife.

Mary dreaded going out to the kitchen when her mother was raging. Mary could hear her. As she worked she sang an old song called "Thanks for the memories". Her voice was loud and angry as she sang and Mary knew that the song was directed at her. It took every ounce of courage she had to enter that room. What did I do now? She would wonder inwardly. Often all it turned out to be was that she, Mary was there, a reminder to her mother that her failure of a daughter was with her under the same roof. For, what else could it be? She couldn't anger someone by getting up.

One morning about a week after Mary came home, Mrs. Sullivan started to haughtily brag about how the Perry's, the people who bought the old house, really liked her. "They have two children, a boy and a girl. The girl, a pretty little blonde, told me that she LIKED me! Can you believe that?" She paced back and forth in front of a nervous Mary. "She said I LIKE YOU Mrs. Sullivan" She then went on to describe incidents from her past where other kids had claimed to like her. "Your Uncle George and Aunt Agnes' children LOVED me!. Children in the stores who wouldn't smile in photo studios would suddenly smile when I smiled at them...But you! You hate filled creature! You never liked or loved me. You never loved anyone except that dizzy nun you were so crazy about!" Stricken, Mary shook her head. She didn't want her mother to believe this (even if it was true). But her mother paid no attention. "I remember when that wonderful Father Mullen lifted you up in the air and swung you around. You pointed your finger downward and yelled YOU PUT ME DOWN! He stopped and said What Mary? And you repeated yourself just as nastily." Mary sat, mouth hanging open in surprise! Had she really been that awful? "What kind of a child acts like that? You were a fiend, not a child. The things you did at St Vincent's. For instance there was that toddler with the orange pants in the playpen. Do you remember him...hmmm? You climbed in there, kicked him in the head repeatedly, why? Because a toy had been taken away from you, and when an explanation was asked, you put your little hands on your hips and said I thought he was a football. He has orange pants on! "Mary remembered this incident. Two young nuns, new to the infant home, were tired of Mary running to them when another child took her toy. When they wouldn't help her, Mary started playing ball in the corridor. The two young nuns didn't like this. One day they dribbled the ball away from her, and tossed it in to the play room. When Mary bawled they told her to go fight for the ball. They wouldn't tell her how, and all Mary knew about fighting was that it involved hurting people. Frustrated and inexperienced, Mary entered the room, and hit some of the kids. When her ball was kept away from her, she climbed in the play pen and repeatedly kicked the toddler that stayed there. Mary thought her mother would make a good prosecutor. She had the personality and body language for it. Sadly she took in all that the prosecutor had to say. She realized that she really must be a terrible person! Could anyone ever love her? It didn't seem likely.

After breakfast came the slow ritual of dressing,, which Mary always did in the bathroom. She tried to drag it out as long as possible. Once seated on the living room floor, her mother usually made her read a chapter or two from a religious book for children. Then she would question her about what she had learned. After lunch Mary was allowed to do all the drawing she wanted to do. She loved to make paper dolls of men she admired. She also made paper dolls of children. Mothers were not included. Fortunately Mrs. Sullivan didn't mention this. One afternoon Mary got so caught up in a paperback copy of Hannah that she didn't bother to draw. She read the book in little less then six hours, sometimes reading parts of it to her mother. Instead of being proud of her like Mary expected, Mrs. Sullivan was furious with her daughter. "You sat there all afternoon reading that book. Yet you can't pay attention in school!! You can't even stay in school!!" She threw things around, stalked in and out of the room, throwing insults at Mary over her shoulder as she went.

By the time Mary's father shuffled in the door after six thirty his wife had supper on the table. Mary didn't know exactly where he sometimes went during the day now that he was retired.

When she was called to the table, she quietly took her seat. She didn't want to do anything to provoke her mother further…Too late. ."Aren't you going to say Hi to Sandy?" Mary said a hurried hello to the dog. "I'll bet if he took a bite out of your ankle you'd say Hi to him!" Mary sagged in her seat.

In the evenings they watched TV together. They usually watched cops and sitcoms, and the Billy Graham crusades. Mary couldn't stand listening to Billy Graham. But her parents loved him.

By ten O'clock they all went to bed. So once again Mary would unfold her roll away bed and put the sheets, blanket and pillow on it. She didn't get to sleep until way after midnight. She laid awake and fantasized about the man she currently imagined was her doting father. Right now he happened to be a singer from the Lawrence Welk show. Her parents loved this show almost as much as they loved to watch The Billy Graham crusades.

One cold day in December Mary and her parents hopped in the car they didn't sell, a black and white 1969 dodge. They wanted to become members at the local Catholic Church. The church was called St John and Paul's. It was only half a mile from the house. It was a small, white, country church. In back were a school and a rectory. All three buildings were separated by a large parking lot. Once in the rectory, the family was ushered in to an office by a burly, man of medium height, with dark grey hair, and a ruddy complexion. Before taking his seat, he shook hands with Mary and her parents. While the three adults talked about the joys of being a member of the church, Mary gazed around the small room and day dreamed about Rhode Island's new governor. A month ago he was voted in. Mary thought he had the most gorgeous smile! Whenever she rode past one of the billboards with his face on it, her heart raced and then melted! Already she was pretending that he was her personal father who went wherever she went, laughed with her, comforted her, and promised that she and he would run away together and have a good home somewhere. She was so busy smiling at the bare wall that she didn't realize that the meeting was over. The burly man turned out to be Father Hoyle. He was the senior priest at the church. Aside from him, there were two younger priests there. Mary didn't hear their names. She was far away once again, walking through the great corridors of the state house, holding the governor's hand. Her mother, aware of the vacant look on her face, shook her roughly as they left.

At home Mary drew pictures of the governor constantly and sneaked them to bed with her. When her mother caught her she took them away, called Mary a dirty, man crazy, tramp, and spattered her in the face with holy water. This was always followed up by a crucifix being waved in her face. Through it all the governor sat on the couch and gazed at Mary with sympathy.

Christmas for Mary was over shadowed by being in a house and town she didn't like. And by her mother's vicious moods. Though she no longer hit Mary, she still managed to make her feel miserable. Her father did nothing to make it easier. The governor did .He was always nice to her. Whenever she was taken out in the car, Mary knew that she would have an opportunity to gaze adoringly at his giant face on a billboard. All too soon her mother was noticing this though. They were driving down the street. She turned her head to the right and was getting ready-"CLOSE YOUR EYES!!" roared Mrs. Sullivan. Mary jumped! She realized just then that her father was joining in on his wife's behalf. "He has a wife and kids, and he doesn't need YOU. SO LEAVE HIM ALONE!!" She cringed and sank down lower in the front seat where she was still made to sit, between her parents. They hardly ever let her sit in the back, though it was so cramped up front.

At the beginning of January Mary was taken in her best clothes, out to rural Coventry where Dr Early lived. It was the start of 1973, but the elderly family doctor was self sufficient. He heated his small, modest, old fashioned home with a wood stove. He reminisced about the old days. Mary had known Dr Early as their family physician since she could walk. But she wasn't interested in how he lived on his farm. So she didn't hear much of what her parents were saying about him. While they visited, Mary's parents talked animatedly to Dr Early about anything and everything. Mary didn't even try to keep up a pretense of paying attention. She stared up at the ceiling continually, smiled broadly at things that crossed her mind, and rocked backward in her chair, so that she was balanced on the hind legs. Often her mother had to stop her from doing this. Mary knew that she was acting weird. She hoped that Dr Early noticed this. Maybe he would arrange to have her committed. If he did happen to notice her behavior, he chose to ignore it.

That evening at home Mrs. Sullivan pointed out the fact that Mary left papers on the living room floor. "Did I?" Mary had forgotten about her art work. However, her mother thought she was being sarcastic and said so. After supper Mr. Sullivan did the dishes, allowing his wife to sit down and concentrate on her sewing. Mary, who was entering the living room, thought her mother was concentrating. Suddenly she was kicked in the behind! The force of it caused her to stagger forward. She quickly took her seat. So, her mother hadn't been concentrating entirely on her sewing.

In February the season of Lent rolled around. Mary's mother gave up chocolate, something she adored! Mary laughed from the back seat where she had finally been allowed to sit. Her father was so funny sometimes. "Hey honey! Look at that chocolate car going by. And look at that chocolate truck over there" Mrs. Sullivan laughed her head off. Mary had to admit that even if they didn't get along well with her, her parents got along great with each other. ."Hey look at that chocolate parking lot over there, topped with whipped cream" Mr. Sullivan promised to give up cigarettes. Mary wasn't expected to give up anything. She just had to keep up with the rosary and the other prayers they all said together. Eating fish on Fridays was a regular occurrence for Mary. Her parents didn't acknowledge Vatican two when it came about back in 1967. They continued to observe the traditional Catholic ways. And one of them was never eating meat on Fridays. Mary didn't mind this. She had recently developed a strong liking for fish.

One evening when they were eating their fish and chips at the cramped kitchen table, Mary dropped her knife. Fearing criticism for being careless, she tried to conceal it, hoping to pick it up while pretending to tie her shoe. It was to no avail though. Her mother, who was sitting beside her noticed, and she pounced. "Ah Ha!" she cried triumphantly. "You see how God works? You were trying to hide that weren't you? You wanted to take the knife for something bad. God made you drop that knife so that I would be alerted" Confused, Mary looked out the window at the dark sky. Did God really do that, if so, why? She wasn't being bad. She shook her head. There seemed no way to figure out this God of her parents. It was clear however, that he never did like her. Why just the other night when her mother was disgusted with her she had looked over at Mary's father, nodded her head emphatically, and declared that Mary was going to hell. Mary felt like a sentence had been passed at that moment, because if anyone had a direct line to God, it was her mother. The fact that her father sat there, saying nothing didn't lessen the effect on her.

Mary often tried to sneak out of the house after her parents were in bed. Mrs. Sullivan was a light sleeper, and always caught Mary. Finally one night, she ordered her husband to sit by Mary's bed. He was to keep watch over her. He wasn't pleased with the arrangement. "Your nothing but a little trouble maker, aren't you?" Mary, feeling frustrated at being caught yet again, said "I am not!! " in an angry hiss. Furious, her usually passive, father smacked her twice across her face! "You've got a mean streak in you, Mary!" he hissed. "Don't you touch me!" Mary hissed back. With that, she rolled over and silently cried in to her pillow. Soupy Sayles, a doting uncle, who she sometimes watched on "What's my line?" stroked her hair sympathetically. He, of coarse was unseen by her father.

Plans to get Mary in to another school somewhere hadn't been forgotten. She had a social worker from the department of education. Her name was Ms. Fornier. She was an intelligent, amiable woman in her mid thirties. She was assigned to Mary about five months after she was discharged from Bradley Hospital. It was she and one of the counselors from state services of the blind that placed Mary in the Boston school for the blind. If only I had stayed there thought Mary miserably. She was sitting in her living room, dressed in a jumper that was too long. She wore a white turtleneck, white leotards, and black shoes with straps. She tried not to pay attention to what Ms. Fornier and her parents were saying to each other. She concentrated instead on her new fatherly heart throb, Willie Gillis, a character from a cop show called The Rookies. About a week ago her mother had finally succeeded in convincing her that the governor didn't nor ever would care about her.

By the time the cozy little gathering broke up Mary learned that in another week Ms. Fornier would be taking all of them up to Connecticut to look at a residential school.

Mary was woken up at the crack of dawn a week later. She was exhausted having stayed awake late, then being caught with a man's picture in her bed again. Her mother spattered Holy water in her face and waved a crucifix at her. Now she was scrubbed, dressed, fed and given the new green coat that her aunt and uncle sent her for Christmas. Her hair, finally grown to a decent length, was brushed hard by her mother.

It was a long ride up to the part of Connecticut where the school was, and they had a lot of interviews to get through in one day. Ms. Fornier drove. Mrs. Sullivan sat up front, and kept up a steady conversation with her. Mary was happier to sit in the back with her father. All the same, when he told her that she could rest her head on his shoulder if she wanted, she quietly refused, feeling very uncomfortable with the idea.

The school was called Devroe School. It was out in rural Connecticut. It was a residential school for boys and girls from ages seven to eighteen. Students with many different types of problems were enrolled there. Mary spent most of the long day sitting in the lobby while Ms. Fornier and her parents were in one meeting after another. She day dreamed, ate when food was brought to her, and watched the comings and goings of the teachers, staff, and students. Once she was taken in to an office where a man in a grey suit asked her questions about herself. He wrote down everything she said.

Later she, Ms. Fornier, and her parents were taken on a tour of the dorms where all the students lived. Mary didn't like the look of the place. It was so modern, sterile bland, no character.

By late afternoon they were all in Ms. Fornier's car, heading back to RI.

About ten days later Mary watched her mother read the letter from Devroe. The letter informed her that her daughter would not be accepted there. It was a good thing that Mr.

Sullivan was at home. Standing there in the kitchen, his arms wrapped tightly around her, he let his wife cry her eyes out. He was her tower of strength. Mary, sitting on the floor in the next room, could see them. She couldn't understand what all the fuss was about. She didn't think that school was worth shedding a single tear over. Yet she was affected by her mother's intense crying. How could she not be? As always she concealed feelings like these. It never paid to show concern. Mrs. Sullivan must have been affected by Mary's lack of concern, because an hour, or so later when they were all in the living room, she expressed her disgust over her daughter's over all attitude. "You know, if you had been born a boy, your father would have knocked you from one end of this house to the other. He's said so several times." Mary, who was sitting on the floor, not daring to touch her art work when her mother was lecturing her, stole a peek at her father. Mr. Sullivan sat quietly gazing at her. His expression was unreadable. She was afraid to ask him if her mother's statement was true. In spite of the comfort, and moral support she received from her husband, it was obvious to Mary that her mother wasn't always happy with him. She made occasional references to his "weakness". "When a fly is in the room your father takes a fly swatter, and taps it. I then have to grab it, and whack the fly!" She sometimes compared him to her brother. "If faced with a burglar, your Uncle George would shoot first, and ask questions later. Your father on the other hand, would ask questions first". Clearly she wasn't impressed with these aspects of her husband. Still Mary's faults remained prominent in her mother's mind. One evening when Mr. Sullivan was out, Mrs. Sullivan was upset with Mary. She was in the bathroom crying hysterically. "You don't care how I feel!!" she screamed. "That proves just how sick you really are!" Mary sat in the dimly lit living room. She wanted to believe that she was too sick to care how her mother or anyone else felt. The more she was called sick, the more it appealed to her. Yet why was there a lump in her throat, and why were her eyes tearing up?

By March Mary wished she was being sent away somewhere, even Devroe. She couldn't stand being in that house any longer. One day Mrs. Sullivan hollered at Mary and called her a dirty pig. She had found a man's picture in Mary's bed again. When her mother left the room Mary burst in to silent tears. She had to get out of here as soon as she got the chance. The chance came that very afternoon when it was decided that she was to go to the lumber store in Artic with her father. It was a mild sunny day, for the middle of March. Mary still had to wear her winter coat though. Hoping desperately for an opportunity to escape, Mary followed her father across the small parking lot. As soon as he started talking to the owner of the lumber store, she turned and bolted back up the hill "Sorry, Daddy." She mumbled, as she turned left and ran down the street. She felt a slight stirring of regret as she heard her father calling her. But it was too late for all that. It had been too late for a long time. Quickly she turned left again and ran through someone's back yard. Soon she was running through many back yards, ducking under clothes lines. She had to lose her father if she was to get away. When she was too out of breath and tired to go on, she hid in someone's cellar to rest awhile. Ten or fifteen minutes later, she crept out, and looked cautiously around and ran until she reached some railroad tracks. She followed these and soon found herself in Artic cemter. She hurried through this area and passed through the mill section of Artic. Her destination was Providence. She wanted to go back to Alabama avenue. What she was going to do when she got there she didn't know. As she walked through areas with a lot of houses and groups of children playing outside, she found that she was the center of attention. The kids, mostly ten or eleven and older, wanted to know who she was and where she from. Suspecting that the police would be looking for her soon, and that they might question these kids, Mary gave a false name and location. She wasn't that stupid, no matter how she acted.

Feeling energetic, encouraged about her mission, and liberated, Mary sometimes walked and sometimes ran through the Crompton section of Warwick and eventually made it to Old spring road.

She turned left and walked up to Harold Avenue, and was passing the medical school. She realized that the route she had taken was the same one she had seen from the car window. No wonder she hadn't needed much assistance. It was all coming back to her now! Just for fun, for the sheer joy of being liberated, Mary sang loudly, made faces at the motorists going by, and shouted out some swear words, words she hadn't dared to say aloud since she left Boston. Now she was like those cool kids she sometimes saw from the car window, the kids her mother frowned at and called trash.

After walking through Garden City Mary was very hungry and thirsty. She didn't have money to get anything. She never had money on her. She had never even held anything of more value then a dollar bill. How would she get anything?

On Reservoir Avenue there was a Mc Donald's. A girl a few years younger then she was threw out a chocolate milk shake. Because the trash can was full, the milk shake was right on top, not even half gone. Mary grabbed it and drank greedily! Still drinking, she continued on her way. Wow, she thought. This must have really been meant to be, her escaping and actually getting away. She felt really good about this. A white car pulled up along side her. A tall, man with dark hair, wearing a tan over coat got out. "Excuse me, can you tell me what time it is?" Mary frowned. That seemed like a strange question for an adult to ask a child. The man held out his arm where a wrist watch was revealed. It was getting dark by now and she could barely see the watch, let alone the face on it. She shook her head and backed away. He reached out and grabbed her arm. "Come with me please". As he drove her to the Cranston police station the only thing she said to him was "So, your taking me back to her, are you?" At the police station Mary tried to tell one of the cops why she ran away from home, but he only said "Sit down kid" and gave her a candy bar.

When Mr. Sullivan arrived, Mary could tell by the way he talked that he was more disappointed in her then angry. He drove her to the police station in Artic, where he had a few discussions with some of the cops. Then he turned to Mary who stood off to the side and said "Now, you apologize for running away and causing these nice men to look for you". Meekly she did as she was told. The cops nodded agreeably and said "Okay you're forgiven, kid". On the way back to Coventry Mr. Sullivan shook his head in a confused way. "Why you do these things, I mean after all we do for you. Two weeks ago saving your pills and then taking three at once to try to make yourself sick and now this?" "I was upset" murmured Mary quietly. "You were upset? That's been the story of your life, Mary" Knowing she would receive no sympathy, Mary clammed up.

The next morning Mary had her usual mid morning breakfast, then went in the living room wondering if she would have to do her religious reading. Her parents, after taking turns having a hushed conversation with someone on the phone, sat down with her. "We have something to tell you". Mary' heart began to race with anticipation! "We had a talk with Dr Early" said Mrs. Sullivan. "He feels that we should put you in the medical center for a while". Mary wanted to jump up and down and cheer. But she managed to sit still and say "Ah, okay". Soon a bag of clothes, pajamas, slippers, and underwear was packed for her. She packed a smaller bag for her toothbrush, toothpaste, drawing paper, crayons and her favorite doll and stuffed animal. She sneaked her latest drawing of Dr Kildare, her latest heart throb, in to her coat pocket. He was now her doting father. However, the governor had made a bit of a come back with her, and was an affectionate uncle.

Her parents recited the rosary in the car on the way over to the medical center. Mary had to participate as always, but she didn't mind seeing as how she wouldn't have to do it after this.

After the long intake process, Mary was taken upstairs and placed on the adolescent ward for girls. She looked around noticing that everything looked pretty much the same as it had when she was last here a year and a half earlier. She didn't know why the grim surroundings and the smell of disinfectant appealed to her, but it did.

When her parents kissed her goodbye and left the ward, Mary turned a cart wheel right in the middle of the day room. She felt so free!!

Chapter Five

Three days in Saint Coldness

Here we go again. Mary thought as she climbed in to the black and white dodge. Her social worker had located another residential school for her to live at. Couldn't they all understand that she just wanted to be left alone to spend an indefinite amount of time at the RI medical center, on the girl's adolescent ward? If it was two years earlier, when Mary was being released from Bradley Hospital, she would have loved to be sent to a residential school. But a lot had happened in nearly two years. It was now April of 1973,, and Mary no longer cared about the future; particularly her future As far as Mary was concerned this whole trip was a waste of time.

Ms. Fornier was accompanying them on this trip. She parked her yellow Toyota next to the dodge and got out, taking her brief case with her. Mary climbed out of the car, feeling awkward and self conscience in the ill fitting, old fashioned clothes that her mother insisted on making her wear. A group of kids, ranging from ages nine or ten, to about fourteen approached and stopped in front of Mary. As they stared at her, she wanted to turn around and get back in the car and hide. But she stood there and tried to look disinterested. "This is Mary" said her mother brightly. "She's going to be with you for a few days" The kids looked her over some more. "How old are you?" asked one of the girls. "Almost twelve" mumbled Mary. "Okay, let's go" said Ms. Fornier eagerly. In spite of the warm April day, Mary put on her coat. She didn't want anyone to see the long, brown jumper over a white blouse with ruffles. The clothes made her look like a fifty year old. "Your going to like it here at Saint Vincent's Mary!" exclaimed Ms. Fornier as she led the way to the main building. Mary looked around as her parents led her. She saw wide spread lawns sprinkled with trees and bushes. There were also some white and blue one story houses. Mary counted four in all. She assumed theses were dormitories. The scene struck her as modern and sterile, totally lacking in character. She knew however, that others wouldn't feel this way. So she kept her mouth shut.

It was already after nine on a Wednesday morning. Students were still on route to their classes. Ms. Fornier knocked on an office door on the first floor. Upon entering, Mary saw a stern, middle aged nun sitting at a desk. Behind her was a window covered by venation blinds. The word that would have entered Mary's mind, had she known it, would have been bleak. As it was, she stood there with her stomach in knots. The nun introduced herself as Sister Mary

Margaret. "I'm the head mistress here at Saint Vincent's" She told the group of people in her office. "Why don't I take you on a tour of my school "The nun led the family out of her office. Ms. Fornier came next, followed by Mary and her parents. They were taken to each classroom, and were allowed to peek in the window that was near the top of the door. Mary's father lifted her up so that she could look in on an art class. She loved art. She had been drawing since she was five, and she didn't let her low vision get in the way.

After they went to look at the gym, they had lunch in the large, noisy school cafeteria.

"So, what do you think, Mary?" Ms. Fornier asked when they were finished eating. What did she think? She knew what she felt. She felt as if a huge bowling ball had been dropped on her stomach! However, she knew what she was supposed to say. Swallowing with effort, Mary said "Umm, it's very nice." Ms. Fornier beamed with pleasure.

In the afternoon Mary, her parents and Ms. Fornier were taken to look at the dorms. "We have two dorms for the girls and two for the boys" explained Sister Mary Margaret. "Boys ages seven through twelve are in that dorm over there" She pointed to a white and blue house nearest to the main building. "Teenaged boys are in that dorm" Mary glanced briefly at the blue house close to the first one. "Over there are the two girls dorms" Sister Mary Margaret led them to a patch of grass. Two small blue houses stood across from each other. "How old is Mary?" she asked. "She will be twelve in two weeks" answered Mary' mother. "Good, she can stay in the older girls' dorm" The nun pointed to the house on the left. A minute later they all entered this house. Mary saw a modern, spotless kitchen. Beyond this was a spacious dinning room and living room combination. The walls were painted white, and the floor was covered with blue wall to wall carpeting. The furniture was very modern, made of a pale wood. It depressed Mary. But she kept quiet about it. To the left was an office where the housemother resided much of the time, Mary was told. A long, carpeted hallway extended past the office. On either side of this hallway were bedrooms, each containing two, and in some cases, three beds. They all back tracked to the office, where they were introduced to a young woman wearing a tan sweater and a pair of bell bottomed jeans. She wore her straight, brown, hair, long and parted in the center. "This is Sarah West. She is the housemother in this dorm" announced Sister Mary Margaret. Sarah shook hands with the visitors. "I must leave you now" said Sister Mary Margaret. "I have a lot of work to catch up on" After she left, Ms. Fornier and Mary's parents got ready to leave. "We'll be back Friday afternoon. These three days are a chance to get to know everyone here and get used to the rules" Ms. Fornier sounded so positive about this trial visit. A lot more positive then Mary felt. Mrs. Sullivan kissed Mary goodbye. "We want this to work for you" she said in a stern voice. Mr. Sullivan kissed his daughter and waved. Mary followed Sarah in to her office and sat down. "We have very strict rules here Mary. If you remember them and obey them you'll be just fine" said Sarah. "We get up at seven, shower, dress, clean our rooms. At eight we have breakfast. Nine o'clock classes begin over in the main building. Lunch is at noon, and lasts for forty five minutes. School ends at three O'clock. You will be expected to return here to do chores. Afterward the girls do homework. At six we have supper. If your homework is completed, you will be allowed a few hours of recreation before bedtime, which is at nine thirty. I do of coarse allow the girls to lay awake and listen to music and talk for a half hour or so" Sarah stopped to take a breather. Before she could continue however, Mary found the tears that she had been holding back, suddenly spilling down her cheeks. Her body began to convulse as she tried to prevent her sobs from becoming audible. Sarah stopped and looked at her. "I understand it's hard to start off in a new school surrounded by strangers. But you will get used to it" There was an air of stiffness about her, as if she was uncomfortable with emotion, and Mary was frustrated with herself for allowing her vulnerable side to show in front of this woman.

By three fifteen the house was filled with half a dozen noisy teenaged girls who were excited because school was over and they had the whole night ahead of them. Mary sat quietly in front of the TV, hoping that she wouldn't be noticed. This wasn't to be however. A chubby girl of about fourteen, with curly, shoulder length, black hair, plopped down near her and said "Hi, I'm Peggy. Don't pay any attention to these girls, they're all mental cases!" Mary could tell that Peggy was only kidding, but she was too shy to say anything. Soon all the girls were milling about Mary, asking her questions about her background. She felt over whelmed. So she went to the room that Sarah had assigned her, and began to unpack. The girls followed her. "Where are you from?" "Rhode Island". "Oh yeah that state's so boring! Its lots better here in Fall River" Mary didn't care. When they discovered that she had been adopted they were all amazed! "You must wonder who your real mother is" Strangely enough, Mary hadn't given it much thought at this time in her life. This shocked the girls. "I would be totally curious if it was me!!" a girl with long blonde hair exclaimed. The others all agreed with her. Mary felt so self conscience! It was as if she had just failed some kind of test, socially. Before going to supper, she hurriedly changed in to the only halfway decent outfit her mother had packed for her, a light purple turtle neck and a pair of navy blue, polyester, bell bottoms that were slightly small for her.

After supper some of the girls sat on the floor in the hallway and listened to records. The chubby girl named, Peggy sat with them. Mary noticed that even though Peggy rocked back and forth to the music, like someone who is mentally retarded, she was very much accepted by the other girls. This puzzled her. After a few records were played, Peggy and three other girls wanted to walk around the campus. They invited Mary to join them. When they got outside, one of the blonde girls, Donna whispered something to the tall blonde girl...Janice Mary thought. "Don't worry, I've got them!" she hissed. Got what? Mary wondered. There were a lot of playful insults tossed about as the girls made their way across campus. They stopped and sat down behind a wide hedge. Mary stood before them uncertainly. Janice took out a pack of cigarettes and a lighter."Hey, Mary, do you smoke? "Feeling uneasy, Mary slowly nodded."Uh, yeah I smoke" After each girl had taken a drag or two, Peggy passed the cigarette to Mary, who promptly took a drag and started coughing her head off. This was met with raucous laughter from Peggy, Donna and Janice. Mary backed away and haphazardly made her way back to the dorm. She didn't tell Sarah what happened.

Later in bed, they all laid awake and listened to Peggy' eight track tapes. Mary was somewhat comforted by the songs. She loved pop music. .She forgave the girls for laughing at her, and was glad that Peggy was her roommate. She was so funny.

The next morning everyone was up at seven. Mary washed, dressed and made her bed, then went to hang around in the dinning room. A red haired girl with freckles was setting the table and helping Sarah get breakfast ready. "Hi I'm Joan. I'm in the room across from you" she informed Mary. Just then Donna came in to the room. "Look Mary" She pointed to some drab, out dated dresses that looked like they were right out of the fifties. They hung from a door knob. "Here are some really cool dresses, Mary" Mary scowled and backed away. "Nah I don't think so" How could Donna say such a thing, did she really think Mary was that naive? Or was she just making fun of her again?

Classes began at nine, though Mary noticed that not everyone was on time, some were very late. Mary's teacher was a tall, lean man with a completely bald head. He was nice, but he tolerated no nonsense. One of the students, a boy who Mary remembered from Bradley Hospital, was very disruptive. He kept talking out of turn, laughing, teasing the teacher and just being silly. When the boy threw a book in to the air, the teacher tore across the room "Steven! I've had it with your shenanigans!" The boy continued to laugh uproariously as the man pulled him from his chair and sat on him. "Have you had enough?" he asked the boy several minutes later. When the boy gave in he was allowed back in his seat; only to find himself back on the floor, beneath the teacher' weight moments later. It didn't seem to bother either of them very much. It actually looked like a game to Mary. This is better then TV she thought as she silently laughed in to her hand.

During recess the students visited other classrooms and had juice and cookies. Mary was passing a classroom when she heard a woman call out to her. It turned out to be Miss Murray, an elderly woman with short, gray hair. She was a kind, patient teacher. Mary had her during her first year at Bradley when she was only seven years old. She learned a lot with Miss Murray. She was so happy to find her here. Miss Murray was once again teaching the younger kids. Five or six students, all between the ages of seven through nine were talking contentedly and enjoying their snacks. Two of the students, a boy named Ricky and a girl named Ellen were very friendly toward Mary. They wanted her to play with them. She wished heartily that she could be in Miss Murray' class and have these innocent, good natured kids for company.

During lunch break many of the kids went outside as soon as they finished eating. It was such a nice day. Mary joined them. Besides the girls in her house, other kids hadn't taken much notice of Mary, now they did. They started by asking her about her clothes and her poor sight. Then a few of them came up to her and stepped on her feet. "Does that hurt?" they asked. "No" said Mary cautiously. They stepped harder "Does that hurt?" Mary managed to act like it wasn't bothering her. Having her feet stepped on didn't hurt that much. It was the intent of the kids who were doing it that bothered her. But she was afraid to show her unease. She was also afraid to back away, walk away, run away, or do anything that would show how they were making her feel. So she stood there like a statue and let them step, then stomp on her feet. "Does THAT hurt?" Mary shook her head and hoped that a teacher would come outside. What saved her was the bell, calling them indoors.

After school Mary did her chores, and then went to watch TV. But Sarah made her turn it off and go outside. "It's too nice to stay inside, and since you finished your homework you should be out in the sunshine" Mary hadn't done her homework and had no intention of doing it. Perhaps if she fell far behind, they would put her in Miss Murray' class. Because that was the only way she could stay at St Vincent's. Reluctantly, Mary went outside. What was she supposed to do? There were no swings and she liked to swing. Unfortunately, the kids had ideas about what she would do. They stomped on her feet some more, laughed at her, asked her if she was retarded, if her parents were retarded, the extent of her vision problem. They wanted her to walk in to a few walls for them. It would be so funny. Through all the harassment, Mary noticed a little girl with short, brown hair, wearing a bright blue jacket. She couldn't have been more then seven. She stood off by herself, and wouldn't look at anyone. "Hey Alice!" another little girl called out "Come over here and help us make fun of the blind retard!" Alice refused. The little girl who tried to entice Alice was about eight. She had shoulder length, light blonde hair, long bangs and an impish face. She trotted up to Mary and said "I'm Tracy; I can kick your ass even though I'm only eight!" She turned to an older girl of about ten, who was chubby, olive complexioned, and had long, black hair. "Can't I kick her ass, Abigail?" The chubby girl of ten nodded eagerly. Encouraged by her friend's support, Tracy approached Mary. "Anna do you want to judge whose the best fighter? "Mary stiffened. What should a person do when somebody half a head shorter challenges them to a fight? Should they pat the person on the head and laughingly tell them to go away? Or say "Ah no thanks. I just got my period today and don't feel up to fighting"? Mary would never know what made her open her mouth and say "Okay" But as soon as she did, the kids burst in to loud, raucous laughter. Tracy of coarse was the loudest of all. She began dancing around like a boxer. "Oh man! I can knock her block off!" Then she froze with a surprised expression on her face. "Hey I can do my karate and jujitsu moves on her!" She began to demonstrate, much to the amusement of the other kids. It was clear that Tracy was well liked by the older kids. She was such a cute, lively, funny little girl. Maybe they even liked the fact that she was an attention getter. When some of the on lookers called Mary a retard, she decided to play along with this judgment. She tried to look and act as clueless as possible, until they ignored her and gave all their attention to Tracy. Feeling safe, she slipped back in to the house.

In the office Sarah was having a dispute with Janice. "I'm sick of that bitch, Linda stealing from me!" "I wish you wouldn't come barging in to my office unannounced like this. I'm trying-" "I don't care! You never listen to me. You always take her side." "I wish you wouldn't speak to me in that tone of voice" In spite of Janice' obvious hostility, Sarah was somehow managing not to lose her cool. Mary supposed that she was used to scenes like this. "And I'm sick this fucking I wish all the time! I wish I wish, can't you say anything else?" Mary tiptoed away from the door and decided that it was safe to put the TV on. Sarah wasn't likely to notice at this point. Halfway through a Doris Day comedy, Joan, the red head that helped Sarah with breakfast earlier, came in the room and pulled a chair up to a window near the kitchen and started up a lively conversation with someone outside. After a few minutes Joan called Mary over. "Hey Mary what color is my friend out there?" Mary looked out the window and saw a young black girl of about eleven. She stood there, smiling up at her. Mary sighed "Black" Did they really think that she was so blind or retarded that she didn't know the difference between black and white? Joan and her friend looked at each other and snickered. When they started talking, sometimes whispering and giggling, Mary walked away. Why was she being such a push over here? If these kids had been at one of her previous schools she would have swore at all of them, and knocked some of them down! What was wrong with her? Soon Mary realized that her problems from outside had not gone away. Peeking in at her from the window nearest to the TV was a small impish face, framed by blonde hair. Beside it was a equally impish face, darker and framed by black hair. "When is our fight going to take place?" asked the smaller impish face. Mary got up from the floor, her heart racing! Oh this was so embarrassing! "Umm, I don't know-tomorrow?" She left the living room and started down the hall toward her room. But before she even reached her room she saw the two faces peering in at her from the window at the end of the hall. "What time and where" shouted a high voice that had to be Tracy's. Mary hurried in to the room she shared with Peggy. Before she could close the drapes, Tracy and Abigail appeared. "We're going to meet in the main building at a quarter of nine in the basement." Tracy decided for her. They weren't going to give up. "Ah Okay" replied Mary reluctantly. She hoped that the adults would stop them from sneaking away from the other students.

After supper that evening Sarah had a friend of hers stop by to cut the girls hair, if they wanted. Mary did, she asked the woman to trim her wavy, light brown hair to a little above her shoulders. A few other girls had their hair trimmed. "Okay everyone." announced Sarah "How about some ice cream?" Everyone agreed readily. They all piled in to the van, used by that particular house. Sarah took them to Friendly's where they had sundaes.

On the way back the girls were talking about school work. When they asked Mary how much she knew about reading, writing, and arithmetic, she pretended to know very little. "You've got a lot to learn, baby!' exclaimed Janice. Mary sighed contentedly and slid down in her seat. She had a sudden vision of Dr Aziz, her favorite doctor at the medical center. He was sitting in the van with them, holding Mary on his lap. She was his little girl who he doted on. He loved her just the way she was. She didn't have to learn now. Her reverie was interrupted by the loud laughter of the girls at a joke told by one of them.

That night the music and talking at bedtime was interrupted by a temper tantrum thrown by Peggy, Mary's roommate. She didn't know that Peggy could get so angry. And what was it about, a simple refusal to brush her teeth? Why would Peggy refuse to do that? But because she did, everyone's music privileges were taken away for the night. This made Peggy more defiant and boisterous. She swore at Sarah repeatedly. Finally the housemother had enough. She washed Peggy's mouth out with soap. It was quite a battle!, a regular wrestling match. Through it all, Mary was rooting for Peggy. What was this was her nerve coming back?

After two days at St Vincent's Mary was starting to find her voice. Sarah wasn't impressed with the change in Mary, and she told her so.

After breakfast the next morning Mary knew with certainty that this was not the school for her. On impulse, she told Donna, the shorter of the two blondes in the house, that she was going to run away. Donna put on a serious expression. "Oh, I think that's a good idea. And if anyone tries to stop you, you just say leave me alone, man. I know what I'm doing!" Mary suspected that Donna was making fun of her. But she didn't care. Soon she would be gone.

Mary was just stepping off the grounds when Janice caught up with her. "Where do you think your going?" "I'm leaving!" answered Mary belligerently. Janice grabbed her jacket. "Let go!" snapped Mary. She had had enough. "No, not until you smarten up! There's nowhere to run. Why don't you give this school a chance?" She held firmly to Mary; jacket. Thinking she was clever, Mary unfastened her jacket and slid her arms out of it. She started to run. However, the April morning was chilly, so she came back and held out her hand. "Now give me back my jacket" Janice tossed it at her. "Be stupid!"

Mary walked down a tree lined street. There were houses with neat lawns in front of them. She felt free, liberated, something she hardly ever was allowed to experience. She supposed that this was part of the thrill of running away, the short lived feeling of independence. Mary must have gone about four blocks when she heard the roar of a vehicle behind her. A navy blue van pulled up across the street from her. "Mary it's me, Sarah. Come here" Mary turned and ran down a side street. The van followed her. She back tracked and ran down another side street. Still the van followed her. When the van caught up with her again Sarah called to her. "Mary, your parents have been notified. They're on their way up here" These words worked like magic for Mary. She got in the van and rode back to school.

Even though Sister Mary Margaret couldn't trust Mary now, she wanted her to continue to attend classes until her parents arrived. So she assigned her an escort to take her to classes and watch her during recess and lunch time. That escort turned out to be none other then Janice, who Mary figured must have finked on her right after she ran off. It was alright though, because her parents were coming to get her. They would bring her back to the medical center, where she belonged. Mary was deposited in the tall, bald teacher's classroom. Steven was still willing to be wrestled to the floor and restrained every five minutes or so. This time though, Mary didn't even keep up the pretense of doing any work. She sat there and stared at the wall and thought about an actor she especially liked. Soon she would be able to watch him on TV anytime she liked. This made her sigh contentedly. She might have even mumbled something too, she wasn't sure.

During recess, everyone was in the gym. Some kids ran and played. Mary stood near a group of teachers, feeling like the coward that she was certain she was. Five minutes ago Tracy's attempt to fight Mary was spoiled by Janice, whose job it was, to watch Mary. Mary felt guilty for being relieved about this. This change of plans didn't totally ruin things for Tracy. Together with her friend Abagail, they continually walked across Mary' feet, stepping as hard as they could, and smiling the whole time. They both were stopped by a middle aged, woman with a firm, but humorous disposition. She shook her finger at Abigail."You better stop, or I'll cough on you and give you my cold. You won't be able to sleep. You'll cough and cough all night." Abigail and Tracy reluctantly backed off. Mary was secretly grateful.

Back in the classroom Mary dropped something and mumbled to herself. A fat girl next to her looked up. "Stop talking to yourself." she hissed. Mary scowled at her. "Leave me alone" She passed some time drawing and thinking about her favorite actor. She couldn't wait to leave this school and return to the life that was becoming more and more normal to her. "STOP TALKING TO YOURSELF!" Mary looked up in surprise! The fat girl was on her feet now. "I wasn't!" cried Mary in disbelief...She hadn't been, had she? The angry, fat girl lunged at her. Mary grabbed a chair and swung at her with it. The teacher grabbed her, pried the chair out of her hands, and led her to the door. He flagged someone down and told them to get Janice out of class. When she arrived, he ordered her to take Mary to Sister Mary

Margaret's office. Mary was still riled about the classroom incident. She didn't go peacefully. "Don't throw a mental fit with me!" exclaimed Janice. She restrained the smaller girl and marched her to the headmistress' office.

Mary sat in the office until her parents arrived. In the mean time she had to hear the nun complaining about what a disappointment she was to everybody. Mary scowled. Couldn't the nun just think she was mental like everyone else did? She noticed that Miss Murray' classroom was right across from the office. Mary looked over at it with longing. The door was open. She could hear the teacher's kind, patient voice as she taught the younger students. If only Mary could have been in that classroom she would have been able to make it at this school.

She was still thinking this when a young, handsome man with wavy, light brown hair, probably a teacher came in to use the copy machine. When he was finished Mary looked up at him and just on impulse, she blurted out "I ran away" in a flirtatious voice. He stopped and looked at her. "Well big deal!! What do you want a gold medal?" Mary gaped. But before she could answer, Sister Mary Margaret said "Yeah, she wants a gold medal "in a hard, sarcastic voice. He might have looked like an actor I liked thought Mary, but he sure doesn't act like him. She was disappointed. She looked at the classroom across the hall until her parents arrived.

Mr. and Mrs. Sullivan said very little as they helped their daughter gather her things. However, once in the car, Mrs. Sullivan started in on her daughter. "What was wrong with this school?" "When will you ever stop being so sick in the head?" She of course went on and on about this all being connected with the nun at the orphanage whom Mary had been very close to. Then she stopped her prosecuting persona, and switched to her parson persona. "While you were still at the school in Boston the doctors called me in for a conference. They wanted to get to know me better. Well I told them all about my faith in God! I gave them such an enlightening sermon that you could have heard a pin drop when I was finished. I wowed them all!" Mrs. Sullivan believed that the doctors saw things her way and realized just what a bad child Mary truly was. "Father McGovern knew. You might not know it, but he washed his hands of you because of all the trouble you caused as a little girl." Mary squirmed in her space between her parents. Had Father McGovern really washed his hands of her? She found herself feeling abandoned by someone she hadn't seen in years. She knew what was coming next. "You haven't been right in the head since you were three!" yelled Mrs. Sullivan. She was being the prosecuting attorney again. Mr. Sullivan groaned to himself as he drove them back to Rhode Island. Mary heard him, though she didn't think her mother did. She wondered if he would go through any red lights. He had done that before, when the yelling in the car distracted him too much. "I don't know how someone could make someone so sick!

But that nun from the orphanage sure messed you up. You've been nothing but trouble since you were three. Nobody could stand you except us!" Mary felt the familiar gnawing feeling in her stomach. Was Mary really such a terrible child back then? Sister Jane had loved her...Oh that's right, Sister Jane was supposed to be bad too.

When the Sullivan's left Mary on the adolescent ward she was so happy. She grabbed her sketch book and crayons and sat on the floor in front of the TV. St Coldness, which is what she called that school up in Fall River, was behind her. Now she would be left to live here at the hospital without further interruptions...right?

Chapter Six

Eden wood School

Mary was sitting in the back seat of her father's black and white dodge. They were on their way to a residential school in Vermont called Eden wood. Mary was twelve years old. It was now almost the middle of August in 1973. She was a troubled runaway with eye sight problems, a combination that made people nervous. After five months in the RI Medical Center where she resisted any kind of discipline or education, the state found a school that agreed to keep Mary no matter how many times she ran away. This was the only thing that seemed to matter to them.

So here she was, on her way to a school that was out in the middle of nowhere. Mary was fond of the city. She was very unhappy with her parent's decision to move from Providence, to a hick town like Coventry. The strange thing was that when they were still living in the city, Mary was fixated on the idea of living on a ranch out west. She wasn't all that fond of the city at the age of ten. By the time her parents were settled in their new house in Hicksville, Mary was back to being a city lover. Why couldn't she be in sync with what was going on? Would she always be this way?

When they were on the outskirts of Plymouth, Mary's father needed directions to Eden wood. He stopped the car near a large field, where a middle-aged, man in overalls, saw him and approached the car. As he was giving directions, Mary stuck her tongue out at the farmer.

Eventually they found themselves on a dirt road with a field to the right, which contained a volleyball court. There were a number of old houses on each side of the dirt road. But none of them were as big as the white house with black trimming that sat at the top of the hill, directly across from the volleyball court. The car made its way up the hill, and stopped in the small area used as a parking lot. While Mary's father struggled with the two suitcases, she was led toward the house by her mother. At twelve, Mary was five feet tall. Her shoulder length, light brown hair was in pigtails…her choice. The outfit however, was not her choice. She was wearing a white, short sleeved blouse with ruffles down the front. She had on a black and white plaid skirt, white socks and black patent leather shoes. She carried a large baby doll. If it wasn't for her height, people would have thought she was eight or nine.

Mary and her parents were brought upstairs by a teenaged girl with long, straight brown hair. She carried a clipboard and seemed to have some authority. The house was Victorian and appealed to Mary. But she would never admit this to anyone, not even to herself. She was too consumed with wanting to be cool. Modern was cool, old fashioned was not cool. So she pretended to dislike old things

Mary and her parents were shown in to an office at the end of a carpeted hallway on the second floor. The room was large, carpeted, and contained old, yet elegant furniture. The director, a thirty five year old Italian man, named Anthony sat down and talked about his school and what would be expected from Mary there. Clearly, Eden wood was a very strict, structured school with high expectations. Mary began to squirm! How could she avoid staying here? She really wanted to know. After the official interview, Mary's parents were told to leave. They said goodbye to their daughter, who was still in shock over the idea that she, was expected to remain in such a place.

Mary sat in a room known as the business office. Teenagers worked hard at typing, filing and answering phones. Occasionally people entered and exited this room; one of them was a young man in his early twenties named, Dexter. He told Mary that he used to be a junkie. Before he came to Eden wood, he jumped out a window. As a result, he was paralyzed on his left side. Students stopped to greet Mary and welcome her to their school. This made her feel a little like a celebrity, which was nice, but was also overwhelming.

A young woman with long, straight, brown hair, wearing a tee shirt, and bell bottomed jeans, approached Mary. "Hi I'm Arlene, the social worker here. Come to my office so that I can explain the program here" She ushered Mary in to a small room that was almost bare. There were two windows, no pictures on the walls, and only two chairs. The room did have wall to wall carpeting though. Mary sat across from Arlene. Before the woman could begin, there was a sudden shout from outside the closed door." GENERAL MEETING!!" Others took up the call. Soon everyone was running and shouting the desperate phrase. Alarmed, Mary ran out of the small office. A fat guy of about eighteen was going around shouting in to a megaphone. "GENERAL MEETING!!" Everyone was running downstairs as though their lives depended on it. Similar noises could be heard from below. Mary sat down in Arlene's office and waited anxiously for an explanation. What were they going to do? She wondered, kill somebody? It sure sounded like it. Arlene settled down in to her bean bag chair." The first thing you must remember is that Eden wood is a school that will stand for no nonsense" Mary squirmed. Already she had a sense of that.

Arlene proceeded to tell Mary all about Eden wood. Weekdays were the most strenuous. Everyone was expected to sign the breakfast sheet the night before. If they did, they had to be in the dinning room by six thirty. If they preferred sleeping through the first meal of the day, they had to be up by seven o'clock. They would clean themselves and their dorms by eight o'clock, and be in the dinning room by nine o'clock, just in time for morning meeting.

This was not optional, everyone had to attend. During this meeting, complaints were voiced, previous and future events were discussed, songs were sung, and the meaning of being at Eden wood was addressed. At Ten classes began. Then at one O'clock everyone had lunch. At one thirty everyone did chores until five O'clock.

In the evenings they had group therapy. By this time Mary wanted more and more to run out the nearest door. What was group therapy, and did they get any time to play or watch TV? "We have two kinds of group therapy here" Arlene explained. The encounter group is for people who are angry at each other. People in these groups can yell at those who they are angry at, with no fear of consequences. They can even request to be put in a group with someone who they are particularly angry at. In these groups students can scream at, swear at, and even express a desire to hurt or kill the person they are upset with. The one thing they can't do is use physical violence." Even without the physical violence, Encounter groups seemed dreadful to Mary. "The other group therapy we have here is called Primal scream therapy." explained Arlene. "In this group session the lights are turned off. A large candle is lit, and placed in the middle of the floor. Like the Encounter group, everyone sits in a circle. Someone starts talking about what is troubling them. When the group leader thinks the person is ready, the person has to hold the hands of the two people on either side of them and begin to chant a phrase that describes their feelings. For instance, they might have to say I'm lonely. They will say this repeatedly, getting louder as they go along. Eventually they will be shouting it, and undoubtedly crying. Someone in the circle will get up and pull the person to their feet, and hold them as they shout and cry about their loneliness". Mary sighed, and put her hand to her fore head. "Will I have to be in these group sessions?" she asked worriedly. "Well of coarse you will, Mary" answered Arlene in a no nonsense tone of voice. "Everyone has to be in them. Now let me tell you more about Eden wood. What you heard a few minutes ago is called a General Meeting. It is a punishment inflicted on a wrong doer, by everyone. We have a lot of punishments here. When none of them work, a General Meeting is used as a last resort. The wrong doer is placed in front of everyone. A director explains the person's actions, or attitude to the audience. They are encouraged to vent their hostility at the person for thinking that they can get away with bad behavior." As if on cue, the sound of many voices was suddenly raised in anger. Mary could hear the sound of many feet running. When she looked alarmed, Arlene explained that although no hitting was allowed, everyone could run up and scream in the person's face. "It's called positive peer pressure, Mary. Everything here is based on this principle. All students are ordered to report anyone who is breaking a rule. It's not finking, it's responsible concern. Students are also expected to not only pick up after themselves; they are also expected to tell others to pick up after themselves. When someone breaks a rule they receive a verbal reprimand. This is carried out by a group of students, selected by, and supervised by a staff member. Each student in turn yells at the rule breaker. Then the staff member sternly sums it up, and dismisses the rule breaker." What have I got myself in to? Wondered Mary dismally. "Sometimes a verbal reprimand is not enough." Arlene went on. "A student might be put in the corner for awhile, or it might be necessary to give them a spanking." A spanking? All the kids here appeared to be older the Mary. She giggled nervously. "Aren't teenagers a little too big to be spanked?" Arlene shook her head. "The student is made to lie across the seat of a chair. Another student, under the supervision of a staff member, proceeds to paddle the offender with a clip board.' Mary gasped! "Well, Mary if this scares you perhaps you'll be able to avoid it by staying out of trouble." There was no sympathy in Arlene's manner. She was calm, laid back, and a very no nonsense kind of person. Mary didn't like her much.

Arlene suggested that they go downstairs for a snack before she finished explaining the program at Eden Wood. The shouting in the dinning room had stopped by this time. As Arlene went to the kitchen, Mary peeked in the dining room. Three teenagers stood at the front of the room, two boys and a girl. The shirts had been ripped off of the boys. They hung in tatters around their waists. The girl looked unharmed. A man with a mustache was talking to the rest of the students, who sat, looking like they wanted to inflict more harm on the three kids before them. Mary would never forget the looks on some of their faces! Arlene beckoned to her to come back upstairs.

Along with reprimands, time outs, spankings, loss of privileges, students will sometimes be made to wear a large card board sign with comments about their bad attitude written on it, or they might have to stand up in front of everyone and recite an announcement about their attitude. These two punishments can go on for a week, or a month, depending on how the student progresses." Mary sipped her milk and listened with a combination of horror and fascination. We have ranks here." continued Arlene. "When you come here, you start off as a worker in one of our departments. You might begin on the service crew. This crew cleans the house and runs errands for the staff and directors. Some students begin on the kitchen crew. They cook all the meals, and clean up afterward. The communications department plans all the recreation activities for everyone. The Business takes care of all the filing. They also answer the phone; take messages, and order supplies for the school. Each department has several workers, a foreman, a department head, and a coordinator. The most elite of all the departments, are the Expeditors. These students are like school monitors, only their on duty all the time…except at night. They consist of a couple of expeditor trainees, a full expeditor, and a chief expeditor. Above them is a coordinator. One expeditor is always going around with a population sheet, attached to a clip board, taking head counts on everyone. The other expeditors are stationed at various locations throughout the house, like cops in the days when they used to walk a beat. These expeditors make sure that people are doing their jobs, not breaking rules, and not talking bad about anyone in authority. They keep note books with a different heading on each page. For instance, liars, thieves, manipulators, ball busters, runaways. People are listed under these titles, and the expeditors keep an eye on them." Arlene asked Mary what she thought of the school so far. "I-I don't think I'm going to like it." Arlene nodded understandingly. "That's okay. No one likes it at first. However, if you cooperate, you can get out of here within a year perhaps a little more. With each rank come more privileges. Eventually students go in to Re-entry. This is the second phase of the program. You continue to live here, but you work, or go to school out in the community. Now that's something to look forward to, isn't it?" Mary felt over whelmed. A year or more!?

Eventually the general meeting ended, and supper was served. Everyone ate, and talked continually. Soon Mary began to notice something very strange going on. Every time one of the three students, who had received the general meeting, got up for anything, they had to interrupt everyone with "Excuse me! I feel better then you!" They didn't do it in unison. They were each seated at different tables. It seemed both funny, and bizarre to see people from different parts of the room, and at different times, stand up and announce to everyone that they felt better then them. Mary, who couldn't help laughing, was corrected for this. She was told that the announcement was their punishment, and had to be taken seriously by everyone. The three unfortunate individuals turned out to be Lisa, Dean, and Allen. They were being punished for having a continually condescending attitude toward people.

For the next ten days Mary was treated pretty much like a visitor. People sat her down and told her more about the things that Arlene told her. Sometimes she was reprimanded when she did something wrong. One day during lunch macaroni and cheese was served. Mary ate some of hers, but decided that she didn't want any more of it. When she tried to throw it away she was stopped. "It's against the rules to throw food away" a chubby expeditor, named Lee told her. "You can give it to someone else if you want. Other wise you have to eat it." Mary made an announcement, informing everyone that her macaroni was up for grabs, but there were no takers. One of the condescending three was announcing that they felt better then their fellow students, when Mary sneaked across the hall, and in to the living room. She spotted the up right piano over in the corner. Quickly she opened the lid, and emptied the contents of her plate in to the piano, and closed the lid. Later on, someone must have tried to use the piano because Mary was called in to the living room. A teenaged, boy with long blonde hair, named Terrence was standing over by the piano. The front of it was pulled up, giving Mary a clear view of the macaroni splattered all over the insides. When Terrence questioned her, she tried to keep a straight face. She laughed in spite of herself. She was reprimanded, and ordered to clean up the mess. Aside from little incidents like this, Mary was allowed to do pretty much what she wanted. She had her dolls and stuffed animals, and her drawing supplies with her. She hoped she wouldn't be made to stay at Eden wood.

One day she over heard Anthony, the executive director telling the other students that he didn't think Mary could grasp the concept of the program at Eden wood. He therefore didn't think she would be staying. Mary beamed with pleasure!

Two terrible things happened to Mary in the middle of August, almost two weeks after she arrived at Eden wood. The first thing was the disappearance of Chrissie, her favorite doll. Mary had been absorbed in her art work for about half an hour when she looked up and noticed that Chrissie was missing. After about ten minutes of frantic searching, two teens approached Mary. They were an obese girl with long black hair, and a slightly chubby boy with shaggy brown hair. The boy was holding Mary's doll, now completely ruined! The stuffing had been ripped out of her middle section. She was covered with shampoo. "Sorry, Mary" the boy, whose name was Kevin said. "I found her lying in the shower just like this." Mary turned and ran to the bathroom where she cried her eyes out! Why would someone do something so horrible to something she loved? The girl with the black hair took Mary outside and had her bury the doll, and say a few prayers over the grave. It soon came out that Kevin was the one who destroyed Mary's doll. He was known for stealing all the time. No one liked him. He couldn't give a good reason for hurting Mary, he just felt like it.

Two days later Mary's care free days at Eden wood ended. She was called upstairs to the Communications department, which also served as the school's library. All three directors and the staff members were sitting in a row. Mary was told to sit in the chair across from them. Mary sat down, and looked at them uncertainly. Anthony, the executive director, started the discussion. "You will be staying here, Mary. Rhode Island doesn't want you back…not until you change." Mary gasped! The state she came from, the one she called home, didn't want her back!? What was she a criminal, a leper? She felt abandoned. Before this information could totally sink in, Anthony had more news for her. "You won't be playing here, and behaving like a little girl anymore." Just then one of the staff, a big man named Paul, walked in. To Mary's horror, he was carrying her dolls and stuffed animals! He had her drawings with him too. "No more toys or art work." said Anthony when Mary gaped at him. This was too much! "You can't do this to me! You're a bunch of fucking assholes, I hate you, and I hope you all die, you rotten Mother Fuckers!!" One of the staff members, a young, black haired, olive complexioned, man, named Marvin slouched in his chair, his arms folded across his chest. "The party's over he said casually. "And to show you what we think of disrespect-"Anthony gestured to a tall girl with glasses, who appeared in the doorway. "Chris here is going to teach you a lesson." He ordered Chris to put Mary over her knee, where she proceeded to spank her. Mary pinched the girl, hard on her leg. "OW!" cried Chris. She was ordered to spank Mary more. Once back in her seat, Mary was informed that Chris was going to be her personal over seer. "She will be with you twenty four hours a day. In the dorm, you will sleep on the top bunk; Chris will sleep right below you." Mary glared fiercely at Anthony. She hated him!

Because Chris was five years older then Mary, she seemed like a big sister. She wasn't a nice big sister though. She got on Mary's case about everything. If she acted silly, she was put in the corner. If she gave back talk, she was reprimanded by a group of her peers, and sometimes spanked. One morning when everyone was getting up, Chris discovered a picture under Mary's pillow. Mary had managed to steal a pencil and a piece of paper the night before. She drew a picture of her favorite anchorman from RI. When Chris found it she took it away, and ripped it up. "You know you're not supposed to have these!" snapped Chris. Without thinking, Mary reached up, and smacked Chris across her face. She was taken up to the library, and under Jeremiah, the director's supervision, she was paddled. Mary was furious! She was also resentful, and hurt. The only thing she still could do was fantasize. Nobody knew that the anchor man was with her all the time; that he was like a doting father to her. When she sat, she was sitting on his lap. When Chris stuck to her like glue, the doting man was also sticking to her like glue. Chris never even knew. In bed at night he held her. Sometimes even things like this could be interrupted. The directors had no qualms about waking everyone up in the middle of the night for a general meeting. Occasionally this happened. Usually someone had to have tried to escape in order for everyone to be woken up in the middle of the night. However, sometimes a director would just want to punish a student for a less serious offense. Depriving everyone of sleep, in order to deal with the troubled student was an excellent way to punish them.

A few days after Chris was assigned to Mary, the staff and directors thought it would be a good idea to make Mary look her age. She was taken to the hair salon, and had her hair cut, and styled in to a pixie. Then she was taken shopping for some modern, adolescent looking clothes. Mary was proud of the clothes, but she didn't like her short hair. She hoped it grew back fast.

At the end of August Chris was no longer Mary's personal over seer. Mary was made a worker on the Service Crew, along with a new girl named, Sue. They did chores together. One day when they were cleaning the living room Mary found a blade from a razor. While playing with it, she accidentally cut the side of her mouth. She was taken up to Anthony's office. He thought she did it on purpose to get attention. After yelling at her, he ordered Paul, one of the staff members, to spank her, and put her in the corner. As Mary sat, crying in the corner, while Sue did her chores, along with her own, she realized just how much contempt Eden wood had for anyone who deliberately tried to hurt themselves. Mary not only cried because of the spanking, she cried because the whole incident had been an accident.

Reprimands were particularly difficult for Mary. Because she wasn't good at establishing eye contact with people, and often went about in a day dream, she wasn't reprimanded the same way the other students were. Each person in line would walk up to her, and yell in her face, and she had to stand there and not react. This went on until the staff thought she was paying attention during reprimands.

Classes at Eden wood began the day after Labor Day. Mary was several grades behind; she had lessons in the living room with three other students who were behind in school. All three of them were boys. They were Tom, Steve, and a new boy named Brian. Lois, a forty year old, blonde woman was their teacher. Across the hall, in the dinning room, the students who were doing well, and keeping up, were taught. A heavy set woman, named Candice was their teacher. Mary didn't like school very much, but she preferred it to the rest of the schedule at Eden wood. One afternoon when school was over, and she was supposed to be doing her chores, Mary was throwing the balls from the pool table out the window. She was trying to hit the tree across the lawn. Tom, one of the boys from her class, was mowing the lawn, going back and forth, getting in her way. Each time he was passing, Mary would wait impatiently, and then throw more balls at the tree. She didn't know if she ever hit the tree or not. Someone reported her for this. She was paddled with a clip board by each of the students who had been selected to reprimand her. She was shocked to discover that they all thought she was trying to hit Tom with the pool balls. They must have hated her for this! How despicable she felt as she stood there with her back side throbbing, as five kids, in turn yelled at her.

Mary wasn't included in the primal therapy sessions during her first few months at Eden wood. Someone explained to her that because she still acted silly and day dreamed so much, she would be an insensitive interruption during a primal group, where someone was screaming out their pain. She was included in the encounter groups. In fact, so many people were angered by her childishness, that the directors organized encounter groups where Mary was the focus. Three or four evenings a week she would find herself in a room with seven to ten students who were angry at only her. Each of them was encouraged to vent their rage at her. Then the group leader would interrogate her about her attitude. These sessions became more and more stressful to Mary, but they didn't improve her behavior.

It was no secret that the neighbors in the small community hated Eden wood School. They were suspicious of hippies, especially hippies with a back ground of drug abuse. They were worried that the students, who sometimes escaped, would destroy their property, or steal their cars. They couldn't stand all the yelling that went on at the unwelcome school. They were particularly upset about the surprise general meetings that sometimes occurred in the middle of the night. Plymouth was a farming community. People believed in hard work, and rose early in the morning. They didn't like their sleep interrupted. In spite of this, Anthony, the executive director, was not only determined to stay there, he also opened another facility over in Pittsford, another farming community.

The new facility opened in November. Half of the students were transferred over to the new house. Because of the friction with neighbors in both towns, they made the move late at night. With half of the students gone, Mary found herself surrounded by only about twenty four other students. She didn't like it, not because she missed the others, but because she would now receive even more attention. At Eden wood, this was not a good thing. It meant that not only was she punished more often, it also meant that she was searched on a regular basis for pictures that she secretly drew, and carried around, concealed on her.

Mary had many opportunities to witness general meetings in the coming months. One evening a chubby, blonde girl, who was an expeditor, lost her temper and threw her clip board in to the air. "I can't take it anymore! I can't take it anymore!" she screamed hysterically. She had to be restrained by a couple of students. The girl, whose name was Debby had been taking head counts. Someone else had to take over for her. A few minutes later, Mary heard the familiar shouts of "GENERAL MEETING!" Everyone was rushed by the expeditors in to the dinning room. Tables were hurriedly pushed to the back of the room. Chairs were arranged in to rows, facing the front of the room. Marvin the staff member on duty appeared at the front of the room. He paced back and forth, his hands behind his back, his head lowered. Mary soon learned that this was characteristic of him. "We have a student here, who is lazy, and likes to act like an animal." He announced. When Debby was brought downstairs, and placed at the front of the room, everyone charged at her, and screamed in her face. Gradually as the mob thinned out, Mary noticed that Debby was crying, and hitting people. "Set up for the boxing ring." ordered Marvin. The chairs were pushed aside, and everyone formed a circle. A girl of about the same size as Debby was called in to the circle with her. They both were given boxing gloves. The girl beat up Debby, who cried, and yelled out "Go on, beat me all you want, you're the animals here!" After a couple of rounds the chairs were put back in place, and everyone sat down. Debby was once again standing before them. It was decided that she wouldn't be demoted, which was what usually happened to anyone who acted as she had. Marvin thought that it would be best for her to continue as an expeditor, and learn to deal with the pressure. "We're not going to put up with a lazy, cry baby, such as yourself" Marvin reminded her of her Two year old son, who was being raised by her parents. "If you want to see him any time soon, you better grow up!"

Several boys tried to run away one night, but were caught by a student, who had earned enough trust to be on night duty. They were given general meetings, put in the boxing ring, and had their hair cut short. When they confessed to trying to escape because they missed their mothers, they were yelled at, and ridiculed. Another boy, named Ricky received a general meeting, not for running away, but for using a racial slur against one of the African American students. Ricky was made to lie across the seat of a chair. The African American student was ordered to paddle him with a clip board. One of the few virtues about Eden wood was their zero tolerance for racism.

Students of all ages were at Eden wood. Mary, being only twelve, was the youngest. Most were between the ages of Fourteen to Eighteen. However, there were some who were in their early Twenties. Everyone there, were either sent there by a doctor, their parents, or a judge. One of the older students was a man named Eddie. He was in his early Twenties. He was thrown out of the navy for being a drug addict. He was blonde, freckled, and had a ruddy complexion. Although he must have been intelligent, he insisted on acting like a good natured imbecile. He wondered the corridors, singing Dean Martin songs, and ignoring orders. He would never give a straight answer to anything. Once, when asked why he got kicked out of the navy, he smiled vaguely, and said "Ah, I think I killed the Captain or something." He was a worker in the Communications department. When he wouldn't keep the bulletin board up to date, he was made to carry it around with him, wherever he went. He good naturedly complied with this, but he still wouldn't up date it. He liked Mary, and used to say "Hi Buddy!" when he greeted her. He liked to put his hand on her leg when they sat together. She liked him because he never criticized her or hollered at her. By the time the new facility in Pittsford opened, Mary was a worker in the Business office. When Eddie, who was among the students being transferred, was leaving, Mary stole a pack of cigarettes from the office, and sneaked them to him. "Hey, thanks, Buddy!" he exclaimed as he slipped them in to his shirt pocket. Mary shushed him urgently, and looked around nervously, but no one saw.

Wanda was a heavy set, young woman with long, straight, brown hair, parted on the side. She had gone through the program at Eden wood, went in to Re-entry, and graduated. She stayed on as a staff member. Mary never saw her do much except run group sessions. When she wasn't doing this, she could usually be found in her cozy little room on the second floor, across from the Communications department. She liked to read, do cross word puzzles, knit, and watch TV. Since group therapy happened three or four evenings a week, students did get a chance to watch TV on the other evenings. Often Mary would go upstairs and watch TV with Wanda. She felt comfortable around the polite, soft spoken, easy going woman. She was surprised that Wanda had ever been in enough trouble to get sent to Eden wood. Mary hated it when her TV privileges were taken away, and it happened over the slightest offense at times, depending on the mood of whoever was in charge.

In December another person in their twenties entered the program. He came from a psychiatric hospital in Maine. His name was George. He had black hair, and was of medium complexion. The thing that caught Mary's attention about him was that he talked out of turn, interrupting conversations, often to talk about something else. Sometimes when one of the directors was lecturing everyone in the dinning room, George would suddenly start loudly talking about the Water Gate scandal. He would be silenced by someone near him, but two minutes later he would start up again. Sometimes George would start talking rapidly about something, to no one in particular. He would get so worked up, that he would kick out at walls, and furniture. He often wandered the corridors. He would up to someone, and start talking nonsense to them. Mary thought George was funny. She hoped that the authorities didn't rein him in too soon.

Chapter Seven

The fire

At the beginning of January 1974 Mary's parents were allowed to come to Eden Wood, and visit with their daughter for a few days. They brought up her presents. They visited with her in Wanda's small room, which meant that Wanda was present some of the time. Mary had been permitted a few phone calls from her parents during the four months she had been at Eden wood. She was lucky to have received this privilege. Phone calls and mail were privileges that had to be earned. All mail was read before it was given to a student, and all phone calls were listened in on, usually by a staff member. Mary enjoyed the first day that her parents visited with her. However, the second day was marred by something tragic. Mary, having signed the breakfast sheet the night before, was in the dinning room at Six Thirty. After finishing her food, she headed back to the dorm and made her bed. When the fire alarm went off, Mary grabbed her tooth brush and tooth paste. She wasn't concerned. It had to be just another fire drill. The week before, the directors had installed an alarm system. Since then, there had been several fire drills. Mary casually made her way to the bathroom. But before she could turn right, where the girls' bathroom was, Dennis, a boy with shoulder length, brown hair came charging down the stairs followed by a huge cloud of smoke! "Mary Sullivan, don't you dare go in that bathroom! The house is on fire!!" He pushed her out the side exit, and ran down the corridor, yelling "FIRE! FIRE! Everyone get out!" Mary made her way down the hill, followed by other students, most of them still in their pajamas. She looked up at the top of the huge, old house. Smoke was pouring from an attic window, staining the sky, directly above the house. It reminded Mary of the smoke that poured out of the factories she used to see when riding on the highway, thick, black smoke that discolored the sky in that area. One of the students, a new boy, named Ed, was staring up at the attic window. He had just got out of the shower, and wore nothing but a big towel. Some of the students had exited out the front entrance. They stood at the top of the hill. Suddenly there was a commotion from up there. Mary was told that Ben, a strange, young man, who had only been At Eden wood for a month, had just tried to run away.

When the fire trucks arrived, all the students were herded down the road, to the executive director's house. Word spread quickly, as they hurried along, that Ben admitted to starting the fire. "That's why he tried to run!" someone said excitedly. Mary noticed a very obese girl named Abby. She was enveloped in a huge, pink bath robe, and was tearfully talking to a girl who walked beside her. Mary quietly laughed at her. She thought jokingly that because Abby was as big as a house, maybe she felt a sense of kinship toward the burning house.

They were all crammed in to the downstairs rooms in Anthony's house. Mary's parents arrived soon after everyone was settled. "Is everyone alright?" asked her mother. Mary told her that a girl, named Cathy had been treated for smoke inhalation. "She slept through all the commotion, and had to be carried out by a fire man!" exclaimed Mary excitedly. She then pointed to Ben, who was sitting near by, staring in to space, with a self satisfied smile on his face. "He set the fire!" For her parent's benefit, Mary strode up to him and asked if he really did set the fire. He nodded his head. "Yelp I did." He sat there, his brown eyes, framed by large, round glasses looking serene. Mary couldn't believe it! Her parents seemed subdued, and had little to say. Eventually they left. Mary found herself doing something she rarely did. She wandered around, talking to people. She wanted to know what they all thought of the fire. One girl, named Marie, told her that before coming to Eden wood, she and her friends used to like to torch people's houses. They never gave a thought to what those people felt. "Now a place that I have come to think of as home has been torched." explained Marie sadly. "I know how those people must have felt". Marie sat there, looking as sad as she sounded. Mary didn't know what to say. She wasn't good at this thing at Eden wood, known as relating. They were all expected to do it. Until now, she had refused to sit down, and relate to someone. Because it was a requirement at Eden wood, it became a bad thing to Mary.

The fire was a bad one. Everyone received progress reports frequently. It was said that one of the neighbors, a woman named Mrs. Iris, who never liked the school, came running out of her house, cheering when she saw the fire. The students were out raged! Because the house was so old, it burned fast. In the end, the only part of it that was saved was the brick structure that had been added on at a later date. It contained the dorms. As a result, everyone's possessions were unharmed. Only Wanda, whose room was in the old part of the house, lost everything.

A school bus was rented, and used to transfer everyone over to the facility in Pittsford. The students that were already housed there were made to stay upstairs, allowing the new arrivals to have supper. After this, Anthony came to the front of the room, and asked for everyone's attention. He told them that the newspapers were informed that the fire was caused by old, damaged wiring in the house. As he paced back and forth, he assured the students that the school would endure. He became very emotional, and cried as he told everyone that Eden wood would continue, and that nothing could keep them down. People felt encouraged by Anthony's speech. Mary did not. She was discouraged, and frustrated. She had hoped the fire would result in the school being closed down. She tried to hide her feelings, as she finished her tomato soup, and grilled cheese sandwich.

Anthony went on to discuss Ben. It was officially confirmed in front of them all, that he did in fact start the fire. "He sneaked up to the attic, poured lighter fluid here and there on the floor. He then set pieces of paper on fire, and tossed them around, then ran" Anthony explained that Ben was a very sick, young man, who had a twisted hero complex. "He truly sees himself as the hero and savior of the neighbors back in Plymouth" Anthony said that he was going to bring Ben in to the room, and let everyone question him. "I don't want you to charge at him like you normally would in a general meeting. We're not keeping him anyway." Ben was being sent back to the psychiatric hospital in Michigan. "The car, with his luggage is waiting outside" went on Anthony. "This is just an opportunity for you to ask him a few questions, and tell him how his actions make you all feel." Ben was brought in, and placed before the students. "So, why did you burn our house down, Ben?" a big guy, named Harold asked. Ben only got as far as "Because I thought it was sick, and–"Almost everyone in the gathering leaped up, as one, and charged at Ben. They screamed at him, and beat him up! Mary, startled by the suddenness of it, burst in to laughter. She was scolded by a boy, named Mitch, who was sitting near her. Mary couldn't understand what was making the furious mob back off, and return to their seats, until she was able to see Marvin. He had dove in and thrown himself on top of Ben. There he sat, with his arms up in the air, fending everyone off. Even in their rage, they had enough respect for a staff member to obey him. Ben was quickly dragged out the door, and shoved in to the car. Someone later told Mary that he was all banged up, with torn clothing, and lots of hair missing.

It was decided that the students from Plymouth would be housed in the three spare houses on the property. It was very tight quarters for them, especially in the house that served as the main house. The two houses that were used as the boys, and girls' dorms, weren't as difficult to move around in. They received their food from the kitchen of the new facility.

It took a little over a month for Anthony to find and purchase property over in Brandon. The property was some what isolated from the farms in the area. Anthony didn't expect to have that many conflicts with the neighbors in this location. The property had once been a residential camp. Woods surrounded the grounds. A large two story house stood in the center of the property. Across the circular drive way stood two houses, side by side. They were much smaller, and had only one floor. In back of the house was a lawn. Scattered down the hill were several cabins. At the foot of the hill was a lake. The first of the two one story houses that stood across from the main house became the head quarters for Anthony and his secretaries, and the nurse. The house next to this became one of the girls' dorms. One of the cabins in back of the main house was also a girls dorm, the rest were boys dorms. Mary was put in the dorm next to head quarters.

Everyone settled in to the new facility quickly. The routine was resumed. Wanda, the live-in staff member, acquired a room on the first floor, in the main house, and Mary was once again allowed to watch TV with her a couple of nights a week. However, like the others, she spent a lot of time in the huge, drafty, echoing, dinning room. It wasn't fancy. It was made entirely of wood, and had old fashioned light fixtures on the paneled walls. There was a big stage at the back of the room. This room was where they held Morning meeting, General meetings, meals, and once in a while, talent shows, movies, and dances.

Mary grew more and more resentful of the small encounter groups that were designed to target her in particular. One evening she ran out of one of these groups. She was chased across the drive way, and carried, screaming back inside. They took turns spanking her. She managed to get a hand free, and proceeded to hurl cosmetics and perfume bottles at her attackers. Another evening she tried to run from the room. A guy jumped up and blocked the door way. Frustrated, Mary hurled a chair at him! A General Meeting was called. It was her first one. She expected to be charged, and screamed at. However, the director only warned her in front of everyone that if she tried to leave her encounter group again, her fellow students would charge her, and scream at her.

Chapter Eight

Friends for Mary

In March a new girl arrived. Mary was in school when she heard a girl down the hall crying, and saying that she didn't want to be there. Mary was extremely curious. She excused herself, saying that she needed to use the bathroom. Instead, she went looking for the source of the crying. She saw a middle aged couple talking to Anthony. With them was a teenaged girl with glasses, and long, straight, brown hair. She was tall, and thin, and wore a red coat. Mary asked the girl what her name was, and how old she was. Before being chased back to class, Mary learned that the girl's name was Julia, and she was eighteen. It turned out that Julia was from Illinois. She had been staying at a psychiatric hospital, called Rosendale. Her doctor sent many of his patients to Eden wood. His name was Dr. Simmons. He knew Anthony well, and liked his brand of therapy. Poor Julia had become accustomed to a drug called Thorizine. Now, at Eden wood, she had to go without it. The only drugs that were allowed at Eden wood were for life threatening illnesses. Julia got off on the wrong foot right from the start. The first day she was allowed to remain in bed. On her second day she was up, and being expected to do what everyone else was doing. Everything made her cry; work, reprimands, group therapy, ETC. Mary felt a surge of pity for this nervous, tearful girl. Julia would interrupt a reprimand to ask for a glass of water, or to be allowed to go to the bathroom. This infuriated the person who was yelling at her. As the reprimand continued, Julia would cry loudly. In the encounter groups, she was targeted by everyone. They screamed, and swore at her for her babyish attitude. Julia would bawl! Mary, who was no longer in her own little encounter groups anymore, would talk comfortingly to Julia, as she was being verbally annihilated. "Stop trying to help her, Mary," the others would tell her. "She has to learn that there are consequences for her actions". Mary couldn't stop herself from helping the girl. Mary found life at Eden wood almost unbearable. How much more unbearable was it for this pathetic girl? She not only stole food, and cigarettes, to give to Julia, she also set herself up as the "look out" when she saw her doing something wrong. One of the directors took an intense dislike to Julia. His name was Jonathon. He was a burly man in his late twenties. He craved authority, and when he took a dislike to someone their days were made miserable! He constantly set up reprimands, and spankings for the new girl. He made her scrub pots and pans. When she bawled about having to do this, he mocked her by imitating her. One evening when Mary was sitting on her bed doing her homework, Julia came running in to the room looking terrified! She slammed the door, and threw herself against it. Mary jumped up, and helped her hold the door closed. Julia looked at her in a puzzled way. Suddenly the door was shoved open. They each fell backward, on to their beds. Jonathon stood over Julia. "If you keep up your nonsense, you're going to receive a good, old fashioned spanking. DO YOU UNDERSTAND!?" She stared up at him in fear, and slowly nodded.

In early April Mary became sick with the flu. Several other students became sick too, but Mary had a bad case of it, and was confined to bed for nearly two weeks. Every morning breakfast was brought to her, on a tray. Every morning Julia was denied food because she kept forgetting to sign the breakfast sheet the night before. Mary would watch the door, and beckon to her friend, giving her the opportunity to eat her food. Mary, who had no appetite, was glad to share her food with her. Sometimes Julia was caught before she could finish it. Once when Cathy, who was just finishing a stint on night duty, was brought some orange juice, eggs, and bacon before going to bed for the morning, turned her back long enough for Julia to grab her orange juice, and begin guzzling it. Cathy tried to pry it away from her, but Julia managed to finish it first. Mary pounded her fist on her mattress, and laughed! Cathy snapped at her before going to report Julia. Being sick did not entitle Mary to peace and quiet all the time. Sometimes one of the coordinators would come in the room with four or five students in lower ranks. They would proceed to call someone in the room for a reprimand. When they were finished, they would call in another student to be "dealt with" as they liked to put it. To Mary's distress she sometimes had to witness Julia being held across the seat of a chair, so that people could take turns spanking her. One evening Mary woke up feeling feverish. She heard an encounter group in progress in the dinning room. People were screaming at Julia. She was bawling and loudly insisting that she wanted to go to bed. She was of course refused this urgent request. Mary felt lucky to be where she was, even if she was sick. Julia was eventually given her first general meeting. When she was placed in front of her peers she pushed her glasses up on her nose, and turned to Jonathon, uncertainly. "W-what's going on?" she asked in a quivering voice. "Face them!" he yelled. With that, everyone charged at her and vented all their frustration on her. Julia screamed, and tried to push her way through the angry mob. She was then held down, and forced to endure all the yelling. This was to happen to her many times. Mary had learned by this time that even though she had no desire to run up and yell at wrong doers, it was necessary to go up there, and lean in to the crowd so that the directors would think she was getting involved. She knew that students got in to trouble for not getting involved in the program at Eden wood. The directors were always lecturing students in data sessions about what Eden wood stood for. They had these data sessions once a week. All of the staff and directors, except for Anthony, had gone through the program, and graduated. They were all referred to as Para-Professionals, because they didn't have any degrees. They taught from experience. Jonathon liked to point out that unlike some behavior modification schools, this school was not barbaric. Mary almost choked the first time she heard this! "We don't believe in shaving heads here. "he said. "Certain schools, like Day top do this, but we think it's too harsh." Mary noticed that for the most part he was right about not shaving heads. Yet this didn't explain why Kevin, the boy who destroyed her doll when she first came to Eden wood, was seen the previous week lying on a cot in the corner of the dinning room with his head shaved, and wearing a sign that read EAT AT KEVIN'S. He wore nothing but swimming trunks, and flippers. She was told that he stole something from a seafood restaurant during an outing. Still this didn't explain his shaved head. Two boys, who had heard that Eden wood was like Day Top, shaved their heads right before arriving at Eden wood. Mary supposed that they wanted to save themselves the humiliation of having it done to them by one of the directors. In these data sessions, everyone was constantly reminded of the importance of confessing all their guilt to someone. It was a system, similar to that of the Catholic Church. When someone did things that no one knew about, they were supposed to go to s student in a higher rank, and tell them all their sins. The person who was hearing the confession wrote them down, and handed them in to a staff member. The person who confessed was then helped to choose some kind of penance. "Remember everyone, "Jonathon would say in the data sessions, "You won't grow emotionally if you don't do this."

At the end of April Mary's parents were allowed to visit her because it was her birthday. At thirteen, she was starting to want to grow up, and be like the other kids. Not knowing how to do this, she began telling the newer students, who didn't know her back at the old house, that she experimented with drugs, broke windows, and shop lifted before coming to Eden wood. Sometimes she was caught in these lies by students who had been there as long as she had. Still Mary stuck to the lies, and tried to act tough, mouthy, and street wise. It landed her in more trouble then ever. First of all, a girl named Patsy, who sometimes treated her like a little sister, used to tease her about her mother being too religious, and sending her ill fitting, old fashioned clothes. "You were never in to drugs." She would say scornfully. "Your mother never let you out of the house!" Mary hotly denied this, and continued to try to make people believe she was something she wasn't. Once when another girl was backing Mary up against the wall, and confronting her, Mary kicked her in the shin. She received her first real General Meeting. Everyone ran up, and screamed in her face. Jeremiah, who was running the meeting, informed Mary that this was what she would receive any time she hit or kicked anyone. He was one of the older directors, being in his thirties. He was a very intense man, who screamed not from his throat, but from deep down in his stomach. He was an unpredictable person. He could be a student's best friend one day and their worst enemy the next day. It was difficult to totally hate or totally like Jeremiah. One couldn't help having mixed feelings about him. Right now Mary hated him. After being screamed at by her peers, Mary returned to her seat with a phony smile on her face. "It didn't bother me" she kept saying. Inside she was shaking. Patsy, the girl who sometimes treated her like a sister, and sometimes teased her, tried to force her in to a seat one day. "I'm an expeditor; you have to do what I say!" Mary pushed her away. Jeremiah had taken a dislike to Mary; set up a reprimand which Patsy was a part of. When it was finished, he told Mary that she couldn't punch people. "But I didn't punch her. I pushed her!" exclaimed Mary. Jeremiah ignored her, and ordered Patsy to punch her. Patsy needed no encouragement. She whacked Mary hard, across her shoulder. Afterward Mary told Patsy that the punch didn't hurt. She continued to refuse to stay in her seat. When a General Meeting was called, Mary feared that it was for her. She was lucky that time. Someone else was hollered at, humiliated, and put in the boxing ring. It was a new student, an African American guy about Seventeen who tried to run away.

Finally Jeremiah decided that Mary needed to learn a lesson. He called a General Meeting one afternoon, and made Mary stand before everyone. "You are going to learn about something called AN EYE FOR AN EYE, AND A TOOTH FOR A TOOTH!" He ordered her to lay on the stage. Everyone who she had talked back to was allowed to come up, and dump left over food on her. Mary knew what this punishment was. Strangely enough, it was called "Food Bath." It was invented by Jonathon, and was often used on Julia. The only thing Mary learned from this experience was how not to throw up when something disgusting was being done to her. Afterward the cook, a kind, humorous, middle aged man, joked with Mary, and told her that she looked like a chef's salad. Laughing with him took some of the sting out of what had been done to her. She noticed that the hired help were a lot kinder to the students then the staff and directors were. Jeremiah, however, wasn't ready to let things go that easily. He came up to Mary during lunch one day, and in a nasty voice, asked her what she thought of the eye for an eye lesson. She reacted with sullenness. There were times when he or Jonathon would make Mary sit in a corner. Everyone who she had argued with, were allowed to go over and swear at her when they felt like it. She was expected to sit there, and take it quietly.

In spite of all this, Wanda was permitted to start taking Mary out in to the community to meet some of her friends. One of them had a daughter who was ten. They all had Sunday dinner together. Mary was occasionally taken to movies, the zoo, or on shopping trips to replace the out dated clothes that her mother sent her. Sometimes she just watched TV with Wanda. On the evening after Mary's eye for an eye lesson, she strode up to Wanda, and asked if she could watch TV with her. Without looking up from her knitting, Wanda asked in a hard voice, "Mary, do you really think you DESERVE to watch TV?" Mary gaped in disbelief at her friend! She had been punished. What more did Wanda want? Feeling betrayed, Mary swore at her. Then she went to the bathroom, and slammed the door behind her. After a few days Wanda and Mary made up.

In May Mary was called in to the expeditor's office. She found not expeditors, but directors, waiting to interrogate her about Eddy, the man who had been thrown out of the navy for abusing drugs. He was apparently still over at the facility in Pittsford. It soon became obvious that the directors strongly suspected that she and Eddy had, had sex back in Plymouth. In truth, the only thing that ever happened was that he used to fondle her leg when they sat together. She wondered what she could have said over the months that made these men suspicious. Did someone else say something? The directors alternated between bargaining with her, and threatening her. Sometimes one of them would talk kindly to her, while another would yell, and warn her of possible punishments for her. Mary, who always struggled with establishing eye contact with people, kept glancing out the window. Spring was in full bloom outside. She longed to be out there, with the other students. She didn't want to be cooped up inside with these big, angry, men. In the end, she told them what they wanted to hear. She said that she and Eddy had sex in the girl's dorm one evening, when everyone was down the hall, watching TV. Mary never did find out what happened to Eddy. She supposed he got thrown out of the program, which was what she wished would happen to her.(They never had her examined. If they had, they would have discovered that she wasn't a virgin. However, it wasn't Eddy, but an older boy at Bradley, who lured a seven year old Mary in to the woods to have sex with her. Mary never told anyone about this) Soon after this interrogation, Mary was awakened late at night, and rushed up to the main house. She noticed that Julia was being led back to the dorm. When Mary reacted with surprise, she was informed that Julia had informed on her, and she better confess to whatever she had done wrong. Four students, all coordinators, were waiting for Mary in the living room. She had to sit across from them. Ed, a tall, brown haired, teen was in charge of the interrogation. "We believe that you, Julia, and Muriel are up to some unsavory acts." He said gravely. Mary was not told what kind of unsavory acts they were supposed to have committed. So she just told the truth. She told about the stealing, lying, bad mouthing directors behind their backs, and sniffing deodorant in order to get high. This didn't satisfy the teens in the room. They wanted more. Mary squirmed nervously. There wasn't more. The coordinators became angry, and began to shout at her. "Muriel killed those baby birds, didn't she?" yelled a blonde, boy, named Mark. Mary didn't know. Muriel, a quiet, intense girl, had been sick a few days ago, and spent the day in bed. Someone had found two tiny birds that had fallen from a nest outside. They left them in the dorm. Because Muriel was asleep in the dorm that day, people suspected that she murdered the birds. "She told you she did it, didn't she?" demanded Cathy, the only girl in the room. "NO!" cried Mary. "She didn't!

We hardly even talk to each other" The group didn't believe her. They backed her against a wall, and yelled at her. Frantically, Mary started making up crazy stories about Julia, Muriel, and herself. This seemed to calm them down. As she was being led back to the dorm, she saw Muriel being led up to the main house.

A few days later the three of them received a very intense General Meeting. They were led downstairs, through a darkened house, and in to an equally dark dinning room. What was going on? Mary knew that there was an audience. She could hear them all whispering in unison. When their voices increased in volume she realized that they were saying "Kill them!" When the voices had reached shouting level the lights were suddenly thrown on, and the audience charged at Mary, Julia, and Muriel. They were pushed against the wall, hollered at, and ridiculed. Muriel was called a witch, even though she insisted that she didn't do anything to the birds. Jeremiah, who ran the meeting, told them that they would all be outside digging ditches for the next few weeks. Upon hearing this, Julia, who hated any kind of work, burst in to hysterical sobs, and was hog tied on the floor as a result. Mary no longer pitied Julia. She actually found her hysterics amusing now. She was screamed at for laughing at the sight of Julia; squirming around on her belly. To Mary, she resembled the bottom of a rocking chair. All they had to do was balance a chair on her back, and the picture would be complete. Mary couldn't stop giggling. She knew she would be punished, but she couldn't help it! She tried not to look at Julia. the floor. They, along with a boy, named Chad, who was being punished for not confronting his mother about issues, when she came up to visit, were taken outside to begin digging ditches. Mary dealt with the stress by singing as she worked. She was made to run laps around the field. Nobody was allowed to be jolly when they were experiencing a punishment. Soon other students, who misbehaved, were included in this punishment. They were known as the chain gang, even though they wore no chains.

In early July Mary was allowed to go home for a week. She felt proud as she told her parents that she was at a school with kids who used to do drugs, steal cars, and break in to houses. She tried not to let the pride show in her voice too much. Her parents didn't like the place, but they took her back when the visit was over. Mary found it hard to adjust to being back at Eden wood. One of the students, a boy, named Bob, who was the chief expeditor, cut her some slack for a day or two.

In spite of the routine at the school, the students were allowed to swim in the lake on many afternoons, since there was no summer school. One afternoon Julia and Mary were in the dorm changing in to their swim suits. Julia started tickling Mary. Then to Mary's horror, Julia stripped, and made her touch her body, including her private parts. Mary went up to the main house, and told on Julia. After the older girl was questioned, the two of them were put in a room with a hidden tape recorder. Julia turned to her in frustrated tears. "Look what you got us in to! If you had only kept your mouth shut about what I made you do, we wouldn't be in this mess!" This was all the directors needed. They quickly got the whole story out of her, and gave her a General Meeting. She lost all her privileges, and had to sit alone in the corner of the dinning room for a couple of weeks. She glared at Mary often.

The only time that Mary reported someone who didn't wrong her was when she noticed a girl, named Joy, acting suspiciously. She was lying in bed, and had a small, shiny object, that she was trying to conceal. Mary asked her what she was doing. Joy said that she wasn't doing anything. When Mary saw blood on Joy's sheets, she went and reported her. Later she saw Joy sitting in the corner. When she asked her why she was there, Joy raised a bandaged arm, and said "You were right, Mary." As was typical at Eden wood, Joy received no sympathy. Instead, she was given a General Meeting, where she was yelled at, ridiculed, and interrogated.

In late August a thirteen year old boy, named Brian, came to Eden wood. He was small, and had long, black, straight, hair. If it wasn't for his light skin, and freckles, she would have thought he was an Native American. He got off on the wrong foot with everyone by trying to act like a tough guy. He didn't like to take orders, he gave people back talk, often swearing at them, and threatening to beat them up. He could also be quite funny though. He was a real clown, and immediately made friends with a tall, African American guy, named David. They both made people laugh in spite of themselves. Mary liked Brian, and David. She latched on to them, and followed them around, acting like them. She was demoted at the time, and had to scrub floors with the other students who were demoted. She often sang as she worked. The people in charge always told her to stop singing, because she had nothing to sing about. She waited until they walked away, and resumed her singing. Brian continued to be defiant. Jonathon took as much of a dislike to him as he had to Julia. He put him in the boxing ring, and had boys take turns beating Brian up. He wanted to show him that he wasn't tough. Once he had Brian restrained on top of a table. He ordered all the girls to get in line, and have a turn at spanking him. Mary refused, and ran out of the room. Eventually Jonathon cut Brian's hair short. He made him dress in black shorts, a white button down shirt, with suspenders, and a big black bow tie. This was to be his costume for the next few weeks. Brian lost his privileges, and had to scrub floors. These punishments went over well enough with Anthony, the executive director, but one day he walked in on a General Meeting, where Jonathon had a group of wrong doers in front of everyone. Two of them were on their knees, waving hub caps, and saying "Let my people go!" The other eight were standing in twos, facing each other, singing "I am a lonely stooge, lonely as can be." The other ones had to respond with "Don't cry stooge, I'll keep you company." At the back of the room, a girl named Barbara was made to kneel, and bark like a dog, with peanut butter in her raised fists. Everyone in the audience was complying with what Jonathon was organizing. Anthony however, was irate! He yelled at Jonathon right in front of everyone, and accused him of turning the school in to a freak show. After that Jonathon had to tone things down, a little.

Jeremiah wasn't challenged though. One morning both Mary and Brian got in to trouble at their dorms. They didn't want to get up. Brian hit the guy on night duty. Mary hit the girl, who was on night duty in her dorm. It wasn't planned, though it might have looked that way, since she copied Brian a lot. A General Meeting was called. Not only were Brian and Mary beat up in the boxing ring, Julia, and a quiet, dirty, girl, who cared nothing about hygiene, named Amy were also beat up. Afterward, for reasons unknown, Julia escaped the food bath treatment. Brian, who received a bloody nose in the ring, was taken up to the nurse's office with instructions from Jeremiah, not to baby him, she was to fix him up, and send him back to the dinning room. When he returned, he, Mary, and Amy were made to lie on sheets. Left over food was dumped all over them. Brian threw up, and started crying. They were made to lay there for half an hour. The fire drill ended their punishment.

In early October Mary was promoted to a foreman in the Business office. She had worked in here before, but only as a worker. Now she was expected to supervise, and give orders. She wasn't up for the challenge. She didn't like to give orders any more then she liked to take them. She felt uncertain and self conscience. She began joking around with her workers, singing to Carol King's "Jazz man," on the radio, and Eric Clapton's" I shot the sheriff." Only they used to substitute sheriff, with expeditor. Mary even acted up with Joanne, one of her workers. They used to sing Billy Preston's "Nothing from nothing". Instead of singing it right, they would sing, "Nothing is a nothing. You gotta have nothing, if you wanna be with me". Mary knew that this was Joanne's silly way of feeling sorry for herself, but instead of correcting her like she was supposed to, Mary went right along with it. It was common among the students to make fun of themselves. Mary often goofed on herself for having eye sight problems, or for being a mistake. "I'm an Oops! Ha Ha. I wasn't supposed to happen." She would say.

Shortly after school started Mary was taken out of the regular classes, and placed in a small class with one other student. His name was Allen. He was seventeen, and needed help preparing for college. Mary was several grades behind, and had a short attention span. Their teacher was a short, bearded man, named Mr. Morton. He was a new teacher. He was married, and had two young daughters. Mr. Morton believed in teaching children to begin reading at an early age. He supported nursery schools with an accelerated learning program. Mary enjoyed being in his class. She found that he was very patient. She learned a lot, and really began to care about school, for the first time in years. In fact, school became not only a place to learn interesting things; it also became a refuge from the chaos that occurred over at the main house.

By November Mary was put on the expediting staff. She was made an expeditor trainee, and had to take head counts when she wasn't in school. She hated it. She felt even more self conscience as an expeditor then she had as a foreman. By this time her confidence had slipped so far that she no longer wanted to grow up. She started regressing back in to a little girl. She was reprimanded repeatedly for this, but it did no good. Once she took her clip board, and threw it down the basement stairs, and skipped away, singing loudly.

In the mean time Anthony was getting fed up with Julia acting up all the time. Once when she was out of control, he ordered someone to mummify her. A long white bandage was wrapped entirely around her face, leaving only a small opening for her nose. She was led around with a rope tied loosely around her neck. Mary had forgiven Julia for what she did back in July. She didn't like seeing her mummified. She went back to acting up with her, being boisterous, and silly. The two of them hung around with David and Brian most of the time. Jane, a short girl, with pale blonde hair, used to act up with them sometimes. One afternoon she received a General Meeting, and was spanked so hard, and by so many people, that she showed all the girls the big, ugly bruises on her back side. Along with Mary, and her friends, others were acting up too. Finally Anthony had enough! He sent Julia, and a temperamental girl, named Regina, and a tough, little trouble maker, named Barbara (The barker with peanut butter in each fist.) over to the facility in Pittsford. This was now a maximum security facility. Although the program was the same over there, the students were rough, and punishments were even harsher then they were at the House in Brandon. Pittsford was often held up as a threat to people who continually acted up. This however, had little effect on Mary, Brian, David, and a few others. One evening a girl, named Donna, who had been at Eden wood for a month, ran away. The trackers were sent out to find her, and bring her back. Trackers were students who had been promoted, and were trusted. Donna was put in to the boxing ring. After a couple of rounds, she had an epileptic seizure. While someone was tending to her, as she lay writhing on the floor, some of the people in the circle jeered at her, and accused her of being a fake. When she recovered she didn't go back in the ring. Instead, she had to go up to each person, on her knees, and beg forgiveness for running away. Mary stared, transfixed, as Donna cried, and hiccupped her way through her apologizes. Mary wanted someone to take pity on her, but they didn't. She stood there, pretending that Cornel Hogan, from a TV show called "Hogan's Heroes" and his men were standing with her witnessing the scene, and shaking their heads in disbelief. Cornel Hogan was Mary's latest father. She didn't have to be an expeditor, or a foreman, or anything with him. She was just his little girl, and his men were her doting uncles. After they finished with Donna, they put a big, blonde boy, named Tom in the ring. He had been in Re-entry, but had been pulled back in to the program because he knew about the drug activity of another person in Re-entry, but wouldn't tell on them. He continued to refuse to tell, and eventually stopped talking completely. Anthony sent him over to the maximum security for some "roughing up".

In December Mary was demoted from an expeditor. After a group session, where she was ridiculed for her attitude, the authorities grudgingly made her a worker in the Business Office. She tried to conceal her delight until she left the room. With the pressure off, Mary did a little better. To her surprise, she was allowed to go home for Christmas. The week at home went smoothly. Her mother was finally starting to mellow out some. Mrs. Sullivan had entered a song in the Official song writers contest. She didn't win. An Artist, named Tim Moore won with his hit song, Second Avenue. Mrs. Sullivan received a consolation prize. It was an album of Tim Moore's greatest hits. She actually seemed to like it, and didn't appear upset about losing. Mary was pleased by her mother's attitude.

Once back at Eden wood, Mary's victory was short lived. 1975 didn't get off to a good start for her at all. Early in January a General Meeting was called. Jeremiah, Paul, and Jonathon, the directors on duty that evening, decided to weed out the trouble makers. Ten or eleven students, besides Mary, were placed in front of the room. Julia, and Regina, who had returned from Pittsford, was among them. While Regina was being paddled, the others stood in a row, facing the wall. Mary who had her coat pockets stuffed with peanuts, and was eating them, tried to pass some down the line, but no one wanted any. It was decided that since the group of students at the front of the room didn't want to fit in, they would be placed in a Day room, separate from the other students. At night they would remain in the Day room, sleeping on mattresses on the floor. Most of them stayed in this room for about Ten days. Regina, who wanted no part of it, isolated herself from the others. After only a few days she was put back with the other students. There were only two boys in the Day room, the rest were girls. Most of the girls were mean, and liked to pick on Mary, Brian, Bob, and a strange girl, named Bernadette. A girl named Cheryl was told to watch the Day Room crowd. She sat near the door, and talked jokingly to everyone. Every few minutes she would take a cigarette, and throw it to the middle of the floor. Because there were no privileges in this room, everyone except Mary, who didn't smoke, dove for the cigarettes like hungry animals. Then Cheryl played a game with them. "When I turn off the light, everyone gets to do whatever they want." She announced. When the light was turned off some of the girls knocked Mary around, and then stopped when the light came back on. The next time it was turned off, the girls went after Brian. However, he was clever. He hid under the couch, and escaped most of the beating. When the light came back on, the girls were so angry they punched him around while the light was on. When Bob, who asked to leave the Day Room, but returned because he couldn't take the pressure downstairs, admitted to it, he received the longest, and worst beating while the light was off.

After nearly two weeks the Day Room was stopped, and the groups of unruly students were put back with the others. They were all without privileges, and had to scrub the house from top to bottom when they weren't in school. Because Mary, who loved school wouldn't stop being silly, and disruptive at the main house, she was taken out of school. Out raged, she yelled "You can't keep me out of school. It's against the law!" She couldn't understand why everyone laughed at her when she said this. She managed to cut back on her acting out enough to be allowed to return to school. It wasn't easy though. The assistant director slammed her against the wall repeatedly one evening because he caught her skipping through the corridor. She had to kick him in order to get free. She was lucky that someone else's bad behavior distracted him from dealing with her further. A girl, named Leslie ran away. She was caught by the trackers, and brought back. She was given a General Meeting, where she was charged at, pushed against the wall, and criticized by everyone. Then Jonathon, and Ed, the assistant director started getting on Leslie's case about being a tom boy, and showing contempt for the other girls. Leslie especially despised the girls who were not only feminine, but wore make up, and came from very sexually active back grounds. She often screamed at them in Encounter groups. "You're a pig! "she would shout. "The sight of you makes me want to throw up!" Jonathon, being Jonathon, came up with a punishment that he knew would hurt her. He made two of the girls take Leslie down to the dorm, and dress her up. When they brought her back she was once again placed in front of her peers. Her long, wavy, brown hair had been center parted. She wore a lot of make up. She had on a blouse with puffed sleeves, and a long, swirly skirt. She also had on nylons, and black platform shoes with straps. Everyone was ordered to yell insults at her. The boys in particular, were made to do this. "Hey ugly you make us sick! We can't stand to look at you!" Mary looked around at everyone. She had no desire to belittle Leslie. Did they all enjoy doing this? Couldn't some of them be simply following orders? She hoped that a few of them felt sorry for Leslie, who seemed to be shrinking before their eyes. "Pick your head up!" yelled Jonathon, "and don't slouch!" Leslie had to dress this way for several weeks. She was demoted, and had to work hard with Mary, and the others.

In March Julia, Amy, and Tom, all patients of Dr. Simmons, from Illinois, were sent back to the hospital where they were, before going to Eden wood. The news wasn't good though. Anthony proudly informed everyone that the three of them weren't going back to an easy life at the hospital. "Shock Treatment" announced Anthony. "They may have got away with not making it here, but they're paying for it now!" Mary didn't like how pleased he sounded. He seemed particularly pleased with Julia, who he had called several days earlier. She was starting to have trouble remembering things. When she grew angry on the phone, he reminded her that she had brought it all on herself, and hung up. Mary was scared for awhile after this. She didn't know if they would do such things back in RI, but she thought it might be possible. She tried to tone down her acting out, as much as she could. She still couldn't bring herself to get involved in many of the aspects of the program. They either didn't make sense to her, or they made her very self conscience. Still, when she managed not to act up, people were so surprised, that they forgot to expect more from her.

People continued to take other people in higher ranks aside, and confess to their guilt, and choose a penance. Confrontations continued to occur, where someone was thought to be guilty, and under intimidation, sometimes admitted to things they weren't even guilty of. During visits home, enough students were able to contact social workers, and report what was going on at Eden wood. One of the states began to investigate the school, and almost removed their kids from the program. After this the directors became nervous, and removed spankings with clip boards, from the program. But there were some good times also. Everyone was allowed the occasional Saturday Night Dance, which took place in the dinning room. Usually movies were shown in the dinning room on Saturday nights during the winter months. The dances happened on summer evenings. Since no sexual relationships were permitted until a student was in Re-entry, No one could get too cozy with another on the dance floor. For the students who had earned enough status, and privileges, outings to restaurants, movies, and the malls were a fairly regular event on weekends. Mary was sometimes included in these more and more often now.

In May three new girls from RI arrived at Eden wood. (RI was among the states that sent a lot of their troubled teens to this school.) Mary remembered one of them. Sandy was a black haired, girl who was almost eighteen. She was at the Medical Center with Mary two years earlier. They weren't enemies, but they had never really been friends either. She was an extremely clean and well dressed girl, who took pride in her appearance. The other two girls with her were Mary Ellen, who though tall, and developed, was only twelve years old! She didn't act or talk like a twelve year old though. The third girl was named just Mary. She was seventeen, but was little, with big dark eyes, and dark hair. Because she was quiet, immature, and had vulnerability about her, Mary liked her best. Mary was still carrying pictures of men around with her in spite of the punishments she received when she was caught with them. When Mary saw one of these pictures she promised not to tell anyone. This sealed their friendship. They spent a lot of time talking together. Mary, who was on the Kitchen Crew, had a stuffed cat that she kept with her at all times. When it was taken away from her, Mary stole it out of a file cabinet, and sneaked it back to her.   Because she got caught too many times stealing candy from the other girls in the dorm, Mary was put in the corner for several weeks as a punishment. She still found time to talk to the other Mary in the evenings. At night they and several other kids had to sleep on mattresses, on the dinning room floor because the authorities didn't trust them. One of the more responsible students was made to sit up through the night, as a guard. After whispering together it was fun to say "Good night Mary." "Good night Mary." However, the friendship didn't last. In early July another facility was opened. This one was over in Northfield. It was to be the new maximum security facility, a state of the art maximum security facility. Three months earlier a new one had opened right down the road from the one that already existed in Pittsford. Neither facility needed to be Maximum security sites; not with the new one opening over in Northfield. Mary's friend was among the students being sent to Northfield. She was devastated! She cried, as she told Mary that she didn't want to be in such a place. She and about twenty five other students left that very afternoon. Mary was lonely without her friend. She couldn't understand why such a quiet, timid girl was being sent to such a facility. Brian and David had been transferred to other facilities over the last couple of months. In order to avoid trouble, Mary started working on trying to be quieter, like her friend, Mary was. It must have helped because people didn't get on her case as much. Also, she was put on the Kitchen Crew. The girl, who was the Coordinator, was nice. Her name was Lisa. Unfortunately, Patsy, the bratty girl, who used to tease Mary about her mother, was the Department head. Mary sometimes got along with her, and sometimes she still argued with her.

A week later another new girl from RI came to Eden wood. She was a short, undeveloped girl, with blonde, straight, hair. Although she looked eleven, she was thirteen and a half. She was Nancy, and turned out to be Mary's little sister! Mary couldn't believe her luck! She promptly made friends with this girl. Nancy came from a family with six other siblings. She was the youngest. Her mother was a drug addict who always had men over at the house. She had little time for Nancy. Nancy spent much of her time roaming the streets of South Providence, with some of her brothers, and sisters, getting in to trouble. She had already spent time in the medical center and the training school for girls. Some of the students knew Nancy, and her family. They talked about Nancy's, and her siblings' problems with the law. To Mary's surprise, Nancy had been made to be a hooker along with two of her sisters, for a year, or more. Nancy acted like a kid. She craved attention. She was always making herself noticed by refusing to go where she was told. Mary remembered one of the expeditors trying to bribe her with candy just to get her to go in the dinning room. Nancy latched on to older girls, and women, trying to get them to mother her. Mary found it amusing that while Nancy was "Mother fixated", her sister Mary had been fixated on fathers. She had crushes on many of the male staff members, and directors. One of the women that Nancy latched on to was Wanda. Mary would see her standing beside Wanda's chair, telling her about some mischief she got in to the night before. When Wanda didn't respond appropriately, Nancy moved on to Julie. Mary had to laugh when she saw skinny, little, Nancy sitting on the couch, at the start of a group that the staff member was running. "If anyone gives Julie a hard time, I'll kick their ass!" She said this several times before Julie said "That's enough, Nancy" in a patient voice. Julie, like Wanda couldn't, or wouldn't give Nancy the individual attention she craved. So Nancy would move on to other females, who were older then her. She accepted Mary's friendship, even though Mary was only a few months older then she was. When they weren't acting up together, Nancy would write sad notes, and have Mary leave them for an older girl, or a staff member to find. When this happened, the girl, or woman would take Nancy aside, and have a talk with her. This seemed to help for a day or two. Nancy also encouraged Mary to fink on her when she did something wrong. "Hey Mary I just pulled the cat's tail. Go tell on me. I want one of those reprimands, where they remind me of how cruel my brother was to animals, and how they want me to be better." It took Mary some time to get used to having a friend who wanted to be told on. Nancy would hide, and send Mary to tell some one that she ran away. "It's true; I just saw her run out the back door!" Mary would say. Sometimes Nancy and Mary would just sit and talk. Nancy would tell her all about her home life, and her neighborhood. "My mom used to hit me, and when she wasn't doing that, she ignored me. She was nicest to my sister, Georgia. Georgia never got in to much trouble. Outside of school, she usually went out on dates, or hung out with Mom." "But the rest of you ran in the streets, and got in to trouble, right?" Mary would ask. "Yeah, except my oldest Brother. He's doing well. He lives on his own. He's a bus driver". Nancy didn't often talk of him. She usually focused on her brother, Walter, or her brother, Billy. She, Mary, and Andrea hung out with them, and got high, stole things, and gave the cops a hard time. "Mom used to hide us from the cops, when they came looking for us." Mary was amazed at the thought of a parent hiding their kids from the law. Other students, who knew Nancy and her family, confirmed what Nancy was saying. "That house was filthy!" exclaimed one girl. Nancy's mother never cleaned anything. She was too busy with the drugs, booze, and the men." Nancy would lower her head, sadly at this. Eventually Nancy and Mary were restricted from hanging out together. This didn't stop their friendship though. They defied everyone, and did what they wanted.

In October Mary, who had tried to run away without much success in the past, ran away one afternoon, and hid in the woods. She was fed up with Eden wood. She wanted to go back to RI. She waited there in the woods, hearing the voices of the trackers in the distance. She would let them get way ahead of her before venturing out on to the road. She fell asleep under some leaves. When she woke up it was getting dark. She left the woods, and started along the road. At first she was proud of what she had done. She would now begin thumbing her way back to RI. However, as she walked along a strange thing happened. Mary found herself missing Eden wood!! She could hardly believe it, but it was true. She didn't miss the excessive discipline, or the over bearing staff, and directors, or even the routine there. She was missing the joking around that often went on in the dorm at night, and the few friends that she acted up with, or just hung out with. She missed the outings that she and some of the other students some times went on. She stuck out her thumb. Soon a car stopped, and a woman asked her where she was going, and why she was out so late. Mary told her that she ran away from Eden wood, and wanted to be taken back. The woman was a nurse, who worked at a nearby hospital. She was on her way home from work.

When Mary returned it was after eleven. Some of the students were still up. Under Jeremiah's supervision, they were taking turns beating up a boy, named Ken, who had been pulled in from Re-entry for suspicion of drug abuse. He refused to confess. Mary was crammed in to a room upstairs, occupied by other students who couldn't be trusted, and therefore, couldn't sleep down at the dorms with everyone else. A guard sat and watched them sleep. Although Mary was demoted, lost her privileges, and had to scrub floors, she wasn't given a General Meeting. This might have been because she turned herself in instead of getting caught, and dragged back. Also, some of the other students were acting up more then she was, one girl in particular, named Belinda, who had been fairly compliant so far, had suddenly turned in to a boisterous sex fiend. She began running around topless, and trying to entice the boys in to touching her. She got in to trouble for writing an extremely graphic sexual fantasy, involving one of the male coordinators. Mary had a crush on this coordinator too. His name was Mike. He had handsome features, and wore his blonde hair long, and had side burns, but she wouldn't have dreamed of expressing her feelings for him in such a way. When the paper was read aloud to everyone, as an attempt to shame her, Belinda reacted with pride over what she wrote. She continued to run around topless, often chasing the coordinator, and other guys. Their harsh rejection of her didn't discourage her. General Meetings and the boxing ring had no affect on her. Group therapy, aimed at her, that sometimes went on for hours, with participants being relieved by other participants, didn't have much affect either. When she stopped going topless she continued acting up, switching from sex fiend to crazy girl. This went on for a few months.

Along with Nancy, Mary sometimes acted up with Belinda, after she gave up going topless that is. She also had a young, African American girl of fourteen, who acted up, to hang around with. Her name was Ellie. She hated it at Eden wood. During her first two days there she either slept, or wailed like a siren continuously. Mary thought she was funny, and when she settled for just being some what disruptive, she became one of Mary's friends, until she decided to behave, and participate in the program. This was how it usually worked with Mary's friendships at Eden wood. She continued to have Nancy as her friend.

By December Mary was doing better. She had been a worker on the Kitchen Crew for a month, and enjoyed it. Brian had been sent back to Brandon recently. Life at the Maximum security facility in Northfield had proved to be too much for him. After getting a bloody nose in the boxing ring, where the blood covered the sheet that was applied to his nose, he was placed back with Mary. They were able to joke around together in the kitchen. In fact the whole crew became friendly with each other, and joined force, making fun of the department head. Still, these weren't offences that got reported regularly. As a result, Mary was allowed to go home for Christmas, as she had the previous year.

Chapter Nine

Tougher times ahead

By the spring of 1976 when she was almost fifteen, Mary started smoking, and as she had two years earlier, tried to act like the street wise students. She once again began lying about her back ground, this time trying to make it sound like Nancy's

Nancy was absent from Eden wood for a month. In February she was allowed to go home for a week. Most students were required to take along a more mature, and trust worthy person when they went home for a visit. Nobody needed this support more then Nancy. Mary, who didn't come from a back ground of trouble with the law, was not required to take anyone. Besides, her mother had made such a fuss when the idea was suggested by a staff member, they immediately dropped the matter. A girl, named Bernadette had been chosen to accompany Nancy home for the one week visit. Three days later she returned without Nancy. She had quite a story to tell! She said that she took Nancy to her house, and they both unpacked. The house was indeed a mess, just as people warned her it would be. The mother was doing drugs, and entertaining various men. There were four other siblings, aside from Nancy, still living at home. Georgia appeared to be the tamest of them all. She was a quiet girl with long wavy hair, and glasses. She made Bernadette feel at home as much as she was able to. Nancy's brother, Walter, was not as hospitable. While everyone else watched, he pulled a gun on Bernadette, and said that he wouldn't tolerate spies in his house. He told her to take her things and leave. "What did Nancy do?" asked Mary wide eyed. "She just stared down at her food and ate." informed Bernadette. "A few minutes later, as I was leaving, Nancy was starting up the street, saying that she was going to start trouble with a cop. She just didn't seem to care!" finished Bernadette. They had to wait until Nancy was picked up, and incarcerated before they could send someone to RI to get her. Mary was glad to see Nancy when she returned. Nancy claimed that when Bernadette left, she tried to leave also, but Walter wouldn't let her. She told Mary that he handcuffed her to the old radiator in the house, and ignored her pleas to go back to Eden wood, and do something for herself. Mary knew Nancy well enough by now to realize that she was probably lying, but she didn't care. She still wanted to be her friend. She liked her impish personality.

Two more facilities were opened right on the property where Mary was. One of them was way down the road. The other, smaller one was right down the hill. Nancy was placed in this one. Mary still saw quite a bit of her. Students from all three facilities had school together.

By early June discipline had disintegrated to such an extent in Mary's facility, that most students, Mary included, ran wild a lot of the time. Spankings were brought back in to the program, this time without the clip boards. It made no difference. So many students in the upper ranks had been demoted that it was necessary to bring in students from other facilities to fill the empty spaces. Mary, and many others, rebelled against the authority of the replacements. Finally one morning when she was getting up, Mary was told to pack her things. She was being transferred to one of the facilities over in Pittsford. It was the facility that she and her friends made fun of. Most of the students there were well behaved, and came from middle or upper middle class families. Mary was devastated! She wanted to stay with the out of control, and street wise kids she had grown used to. The other girls talked her in to packing her things, and leaving in a cooperative way.

The Pittsford facility was everything Mary feared it would be. It was run by a very strict director, named Paul, who remembered Mary from her days in Plymouth before the fire. She remembered him too. He had a sick joke he used to pull on new boys, who acted up, and received a General Meeting as a result. After all the yelling was over with he would ask the boy to ask him if his father did the Irish jig. When the boy asked him this, Paul would roar "MY FATHER DON'T GOT NO LEGS YOU MOTHER FUCKER!!" The boy would cringe, and the audience laughed their heads off. She noticed that things like back talk, or stomping one's foot, earned a person a spanking. Over in Brandon this would have only resulted in a reprimand. Mary did what she had always done when in an undesirable situation. She acted up, and tried to get herself sent back to the house in Brandon. She even tried to run away. All this got her were spankings, harsh reprimands, and a General Meeting where she was put in the boxing ring. In the end, she and another girl, named Julie, who came from a wealthy home with decent parents, but fell in with the wrong crowd of kids during high school, was known for throwing temper tantrums, were dressed up as the Bobsey twins. They had to scrub floors side by side, and could only talk to each other. If they needed to talk to anyone else, they had to ask permission to speak before they could say anything. They had a personal over seer (PO) who was with them constantly. If one of them did something wrong, they both got punished for it. It was a good thing Mary liked Julie, or what Paul hoped would happen, would surely have happened. Julie would have driven her bonkers with her constant talking, whining, and complaining. The only thing that got Mary through these difficult weeks was her preoccupation with Thomas Jefferson. She had a crush on him, and either drew pictures of him, in secret, or tore pictures of him out of history books. She was often searched though, and the pictures were usually found. One evening a staff member decided to really stress Mary, and Julie out. She called them in to the living room, and knocked all the books off the large book case. "You both have five minutes to put them all back!" she announced. As she sat on the couch loudly counting, the two girls frantically tried to put all the books back. Each time they failed to reach the dead line. When all the books were knocked back on the floor, Julie burst in to tears of frustration. Mary did this too, at first. Then it suddenly dawned on her that nothing lasts forever, even this wouldn't. It seemed to her that Thomas Jefferson himself was imparting this information to her. With this new thought in mind, she was able to calmly go through the motions of returning the books to the shelves.

Mary was taken off of this punishment after two weeks. Julie remained on it for another week. So for one week they were enemies because of Julie's envy, and resentment. After weeks of tears, tantrums, and extreme stress, Mary was allowed to take a breather. She didn't act up, but she continued to keep up the pretense that she came from a back ground similar to Nancy's. She managed to fool many of the students at this facility because they didn't know her earlier. She had to be careful about what she said in front of the staff, and directors. Once in a while she was caught in a lie, and had to work at rebuilding it. Mary, who still liked Thomas Jefferson, had developed a crush on an older, good looking, boy with a funny sense of humor, named Charlie. At first he was nice to her, and sat and talked with her. He soon grew tired of her following him around, and doing things to get his attention.

Unlike Brandon, Pittsford wasn't surrounded by woods. So what went on in the two facilities in Pittsford could be heard by the farmers in the area. They complained often about the noise. One man, who lived across the road from Mary's facility used to yell through a megaphone, mimicking some of the things he heard the staff, directors, and students shout.

In August plans were made to place Mary in Re-entry. It was decided that she would be placed in a foster home. There was a man who worked as a janitor over at the maximum security facility in Northfield. He lived about fifteen minutes away, and had a wife, and daughter. His name was Gabriel. Everyone just called him Gabe for short. He was a short, stocky, man in his mid thirties. He had a mustache, and beard, wore jeans, plaid shirts, and drove a pick up truck. At first Mary spent weekend with them. His wife, Sandy was a secretary at a nearby hospital. She was rather tom boyish outside of work, and was sharp tongued at times. Their daughter, Natalie, was six, and would be starting the first grade in a few weeks. The house they lived in was small. It was a red, one story house on a road with only a few other houses. The screened in front porch was where they ate their meals. Beyond this was a small living room, and to the left of it were a bath room, and two tiny bed rooms. Mary shared the back bed room with Natalie. Natalie was small, slim, and had straight blonde hair. She was a friendly little girl, but she whined a lot, and asked Mary dozens of questions regularly. It soon began to get on her nerves, but she tried to hold in her irritation. They all went for walks together. Gabe showed Mary the high school that she would soon be attending. Mary liked the family she was now moving in with. She wanted to please her new parents, and eagerly helped out with chores. She was allowed a few new out fits for school. She soon found out that she was going to be expected to dress very respectably in school. They wanted her to wear dresses, skirts, and blouses at least three days a week. The other two days she was permitted to wear dress pants and a sweater. The jeans and T shirts that she liked were thought of as "knock around clothes." She could only wear these after school, and on weekends. She was taken to have her thick mane of hair cut in to a shag style.. Her foster parents went out in the evenings now and then. When they did, they left a girl, named Debby in charge, even though she was the same age as Mary. This might have been because Mary had confessed to being reluctant to be in a position of authority. Still it was embarrassing to be baby sat by a girl she went to school with. Luckily, Debby didn't make fun of her, or tell the other kids about it. She did tell on Mary when she did something wrong at school, and at home. Once when Mary sneaked her denim jacket to school, wore it there, then hid it in her locker, and wore her other jacket home, Debby confronted her about it in front of Sandy. Mary was shouted at by the easily provoked woman. She was made to bring the denim jacket home the next day. From then on, Sandy searched her every morning. Sandy could get provoked very easily, and would shout at Mary and Natalie for almost nothing. Gabe had to be the referee, defusing family conflicts.

Because Mary was still having some problems keeping up in school, mainly because of her eye sight, she had her academic classes with the freshmen and her nonacademic classes with the sophomores. Fear of being made fun of caused her to be quiet, and shy at school. On the noisy bus she buried her nose in a book. However, because she smoked, and Gabe only gave her one pack of cigarettes a week, she had to summon up enough courage to bum cigarettes off some of the kids. Often she stole them out of the other girls' pocket books. At other times she would skip lunch, and use her lunch money to buy cigarettes. Her foster parents always knew when she did this, and would demand an explanation. Someone was watching her at school, and it might not have only been Debby. Debby couldn't watch her all the time. She had a social life.

It soon became clear Gabe liked Mary, in spite of his strictness. He actually liked her too much. He started putting his arm around her when they went out for walks. Then he started feeling her up when his wife was in the other room. By October he was fondling her, and making her give him hand jobs whenever his wife wasn't at home. Mary found him repulsive! She was afraid of him though, and knew that his wife wouldn't believe her if she confided in her. Sandy didn't like Mary, partly because she smoked, also because she was sometimes sneaky. The main reason though was because Mary had recently become fascinated with

Nazi Germany. Mary wasn't a bigot. She was prepared to like anyone who accepted her, but she was drawn to those powerful men with their high black boots, black coats, and insignias on them. This made her repugnant to Sandy. Even Gabe would angrily confront her about this. As time went by, Sandy continued to be temperamental with everyone, even Gabe. He continued to molest Mary, and make her kiss him, and give him hand jobs. Natalie became more irritable, causing Sandy to not only yell, but sometimes spank her. Mary was always the first one home in the afternoons. She was expected to get right to her home work. She did, once she put on the stereo, and tuned it to the local top forty stations. On some afternoons she would call Edenwood, and talk with Anthony's secretaries. While she was engaging in small talk with them, she really wanted to tell them what Gabe was doing to her, but she never got up the courage to do this.

Because Gabe was employed at the facility in Northfield, he sometimes took Mary to work with him. She was able to see Nancy's older sister, Mary, and rekindle their friendship. She couldn't bring herself to even tell Mary what was going on at home. However she enjoyed hanging out with her. Mary was still fixated on fathers. She had, had a crush on Jim, the former director at the facility, who recently left. Now she was developing one on Jonathon, the new director there. She laughingly told Mary about the things she did to get his attention. She also liked the security guard, who worked there at night. They often lay on Mary's bed with their feet on the wall, talking while listening to Helen Reddy.

A few days before Thanksgiving Mary got caught stealing cigarettes out of her home EC teacher's pocket book. The teacher yelled at her in front of everyone. This brought up another conflict because one of the girls in that class had also caught Mary stealing cigarettes from her. Gabe and Sandy were notified. That evening they had it out with Mary, right in front of Natalie. Gabe and his wife were friends with a family who lived in a trailer park near the high school. Mary always went over there whenever the school had a bomb scare. Gabe accused Mary of stealing cigarettes from the woman. This wasn't true. The woman, whose name was Phyllis, and was very nice, often shared her cigarettes with Mary when they sat, and talked. But because a pack had disappeared, Mary was blamed, not by Phyllis, or her husband, by her foster parents. Now they were telling her that they were fed up with her, and didn't want her in their home anymore. Sandy grabbed little Natalie, and stalked from the house saying that she never wanted to see Mary's face again. Because Gabe worked at the facility in Northfield, this was where he took her. To embarrass her, he made her carry a big, pink dog that someone had given her when she first joined the family. She hated carrying the big, pink stuffed animal through the door of a maximum security facility. She threw it aside the first chance she got. She remained there for two days. Gabe didn't hesitate to tell everyone how Mary had messed up. Every time he came near her during meals she found that she couldn't finish her food. People thought it was her conscience that made her act this way, but it wasn't.

Once back in the Pittsford house that she had been in during the summer, Mary started to act up. She was very upset about what happened to her in that home, and so far, she hadn't told anyone about it. A week or so after Thanksgiving she told two of the girls, who were scrubbing pots and pans in the kitchen, what Gabe did to her. They urged her to go to someone in authority immediately. She took their advice. The next thing she knew, she was over at Headquarters, in Brandon, telling Anthony what had been done to her. He believed her. He told her that some of the girls over at Northfield were complaining that Gabe was coming on to them. He was promptly fired. Mary received her report card from the school she had been attending. In spite of everything, she managed to get Bs and Cs. As pleased as she was about this, she had other things to think about. Her crush on Charlie, the older boy she used to follow around, had returned. He wasn't as patient with her this time though, and soon he became an enemy. She got demoted, and had to scrub floors again. One of the new students, a tall, handsome, Jewish man with thick wavy black hair, named Mark, took an interest in her. He often sat with her, and asked her how she was doing. He was in his twenties, and had been a junkie before he came to Edenwood. He was extremely smart, an intellectual, who had gone to college. Mary was flattered that someone like this would talk to her. As luck would have it, Mark was transferred over to one of the facilities in Brandon.

In February of 1977 Mary calmed down. She was put back in Re-entry, but it was a different kind of Re-entry. She worked in the laundry room, every day except Sunday, and earned a stipend. In the evenings she was sometimes taken on outings. One evening she visited the facility in Brandon that Mark had been sent to. When Mark was finished talking to the guy who had rode over with Mary, he suddenly turned to her, and said "And you!" he gave her a bear hug! This was when Mary knew that she really liked Mark. Although it was March by this time, it still snowed a lot because they were so far up North. As Sam slowly drove through a snow storm, Mary listened to "Blinded by the light" "The things we do for love", "Carry on my wayward son" and other songs, as she stared out the window, thinking about Mark. She thought about him all the time. Once or twice he was allowed to visit her facility. After talking to other students, he would talk to Mary, and give her a big hug. She could hardly believe her luck!!

Late in March plans were being made for Mary to go back to RI. She would be living in a group home in Cranston. She was very excited about this! Once when she was allowed to visit the maximum facility where Mary was, she was told that it was a pretty good group home. Mary, who had been there before being sent to Edenwood assured her that she would like it.

Then to Mary's complete dismay, she was in formed that she wouldn't be going there. Other plans would have to be made. Mary became discouraged. Would she ever leave Edenwood?

In April, when Mary turned sixteen, her parents were allowed to come up, and spend the day with her. Mrs. Sullivan had under gone major surgery the previous year. She claimed to be doing much better. Mary noticed that she was wearing a wig, but she didn't say anything. As they sat in the motel room, Mary's parents told her that they had been opposed to Mary going to the group home in Cranston." We didn't think that it was the place for you "Mr. Sullivan said in his quiet voice. "We didn't like the location, and we thought the other girls there might not be appropriate companions". Mary tried to hide her disappointment over this. She had learned a long time ago that it wasn't a good idea to challenge her parents about anything. As they ate cake, and Mary opened her presents she managed to put the group home in the back of her mind.

As spring continued, Mary joined the girls' soft ball team. There was a lot of practicing to be done. Every afternoon they practiced in the field in back of the house. Their coach, a director, named Morris, worked them hard. Mary wasn't very good because of her eyes, but Morris let her stay on the team. She was extremely glad about this, seeing as how she joined mainly because the actual games were played over in Brandon, where Mark was. She would get to see him every week! She would also be able to see Nancy too. Once when a game was in progress, Mary, who played a substitute on the team, noticed that Nancy's sister, Mary was watching. Mary went over, and sat with her. Mary was feeling down. She told Mary that one of the staff members at her facility heard her referring to another staff member as her "Daddy". "He's not your Daddy!" the staff member said. "Besides, he wouldn't want an ugly daughter like you!" Mary was out raged, and wanted to slap him upside his head!!

Everyone at Eden wood smoked as far as Mary could tell, except for a boy, named Elliot. He suffered from asthma. During Morning Meeting he insisted on sitting just outside the open door of the living room. He could hear everything, and often participated, but everyone would laugh afterward at how funny it must have looked to motorists going by, to see a boy sitting in the parking lot, facing an open door, and raising his hand, then standing up to speak.

As summer approached, Mary acted up and was pulled in from Re-entry. She was demoted, and lost her privileges. As was the policy concerning sports, she remained on the team, and not only went to every practice, she attended every game over in Brandon, whether she was allowed to participate or not.

Mary sometimes hung around with, and acted up with three other girls. They were Hannah, Miriam, and Sandy. One night in the dorm Hannah, who was being punished, and therefore had to sleep on a mattress in the hallway, called out to Miriam, who was looking for an ash tray. "Just flick your ashes in my mouth". Laughing, Miriam did it. The next day a General Meeting was called. Mary, Sandy, Hannah, and Miriam were called to the front of the room. It seemed that the incident from the night before had been the last straw as far as the director was concerned. By telling Miriam to flick ashes on her, she was saying that she was trash. When Miriam complied, she was agreeing that Hannah was trash. Mary and Sandy were included because of their dealings with Hannah and Miriam.

The four girls received a General Meeting. After being yelled at and shoved against the wall by their angry peers, the director focused his attention on Mary. He informed everyone that when she first arrived at Edenwood, she had been diagnosed as semi autistic. Mary, who knew what this meant, wished the floor would open and swallow her up. She was still working hard at making the kids think that she was cool and somewhat street wise. She hoped that most of the audience didn't know what autistic meant.

After being yelled at and humiliated for a while longer, the four of them not only were made to scrub floors under the supervision of a PO, they had to recite an announcement every time everyone was assembled in the dinning room. It went "Eeny meeny miny moe. We're all so negative that we don't grow." "I'm Miss Negative" Hannah would say." I'm Miss Nasty" Miriam would say. Sandy came next. "I'm Miss Dike". Then Mary with "I'm Miss Punk" Then in unison they all would say "We all wanted to goof around together, so now we're all sunk". Whenever they went some where they had to march in single file. This went on for three, or four weeks.

One afternoon when everyone was in the living room waiting to be assigned to encounter groups, Mary was day dreaming, as she often did. A boy named Scott was demoted just like Mary. He asked her why she wasn't talking to anyone. It was a rule that when people were assembled somewhere, they were supposed to talk to each other about their problems. Mary sighed, and rolled her eyes. "You wanna not cop an attitude when I ask you something?" Scott couldn't order her to do, or not do something because he was on the same level as her. "Oh leave me alone" answered Mary. "You wanna not answer back?" said Scott peevishly. Mary turned her back on him. "You wanna not turn your back on me? That's rude." Mary stomped her foot in exasperation! "You wanna not you wanna me your you wanna's!!?" Scott's jaw dropped. "Mary Sullivan, I'm telling on you!" Mary sighed, as he hurried from the living room. Ordinarily she liked Scott. She felt bad for him because he, like her, was father fixated. But right now he seemed like a brat who was trying to score points in order to get promoted. A few minutes later Mary, Hannah, Miriam, and Sandy were told to knock on the door of the Coordinator's office. As was the custom when receiving a reprimand, someone behind the closed door would yell "Whose out there?" even though they already knew. On this occasion the people behind the door heard "Hannah", "Miriam", "Sandy", and "Mary you wanna not!..." The door was flung open, and Mary was scolded. Then they all had to say their names again.

In August a new girl arrived. She was from New Hampshire. Her name was Candice. She was Fourteen, and had thick, dark hair that she always wore back in a braid. She was somewhat pudgy, and could still have passed for twelve. She had started out at the maximum security facility, but after a few days she was transferred to Mary's facility. "Those girls over in Northfield are tough aren't they?" asked Hannah. "You're telling me!" answered Candice emphatically. Mary took an immediate liking to Candice. They became friends. Candice joined the soft ball team. One day Morris sent them both up to the house to get some pitchers of koolade. They were starting back down to the field when Mary realized that they forgot to stir the koolade. "Give me your pitchers." urged Candice hastily. She stuck her arm in her pitchers, and stirred the powdered drink mix. Then she did the same with Mary's. They both laughed, as Candice did this. Later they tried to contain their laughter, as they looked at each other when Morris, the coach, had the first sip. Candice was a lot of fun. Not only was she mischievous, she liked to sing, and could sing on key. She wrote poetry, and liked to listen to Fleetwood Mac. She wore cool T-shirts, corduroys, and wooden sandals. She also liked sweaters with hoods. Candice told Mary about her abusive mother, absentee father, who she couldn't remember, and about her two little brothers who looked up to her. After coming to school with facial bruises too many times, her fifth grade teacher reported it, and Candice began living in foster care. She ran away from the homes, and was eventually hospitalized. Mary realized that Candice came from a similar back ground as herself. Mary stopped lying about her back ground because she discovered that there were now a few students with her who didn't have major trouble with the law before coming to Eden wood. Unfortunately Candice had a bad temper which caused her to receive a lot of reprimands, spankings, and General Meetings. Jeremiah took an immediate dislike to her, and punished her frequently. Mary used to see her sitting in a corner crying her eyes out after one of Jeremiah's supervised spankings. Candice was a fighter, and didn't like to be pushed around. Some of the students used to provoke her on purpose, just to see her get punished. Mat, a boy with a bad case of acne, was the senior coordinator. He never smiled, and was quite a tyrant. He chewed up people like Mary, and Candice, and spat them out! It was no picnic to be in his company. Once when someone snapped at him, and he became offended, Candice, who was sitting in the corner, turned around, and said "Ha! Now you know how it feels to be vomited on!" Mary burst out laughing. She almost fell off the couch! Many of the students hated mat. There were those who argued with him, and there were those who took a sneaky approach. One day it was revealed that someone wrote "Mat sucks dick for lunch!" in a dictionary. Everyone had to sit silently in the dinning room until someone confessed to doing it. Someone eventually confessed, but Mary didn't know if the real culprit confessed, or someone who was bullied in to confessing.

After a month of being Chief Expeditor, it was decided that Mary truly was the worst Chief Expeditor in the entire history of the school. It wasn't that she was lazy, she wasn't. She just couldn't take being in a position of authority. She hated bossing people around. Because she didn't act up during the extremely uncomfortable experience, she was put back in Re-entry. Once again she worked in the laundry room, and earned a stipend. She went out on Fridays, and Saturday nights, with the other students who were in Re-entry. For the past year classes had been held in the evenings from 6-10. The Para Professionals apparently didn't consider school as much of a priority as "Good old therapy", and they didn't want it interfering with the rigorous schedule that occurred during the day. Often after classes Mary would stay up late watching TV with some of the other Re-entry people. She still had to be up by seven like everyone else though. She enjoyed working in the laundry room. She was left alone a lot of the time. She had the option of inviting friends in to visit. Sometimes she was completely over looked when Group Therapy was being organized. Most of all, she could draw. By now she was in to John. F. Kennedy. She read about him, and drew pictures of him. Nobody thought to search her, and take the pictures away.

In the spring of 1978 Mary turned Seventeen. She hadn't been allowed to go home for Christmas. Now she only received a phone call from her parents, and a few gifts in the mail. What was going on back at home? As an assignment for school everyone was made to watch a mini series on TV called "The Holocaust". In spite of herself, Mary found herself being drawn back in to her old fascination with Nazi Germany. Nobody was more upset with her for this then Jeremiah, who was Jewish. During an Encounter Group he yelled at her, accused her of being mad at the world because she couldn't see well, and told her that one day she was going to grow up to be a mass murderer. The students in the group agreed with him. When the group ended, Mary continued to sit on the couch with her head lowered, feeling like she didn't have a friend in the world. She couldn't really blame them though. She knew she was bad for liking men like the Nazis. But she wasn't anti-Semitic. She still found Mark attractive even if she no longer had a crush on him. At supper Mary imagined that John Kennedy was sitting across the table from her. He didn't approve of Nazis, but he wanted her to know that she still mattered to him, and he would stick by her. The only thing that distracted her from her loneliness was a girl, named Debby. She was being punished for falling asleep on night duty. Whenever she entered a room, she had to get everyone's attention, and yell "Hickory Dickory Dock. Responsible I am not. I fell asleep like a little sheep. Ask me why I'm a dummy". Someone in each room had to ask her why she was a dummy. She had to say "Because I fell asleep while on night duty." The big card board sign she wore read the same thing. Another girl was being punished at the same time. Her name was Addie. She came from RI like Mary. She had a big appetite, and was very over weight. This didn't seem to bother her. She enjoyed her food too much to care. For awhile she was made to wear a cow bell around her neck. Then one morning someone noticed that it was no longer ringing. They wrestled with Addie, and found that she had stuffed a doughnut inside of it. The bell was removed, and Jeremiah came up with another punishment. When ever everyone was assembled in the dinning room Addie had to get up and recite an announcement. She started off by growling out "FEED ME, I'M HUNGRGY". Then while stomping her foot rhythmically, she had to chant "I came from out of space, looking for something to eat. I landed in RI. I thought it was a treat, it was sweet." Then in a growl, she finished with "AND IF I'M STILL HUNGRY, THE WHOLE COUNTRY IS DOOMED!' She said it with the same finesse that she said the other announcements that were assigned to her as punishments. None of it seemed to faze her. There was one thing that fazed her though. One evening the Kitchen Crew gave her fried chicken by mistake. When it was taken from her, Addie had a fit! She didn't want the baked chicken that she was given instead. She threw her grape fruit at someone's head, and ran from the dinning room screaming. She was dragged in to the laundry room where Mary was working. Instead of sitting quietly in the corner, Addie ripped a shelf away from the wall, and hurled it across the room. Mary got out of the way, as people were called in to restrain Addie so that they could spank her.

Two days after the humiliating Encounter Group with Jeremiah, Mary noticed her friends drifting back to her. Aside from Candice, Addie was her friend, as was a Twelve year old boy, named Mike, and a young man, named Chad. Unlike the girls, Mike, and Chad weren't quick to act up. They were easier going. Chad was a transvestite, but he was forbidden to act this out at Eden wood. He was ridiculed for it. He told Mary that his Grandmother, whom he had been very close to, died when he was Five. She used to dress him up like a girl all the time. The effect she left on him couldn't be undone by his parents, or any of the doctors he was taken to.

Late in April Mr. Morton, who used to be Mary's tutor sat down to talk to her. He had been promoted to the head of the school department at Eden wood. He in formed her that a school had been found for her. "It's in Massachusetts, and it's called Perkins school for the blind. You'll like it there, Mary." Mary needed little convincing. She was looking forward to getting out of Eden wood once and for all. Besides, she had a good feeling about Perkins. "If all goes well you'll be starting there late in June, for the Summer school session." Mary thanked Mr. Morton, and went to tell everyone her great news!

Late in May Candice escaped in the middle of the night. Trackers were sent out to find her, and bring her back. The following evening, a Saturday, Jeremiah called a General

Meeting. It was very hard for Mary to watch Candice being charged at, screamed at, and pushed against the wall. Being easily provoked, she fought back, and was put in the boxing ring as a result. Jeremiah interrogated her. Others followed his example, and joined in. Finally being dissatisfied with Candice's answers, Jeremiah ordered a couple of girls to throw Candice in the shower with her clothes on. As she was being led from the room, Jeremiah suddenly noticed Mary. "Hey Mary, wanna watch?" Her jaw dropped! How could he ask her such a thing? She mumbled "No". Returning soaking from head to foot, Candice was told that she had to take her hair out of her braid. Horrified, she refused. A girl, named Mary Ellen quickly undid Candice's hair. Jeremiah held up a pair of scissors. He told her that if she didn't answer questions properly he would start cutting a little of her hair off. Frantically she tried to answer the way they wanted her to, but she was either too slow, or didn't give the right answers. Jeremiah had one of the girls cut a chunk of Candice's hair off. By the time the General Meeting ended Candice had chunks of hair missing from the back of her head. Since the rest of it was still long, she was able to braid it again. For some reason Jeremiah came to the conclusion that Candice was a hippie. She vehemently denied this, insisting that she was a gypsy. Seeing how upset she became over this, he insisted that she was a hippie. He made her wear a tie dye shirt, jeans, and a big floppy hat. Mary felt sorry for her friend.

On a Monday morning, June 28th, 1978 Mary gathered her luggage, and got ready to be released from Eden wood. She had said her goodbyes to her friends the night before. She wore one of the new summer dresses that she had chosen on a recent shopping trip. All the clothes she was bringing were new, and were her own choices. Unfortunately Mary was going to have to return to Eden wood for the month of August because Perkins shut down for vacation then. She was not told why she couldn't just go home for the month of August, but at least she would spend the month in Re-entry, and would be returning to Perkins when the fall classes began. In the mean time Mary was looking forward to a month of new experiences, new friends, and opportunities. She would be able to draw without anyone stopping her ever again!

Chapter Ten

A little piece of Heaven, here on Earth

Early on Monday morning Mary arrived at Logan Airport, in Boston. It was a warm, sunny day late in June. The year was 1978, and she had a very good feeling about it. As she stood with her luggage, a young man with wavy dark hair, and a young woman with a round face, framed by short, black hair approached her. "Are you Mary the man asked. "Yes" answered Mary eagerly. They took her luggage, and had her follow them out to a small red car. They were teachers at Perkins School for the blind. Before driving to Watertown, where the school was, they all stopped at McDonalds for breakfast. The man and woman taught over in Secondary Services. "Your going to be in the Junior/Senior high program." said Miss Bartlet. "You'll have Mr. Kennedy as your supervisor, and will be in Bridgman Cottage. "explained the man, who turned out to be Mr. Jackson. Mary listened eagerly, and asked questions about what the school looked like. "It's a beautiful campus!" both teachers told her with enthusiasm. Mary beamed with pleasure. When they reached the campus, Mary saw for herself just how lovely it was. At the entrance was a pair of big wrought iron gates. Beyond were wide spread, well kept lawns. To the left, just inside of the entrance was a red, modern building. "That's the Northeast building" said Mr. Jackson, "There's a cafeteria in there. On the second floor is a dorm for students in the Adult Rehab program." Miss Bartlet pointed to another modern building, on the right. "That's the North building. Students learn work shop skills in there." Ahead of them was a long drive, lined with trees, and side walks. At the school of the campus stood a magnificent, old building that had been built at the beginning of the Nineteenth century. A large bell tower was on top of it. The chimes rang every quarter hour, half hour, and hourly. "This is the Howe Building." explained Miss Bartlet. "It was named after a doctor who worked here in the last century." "All the buildings, except the two new ones you saw, were named after famous doctors, teachers, and students from the past." To the left of the Howe building was the East Close. It consisted of four buildings, two on one side, and the other two across a brick path. Stone walls, three feet high, were in front of these buildings with openings at the entrance to each building. "These are Bridgman, and Tompkins cottages," said Miss Bartlet, as she pointed to the left. "The two buildings on the right are Elliot cottage, and Moulton cottage, you'll be staying in Bridgman. It was named after a deaf/blind student, named Laura Bridgman." Mary was then told that on the other side of the Howe building, also known as the main building, was the West Close. It was shaped like a U, with two cottages facing two other, and a fifth one at the end. They were Fisher, Oliver, (This cottage housed the students in the Deaf/Blind program) Bennet, May, and Brooks. In back of the West Close stood the Keller/Sullivan building and beyond that was a factory called Howe Press, which made braillers. Mary, who loved old arcutecture, was delighted that all the buildings, except for the North, and Northeast buildings, were Victorian. "We have a lower school too, but that's on the other side of the campus. You'll see that later." said Mr. Jackson. He dismissed himself, and asked Miss Bartlet to take Mary to her cottage.

Breakfast was nearly over when Mary was brought to Bridgman. Upon entering, she saw a stocky, blonde, boy of about fifteen. He was carrying a transistor radio, and saying that if people didn't like his kind of music, it was just too bad. "What's wrong John?" asked Miss Bartlet. "Did you get thrown out of the dinning room for playing your radio at the table again?" John gave her a sullen "Yes" The house mother was a young woman with short, straight brown hair, named Nancy. She welcomed Mary in a cheerful manner, and asked a thin, girl with straight brown hair, parted on the side, named Carol to take Mary up to her room. "It's the second room on the left" she said. Mary said Goodbye to Miss Bartlet, and thanked her. Then she followed a complaining Carol upstairs. She took her luggage from the girl, thinking that this might improve her mood, but she soon learned that Carol was a chronic complainer. Like her previous school, her room contained bunk beds. She didn't mind, even though the other rooms contained single beds. In spite of the two bunk beds, Mary learned that she had only two roommates. Carol slept on the top bunk above the bunk that was to be Mary's. The other person in their room was a woman in her mid twenties. Her name was Diane. She had a very likable, motherly personality. The cottage was co-ed. Among the boys, was a thin, blonde, boy with glasses named Bill.. Diane looked out for him, and gently chided him when he was running late, as he was that morning. Bill seemed to welcome Diane's gentle authority over him. He was a good natured boy, who said a cheerful "Hello" to Mary. As Mary unpacked, Diane told her a little about herself. "During the school year, I'm in the Adult Rehab program over in the North East building." "How long have you been a student at Perkins?" Mary asked her. "I've been here since I was Five." She told her that her mother died when she was a baby. She and her father were very close. When she was home on weekends he took good care of her, and told her stories. This really interested Mary, who was quite taken with fathers.

Once downstairs, Mary was introduced to David, the other house parent. He was young, man and had a mustache, and beard. He was an open, friendly person, liberal in his thinking, which made him popular with the students in Bridgman. Nancy, though nice, was a little on the strict side. "Mr. Kennedy is the supervisor of our cottage" David told Mary. He ushered her in to the office where a man with a darker mustache, and beard, and a slightly stern face awaited her. Mary was asked to take a seat. Mr. Kennedy got right down to business. "At Summer school you won't be receiving that many academic courses that will come in the fall." He looked down at some notes on his lap. "With the exception of typing, most of your classes will be in independence skills, such as Mobility, Home Economics, doing cottage chores, and Work activities. This last one is a class that will help you to learn to do piece work like they do in a factory. You will be paid a little money for this." Mary beamed. "I like to work, and I'm a hard worker! " Before she could stop herself, she eagerly volunteered to wash the windows in the office. Mr. Kennedy allowed her to do this. She even cleaned the outside of the windows. Mary wasn't trying to show off. It was just that having been released from Hell, Mary was anxious to prove herself worthy of Heaven.

After her stint on the windows, Mr. Kennedy asked her to sit back down. "Since you like to work so much, I have an idea for you. I'm sending you over to Personnel. I heard they need some one to clean Moulton Cottage, across the way. It would only be for an hour, or two each day, but you'll pick up a little extra spending money." Mary thanked him then was taken to the main building to start classes. During the first recess she was shown to Personnel, where a friendly, informative, man told her about the job, and said that she would be paid minimum wage, which was $2.75 an hour. Mary was eager to begin.

Later toward the end of lunch, Mary was approached by a thin, blind boy, who had difficulty walking, and had to use a cane. He didn't know how to get to the North building, where his next class was. Mary, who already knew where this building was, walked him over there. She was feeling confident, and happy with the world. As they walked, the boy, whose name was Kenny told her how happy he was at Perkins. He said that at his school in Connecticut the staff and teachers weren't teaching the students much of anything. He felt that the school was going down hill, and hoped to be returning to Perkins in the fall.

When classes were over for the day the students were taken to the beach, the movies, amusement parks, and on picnics at nearby parks. At the end of Mary's first day at Perkins her cottage was taken to see a movie called "Grease". Mary loved it! It was a musical set in the late fifties, about a high school. John Travolta and Olivia Newton John starred in it. There were many outings that summer. One afternoon the students in Mary's cottage were taken to a large yard sale on the outskirts of Waltham. Not only did she find some nice trinkets, and clothes she also had her fortune by one of the two elderly women, who were doing everyone's fortunes for a small fee. Mary was told that she would meet, and marry a wonderful man when she was Twenty One. They would have two or three children. Later everyone went on a hay ride. Mary felt like a Queen sitting on top of the hay.

In the evenings, when there wasn't a dance scheduled, they would all sit out on the stone walls in front of the cottages. Some of the students from Secondary Services, who lived over on the West close, would hang out with the students from the East Close. This was how Mary was reunited with an old friend. A girl with short, wavy medium blonde hair, who was some what bigger then Mary, sat next to her. Mary gazed at her, thinking that she looked familiar, but didn't say anything until some one referred to her as Beth .She turned suddenly. "Are you Beth from the Boston Center for Blind Children?" When the girl said "Yes" Mary introduced herself excitedly. Mary had spent Eleven months at the school. Beth remembered her. She cocked her head at Mary. "You were sighted back then, weren't you?" Mary told her that she still was. Soon they were talking, laughing, and reminiscing about the time they spent at the school. After this she and Beth became a twosome. They hung out together when ever they weren't in class. Mary also acquired a boy friend. He was a slim, out going boy who could be a smart ass sometimes. His name was Harold. He wasn't especially good looking, but she thought he would be fun to hang around with. However, in going out with Mary, Harold was causing his former girl friend, a small, blonde student in Bridgman, named Amy, a lot of resentment. Mary wasn't too uneasy about this at first, so she spent a lot of her free time with Harold, Beth, Bill, (Diane's pet), and an African American girl, named Anna, who loved Disco. She used to place the speakers of her stereo in her open bedroom window, allowing everyone to enjoy her music. It added to the general atmosphere of a fun filled, liberated summer. Mary loved it. The only thing that so far marred her pleasant experience at Perkins was her typing class. She had never typed before. She found it very challenging. What made it more challenging was her typing teacher's attitude toward her. The woman was young, intense, and didn't have much patience. She decided that Mary just didn't want to learn. This hurt Mary. She felt discouraged, but not wanting to act up, and ruin things for herself at this wonderful school, she did the only other thing she knew how to do. She with drew, and became very quiet in this class. Her other classes weren't very difficult because she had been given plenty of independence skills while she was at Eden wood. .She already knew how to make a bed, do laundry, keep her room clean, and assist with meals in the evenings. Once during supper preparation a short, thin, deaf/blind girl, named Katy continued to work with her yarn, and loom. She did this every chance she had. When Nancy signed in to the palm of Katy's hand that it was time to help make supper, Katy signaled that she understood. However, she continued to work on her loom. As a result she wasn't allowed to have supper. Mary watched her go over to the snack bar in the main building to buy herself a soda. She hoped the girl would be able to get a snack later on.

 Later that evening Mary walked around the campus with Harold, and some of his friends. As they passed the fenced in pond they heard the bull frogs. "There's your typing teacher!" called out Harold, gesturing in the direction of the pond. Mary laughed, as she always did when he said this. Walking around with Harold gave her the opportunity to see the rest of the buildings. The West Close looked identical to the East Close, except that it had an additional building at the end. This was Bennett Cottage. "That's where some of the lower school kids go when they're still too babyish to really be considered Upper School students." Harold told her pompously. In back of the West Close was Brooks Hill. This was where the students who weren't yet eighteen went to sneak cigarettes. "If you get a permission slip from your parents, you can smoke out in the open when your sixteen, and older." said Harold. He showed her the lower school, which was across the street from the West Close. The lower school consisted of a cluster of buildings that were Victorian like most of the other buildings. They even had their own main building. It was a slightly smaller version of the Howe building. Bradley, Glover, Potter, and Anagnus were the names of the lower school cottages. There were two play grounds down there, one in back, and one in front. Mary expected to see them there. What surprised her was that behind the East Close was another playground. It faced a track. Within the track was a base ball diamond. She was also surprised to find that some of the upper school kids occasionally went down to the lower school to use the seesaws, the big, wooden rocking boat, and a super long swing that could hold five or six people . They sat astride this, and could really make it go fast! The rocking boat was their favorite. "Once a few kids were using it, and they rocked it so hard that it tipped over!" Harold and his buddies informed Mary. As much as she tried to hide it these days, Mary still liked childish things. She took part in her friend's antics with a "Well, if you want to I will also "attitude.

True to her word, Mary spent a lot of time drawing. She covered page after page of the sketch book she bought with her work money. Sometimes her pictures were of kids having fun together. Other times she drew fathers holding, or playing with their kids. A few of her drawings had a darker side to them. In them men wearing long black coats and black boots were raiding Eden wood. Some of them were beating the staff, and directors with clubs. Others were rescuing the students. In one of the drawings a man was holding a sobbing girl, and telling her that he was going to get her out of there. The girl was her friend, Candice. Mary couldn't get her mind around the fact that these men would most likely be beating up on her friends, not the directors, especially her friend, Candice, who it was rumored was a quarter mulotto. When she showed these particular pictures to Nancy, her House Mother, the woman glanced at them, and said "Cute", or "Nice". Mary knew that they weren't cute, or nice. So why was Nancy responding this way? She wanted the House Mother to sit down, and talk to her, but she didn't.

Finally the friction between Harold, and his ex girl friend, Amy came to a head. One day he got tired of her waylaying him, in order to insult him, or make fun of him. Once she tried to slam a window on his fingers! He and his buddies gathered beneath her window. They wanted Mary to join them. They were throwing rocks, laughing, and calling Amy names. It was six against one, and the most important one had recently dumped her. Mary ran in Bridgman, and burst in to tears. Nancy was just coming out of the dinning room. "What's wrong, Mary?" she asked. When Mary told her, she suggested that she go upstairs, and comfort Amy. Amy welcomed the company. Mary, who had never learned how to be demonstrative could only sit, and listen to Amy sobbing out her feelings about Harold, and previous boy friends. "All those break ups, and make ups" she said through her tears. "This is the worst one yet." After fifteen minutes or so, the boys down below got bored with picking on Amy, and wandered off.

Mary still hung out with Harold, and his friends sometimes, but it wasn't the same anymore. She lost respect for Harold after what he did to Amy. More often Mary stayed by Beth, and her friends. One of them was a girl with long, pale blonde hair. She was partially sighted and liked to act more blindly then she was when she was around boys. Because she was attractive, and dressed in cool clothes, the boys couldn't do enough for her. Once when they were all sitting out on the wall in front of Bridgman, Trish, the girl who played helpless around the boys said that she couldn't wait to get her SSI check. "Me too!" exclaimed several others. Mary had never heard of such a thing. She learned that everyone who was eighteen, and older received checks every month from the government because they were disabled. Mary, being seventeen, supposed that she would start getting a check the following year. Things were looking better, and better!

On the last day of Summer School Mary and some of the other new students were told by Mr. Lully the supervisor above Mr. Kennedy that they had been accepted, and would be returning in the fall. Mary was thrilled! They had a dance over in the main building that evening. It was held in Dwight Hall, a huge room with a high ceiling and windows that were high up on the walls. Along the walls were old fashioned lights. There was a stage at the front of this room. On the stage was a grand piano. To the right of the stage was a huge pipe organ. Everyone danced to disco music, and had a great time. At one point Mary noticed a little girl with short, light blonde hair and glasses. She couldn't have been more then five. Mary had seen her many times during the past four weeks. She wondered why a lower school student was with the older students. When Mary talked to the girl she found out that her name was Madeline, and that she was going on fourteen! "I'm going to be in the upper school this fall." She said in her high, excited voice. "I'll be in Bennett Cottage". This was the baby cottage according to Harold.

Mary flew back to Vermont the next day. She was scared, having only been on a plane once before. She turned, and clutched the side of her seat, her eyes squeezed shut. A man asked her if she was alright. She nodded her head. She didn't want to make a scene. She was so relieved when the plane landed. She was returning to Eden wood for the month of August. Mary was glad that she would no longer be in the program. She would work in the laundry room as one of the hired help, and earn some money. What she couldn't understand was why she couldn't just wait out the month at home. Didn't her parents want her there? No one told her much except that it was thought best for her to stay, and work at Edenwood.

A van full of kids from one of the facilities in Brandon picked her up, and drove her back with them. Later someone from Pittsford would be picking her up. While there Mary saw a lot of familiar faces. One of them was Ken, a man who had been in the program when she first went there as a twelve year old. He graduated when she was thirteen and decided to stay on as a staff member. He was now a director. Ken was a jovial man with brown hair, and glasses. He was some what on the stocky side, and had a slightly more liberal out look then the other directors. Once when Mary was just turning fifteen and was trying to make everyone think she was like the older, street wise kids there, Ken held a data session in the dinning room. Everyone was present. When he was finished with this, he decided to read off all of the addresses in a metal box that contained index cards. He eventually came to Mary's phony address which was located in South Providence. She called out to claim it as hers like the others were doing. Then Ken called out her real address, located out in Coventry. Mary cringed! He called it out again, then after a pause, he moved on to another address which somebody claimed. Mary heaved a long sigh of relief. He let her get away with it. Sometimes she still thought about this, and wondered why he did it. She felt a mixture of gratitude, and puzzlement.

Mary worked through August, and went on outings during the weekends. She was upset to discover that her friend, Candice had been transferred to the maximum security facility because she was acting up too much. Still Mary had her other friends, Addie, Chad, and Mike to talk to, and joke around with.

When word got out that Mary not only made friends at Perkins, but had a boy friend as well, Jeremiah, the director, received this news with a mixture of pleasure, and surprise. Mary wasn't all that pleased with Harold, and wasn't sure if she still thought of him as a boy friend, but she was willing to let Jeremiah, who had belittled her often, believe that there really was something between Harold, and her. Although Jeremiah was kind to Mary at times, like when her mother called her and spent the ten minutes allotted, insulting her, Jeremiah was sympathetic. "You know how your mother is. So go get a coffee and a doughnut and sit back and say fuck it. We both know she isn't going to change." On the other hand, when Jeremiah became angry, he could act very brutally. One evening he found out that Mary gave a pack of cigarettes to a boy whose privileges had been taken away. "I'm sick of you doing this!!" roared Jeremiah. He ordered everyone in to the dinning room and made them form a big circle. Mary was forced to stand and watch while Steve, the boy who she gave the cigarettes to, was beat up by a more experienced boxer. Feeling over whelmed, Mary lowered her head.

Seeking Love and Acceptance on a Path of Adversity

"LOOK AT HIM!" screamed Jeremiah. Mary tried to keep her head up, but she was horrified over someone being punished for something she had caused. Jeremiah continued to scream at her for lowering her head. After three rounds in the ring, Steve stood before Mary, crying and hiccupping. Jeremiah wasn't finished yet. "The best punishment I could come up with for you would be to drive you back to RI and dump you on your mother's door step! This would be more affective then any punishment we could concoct for you here." After this Mary was demoted and lost her privileges. Oddly enough when Jeremiah saw her cleaning the floor the following evening he seemed perplexed. "What are you doing Mary? Why aren't you being an expeditor?" Mary's jaw dropped. She reminded him that he had demoted her the previous evening. Jeremiah good naturedly brushed off her punishment and restored her status as an expeditor. Mary felt both grateful and confused. Now she found herself hoping that she could get through the month of August without upsetting Jeremiah.

A week before returning to Perkins, Mary wrote her parents a long letter. She was still puzzled about why she wasn't spending the month of August at home. She wanted them to know how good she was doing, and how well she had behaved at Perkins during the summer session. "They accepted me there!" she wrote excitedly. "I'm going back there next week. During Summer School I had Mobility classes, cooking, typing, and money management. I also had work activities. In this class I learned how to drill holes in plastic knobs that will go on Braille writers." She told them about the trophy she won in bowling, and how she enjoyed swimming, and base ball. "They play it with a soccer ball because the kids have eye sight problems like me." She went on to tell them about her job in the laundry room at Edenwood, and because she didn't know if they had been told, she informed them of her grades for her final term before Summer School. She received a B- in US History, a C- in Math, a B+ in English, and a C in Science. "I'm going to do even better at Perkins" she told them. After apologizing for not writing sooner, Mary signed the letter, and gave it to a staff member to be mailed.

On September 5th, Labor Day, Mary was taken to a bus station to begin the long ride that would take her back to Boston, and her new life.

Chapter Eleven

Returning to Heaven

Mary had been back at Perkins for nearly two weeks. She was in the JR/SR High Program. This program's students were divided among two cottages, Elliot for girls, and Moulton for boys. Mary was directly across from Bridgman, which was where she spent the Summer School Program. Now Bridgman and Tompkins were part of the Adult Rehabilitation Program. Adult students who needed more assistance in independence skills lived in these cottages, and on the second floor of the Northeast building. The Northeast building also had a cafeteria where students, teachers, house parents, and administrators had lunch every day. Many students were taught food service skills in the cafeteria, Mary was one of them. She worked in the kitchen, and cleaned the cafeteria every Thursday morning from 8:25-9:35. She enjoyed this very much.

Mary arrived at the school on Labor Day the previous week on September 4th, 1978. Because she was Seventeen, she expected to be made a senior, but to her surprise, Mary was told that she would be a junior. They wanted to be sure that she hadn't missed anything the year before. Mary was pleased with this arrangement. Two years instead of one in this marvelous school!

Her schedule went as follows

Monday- Mobility, Wood Working, Recess; Metal Work Shop, lunch, Typing, English, Math, Counseling.

Tuesday- English, Study Hall, Math, Study Hall, Recess, Career Ed, Cottage Chores, Gym.

Wednesday- Mobility, Typing, Recess, English, Study Hall, Long Noon Hour, Math Tutor, Low Vision Drawing.

Thursday- Work Experience, Mobility, Recess, Mobility, Home EC, Math, English, Cottage Chores.

Friday-Work Activities, Home EC, Math, Assembly, Cottage Chores, English, Study Hall.

Classes ran from 8:25-4:10, except on Tuesday, when the school day started a half hour earlier because of Chapel. Classes were a half hour, or an hour long, depending on the class.

Mary was happy with most of her classes. She was learning to make a wind mill in Wood Working, and a xylophone in Metal Shop Class. Her favorite class was Low Vision Drawing, and her least favorite class was Math.

The girls in Elliot ranged from ages 14-20. Students at Perkins began JR High two years late even if they had been attending since the age of five, or six. Mary could tell who the new arrivals were from Lower School. It wasn't just because they were younger looking, they also acted younger. Pearl and Abigail were both fourteen, and acted more like eleven, or twelve, especially Pearl. She was a prissy, prim gossipy, girl from the South. She refused to tell her age. She wanted people to think she was older then she was. She frequently preached about God, and acted shocked when the other girls used foul language. She scolded them like a mother would. "I'm surprised at the language you kids pick up!" she often exclaimed. This of coarse made them swear more. Often a group of girls, led by Shirley, who loved to mimic Pearl, led the other girls in a loud obnoxious chant. They would all surround Pearl, stomp their feet, clap their hands, and chant obscene phrases, usually taking the Lord's name in vain. Mary sometimes joined in, being rebellious toward religion herself. Abigail, an African American girl wasn't so bad, but she had an explosive temper. She and a girl named Kasey, who was going out with an older boy named Dennis, was also fresh from Lower School were Mary's room mates. Abigail only had light perception, but this was enough for her to insist that Mary turn the light off early. This led to arguments. In the end Mary took her book, journal, or drawing pad, and sat in the bath tub until she got tired, and dozed off. Mindy was in her mid teens, and already was developing quite a smoking habit. When she wasn't in class she could usually be found in the smoking room which was on the first floor in Elliot. She was Pilipino, and had recently changed her name because the kids used to tease her about her original name. She, like Abigail, had a very explosive temper. Laurite was a nice likable girl, but she was boy crazy and very vain about her appearance. Diana was a bully who got in to a lot of trouble. Mary considered herself lucky that Diana had taken a liking to her. Lorena was a quiet some what chubby, Portuguese girl, in her late teens, who never wore pants. She always wore dresses, or skirts. She was warm, affectionate, but tended to be rather cynical at times. Lynette was in her mid teens. She was known as a hypochondriac, who told tall tales to get attention. Charlene, a tall, slim, African American girl was a senior. Because she often helped the totally blind girls get around, Mary thought she was a house mother the first day she was there. She discovered that even Charlene became fed up with Pearl's prissy, obnoxious ways. She sometimes criticized her along with the other girls.

Their House Mother was a strict, often irritable, elderly woman named Mrs. Lyman. Mary had already had a few conflicts with her over being late for breakfast, and insisting on following crash diets. Once Mrs. Lyman yelled at her for taking diet pills, but Mary, who was afraid of getting too big, or too fat continued to take them to suppress her appetite.

On Thursday afternoon, when Mary was finishing up her second week at Perkins she was called out of Math Class. She found her father waiting for her in a seldom used class room on the first floor. "HI!" they both cried in unison. After they hugged Mary found herself sitting across from Mr. Sullivan. He still looked the same with his grey hair, horn rimmed glasses, and Sunday suit. He told her that Mr. Rossetti, her counselor from Services for the Blind came up with him, but was wandering around the campus so that Mary and her father could talk privately for the time being. For the next five, or ten minutes Mary felt as if she were being interviewed for a job, or something. Mr. Sullivan took out a small pad, and a pen. He began to ask her questions. "Are you happy here at Perkins? Do you want to come home on weekends?, if so, how often?, Do you want to go to church with me?, Do you want to continue your religious education, and receive your first Communion, and later your Confirmation?" Mary dutifully said "Yes" to all of his questions. Then Mr. Sullivan gestured for her to approach him. He pulled her on to his knee. Because she had never received this kind of affection from her father before Mary perched tensely on his knee, and waited for him to talk. "I have to tell you something about Mama…God called her" If she had been raised by modern parents, Mary might have responded with "called her what?", but she knew that her father was telling her that her mother had died. Mary felt shock, surprise, but she felt no grief. Still she tried to act concerned. She wanted to know what happened. Mr. Sullivan told her that her mother had been ill for a long time. "She had a heart condition, Mary" he said slowly. "It became worse during the past year". When Mary learned that Mrs. Sullivan died on the 28th of August she was incredulous. This was the day she wrote a long letter to her parents, telling them all about her summer. Only her father received, and read that letter. Her mother didn't know how well she did during Summer School at Perkins. "She knew about you coming here for Summer School" said Mr. Sullivan "and we did receive the report. So don't worry". Mary felt a little better hearing this. The conversation changed coarse. They discussed the foster home Mary spent three and a half months in when she was fifteen. Mr. Sullivan felt bad about the foster father molesting her. This led him to bring up her real mother, something he had never discussed with her before. "As far as I know, your mother had a boy friend when she was around thirteen. One day they were at her house alone, and he got her pregnant. She had you at fourteen." Mary was surprised that her mother had her so young. "Her name was Nancy. I don't know what her last name was, but she lived some where in Cranston."

Mary and her father found Mr. Rossetti waiting outside. He was a stocky middle aged man of medium height. He wore thick glasses, and was legally blind. He had been her counselor for years, finally taking over her case from Mr. Loreto, who was older, and totally blind. He was assigned to Mary when she was only five. She remembered how she used to hide his brief case so that he wouldn't leave the house until her father came home from work. Poor Mr. Loreto probably thought she was doing this to make fun of him because he was blind, but this wasn't true. She was afraid to be left alone with her mother much of the time because her moods were so unpredictable. Sometimes Mr. Loreto unknowingly defused a violent scene by showing up for their scheduled appointment. She wanted to tell Mr. Rossetti to tell him this, but with her father present she couldn't. He never liked her to say anything unpleasant about her mother. For the sake of herself, and out of sympathy for her father who was grieving, Mary kept quiet about this.

Mr. Rossetti informed Mary that he attended Perkins as a boy. In fact, he was in the same cottage as she was. "Elliot used to be a boy's cottage back in the day" he cheerfully told her. Apparently Mr. Rossetti had a pocket sized telescope which he always kept with him. During the ride up to Perkins he used it to direct Mr. Sullivan on the highway. Mary was impressed. Along with his job as a counselor, he also played the organ at his church. The three of them went in to Elliot, and sat in the smoking room. Mr. Sullivan knew that his daughter smoked. "I'm not going to forbid you to do it, because like most teenagers, you'd find a way of doing it anyway". Mary felt grateful, and relieved. He wrote a note stating that she had his permission to smoke, and gave it to Mrs. Lyman. They hugged again, and Mary shook hands with Mr. Rossetti.

After they left Mary sat on the back steps of Elliot, and wrote in her journal, as she enjoyed a cigarette. She couldn't believe all the things she went through before finally winding up here at Perkins. Mary wished her case worker had thought of sending her here when she was ten, and just getting out of Bradley Hospital. She was the closest to being well after three years there, as she ever was in her entire childhood. If she had come here, or been sent to the Franklin Perkins School in Lancaster she never would have been in those other schools. In June of "71" she wasn't yet a run away. She would have made it in a residential program, she knew she would have. How did the system manage to screw things up for kids? It happened often. Her previous friends were proof of it. She decided then, and there that nothing would cause her to get thrown out of Perkins. She was here…better late then never!

Mary saw a guidance counselor the next day. His name was Mr. Dee. He was a nice, over weight man with brown hair, and a mustache, and beard. He talked with her about her mother, and informed her that all her teachers knew about the death, and if she was caught not paying attention in class they would go easy on her for a while. Mary thanked him. She broke down as she expressed concern about her father being alone in the house. "He has to get rid of the couch in the living room because she used to sleep on it. This gave him easy access to her when she needed him in the night". Mary felt embarrassed about crying, but Mr. Dee was very understanding.

Her regular counselor was Mr. Davis. He was a tall thin man in his late fifties. He had white hair, and a mustache, and beard. Although he had bad breath, she liked him. He had a deep voice like a frog. She could do a pretty good imitation of him saying "Mary come in to my office for a little chat" in his croaky voice. Once when she was angrily telling him that some one she was up set with couldn't make her do something, Mr. Davis looked thoughtful then said "I'll bet there were many times in the past when people made you do a lot of things". Mary, feeling comforted, settled down.

As the days went by Mary got used to being bumped in to by students who, couldn't see as well as she could. She got used to house mothers, who gave her a tiny glass of orange juice at breakfast, and said that this was her daily requirement when she wanted more. She started making friends with some of the students outside of Elliot. Often they were from the West side of the campus. She continued to be friendly with Beth, a girl she knew when she was at the Boston Center for Blind Children six years earlier. Because Mary had recently read Harriet The Spy, and told Beth about it, Beth thought it would be fun to start a spy route right there on campus. Mary, who had already started one, agreed. When they weren't in class, or doing chores they went around spying on students, and taking notes on them. Later they held a secret meeting, and compared notes. It made them both feel very important. They never turned in any of the students when they did bad things, just knowing gave Mary, and Beth a feeling of power over them all. They found out things that they could have reported too. Aside from spying on the gossipers, they followed Harold, and his friends, and discovered the places where they not only smoked cigarettes, but also drank beer, and smoked pot. They found out that a good looking popular boy, named John bought the dope, and beer, and sold it to kids, usually his friends. One evening Mary went with them to one of their secret places. When Harold invited her, she saw it as an opportunity to try to find out who John was buying everything from. She only knew that the person lived off campus. It would have been fun to return to Beth with some new information, but the kids, even when high as kites, didn't reveal much. Dismissing herself to return to the dance over in Dwight Hall, Mary ran off in to the darkness, and smacked in to a fence! The good thing about this was that the kids saw this, and laughed at her because they thought she was stoned. They didn't even suspect her of being a spy. Aside from this Mary participated in Base Ball, and the bowling league. Beth worked part time in the snack bar, located in the main building. She also had a volunteer job over in Bennett Cottage helping the house mother with the students. These students were slow, and needed more help during their first year in upper school. Mary asked Beth how little Madeline was doing. She had met Madeline during Summer School, and was amazed that the girl was almost fourteen, and only looked five. There was a boy in this cottage who was a year older then Madeline. His name was Jimmy. He came from RI like Mary did. He also looked a lot younger then he was. At fifteen he could have passed for nine, or ten. The both of them were mentally challenged to some degree, and as a result, acted younger then they were. "You'll never guess who else is in Bennett" exclaimed Beth in credulously one day. "Who?" asked Mary. "Peter from the Boston Center for the Blind. Do you remember him?" Mary remembered him alright. He had been only nine at the time. He was one of the kids who used to tease everyone, Beth especially. He had no eyes, but could talk, and get dressed without supervision. Many other students couldn't do this.

One Wednesday afternoon when Mary was in Low Vision Drawing, she saw Madeline being led out of Work Activities. The woman was asking her if she knew why she was being taken to get weekly shots. In a loud, brave voice Madeline said "I know why. It's because I'm short, but I won't cry. I'll just say ouch!" She wondered if Jimmy was receiving shots. Now that she thought of it, she realized that she had met Jimmy six years ago when he did his ten day evaluation at The Boston School. He must have come to Perkins several months later. Like Madeline, he was very short for his age.

When Mary started going home every other weekend she found that the RI students were picked up late on Friday afternoons by a school bus which was supplied, and paid for by the Lions Club. It dropped everyone off at the main post office in Providence where the parents would then take their kids home. On Sunday afternoons the students would once again board this bus at the same place, and ride back to Perkins. Mary found that the bus ride was a real trip in more ways then one! First of all the bus bounced so much that Mary felt like she was being bounced on the lap of a mad man! Some of the students on the bus were loud mouthed big shots, who hung out together all the time. A few of the quiet students simply lay on their seats, and slept. Jimmy was one of these. Then there were the students who rocked back, and forth, and made noises. However the most outrageous one of all was a deaf boy, named Brian. Mary nick named him the Bird Boy because he screeched excitedly like a wild bird from a jungle. He swung on the seats, and sometimes banged his head on the window. Mary thought that some one should have captured the Bird Boy, and put him on the Wild Kingdom Show so that Marlin Perkins could talk about him. To pass the time on the long Friday afternoon ride, due to all the traffic, she played her transistor radio which she always had with her.

During her first visit home Mary had a nightmare. In it she saw her mother's ghost. She was walking down the hall with her clothes on hangers, hung over her shoulder. It looked like she was moving on. As she turned to look at Mary, her face was expressionless. Mary was now sleeping in her bed, no more roll away cot in the living room for her when she came home.

She liked having her own room, but she hoped she wouldn't have more nightmares. On Friday evening Mr. Sullivan took Mary out for fish & chips. The diner was in Artic. Then they went to a near by church to play Bingo. Later they went home to the one story, yellow house at the end of Kilton Lane., and watched TV until Ten, or Eleven. On Saturdays they went bowling for a few hours. This gave Mary a chance to improve since she was on a league at school. Sometimes they attended the Saturday Evening Mass instead of the Sunday morning one. Either way, they usually had pizza on Saturday nights. This turned out to be a typical weekend at home. Sometimes on a Saturday before, or after bowling they would visit a few of Mr. Sullivan's friends. Mary found this boring, but she tried to be pleasant about it. Although she was polite, she felt uncomfortable around the couples, and in some cases, single men. They were all old, and sort of religious like her father. There was one exception. Mr. Sullivan liked to take Mary to visit a young nurse, named Donna. She had a husband, named Tom. They had two little girls, and a baby boy. What made Donna special was that she worked in the nursing home where Mrs. Sullivan spent her last few months. Donna not only took good care of her, she also talked to her a lot. Later she comforted Mr. Sullivan, and told him that he could visit her family when ever he wanted. Mr. Sullivan took her up on this. Every time Mary was home he brought her over there. She found Tom funny, but rather intimidating, but the kids were cute, and she liked to help Donna in the kitchen. Mr. Sullivan took pride in the fact that Mary always did the dishes for Donna after they ate.

Even though Mary hadn't received any formal Catholic education, her father talked to Father Hoyle, who was the head priest at St. John & Paul. Because of what she had gone through over the years, and because she was attending church now, Father Hoyle gave Mary her first communion in the chapel at the rectory. Only her father was present to witness the event. Afterward she was given a small gold ring with a tiny chalice in the school of it. Mary was grateful, and saw Father Hoyle as a caring person.

Mr. Sullivan knew about the journal that his daughter was keeping. He liked the idea that she was reading a lot, and taking an interest in writing, but he was concerned that one of the sighted students might take her notebook, use the copy machine, and pass out copies of her notes, and soon everyone would know what she had been writing about them. He urged her to keep the journal with her at all times. Mary supposed that her father was concerned because she had read a large print copy of Harriet the Spy to him one day. He must have been afraid that she might suffer the same fate that Harriet did. She knew her father was right. She promised him and herself that she would always be careful.

By the end of her first semester at Perkins Mary found to her complete surprise, and delight that she had made the honor roll! Everyone was happy for her, especially her father. She continued to study hard, but she still hung out with Beth, and other students. One night she and two boys from the JR/SR High Program sat in the rocking boat down at the lower school play ground, and told ghost stories. On that chilly autumn night, with the smell of burning wood in the distance, telling ghost stories seemed like the perfect thing to be doing.

By December snow was on the ground, and everyone was getting ready for the various Christmas plays and concerts that Perkins had every year. A giant wreath was hung on the front door of the main building. A tree stood decorated in every cottage. One day in Assembly the students from the special program put on a play called A Christmas Carol. Mary had always loved this story. She noticed that some of the students from Bennett Cottage were in the play. At the end Peter, who played Tiny Tim, yelled "God bless us, everyone…NOW DO I GET MY CHECK?" The audience laughed. Most people knew that the students in Bennett were on the reward system. They needed rewards to get ready in the morning, to behave during meals, go to class on time, and behave there. The reward usually came in the form of a piece of paper saying that the person had earned a trip to the snack bar for some soda, and candy, or chips. This paper was called a check. As Assembly broke up, and students began to leave, Mary caught up with Little Madeline. "And now I get my soda!" sang out the girl happily. Mary led her to the snack bar. A boy a little bigger then Madeline latched on to Mary's other arm. He looked about ten but had to have been older because he was from Bennett too. His name was Bruce. He was totally blind, and must have been in some sort of accident years ago because his forehead was pushed in, and there was something wrong with his sinuses, causing his high voice to sound unclear. He too was talking about a check.

Mary was looking forward to vacation, but she loved the campus at Perkins, and the concerts. Being on the Perkins campus made her feel as if she had stepped back in time. It was easy to imagine what the Victorian Era must have been like. The buildings were from this time, and the traditional music played at the concerts made it even more real to Mary. She sometimes fantasized about what it would be like to have lived back then. Mary realized that she had fallen in love with Perkins that very first day of summer school back in June. She began to fantasize about the Victorian Era, and wear long dresses and slender boots occasionally.

They had a final assembly at Ten O'clock on the last Wednesday before Christmas. Then everyone's transportation arrived early to take them home. Mary and the other Rhode Islanders waited in front of the main building for the Lions club bus. It was late. This occasionally happened. The one student who became agitated about this was Jimmy, the boy who Mary first met at The Boston School for Blind Children six years ago. He was normally a very passive, easy going boy, who didn't act up. He went about the school looking, and acting apathetic, and only came to life when he had his music classes. However, once Friday rolled around, he wanted to get home, and that was that! Even now he didn't exactly act up. He simply asked repeatedly where the bus was. When he didn't receive an answer he would rock his suitcase back, and forth on the side walk, making a thumping sound and saying "Hello? Hello?" The first time he did this Mary doubled over in laughter because she thought he was pretending that someone was in his suit case. Then she realized that he did this to get the attention of people around him. Eventually someone would reassure him that the bus was on the way. This would satisfy him for about three minutes. Then he would start nagging people again. Because Jimmy was short for his age, and only sounded about ten a few of the bigger boys would grab his arm, or shove him around. Once he sighed, picked up his suit case, and walked out in to the street groping around for a bus that wasn't there. Someone had to bring him back on to the side walk.

The first two days of vacation were uneventful for Mary. She and her father went to Mass each morning then went out to eat. Later they played board games like "Sorry", and "Parcheesi". Then they watched TV. On Friday Mr. Sullivan took Mary to visit his friend, Louie, the big, friendly ox, who lived up the street from them. Mary was bored, but she acted polite. Later in the afternoon they went over to St. John & Paul's, and with three other men cleaned the church. Mary enjoyed it, and didn't even mind staying to light candles with her father afterward.

On Saturday they made Christmas wreaths, and drove to St Ann cemetery, in Cranston to place them on graves of relatives. Mary was bored with this, but she reminded herself of how pleased her mother would have been with what they were doing. The afternoon took a turn for the worse when Mr. Sullivan, who was in a religious mood, lectured Mary on the Ten Commandments, and the evils of sin. He went on, and on, sometimes repeating himself. When it was over Mary felt scared. Would her father start acting like her mother used to? She was suddenly anxious to get back to school. In her room she took comfort in the picture she had of John F Kennedy.

The day before Christmas Mary, and her father wrapped presents for Dr. Early, and his family. He had been their doctor for years, since before Mary was born.

Christmas was a pleasant day for the both of them. They exchanged gifts, but received nothing from anyone else. Where were their relatives? They appeared to have abandoned Mr. Sullivan, and his daughter after Mrs. Sullivan died. They never even called. Once in a while Mr. Sullivan's niece, Barbara, her husband, Frank, and their kids wrote to him, and Mary, but that was it.

The day after Christmas they went to clean St. John & Paul's school which stood across the parking lot from the church. Mary enjoyed all the work, and the people she, and her father were working with were fun to be around. They were there from nine in the morning until after four thirty. When she was alone in the school library Mary seized the opportunity to steal a large picture of John Kennedy, and smuggle it home.

The following day Mary received a visit from Barbara Ridge, her new counselor from Services for the Blind. Before the woman arrived, Mary was given an extensive lecture by her father on what to say to Barbara, and how to say it. She was forbidden to say anything about her mother. If Barbara asked about her, Mr. Sullivan would say only that the Good Lord called her. Mary was afraid that the woman would see them as a couple of fanatics.

Later in the evening Mary passed the time in church by noticing some of the other people there. There was a short woman in very high heels, who talked like she was from Texas, there were two old women behind her, who started whispering to each other every time her kneeler squeaked, a man near by crossed his arms, and his legs, and went to sleep. It looked deliberate to Mary. Last, but not least was the church show off, who wanted everyone to notice him when ever he did a good deed.

During the next few days they finished cleaning the school, then the church. After Mass one evening Mary went to her room, and cried. She liked the work, and had to reassure her father that it wasn't too much. Why didn't he worry about all the religion he was exposing her to? She felt guilty about resenting it.

The next few days were spent going to Mass, visiting Mr. Sullivan's friend, Louie from up the street, going to a thrift store in Artic; followed by some bowling, then back to cleaning the church again.

Finally it was the first of January 1979. Mary packed the stolen picture of John Kennedy in her suit case, and returned to Perkins. She was so happy to be back! She was totally sick of religion, and felt liberated. She could now go back on her diet too. Her father didn't approve of her dieting, and was always pushing food at her. He also didn't approve of her washing her hair every day. "I only wash my hair once in a while. Girls and women are too vain about their hair" he stated one day when he saw Mary with a towel wrapped around her head. "And think of the water, and heating bill, will you?"

Needless to say, she wasn't happy to be going to Chapel on Tuesday morning, but this was the only time she had to concern herself with religion at Perkins. So she enjoyed the singing then wrote in her journal during the sermon. Other then Math, and Gym, Mary's day was free because a few of the teachers didn't come in. She felt uneasy about the extra free time, but she busied herself with listening to audio novels from the school library. The following day Mary started her new job. Every morning she was to go around posting the absentee list to various parts of the school. She liked doing this, it made her feel important. As she posted the copies of the list, she thought about how lost Steve looked without Lorena, his girl friend, who was home sick. She thought about the angry lecture Mrs. Lyman, her house mother, gave the girls in Elliot because someone gave Pearl a bar of soap for Christmas. Mrs. Lyman thought this was mean. The girls thought the gift suited Pearl because she was always too busy preaching religion, and yet also gossiping to take a shower. Mary stopped, and wrote "Extra! Extra! Read all about it! A certain student here was rushed to the Mount Auburn Hospital for over dosing on religion. She had to get her brain pumped…can anyone guess who I'm talking about?" She put her notebook away, and observed an argument between a nasty boy, named Richard, and Mindy, the heavy smoker from Elliot. Mindy had a bad temper, but if she kept smoking the way she did, she soon wouldn't have enough breath to argue.

After school a teacher took Mary to the Boston Public library to get a book that she had been dying to read. It was called "Maud Shaw: White House Nanny. The book told about the years Maud took care of John, and Caroline Kennedy. Mary loved it! She enjoyed reading about what a devoted, fun loving father John Kennedy was.

On Friday Mary became furious with her Work Activities teacher, Mr. Landis. He accused her of coming to class only to make her money, and leave. Why wouldn't she want to make money? This was what they did in Work Activities. She couldn't help it if she was faster then some of the other students. Now she supposed that Mr. Landis hated her like Mr. Dickson, her Wood working teacher did. One day in Wood working class a deaf/blind boy, who also had that class was feeling Mary up. This had happened before, and Mary was fed up. He reminded her of the man who molested her in a foster home two years ago. She didn't like the old feelings that came back when the deaf boy touched her. Finally in frustration she said "He gives me the creeps! Why doesn't he stop touching me?" Instead of asking her why she said that, Mr. Dickson told her that she probably gave the boy the creeps, which was a stupid thing to say because if she gave him the creeps, he wouldn't be touching her. When Mary protested, Mr. Dickson said "Well, Even Steven. You said it about him, so I'm saying it about you!" Mary didn't want to risk getting in to a heated argument with a teacher. As a result, she told one of the other shop teachers that Mr. Dickson sniffed glue, Even Steven indeed! Since then Mary hated Mr. Dickson, and she was sure that he hated her too.

As if the incident with the deaf boy wasn't bad enough, someone had put her in a Sex Ed class with all boys, no girls. Mary was so embarrassed, and uncomfortable that she wouldn't pay attention, or participate. Because of the various assaults that were done to her over the years, Mary wasn't even happy about becoming a woman, and she certainly didn't want to talk about any of it in front of boys. Fortunately as the weeks progressed the subject began to shift away from sex. Mrs. Salmon started teaching about the different kinds of relationships people have with each other. It became almost like a psychology class. Mary liked this.

Two weeks after vacation ended Mary found herself at home again. Something had changed, and now she was happy to be home every other weekend. Recently she spotted an article about Father Hoyle. He had received an award from the Bishop. His picture was in the paper. Mary tore the picture out, and kept it. She realized suddenly just how much she admired, and liked this priest, who bended the rules, and allowed her to receive her first communion a few months ago. John Kennedy was now taking a back seat to Father Hoyle in Mary's affections. She eagerly went to Mass with her father, hoping that Father Hoyle would be saying it. Sometimes it turned out to be one of the younger priests, Father Kelly, or Father Davis. Mary began requesting that her father take her to the Masses that were said by her favorite priest. Mr. Sullivan complied. Once at Bingo Mary won Fifty Dollars. Instead of keeping it, she donated it to St. John & Paul's. One Saturday afternoon Mr. Sullivan sat in the car in the church parking lot while Mary, using a pocket sized telescope, drew a detailed picture of the church, and gave it to Father Hoyle.

At school Mary thought of Father Hoyle all the time. When ever she saw the students in the Adult Rehab Program, who acted like whining old people, and even dressed in old style clothing, she wondered what the priest would think of them. When she saw students who looked a lot older, or a lot younger then they were, she wondered what he would think of them. She also wondered what he would think of the nasty, loud mouthed big shots that were mostly in the JR/SR High Program with her. Mary made things for Father Hoyle in her drawing class and in her cooking class if it was close to a Friday that she was going home. To avoid any jealousy she also made gifts for her father too. Mary still spied with Beth sometimes, and took notes which they compared later. Once again she found herself wondering what Father Hoyle would think. She hoped that he would think that she and Beth were careful, talented, brave spies. Mary desperately wanted Father Hoyle to see her as unique, different from the other teenagers, special even. Instead she often felt inadequate around him, like she couldn't do anything funny, or clever. When ever she saw him she told him about all the things she was in to, and how adventurous she was. He responded pleasantly, but didn't talk as much as she hoped he would. At school Mary drew pictures of the priest. Father Hoyle was about sixty. He was of medium height, with grey hair, and a ruddy complexion. He was rather chubby, and had a round, clean shaven face. Mary had to laugh as she imagined Father Hoyle visiting Perkins. He would hear Denise yelling "Sit on it! "at the students, in her hoarse, monotone voice. He would hear her asking everyone if they were a guidance counselor even though she knew they weren't. She often said silly things just to get the other students to yell at her. Then she would walk away laughing in her monotone voice. She was a day student, and always brought her tooth brush, and tooth paste. Every day she would ask if anyone had seen her tooth brush. When everyone yelled, and insulted her, she would go in the bathroom, and pick up the tooth brush knowing all along where it was. Although she was white with blonde hair, Denise was obsessed with the Spanish culture. One evening she stayed on campus for a fiesta that she thought was occurring in Dwight Hall. Out of curiosity Mary followed her over there. The lights were off, and no one was around. Denise stood there in the dark room and said "Where are all the booths, and hot air balloons? Where is the music, and the people in costumes?" Mary could only shake her head at Denise's bewilderment.

When spring came some changes came as well. First of all Leona, the cook from Moulton Cottage, where Mary, and the others from Elliot, and Moulton ate their breakfast, and supper, was transferred to Anagnus Cottage. She had been a good friend to Mary. They often talked, as they did the dishes, and cleaned the kitchen. Now Mary was going to be helping a cook who resembled the man who molested her two years earlier. Was there any rest for the weary?! She would just have to be on her guard around him.

Mr. Babcock, the director of Perkins lived in a weird, modern looking house on the edge of the campus. He started inviting students to his house for supper. Mary didn't go because of her diet, but some of the other students went, and came back stuffed. One evening Shirley and Abigail returned, and lay on the floor of the smoking room complaining that they ate too much spaghetti, and meat balls.

A popular boy, named Jonathon, who was small for his age took a liking to Mary. He actually seemed to have a crush on her. Mary liked him, but she wasn't interested in going out with him. She didn't want to go out with anyone at this time in her life. In site of his size he was very active in all the sporting events. Mr. Regan, the gym teacher called him "Numeral Uno" which meant Number One.

The governor came to Perkins because there was a celebration on account of the school's One hundred, and fiftieth anniversary. He gave a speech. Then the upper school and the upper school choruses sang for everyone. Later someone heard the governor say that he never knew that blind children could sing. After he left people were bashing him, and making fun of him for his ignorance.

One evening Mary experienced a real blow. For weeks Diana, the bully, who had taken a liking to Mary, started to change toward her. She hogged the TV, and didn't care when Mary complained because she wanted to watch something else. One evening when Diana, Mindy, and Mary were in the smoking room Mindy started an argument with Mary about the ash tray. Mary argued right back. Diana sided with Mindy, and yelled at Mary. "I'll kick your ass!" This was too much! Feeling betrayed, and hurt, Mary couldn't think clearly. Instead of telling Diana what she thought of her, she pointed at Mindy, and said "No, I'll kick her ass!" Mindy walked up, and grinned in her face. Because her fight wasn't really with Mindy, but with Diana the phony friend, the betrayer! Mary left. She ran out of the cottage, and made her way down to Lower School. She sat outside, and cried for a long time. A cat came over, and rubbed against her legs until she stopped crying. After awhile she began to pet the cat, feeling grateful for its comfort.

After this Mary wanted nothing to do with Diana, or her other friends. She could now understand why Diana's family had so many problems with her, and dreaded having her with them for the holidays. She probably treated them badly too. Only her sister enjoyed being around her. She had a little girl, and a baby boy. Diana visited them on some weekends. She claimed to be a tough baby sitter, who tolerated no nonsense from Three year old Mandy. Mary pitied the toddler. Diana wasn't even finished with Mary yet. A few days later Mrs. Lyman asked Mary where Kasey was. Without thinking Mary said "Upstairs getting ready." Kasey was reprimanded for being late for breakfast. Afterward Mary found Kasey and Diana in the smoking room. While Kasey sat looking like a wounded princess with her long, blonde hair, and pink cheeks, Diana yelled at Mary for getting Kasey in to trouble. Trying to explain her side to Diana did no good. In the end Mary stormed out of the room, and went to short sheet Kasey's bed. Then she squirted tooth paste on the sheet that remained. That would teach Kasey not to get other people to fight her battles for her! Who fought Mary's battles for her? No one did.

Mary made friends with Lorena, and Steve. Lorena was the nicest girl in Elliot, even if she was quiet, and Steve, next door in Moulton, was one of the nicest boys. They were going together, but they liked having Mary as the third wheel most of the time. She never had to walk on egg shells with them like she did with Diana, and her friends. Even though Beth had given up their spy route by then, she, and Mary were still friends.

In May Mr. Sullivan came up to Perkins with Barbara from Services for the Blind. Every student had a meeting with their program supervisor, teachers, and state counselor. Parents were encouraged to come too. In the meeting Mary was told that she wouldn't be in the Summer School program this year. It had been an evaluation period to determine whether or not she would be accepted in the fall. When Mary mentioned that many students, who had been there for years attended summer school, she was told that she didn't need it. She also learned that during her senior year she was going to be in the supervised apartment program. Every cottage had an apartment on the first floor. In this program she and two other students would live in the apartment, and learn how to be independent. Leaving the meeting with compliments on how well she had been doing, Mary didn't feel flattered. Maybe she shouldn't have tried so hard. If she had held back she might have been allowed in summer school, and she wouldn't be considered capable of going in to the apartment program in the fall. So now she was going to have to prepare herself for a lonely, restricted, religious summer with her father. Mary felt some what abandoned by her favorite school, the one she had always thought of as Heaven.

In late May Mary and most of the other students in her program went whale watching in Province Town. They had a great time.

In June there were a few more boat rides, a school picnic, and the Junior Prom. Mary attended, and had a good time. She didn't have a date, but she danced any way. Mr. Flannigan, a fairly new guidance counselor, who Mary had been seeing for a few months, had a rock band. They played at the prom. Mary thought Mr. Flannigan was cool. She liked talking to him. She didn't even mind when he dedicated "Land of Fantasy "to her instead of "Yellow Submarine". Mary had been quite taken with Admiral Nelson from a TV show called "Voyage to the bottom of the sea" Admiral Nelson seemed like a better father figure then Father Hoyle, who had no time for her. Mary supposed that as a guidance counselor, Mr. Flannigan couldn't encourage her fantasy too much by playing the submarine song for her. The other song was intended to be a compromise. Mary happily danced to it.

Chapter Twelve

Home for the summer

When Mary got off the bus in Providence she was nervous. After much contemplation, she had decided to cut her hair short, and part it on the side. Because her parents had always been upset with her when she cut her hair in the past, Mary quickly came up with a lie to prevent her father from scolding her. When Mr. Sullivan stepped forward to take her luggage from her he noticed her hair. She told him that she had to cut it because she got bubble gum stuck in it the previous day. When Mr. Sullivan accepted this story Mary heaved a sigh of relief. They set off for an entire summer together.

By June of 1979 the gas crisis had become so bad that Mary's father had to break a promise to her. For the past two months Mr. Sullivan had been planning to take a trip to Buffalo, New York. He was born there, and lived there until he was eight. Then his parents had decided to move to Rhode Island. Although his parents had been dead for years, he had relatives who still lived up in Buffalo. He wanted to take his daughter, and spend a week up there. Mary had been looking forward to seeing people who she hadn't seen since she was two years old, but with the gas shortages it was impossible. This was a double blow to Mary, who had been denied summer school at Perkins. She supposed she would be stuck in the dismal town of Coventry all summer. The thought depressed her.

Even though Mary had moved on to Admiral Nelson, from Voyage to the bottom of the sea, as her significant father figure, with his men as doting uncles, she still had feelings for Father Hoyle. On her first afternoon home from school she found herself helping her father clean out the garage of the rectory. Father Hoyle said a cheerful "Hello" to the both of them. He talked a little to Mr. Sullivan then said he was on his way out to his house in Point Judith for some rest. He hurried away without saying goodbye to Mary. Already feeling abandoned by Perkins, Mary dissolved in to silent tears at Father Hoyle's rebuff. What was wrong with him? Did he think of her as just another teenager? Maybe he didn't like teenagers. Well she couldn't help her age, could she? She felt like screaming "EXCUSE ME FOR BEING EIGHTEEN!!" at him. She kept her mouth shut, and wondered if he even noticed that she was crying as he left. If he did he ignored it. She decided that she was better off with the Admiral.

In the next few days Mr. Sullivan took Mary to Colt State Park, and a few other beaches. They did some core hogging at one of them. She found that she was happier when she was away from Coventry. Mary had been home for almost a week when she became sick from drinking too much apple juice. She was confined to bed for a day. In the evening her father surprised her by appearing in her room with an old wooden lamp. On the front of it was a ship's wheel. The lamp was turned on, and off by turning the wheel left, or right. Mary was delighted with the lamp. When she had it on she felt like she was in the cabin on a ship far from Coventry.

Mr. Sullivan pretty much had Mary's schedule mapped out for her. They went to Mass every morning. Then they either helped with the land scaping on the church property, or they went to visit his friends. One day Mr. Sullivan surprised Mary by taking her to see Father McGovern. He greeted Mary and her father warmly. The three of them stood outside of the church he now worked at. Father McGovern told them that Sister Jane and the other sisters from her order had been transferred back to Kentucky in 1970. Mary concealed her disappointment about this. Instead she excitedly told him about the activities she was involved in at Perkins. Father McGovern laughed and ruffled her hair. Back in the car Mary turned to her father. "Years ago Mom told me that Father McGovern had washed his hands of me. He doesn't seem to have done that though". Mr. Sullivan sighed and then said " Sometimes parents say things like that to make their kids smarten up and start doing the right thing". Mary felt a flash of anger at her mother. However this was replaced by a feeling of relief because the priest hadn't abandoned her after all.

On Wednesdays they always went over to Dr. Early's farm in rural Coventry. They left right after Mass so that they could spend the whole day down there. Mr. Sullivan looked forward to getting together with Dr. Early, and the other guys. They worked on machinery, and stopped to have spam sandwiches for lunch. Dr. Early was really immersing himself in becoming a hick. He loved it! Mary didn't spend the day with the men. Mr. Sullivan always dropped her off at the doctor's daughter's house which was right on the same property. Her name was Charlene. She was in her twenties, and was married to a man named Tim. They had a tree year old daughter, named Jenny, and a baby boy, named Jeremy. Mary was left to follow Charlene and the kids when she did her shopping, or sit, and color with Jessica while Charlene did her house work. When Jenny was put down for a nap, or went on errands with her father in his truck Mary was free to draw, or write in her journal. Charlene was in to healthy living. She bought health food. She often took Mary and the kids down to a small creek. She would let Jenny, and her little brother go naked. Once while in the car, little Jeremy, who had nothing on let out an upward stream of urine causing Charlene to quickly grab a towel, and put it over him momentarily. Mary was bored with having to spend every Wednesday at Charlene's. She checked her watch every time Charlene's back was turned.

Along with daily Mass, Mr. Sullivan, and Mary said the rosary together every afternoon, or evening, and always said Grace before each meal. No matter what else they did, they're activities always reverted back to the church. One day Mary, and her father went strawberry picking with some of the other parishioners. She enjoyed this activity, and was relieved when Father Davis accompanied them instead of Father Hoyle. She didn't need another rebuff to spoil the day for her.

Mary loved rain. It was an excuse to stay home, and listen to novels from the library for the blind, watch TV, write, and draw. She had to do everything out in the living room. On several occasions she had decided to draw, write, or listen to stories in her room, and found herself being questioned, or even yelled at by her father. Once he walked in when she was changing her shirt. She had to turn quickly to conceal herself from him. He couldn't understand why she would be in her room if it wasn't bed time. When she told him that she liked to have privacy sometimes he yelled at her, and said that what she was saying was a bunch of nonsense. She recently caught him trying to read her journal. She was dumbfounded. Months earlier he had warned her to be careful that no one read her journals, and here he was doing it himself! After he left Mary burst in to tears, and hurled her pen at the wall. Mr. Sullivan not only hated the idea of privacy, he also got upset when Mary washed her hair, or did anything that involved using a lot of water. When they did their washing they went to a small laundry room which stood in back of Dr. Early's office. Mr. Sullivan would take Mary's laundry, and go through it as he unceremoniously dumped it in the two washers, underwear in one, clothes in the other. Mary having unsuccessfully convinced her father that she should do her own laundry, turned away, and cried quietly because she was embarrassed at being a teenager, and having her father handle her underwear. He had no idea about privacy! Mr. Sullivan did his own laundry, not that there was a lot of it. His wardrobe was small these days, and no longer consisted of nice clothes. He now wore baggy trousers, and short sleeved button down shirts. Around the house he removed the button down shirt, and sat around in a sleeveless undershirt, smoking cigars. "(He used to smoke cigarettes, but thought cigars were less harmful.) He no longer had any teeth, and with his oily hair, he looked nothing like the man she knew when she was growing up. His personality had changed too. Mr. Sullivan was much more out spoken, and out going with people since his wife died, but he was also more irritable with his daughter. Not only did he give her religious lectures at times, he was quick to snap at her when she was clumsy, or forgetful. Sometimes he would say "Can't you do anything right?" or "Your so sloppy, what's wrong with you?" He hated having to repeat himself when Mary failed to hear him the first time. Once when one of her friends called Mr.

Sullivan angrily told her to hurry out of the bathroom, and pick up the phone. Mary rushed in to the room, and accidentally knocked over her father's glass of iced tea as she was taking the receiver from him. He swore loudly, and threw his chips across the room. Mary found it hard not to cry as she talked to her friend. She couldn't tell her how she was doing either because her father was hovering nearby.

At the end of June Mary and her father were invited over to Jimmy's house. Jimmy was in Bennett Cottage at Perkins, and always rode the Lions Club bus with Mary during the school year. Jimmy, his parents, and a brother, and sister all lived over on Merry Ave, not far from Mary. When they arrived Jimmy, his mother, and sister, Carrie greeted them. Jimmy, who had a natural talent for music, played the organ for everyone. He was almost totally blind, but could play better then many sighted kids his age. His mother said that he was born with perfect pitch. The house they lived in was a split level, built in the fifties. In spite of its modern look, Mary liked the upstairs living room where the organ was because it was very elegant with a Grandfather clock, and antique looking furniture. Later they all went outside and went for a swim in the built in swimming pool. Jimmy kept getting out, and asking Mr. Sullivan to throw him in. "Do it again, Mr. Sullivan "he said repeatedly. Mary's father grew tired of this after a while. Jimmy could swim as well as he could play the organ. He was like a fish in the water. After an hour, or so they all sat at the picnic table, and had a big lunch. Jimmy loved eating. His favorite food was pasta. He also loved cake, and pastry, but he didn't like candy, cookies, or gum. Mary had never met a kid who didn't like candy. He told Mary that she shouldn't eat it either. "It's bad for your teeth" he said wisely. His mother agreed then she started talking about why Jimmy was so small for a fifteen year old. She said that his pituitary gland stopped working years ago. In August he would begin receiving growth hormone treatments. Mary was disappointed. She thought he looked cute the way he was. His mother was concerned though, because he was only four feet, and five inches tall, and weighed only seventy five pounds. He still had many of his baby teeth, and a high voice. He of coarse didn't shave yet either. "He will start off taking pills "said Kathy, his mother. "Then as he begins to grow he will receive shots to speed up final stages of growth. After that he will have to receive injections of male hormone." Kathy wanted Jimmy to grow to at least five feet, and six inches tall. She said that this was a socially acceptable height for a man. Mary, who liked Jimmy, and was already desiring him as a cute little brother, who she could dote on, and show off to people wasn't happy about Kathy's plans for the future, but she knew she couldn't disagree too much. Soon they were talking about diets because this was a subject that interested the both of them, and Mary figured that it would avoid a conflict. However Mr. Sullivan saw it as an opportunity to criticize his daughter for smoking. "If you can give up food, you can give up cigarettes". Mary felt annoyed with him, but she kept it to herself.

To top it off he said that she looked large framed to him after Kathy had just finished saying that she was probably small, or medium framed. Mary was sure that he said this to upset her because she was obsessed with being small. Mary couldn't wait to go back to school! Later that evening Mr. Sullivan took Mary to a wake. She didn't know the person who died, but her father apparently did. She couldn't understand why her father couldn't have dropped her off at home on his way to the wake. She sometimes wished that he would leave her with someone else for the summer. Then he could go to all the wakes, and church activities that he wanted, and not have to drag her along. The wake was from seven until nine. Mary hoped that they wouldn't have to stay the entire two hours. She wanted to get home, and watch Voyage to the bottom of the sea. She fidgeted, looked at her watch, and tried not to cry. They made it home by eight twenty. Mary hurried to put the TV on. She had only missed the first twenty minutes of the show.

The following evening which was a Saturday, St. John, and Paul church had a big dinner over in the school auditorium. Almost every parishioner was there. Mary helped some other teenage girls set all the tables. When Father Kelly urged them to hurry up, one of the girls, who had a real attitude, glowered at him, and said "Yeah, you give all the orders, but do none of the work", but she didn't say it loud enough for him to hear. Mary smothered a laugh. She kind of liked this girl. Once everyone was seated a prayer was said. Then people got in line for the buffet style dinner. Since Mary's table was near the head table where the priests sat, she was able to give Father Hoyle some spine chilling looks. She knew that he noticed what she was doing because he looked at her in a bewildered way. She hoped he would confront her, but he didn't. When the dinner was over Mary was among the cleaning crew. At one point Father Hoyle was coming down the aisle, Mary was coming toward him, as he was passing her, she tripped on his foot, and fell on her face! When he asked her if she was alright, Mary laughed self consciously. Father Hoyle walked away without looking back.

On July Fourth Mary and her father went down to Bristol for the parade. The parade was fun, and exciting, but even without it Mary still would have wanted to go to Bristol. It was such a quaint, charming town. Mary felt totally at home there.

After the parade ended Mr. Sullivan took Mary to see an old friend of his. They went to a large, white house with many rooms on the first and second floor. The house was a hotel run by an old man, named Charlie. He knew Mary's parents for many years. When they adopted Mary Charlie donated the baby furniture that they would need. Mary thanked him. It was a nice thing to do. Still she was more interested in the hotel then she was with the owner. The hallway had a long, dark red carpet. She liked the spiral stair case, and the antique furniture, but most of all she liked the house itself. It was a colonial house that was well preserved. Mary wished that they could stay there for a few days, but she knew that her father was eager to return to their modern, boring, small town life in Coventry.

The next day, Thursday, Mary felt like a caged bird that was about to receive her freedom. She had a friend who worked at Perkins. Her name was Sue. She was a secretary, who liked Mary, and had many talks with her. She understood how unhappy Mary was at home. By pulling some strings, Sue was able to arrange for Mary to spend a long weekend at Perkins. Mr. Sullivan drove his daughter up to school Thursday morning, and told her that he would be back to get her on Sunday. As was to be expected, Mr. Sullivan had to visit the church in Watertown square first. Mary waited patiently, as he lighted candles, and prayed. Then they said their goodbyes at school.

Mary stayed in Bridgman Cottage just like the previous summer. She was given a single room with a TV. The only time she watched it was from eight to nine on Thursday, Friday, and Saturday nights to see Voyage to the bottom of the sea. She wanted to spend as much time outside of her room as possible. She only had three days, and she was going to make the most of them. Kathy, a young woman, who had been Mary's mobility teacher during the second half of her junior year, was there. She had found Kathy to be a fun, and helpful teacher. She taught Mary how to cross streets safely, and how to ride the busses. Later they started taking the subways together. Kathy would have her take a subway to a certain place on her own, and meet her there. Then they would discuss how Mary handled the experience. Kathy also worked as a house mother in Anagnus Cottage down in lower school. She lived there, and went home to her family in Springfield on the weekends. Mary used to go down there, and hang out with Kathy. Of all the students in Anagnus, three stood out. One was an African American boy of about thirteen who lived in a fantasy world because he had no family, and had grown up in foster homes. His name was Mike, and he often talked about a made up place called Weasrerland. Apparently one of the pass times of the characters in this place was clapping their feet because Mike stopped to lie down, and do this a lot. This earned him many reprimands from the house parents. Mary could identify with Mike because she too lived in a world of her own. The other two students who caught her attention were a twelve year old girl, and a thirteen year old girl. They both talked to themselves constantly. What puzzled Mary was that one of them was corrected for this, but the other one wasn't. Now Kathy was working as a house mother in the upper school for summer school.

On Thursday afternoon Kathy took Mary and a few other students to the beach. They had a lot of fun, but on the way back Kathy's car broke down. They had to ride the rest of the way to school in a tow truck. Mary saw it as an adventure. Kathy didn't. She was so angry she wanted to throw her keys in the Charles River! In the evening, before, and after her favorite TV show, Mary sat out on the stone wall, and talked to some of the other students. She saw

Abigail, her former roommate from Elliot Cottage. Their former arguments were forgotten. Mary was glad that Abigail had been allowed to attend summer school. Her home life was as dull and unfulfilling as Mary's was.

Friday Sue took Mary to Harvard Square for lunch. Sue liked Mr. Sullivan, and respected him, but she understood that he wasn't offering his daughter a very good home life. She tried to be sympathetic to Mary while continuing to have a good opinion of her father. After they ate they did a little shopping. In a book store Mary bought a magazine that had pictures of Admiral Nelson. She was thrilled with it! When they returned to Perkins Ms. Standish, the supervisor of the Junior/Senior Program was there. She was Sue's boss, and this was how Mary had met, and formed a friendship with her. She didn't always feel so friendly toward Ms. Standish though. She often felt like she didn't understand her, and just wanted to push her through the program, and out. On this occasion Ms. Standish was in a very friendly, talkative mood toward Mary. This made her feel like confiding in the woman. She told her about her longing to have a doting father figure. Ms. Standish seemed sympathetic, and was pleased when Mary said that she would give up her pictures and fantasies of the admiral if she found someone real. Mary told her that she was attracted to older men, and had been for years. "I'm still looking for a father figure, not a boy friend. I guess that's why I push boys away". Ms. Standish agreed.

On Saturday the school had a big picnic followed by a base ball game played the Perkins way with a soccer ball, and no gloves. During the picnic Mary sat next to a chubby girl of about thirteen. She had short, straight light brown hair, and was totally blind. Her name was Judy. As they talked it became apparent that Judy was obsessed with base ball. She pretended that she was a famous ball player for the Red Sox. As Mary guided Judy over to the ball field in back of Elliot Cottage Judy asked her if she wanted to interview her. So Mary pretended to be a reporter, and tried to ask Judy the kind of questions a reporter would ask a ball player. In spite of all her talking, Judy couldn't play base ball. A partially sighted boy, named Billy helped her swing the bat. Then he helped her run the bases. Judy was delighted, and saw herself as a Pro.

That evening at supper Judy dropped a plate of food on the floor. The dinning room erupted in applause. As Judy cleaned up the mess she was bewildered. "Why did they clap?" she kept asking. Sarcasm was something that was difficult for Judy to understand.

Sunday came, and Mr. Sullivan arrived to take his daughter home. Things continued to be the same at home. Mr. Sullivan's moods flocculated between being nice to being very irritable, and critical of his daughter. Mary eagerly looked forward to rainy days because they stayed home, allowing her to listen to novels on records that took her far away from Coventry if only for a little while. They continued to go to daily Mass, and to visit Mr. Sullivan's friends. One day Mary got away with sleeping until noon. It gave her an idea. If she could do this until school started up again the summer would only be half as long. However she gave up the idea as soon as she got it. Her father would guess what she was doing, and put a stop to it. So she watched movies, and cried over a sad one called The Summer of my German soldier. She felt so bad for Patsy, an abused, lonely teenager, who hid an escaping soldier from the nearby prison camp. The soldier, a handsome, blonde man, was kind to the girl, and even ran out of hiding to stop Patsy's father from beating her. Then he thought better of it, and returned to the hide out. This was supposed to show that he cared about her, and wasn't just using her. He wasn't even a Nazi, and liked her despite the fact that she was Jewish. In the end he was found, and shot. Mary cried herself to sleep.

On the second Wednesday of July Mary was once again at Dr. Early's farm. She cried for a while, as she wandered around the property, surrounded by dense woods. Then she went, and had lunch with the guys. Several times Mary tried to strike up a conversation with the old doctor when no one was around, but each time he ignored her. Feeling embarrassed for trying, Mary slunk away. Why would their family doctor, who liked her parents, but not her want to talk to her? What bothered her was that she had tried, and thought she would succeed. Now she felt stupid!

Two days later Mr. Sullivan surprised Mary by taking her to Rocky Point. He even went on some of the rides with her. Then he sat down, and told her to go off, and have a good time. This was a remarkable day for Mary!

By the middle of July Mary had made up a comic script about Admiral Nelson. She gave him a wife, older brother, and a teenaged son. Then she had him take in eight disabled or abused foster children. Because there were twelve of them living in a grand house, Mary called the comic script The Baker's Dozen. She worked on it every chance she got. When he was in a good mood, Mr. Sullivan complimented his daughter on her art work. Still Mary had to spend most of her time doing what her father wanted to do. One of the families he occasionally visited was in West Warwick. Molly was a woman in her late thirties, who was separated from her husband. She had an eight year old daughter, named Terry, and a five year old son, named Jeffery. Terry, a cheerful, funny, blonde, missed her father, but Jeffery seemed more affected by the separation. He acted defiant toward his mother all the time, and often laughed when she spanked him. Mary spent more time with Terry, coloring with her, and listening to her jokes, and riddles. When Maxi's father died Mr. Sullivan took Mary to the funeral. She felt bad for Terry, who was closer to her Grandfather then her father. The little girl was crying. Jeff seemed kind of unaffected by his Grandfather's death. He fidgeted, and whispered like he normally did in church. Molly's mother moved in with them. She was a glum woman, who liked to instill guilt in to people. At home when Mr. Sullivan put Mary on the phone with her, the woman always ended the conversation with "I'll let you go. I know you don't want to talk to me. No one wants to talk to an unwanted old woman like me". She refused to listen when Mary tried to disagree with her. Mary dreaded these phone calls. She was made to feel like an insensitive, clueless teenager.

Mr. Sullivan had a friend named Jim. He was unemployed, and couldn't find a permanent job anywhere. He haunted the unemployment office. Mr. Sullivan not only felt sorry for the unshaven, unkempt, sad man, he also seemed to like him. They sometimes spent several hours in the kitchen, smoking, drinking coffee, and talking. Jim wasn't an out spoken man, but he was a very good conversationalist when he was around Mary's father. Jim didn't say much to Mary, but he was polite toward her. She liked it when he came over because she was left to do as she pleased. Jim lived in a motel nearby, and sometimes went to the beach with Mary, and her father. Mr. Sullivan core hogged, and fished with him, allowing him to take whatever they both caught home with him. Jim apparently had a small stove of sorts in his motel room. Mr. Sullivan occasionally slipped Jim some money to help him out. Though he liked being around Mr. Sullivan; Jim never smiled. He seemed too weighted down by his troubles.

By the third week in August Mary was happy to see summer vacation winding down. The proof of this was when she heard her father call the Lions Club to confirm that they would still be transporting Rhode Island students to, and from Perkins. He checked to make sure of the schedules, and then took Mary to the thrift store in West Warwick for some back to school clothes. Unlike her mother, her father allowed her to choose her own styles. Then they went to another store to buy some pens, a notebook, and a folder. Mary wanted a folder with sail boats on it, but her father wouldn't let her have it because it was more expensive then the plain folder he picked out. Mary begged him to change his mind. He became angry with her. She grudgingly gave in. She saw him as unfair, and too controlling. She couldn't wait to return to school. The previous day she had come close to packing her things, and running away. They were cleaning the living room. Mr. Sullivan was dusting the piano, and Mary was using the old carpet sweeper. She accidentally lost her grip on the handle. It fell against the lid of the piano. Mr. Sullivan screamed at her, and called her clumsy, and careless. Mary ran to her room in tears. She started packing her things. She was going to sneak back to Perkins, and hide on campus until classes resumed, but in the end she gave up the idea because she knew that her father would go right up there, and get her. Standing in the store Mary realized that she would just have to bare up until Labor Day.

On the twenty first of August Mr. Sullivan took Mary to Block Island. He had a friend, who used to be a state trooper with him. He lived on Block Island with his wife. They were both in their seventies like Mr. Sullivan. The visit was like the visits with the other friends of her father, dull. They sat, and talked for hours about their younger days. Mary became restless, but tried not to show it. What she loved about the day was the boat trip to, and from the island. She also liked all the picturesque shops, and restaurants around the harbor, but the rest of the island was boring, consisting of a few houses here, and there.

On August twenty fifth Mary went to Springfield, Massachusetts to spend the weekend with Kathy, and her family. Mary was late getting there because she and her father were waiting at the wrong platform. Mary called Kathy, and told her that she would be arriving an hour late. She sensed Kathy's disapproval. As Mary's former mobility teacher, she must have expected better from her. Kathy was there to meet Mary. She still seemed moody. Mary hoped she wasn't holding her mistake against her. Kathy lived with her parents, and brothers in a house in the suburbs of Springfield. They had two TVs. Mary wished she had her own TV at home. Her father didn't like many of the shows she liked. Kathy's family was very nice to her. What she didn't like was the way they were always trying to do everything for her. She didn't like feeling helpless. She discovered that they weren't very fond of the Governor. Mary hadn't given him much thought until last February when he visited the campus, and said that he was surprised that blind children could sing. It was inevitable that Mary would have to attend Mass during her visit. Kathy came from a good Irish Catholic family, who attended church regularly. Mary thought it was a small price to pay, since she was away from home, and happy about it. In the afternoon she and Kathy took a walk to Forest Park which wasn't far from the house. They sat by a stream, and talked. Mary was unhappy to find out that Kathy still believed that she had been angry at her one day in the spring when she threw a bit of a tantrum because she couldn't find a book with Admiral Nelson's picture in it during an outing in Harvard Square. Mary tried to reassure Kathy that she hadn't been angry at her, just frustrated at the circumstances that wouldn't allow her to obtain the admiral's picture. Kathy seemed some what convinced. Mary, who apologized for the incident when it happened, apologized once again. Why was it so hard for people to forgive her sometimes? The next day Kathy took Mary to pick out a school folder before taking her to the bus station. Mary couldn't find one with sail boats, but she did find one with the ocean, and a surfer on it. She thanked Kathy, and boarded the bus. She didn't cry during the ride because she knew that school would be starting in only a week. Surely she could hold up until then.

On September third Mary packed her big suitcase, and rode with her father to Providence. She couldn't wait to return to Perkins! It had been quite a week between worrying about Hurricane David, and whether it would reach New England, or not, and having to go to Dr. Early's farm twice instead of once. Charlene was in a bad mood one of the times Mary visited, and kept snapping at her daughter. She made Mary go shopping with them instead of leaving her on her own. What did she think Mary was going to do, wander off in to the woods where the wild pigs ran free? What a dreadful place! Her father drove her crazy with his disrespect of her privacy, and she drove him crazy with her clumsiness, and day dreaming. At one point she almost shop lifted a post card with sail boats on it, but managed not to. Her father would have had a right to be upset with her then.

Mary heaved a sigh of relief as the big, yellow school bus arrived at the main post office on time. The driver had decided to bring his wife along for the trip. She was a very obese woman. Mary figured that most of the students better sit on the opposite side so that the bus didn't tip over! She quickly made a note of this in her journal. Then she said goodbye to her father, and happily boarded the bus eager to return to civilization.

Chapter Thirteen

Anxiety about apartment living

When Mary returned to school she was surprised, and relieved that no plans had been made to put her in the apartment yet. Last spring Ms. Standish told her at the end of school review that she wanted her to try at least one semester in a supervised apartment program. Mary didn't want to do it, and said so.

Mary was told by Arena, the young house mother on duty in Elliot Cottage that she was in a single room upstairs with the other girls. Mary unpacked, and wondered what classes she would be in this year. She was certain that most of them would be of the vocational variety. Because her curiosity about the apartment was getting the better of her, she crept back downstairs, and went to the back wing of Elliot. Finding the door to the apartment unlocked, she went in, and looked around. To the right was a small kitchen. Mary thought it a good sign that the refrigerator and cupboards were entirely empty. To the left was a small living room. Straight ahead was a bathroom. On either side of this were two bedrooms. Mary didn't wonder what bedroom she would be in because she had no intention of living in there. She wanted to be a regular student like everyone else.

That evening there was a cook-out in back of Elliot, and Moulton Cottages. Everyone was invited. The assistant director, Mr. Lasorda, and his wife, and kids were there. Among the many students was Abigail, Mary's former roommate. A loud boy in his late teens, named John was singing like a lunatic inside Moulton. Mary could hear him from the lawn. His nick name was Kause. He drank tons of coffee, was fascinated with people's watches, and asked questions, then apologized for asking. Because he got lost one day on his way to the North building, he was sometimes referred to as the "Lost Kause". He was a friend of Lorena, and Steve, two students who were going together, and had included Mary as their friend last spring. Mary was happy to see them. They all had a lot in common. In fact the only two things they didn't have in common were that Mary liked to watch science fiction shows, and they didn't. Also they didn't like Perkins as much as Mary did. They felt that it had changed since they were in lower school. People in charge didn't seem to care as much, or take the time to listen the way they used to. Lorena seemed most effected by this, and it made her cynical at times.

By the next morning all of the students had returned from vacation, and were ready to begin school. The school day would consist of eleven periods just like the previous year, but lunch time was going to be shorter, as a result the day would be a little longer. The school day would begin ten minutes earlier, and end twenty minutes later. As happy as Mary was to be back, she wasn't happy about this. After classes ended students would be expected to choose at least one elective to sign up for, such as music, arts & crafts etc. Because of this the school day would now end at Five O'clock! Still Mary preferred this to being at home. Of all the teachers, Mr. Ackerman, Mary's English teacher agreed with the students that Ms. Standish was expecting too much from them. Mary found out what her schedule would be. She started off every day except Tuesday with Home Room, run by Miss. Jackman. Tuesday began with Chapel, run by Mr. Babcock, the director. She no longer had General Metals, or Sex Ed. On Mondays she had Career Ed with Ms. Futon, English with Mr. Ackerman, Guidance Counseling with Mr. Flannigan, Home Ec with Mrs. Salmon, Math with Mr. Quake and Gym with Mr. Regan. Tuesdays she had Community Experience (field trips) with Ms. Herman, Crafts with Mr. Walsh, Math, and in the afternoon she worked with the school janitor, Pat as part of her work experience program. On Wednesday Mary found that she had English, Food Service, Home EC, Math, and in the afternoon she had two new classes. Production Industries with Mr. Bowdoin, and Family Life, which was a basic psychology class taught by Ms. Herman. Thursday Mary spent the whole morning down at the Northeast building in her Food Service class. She enjoyed preparing food with Ron, the cook. She liked washing the dishes, pots, and pans, and cleaning the cafeteria. In the afternoon she had Math, then Arts & Crafts. Fridays Mary had Mobility, but not with Kathy this time. Instead she had Miss Richardson Another student was in this class with her now. She was a junior named Lynette. She talked constantly about nothing important, and was known for being a hypochondriac. Mary soon earned the right to not only go to Watertown Square without supervision; she could now go to the mall on her own. After Mobility she had Family life. This was run by Ms. Herman. Although Lynette was in this class too, so was Mary's friend, Lorena. Later she had English, then Math. The day ended with Senior Seminar, run by Ms. Standish. Mary, Lorena, and Steve were the least enthusiastic about this. They found it a waste of time. Ms. Standish ran it, but she never seemed to take people's suggestions; or complaints seriously. Every other Friday Assembly was held for the students in the Junior/Senior High Program. On alternate Fridays they had Coffee hour, but the seniors had to be in charge of it. Mary enjoyed helping out, but she hated to be in charge of anything. She had other things on her mind, like dreading the apartment program, and being asked by her case worker from Rhode Island if she wanted to go, and be interviewed by NBC. They wanted former students to come forward, and talk about what it was like being at Eden wood School. Mary having been there nearly five years could have told them a lot! However she was afraid of possible repercussions, and she felt over whelmed about having cameras trained on her. She took a few days to think about it. She even called her father, who thought it best for her to concentrate on her studies. This was all she needed to hear. She called her case worker back, and said that she couldn't go through with it.

Mary's friend, Sue, Ms. Standish's secretary, was also working part time as a house mother on Saturdays. She was in Elliot, which made Mary happy. She liked Sue. On the first Saturday after school started Mary waited until evening, and then she sneaked in to the Elliot apartment, and dumped a gallon of milk all over the floor. Then she cut the cords in back of the refrigerator, and stove. She figured that the damage would cause more of a set back in getting the program started. Then she went to watch Voyage to the bottom of the sea. Sue watched it with her, getting up to check on other students during commercials.

As Mary became better friends with Lorena, and Steve, she found her taste in music changing. They hated Rock, and Disco. They always listened to oldies, and were fond of WNTN, a local radio station from Newton that played oldies. Soon Mary turned against Rock, and Disco, and listened to oldies. She also began to explore old music from the Eighteenth, and Nineteenth centuries. Because of this, and her obsession with Admiral Nelson, she found herself being teased unmercifully by many of the boys in the Junior/Senior High Program. At first she was able to ignore them, but as time went on she began answering back, then on some occasions getting in to fights with her tormentors. She was reprimanded for this, and sent to see Mr. Flannigan; her new guidance counselor for some extra counseling.

Room changes were made. Mary found herself back in her old room from the year before. Happily she grabbed her old bed. Her room mates were Prissy, Gossipy Pearl, now Fifteen, who was now paranoid as well (she thought the boys were going to kill her, either through physical assault, or poison), and a new girl, named Kama. She was Fourteen, and wore small, square glasses. She didn't like living at school. Mary once over heard her father warning one of the house mothers to keep an eye on his daughter because she was threatening to run away. As unhappy as Kama was, she managed to keep everyone entertained with her jokes, silly songs, and riddles. She could also make animals by folding paper, or napkins many different ways. Mary didn't mind having Pearl for a roommate, and was happy to have Kama because of her funny personality. She still saw, and spoke to her old spying partner, Beth, but they had drifted apart since the previous spring.

On the last Friday of September some of the students from the Junior/Senior High, and Secondary Service Programs were invited to spend the night at the marina of a minister who lived out in West Yarmouth. The next day they would go sailing, and have a cook -out afterward. Mary was of coarse one of the students who signed up. While Mary was packing

Pearl came upstairs, and asked if anyone had pulled a knife on her, or Kama, or tried to strangle them. When Mary and Kama laughed, Pearl wondered aloud if they were involved in the plot to kill her. She wanted Kama to start staying up at night to guard their room. Mary knew that the boys jokingly claiming that they were going to kill Pearl were adding to her problems. Everyone talked excitedly in the van, as they rode to West Yarmouth. Mary closed her eyes, and imagined Admiral Nelson telling Captain Crane that he invited his niece, and some of her classmates to visit his marina, and do some sailing. At one point someone mentioned the Elliot Apartment. "Your going to be in there, aren't you, Mary?" "I guess so" murmured Mary reluctantly. She imagined the admiral looking worried that his little niece was going to betray him by growing up. "I won't!" she mumbled to herself determinedly. Everyone slept two to a yacht. Mary was stuck with Anna, a short, stocky girl from Secondary Services, who snored loudly. Soon Mary was able to focus on the gentle swaying of the yacht, and the sound of ropes hitting the poles outside. They got up at Six thirty to find it foggy outside. They had breakfast in the minister's house. He, his wife, and two little girls lived there year round. The weather cleared later in the morning, and they all went sailing, three students, and an experienced sailor to a yacht. Mr. Stocky was one of the teachers who came on the trip. He was on Mary's yacht. Because there were no other students with them, the owner let her not only learn how to steer the rudder, she only had to share it with Mr. Stocky occasionally. They sailed for five, and half hours. Afterward they had a cook- out, and Mary was able to watch Voyage to the bottom of the sea that evening back at school. The following day Mary took up a new hobby. She wasn't sure why, but she started going around recording people's conversations. She recorded a rowdy conversation between some of the big shots. Then she recorded one of Pearl's freaky discussions with her friends. Next she recorded an intense argument between Mindy, and Lynette. It got so out of hand that Mindy had to be tackled by Dennis, and another boy. Mary sneaked away realizing that she would have to practice shutting off her recorder quietly so that she didn't get caught.

On Monday the first of October the Pope came to Boston. Students who wanted to go hear him were taken to Boston. Afternoon classes were canceled because of this. Mary didn't mind that the Pope was also being aired on TV until it was time for little house on the prairie. Then she became impatient with the whole thing!

Mary was tired of her Community Experience Class opting to go to Watertown Square for coffee. Every time she suggested one of the many historical sites that Boston had to offer her classmates said that they weren't history buffs. Apparently Ms. Herman wasn't either. She must have enjoyed coffee as much as Kause did. He, Lorena, and Steve were in this class with Mary. On their way down to the square one Tuesday they ran in to one of the mobility teachers. Mary couldn't stand the man! She had an altercation with him on the stairs one day, and was still angry at him, but Ms. Herman liked him. Sue, Ms Standish's secretary, and Mary's advocate, wanted her to try to work things out with him. She was arranging a meeting to accomplish this. Once on a Saturday evening when the students were eating at the Northeast building, the cook, a middle aged man with a mustache, and beard scolded Mary for arguing with him for not giving her more olives. When she answered back he threatened to smack her face. Here was a man who looked just like the foster father, who molested her three years earlier, even saying the same thing he used to say. It was too much! Mary swore at him. Then she threw her orange at him. Later Sue made her go back, and apologize to the cook. Reluctantly she returned, and offered a belligerent apology, then ran out before Sue could stop her. As a result she wasn't very confident about this meeting Sue was planning.

Mary learned that Diana, a tough girl, who used to be her friend, but turned against her last spring, was over in Mount Auburn Hospital because she over dosed on drugs. Mary supposed that the girl had grown tired of hurting the weaker students, and had decided to hurt herself instead. At least her little niece, Mandy wouldn't have to put up with her as her baby sitter for a while. Diana often bragged about not taking any crap from her little niece. Once she claimed to have smacked Mandy across her mouth for giving her back talk. Laughingly she said that Mandy had stolen a couple of her pain pills, but her mouth still ached. As Mary went to buy some batteries for her tape recorder she found herself wondering why the girl was so mean.

Mary was upset with the changes that were being done to the school. They were planning to replace one of the spiral staircases in every cottage with a straight staircase. They were planning to modernize all the kitchens; and bathrooms too. They were already covering the front corridor of the main building with paneling. Most of the old fashioned furniture in all the buildings had been replaced with modern furniture. Fluorescent lights were going to be put in all the cottages. To Mary Perkins was a beautiful, historical place that should be preserved, not made ugly with sterile, cold modern features. Couldn't anything retain it's historical charm anymore? She often complained about this. Mary supposed that if she retuned to Perkins ten years later she wouldn't even recognize the school. It was bad enough that the campus already contained three modern buildings. The Northeast building, the North building, and the director's house, which looked like something from outer space!

Mary went home on the second weekend of October. On Saturday she and her father went to a flea market run by The Involved Tax Payers of Coventry. Mr. Sullivan belonged to this organization. One of his friends, a good natured, middle aged woman, named Pauline had invited him to join. She was out going, and had an infectious laugh. She, and her husband Claude, a quiet, easy going man, had three children, two of which were grown. Mr. Sullivan looked forward to visiting this couple, which he did often. One of the other women in this organization brought her Thirteen year old daughter to the flea market. She was mildly mentally challenged, and was small for her age. She spent most of the afternoon running around the room wailing like a siren just for the fun of it.

Once back at school Mary heard Kause's booming voice from down the hall. During supper she, and a girl, named Laurie giggled, and acted silly together. They both wound up with the hiccups. Laurie was always talking about Sue. Once when Laurie was feeling nauseous, Sue grabbed her arm, and rushed her to the bathroom saying "Oh run run run to the bathroom, and don't forget to flush!" in a silly sing song tone of voice. If Laurie was telling the truth, Sue must have started to find it stressful working as a house parent on weekends, as well as working for Ms. Standish during the week. Mary noticed that she had recently taken up smoking. Mary wondered if she was aware that Kasey, the princess, and her boy friend, Dennis spent most of their free time making out on the couch in the Elliot living room. The couch faced away from the door, obscuring anyone's view of the people on it. They spent the previous year doing this. Mary felt like telling the boys who teased her about the admiral to go spy on, and then tease Kasey, and Dennis instead. A girl on campus had recently given birth to a baby boy. Her parents were taking care of him during the week. Now the girl had to attend classes with the father, who no longer cared about her. Yet people still thought that Mary's obsession with the admiral, and the long Victorian dresses that she sometimes wore were worth making an issue of.

Finally Mary couldn't keep her secret about the vandalism in the apartment anymore. She told Sue what she had done. She was tired of feeling guilt ridden. She had been snapping at people, and being very impatient. Afraid that she would revert back to acting up as she had at Eden wood, she talked to Sue, who then talked to Ms. Standish. It was decided that Mary would have to pay for the damage. The cost was thirty dollars.

Because Lynette was absent Mary had a fun mobility lesson with Miss Richardson. They took the subway in to Boston. Soon she would be cleared to take the subway on her own. She found this exciting! She wasn't surprised that Lynette was absent. Lynette was absent a lot. She claimed to be ill much of the time.

At the end of October Mary, Lynette, and Jolene moved in to the Elliot apartment. (The night before Pearl, who was still acting paranoid, told Mary to let her know if she noticed anything strange happening in the apartment.) A woman named Barbara was to be their supervisor. It was her job to take them grocery shopping, teach them about budgets, help them prepare meals, and make sure that they kept the place clean. Mary ended up rooming with Jolene, who didn't get along with Lynette. While Lynette often avoided classes she didn't like, she was totally enthusiastic about living in the apartment. She eagerly did everything that was required of her. Jolene tended to sometimes shirk responsibility like Mary. One night as they both lay in bed pretending to be asleep, Barbara, and Lynette, who knew that they weren't asleep, yelled at them from the kitchen about their lousy attitudes. After this Jolene began to show some enthusiasm, but Mary continued to do only the minimum of what was expected of her, and usually had an attitude about it. Soon she started taking her blanket, and pillow, and sleeping on the couch out in the living room of the cottage. (Kasey and Dennis's couch) When she told Lorena about this, her friend joined her in what they called "The secret place ". Mary let Lorena take the couch while she slept on the thick rug. They talked until they fell asleep. No one knew about this, or if they did, they ignored it.

Mary wasn't thrilled with Production Industries, and she noticed that her classmates John, Lorena, Steve, and Diana didn't like it much either. Mr. Bowdoin had them working on wooden games which would later be sold. Everyone was supposed to go around during the week showing people a model, and asking how much they would pay for it. John was the only one who did this assignment. The class was made to accompany Mr. Bowdoin to his office so that John could call the lumber company about the wooden toys. Lorena stayed behind, causing Mr. Bowdoin to go back for her. As John was making the call, Mary noticed Lorena edging toward the door. When she looked again Lorena was gone. Mary stifled a laugh. Back in the classroom Lorena and Mary started clowning around. John gave up his "Good boy act ", and joined in. Lorena kept taking the handle of the vice, and saying "Mr. Bowdoin is nothing but a-"then she let the handle go with a bang! Mary grabbed a hammer, raised it above her head, and said "Mr. Bowdoin is nothing but a-"then she brought the hammer down with a bang! John had a piece of sand paper. He rubbed it rapidly on the table, saying that it sounded just like the voice of one of his other teachers. He pretended to have a conversation, talking in his voice, then answering with the sand paper. Steve thought the whole thing was funny, but Diana looked disgusted, and accused them of acting like Ten year olds. No one cared. After all her friend, Joe kicked a slowly passing car a few days earlier just because he felt like it. When the angry driver demanded an explanation he simply shrugged, and said he didn't like the car. He was always getting in to trouble which didn't make Diana like him any less. Apparently there was a double standard here, and Mary and her friends weren't going to be taken in by it.

The Halloween party was a flop!. Some students dressed in costume. Mary was a pirate, and she helped Pearl dress up as a boy. (Mary wished she wasn't so prissy.). The costume might have suited her.) After supper candy and popcorn was put out for students to help themselves to. Over in the main building there was a haunted house set up. Aside from this nothing much happened. It didn't feel much like Halloween. The previous year the house parents organized a big party for the students. Everyone played party games. Then they were taken on a treasure hunt. Afterward ghost stories were told, as everyone ate snacks. Almost all the students were in costumes. This year it felt like the Jack o lanterns were in mourning! Where was the festive spirit?

Mary and Kause simultaneously resigned as members of the senior class, thereby joining Lorena, and Steve, as nonmembers. When Diana found out she yelled at Steve down in the gym, and accused him, and Lorena of influencing Mary. This made Mary furious! Lorena, and Steve had turned out to be better friends to her then Diana ever was. Why should she care if Mary hung out with people who Diana thought were dragging her down? She had turned against Mary last spring. Mary resolved to be even closer to Lorena and Steve then ever! She hung out with them more then she was in the apartment. Lynette's constant chatter got on her nerves, Jolene had a maddening habit of calling out "Who goes there?" every time Mary, or Lynette entered, and boys were always in there, sometimes the mean ones. Mary couldn't have much privacy. She started taking showers upstairs with the regular students. Barbara wouldn't let the girls use the toaster, or the kettle without supervision. She always took these with her when she left for the night. What did she think they would do, burn the apartment down? So the girls used a pan to heat water for coffee, or tea.

Pat, the janitor had taken a liking to Mary as she worked with him on Tuesday afternoons. One Sunday he invited her over to his house to meet his wife, and kids. They lived in Waltham. They were a good Irish Catholic family. They took Mary to Mass with them. Then they all returned to the house for a Pre-Thanksgiving dinner. Afterward they watched TV together. Only two of Pat's five kids still lived at home. John was Twelve, and Katarina, who was mentally challenged, was in her twenties. The only member of the family who didn't welcome Mary was their big dog, Peppy. He didn't like strangers.

School ended at noon on the third Wednesday in November. Everyone went home for Thanksgiving Vacation. When Mr. Sullivan picked Mary up at the bus stop in Providence he told her that Father Hoyle had a chore for the two of them to do. Apparently he even said that he was glad that Mary was home for vacation. Discovering that she still felt fond of Father Hoyle, Mary happily helped her father saw wood for the church. The next day was Thanksgiving. Mary and her father had turkey, stuffing, yams, and cranberry sauce, followed by pumpkin pie. The only thing that bothered her was that no one else was there. They spent the holiday with only each other, but once the TV was put on Mary felt better.

On Saturday Mary and her father visited Bradley Hospital. The grounds looked the same. Mary found this reassuring. The inside of the building was much the same as well. However, the two girls units had been merged in to one. She still sometimes missed the three years she spent there. She had been with the Pixies, who were the youngest of the girls. (All the units were named like this). With Mary there were five pixies. Now all the girls, little, or big were in the Debs unit. Miss Ribera and another woman were in charge of the ten, or eleven girls that day. Mary was happy to see, and talk to Miss Ribera. She hadn't changed much in eight years. Although most of the girls seemed fairly normal, some of the boys at Bradley had some degree of autism. Bradley was now accepting the more disturbed children to be residential patients. Miss Ribera laughed as she recalled an afternoon when she took the Pixies to an amusement park. Mary got lost. When Miss Ribera found her, she was running after a woman, who looked just like her from behind. As Mary and her father were leaving, she saw some of the autistic patients going downstairs for supper. They were with drawn, and had to be urged to move along. The youngest of them, a little boy with blonde hair, wearing overalls, seemed totally absorbed in his own world. The unit leader, a young woman with long, brown hair kept yelling at him to come down the stairs. He stopped frequently to stare vacantly at the wall. In the dinning room the woman slapped his hands for touching something on the table. He didn't cry, or even look up. Mary disliked the woman. How was yelling at, and slapping a kid supposed to make him come out of his world? She figured that it would make him more with drawn, and reluctant to join a hostile environment.

On Monday Mary had Career Ed. She was becoming quieter these days, and her teachers didn't like it. Both Miss Futon and Miss Stately were always getting after her about this. It only made her more stubborn about it, which made them more irritated with her. Another student in the class was having problems too. Lynette, who was in the Elliot apartment with Mary wanted to become a water ballerina. Both teachers informed her that this goal wasn't practical. They wanted her to choose something else. Lynette sat there looking like her dream had been ripped from her, and dashed upon the floor!

Mary was making a lot of progress in Mobility. After she took the bus, then the subway, and met Miss Richardson at the Boston Museum of Science she was told that she would probably complete the course by the end of the semester. Mary felt proud. She loved taking the subways, and rarely got lost. English and Craft Class were successful for her too. As usual Math Class was the only obstacle. Kause made it worse by bragging that he knew the answers. He couldn't understand why Mary didn't. Admiral Nelson was slowly being replaced by Queen Victoria, and Benjamin Disraeli, a former prime minister. Because Mary was imagining them there in the classroom, Kause's comments were harder to tolerate. Mary felt humiliated. The next day she cut Math Class because Mr. Quake was absent. She pretended not to know that someone was filling in for him. In Production Industries Mary and Lorena felt so bored, and resentful that they both proceeded to count to Sixteen Hundred. It drove Mr. Bowdoin, and Fawn crazy! When Diana called them a couple of babies Lorena stopped counting long enough to say "Better to be a baby then a snob!" Diana lost her temper, and yelled at Mary, and Lorena. They ignored her, and continued to count. Later Diana told Mary to stop hanging around with Lorena, and Steve because they acted immature when they were together. Mary disregarded her. Why should she have cared anyway? She was a bully, who could turn on a person for little or no reason.

Over the weekend Pat, the janitor took Mary to Mass with his family. Then they went bowling together. Mary enjoyed it. That night she had a terrible dream. In it a man crept in to the Elliot apartment, and stabbed Mary. When he left she got up, and went outside. Two students were talking. They said they heard that Mary had been stabbed to death by an intruder. Mary tried to talk to the students. Even when she shoved them, and stepped on their feet they weren't aware of her presence. She realized that she was a ghost! As she slowly walked toward the main building she felt afraid, and lonely. The sun was out, and she could feel the warmth of its rays on the back of her lowered head. When she looked up she saw a man in the distance. He was coming toward her. Mary couldn't see his features, or tell exactly what he was wearing, but she could sense that he was a good man, who meant her no harm. He took her hand, and led her toward the main building, but she didn't know if they entered it, or passed it because she woke up. While the dream was fresh in Mary's mind, she had the distinct feeling that the man was leading her far away from Perkins.

Something was wrong with Lynette. Mary wondered if she was taking drugs, or perhaps was having a nervous break down. She had always acted a bit odd, but lately she seemed to be losing control of herself. Everything was going along in the usual way in Career Ed. Miss Futon was helping Kause, Lorena, Steve. Miss Stately was working with Lynette, and Mary. Lynette was ignoring the fact that she hadn't taken lessons as a water ballerina when she was growing up. Miss Stately pressed the issue. Suddenly Lynette jumped to her feet screaming! She threw a book at the teacher. As both teachers approached her she struck out at them, and had to be restrained. As she was taken away her hysterical screams echoed in the corridor making the school sound like an insane asylum! Later Mary heard her telling Mindy what she did. She claimed that she wasn't going to apologize. Later in Math class she hollered at Mr. Quake: grabbed her books, and ran from the room. Mary wondered if Ms. Standish's rigorous schedule was getting to her. There was a lot of tension among the students. Two of them had recently been suspended for violent behavior. Mary supposed the pressure was already getting to her. She didn't like this school year as much as she liked the last one. Her moodiness over it sometimes even affected her favorite classes. In Mobility Miss Richardson scolded her for lagging behind when they were taking the subway to Logan Airport. Mary wanted to go on the trip. She liked the idea of becoming familiar with an airport, but she felt cross because she and Lynette weren't allowed to have lunch that day. (The previous year this wouldn't have bothered her much) So she stalked along behind Lynette, and Miss Richardson sulking. Finally the teacher gave her some quarters at Park St, and told her to go back to school because she was sick of her mood. Mary felt no regrets. They would have only continued to snap at each other. So she headed back to school. However she stopped at Friendly's, and had a Banana Split first. This cheered her up a little.

In Senior Seminar Mary was able to read a whole chapter of a history book before Ms. Standish stopped her. In disgust Mary threw the book under her chair, and glared at the supervisor. Soon after this Ms. Standish stopped her from drawing, and told her to write down what they were talking about. Mary wrote sloppily. She told Ms. Standish that she was going to throw the paper away later. Diana lost her temper, and told Mary to shut up! She did shut up… after telling Diana that she hoped her face exploded! She hoped that she didn't become like Lynette. She felt angry, over looked, and unimportant to the people in charge. She couldn't take criticism anymore either. The boys continued to tease her about the admiral, and were often allowed in the apartment by Lynette, and Jolene. Mary couldn't stand it! After Senior Seminar was over Miss Jackman invited the seniors to her house for a Christmas party. Everyone except Lorena went. She went home for the weekend. Mary stayed near Steve, and talked to him the whole time. The food was good, but the hostess was awful. Miss Jackman banged in to Mary, and yelled at her for being in the way. Later when she and Steve wanted to return to school Miss Jackman said she would call a cab soon. When Mary reminded her ten minutes later Miss Jackman snapped at her. Mary snapped right back and found herself being yelled at in front of everyone! On Monday morning Miss Jackman had her revenge. Mary was one minute late for Homeroom, and was made to stand in the corridor. This was done to Kause frequently. Mary noticed that some of the other seniors weren't punished when they were late. Two of the seniors, who were angry on Miss Jackman's behalf, teased Mary to such an extent that she over turned all the tables in the snack bar, and threw chairs at her tormentors. One of them threatened to beat her up if she didn't clean up the mess. She ran out of the snack bar.

Mary was glad that she stopped recording people's conversations. Two other students were caught doing this, and had to go see Ms. Standish about it. Finally a meeting was held over in Moulton Cottage. Students from Elliot had to attend also. Ken the house parent over there reprimanded everyone for not respecting each other's privacy. He said that everyone in the JR/S program had rotten attitudes, and he was sick of all the fighting, and stealing that was going on. Mary wondered if Kause was going to be reprimanded for fighting in the smoking room the day before. Dennis and his buddies were teasing him about all the coffee he drank. Kause lost his temper. He punched one boy, pushed another, and when Dennis tried to tackle him, Kause slammed his head in to the coffee table! Dennis's head was bleeding. If Kause was punished Mary hoped that Dennis was punished for starting the whole thing. Ken didn't mention this. He warned the pot smokers among them that they better stop what they were doing. "You know who you are, and you will be caught. The penalty will be harsh." He also mentioned an incident where a student was caught trying to steal a tape recorder from a teacher. Mary knew about this. John, from her Production Industries class was caught by one of his other teachers stealing a tape recorder from a classroom. Ken finished by saying that there was going to be a lot of changes in the rules when everyone returned from Christmas Vacation. "Some of you might not want to hurry back to school. You won't like what you find when you return." After the meeting ended Mary heard Ken's angry voice coming from someone's tape recorder. They were half way down the corridor. Mary couldn't see who it was, but they were very reckless.

On Friday, the twenty first of December everyone was dismissed for Christmas Vacation. The night before Mary attended the last of the three concerts that were held every year. She loved the Hand bell concert that was held in the museum area before the audience went in to Dwight Hall to hear the Upper, and Lower school choruses sing. The bell ringers and singers all wore red robes. Dwight Hall was decorated with Christmas wreathes, and other ornaments. Mary wished she had recorded the concert, it was that good! Now as she boarded the bus bound for RI she hoped that she wouldn't regret returning to school in January. Maybe Ken was exaggerating, or maybe Ms. Standish would have such a nice vacation that she wouldn't want to crack the whip when she came back… maybe.

Chapter Fourteen

Tensions mount at school

Mary was hoping for a less predictable Christmas Vacation. On her first day home she and her father helped put up the Christmas lights at Saint John & Paul's. Mary was very cold, but refused to admit it. Being cold made her irritable. She hid this too. When they were finished Mr. Sullivan took his daughter with him, and went to visit The Involved Tax Payers of Coventry. Mary had met these people back in October. Because she didn't know much about what they did, they seemed like a country club to her. However, she was glad to get out of the cold, and have some coffee.

The next day after Mass Mary and her father decorated eight wreathes. They visited three different cemeteries to distribute them to Mr. Sullivan's dead relatives. This took up most of the day. Mary, who had held in her boredom, and frustration, hoped for some privacy, and time to herself. After their grave yard adventure they went to get pizza for supper. A few of her father's friends met him in the parking lot. When Mary came out with the pizza they were still there talking. They were an elderly couple, who wanted Mary, and her father to visit them the following day. This was exactly what they did. Mary groaned inwardly. Her father sometimes stayed at a friend's house for three, or four hours! This visit wasn't as tiresome as the others though. Myrtle, a heavy set woman served Mr. Sullivan, and his daughter cake. While her husband, Fred sat, and smiled pleasantly she talked about how people's moods can be affected by the moon. She mentioned a man she knew, who was usually very helpful, and good natured. Then when the moon became full he became mean, and selfish. Myrtle claimed that not everyone was effected by the cycles of the moon, only people who are slightly, or not so slightly unbalanced. Mary figured that this might explain the unpredictable behavior of some of her class mates.

At the start of the week Mr. Sullivan's friend, Jim came over for a visit. They sat out in the kitchen drinking coffee, and smoking. Mr. Sullivan puffed on his cigar while Jim chain smoked cigarettes. Mary was left to draw, and watch TV. She liked it when the sad, unkempt, unemployed man visited.

Mary didn't have to celebrate Christmas with just her father. Jim came over again. After they returned from Mass he showed up looking like he just woke up. Mary thought it was funny how Jim was always on time for meals, but he hardly ever got to work on time. Maybe this was why he found himself unemployed so often. Sometimes her father had to go over to his motel room to wake him up in the morning when he had a job. He had a hearty appetite. They all had turkey, stuffing, yams, and cranberry sauce. In spite of all the eating he did, Jim never stopped talking to Mr. Sullivan.

The next day Mary was allowed to visit a park that she used to go to during her three years at Bradley. They didn't stay as long as she hoped they would, and she came to the conclusion that her father never really wanted to go in the first place. He became angry with her when she wanted to clean up the litter. Well why wouldn't he? After all, it was her favorite childhood place, not his! Later Father Hoyle came over for supper. Mary was delighted, and welcomed him enthusiastically. She hoped he would hug her, and when he didn't she felt a foolish lump in her throat. Why couldn't he act like a doting Uncle toward her? He was polite to her, but he mostly talked to her father. She felt totally disappointed, and unimportant.

During the next few days Mary tagged along with her father when he visited his friends. Finally on the last day of December she found herself over at Dr. Early's farm, in rural Coventry. Charlene wasn't home. So Mary stood outside of Dr. Early's garage blushing, and trying to hide every time a car pulled up. Her father was in the garage working on a greasy, old machine with the elderly country loving doctor. She hated being where she was. All she saw were trees, fields, dirt roads, tractors, and old jeeps. She decided to hide behind the garage so that visitors wouldn't stare at her. Later at home Mary played some records she had bought at a flea market the other day. Jim came over for supper again. Mary was worried about Ken, the house parent's warning, but she still couldn't wait to return to school. She didn't belong in a hick town visiting the elderly, and attending Mass every day. She was willing to take her chances at school.

The next morning not many people were in Church. Mr. Sullivan said that a lot of them must have stayed up celebrating the New Year. He thought this was foolish. He believed it made more sense to get up on New Year's Day, and yell "Happy New Year!" instead of staying up after midnight. Mary supposed she agreed. She was just eager to get out of Coventry, and go back to Perkins. She wondered what kind of year 1980 would turn out to be. The fact that she would no longer be a student after June made her very nervous.

When Mary entered Elliot she found everything covered in saw dust, and pieces of plaster. Mary Lu, the new house parent said that the construction workers were narrowing all the doorways. This made no sense to Mary. The changes being made to the cottages were supposed to be for the sake of safety, and convenience. What if there was a fire and everyone had to get out in a hurry? She could imagine students getting stuck in those narrow doorways. That would surely start a panic! Were the work men senile?! Mary went over to the snack bar, and was nearly over come by a foul stench! Someone told her that the refrigerator was broken, and all the food was spoiled. The person who told her this opened the refrigerator, and ran outside to throw up. Mary wondered what other unpleasant changes she would find. She continued to sneak out of the apartment at night, and sleep on the couch in the living room. Lorena joined her. They talked about vacation until they drifted off to sleep. Students, mostly boys were still teasing her about the admiral, and her choice of music. She didn't even like the admiral anymore because she couldn't imagine him supporting, and comforting her over the teasing, Mary found herself not only losing interest in him, but actually starting to hate him. She began to see him as being critical of her for being the kind of person, who was teased a lot, another wards as someone who was different. She not only felt different, she also felt ugly with her thick, coarse hair that was often unmanageable and large front teeth. Her clumsiness added to her low opinion of herself. Because of this she really didn't need all the teasing. Two of her worst tormentors were popular, responsible seniors. They lived off campus. They shared an apartment in Boston, and took public transportation to, and from school each day. They couldn't wait to graduate, and get on with being adults. They were scornful of Lorena, Steve, Kause, and especially Mary. They saw them as babies. So Mary was very suspicious when these two boys invited Kause over to their apartment for dinner one night. She feared that they were going to play some mean trick on him. Kause wasn't suspicious, and was looking forward to going. Mary hoped that he knocked them both out if they tried to pull anything. One thing Mary felt she had control over was her ability to prevent herself from being lazy. When she started getting in to a rut where she didn't help out with chores, she became discontent with herself, and started making herself do more then her share. Because of this ability Mary felt certain that she could get a job working on campus after she graduated. Her guidance counselor promised to help her make plans for this. She already had a part time job at Howe Press. This was a factory, located at the back of the campus. They made brailers there. Since the first week of January Mary worked there on Tuesday afternoons, and all day Thursday. She loved it, and hoped to either stay there permanently, or work as a maid in one of the cottages after graduation. Her father knew of her plans, and acknowledged that she was happier at Perkins where everything was familiar to her. She promised to come home every other weekend as she had been doing all along. In the mean time she worked hard at Howe Press. She loved the people there, especially the men. They talked with her, and joked around with her. Larry, the foreman was very nice. No matter what kind of friction she was experiencing up at school she could always count on the guys at Howe Press to cheer her up.

By the third week in January Mary was allowed to leave the apartment, and move back upstairs with the other girls. Although she had won this victory by being stead fast against Ms. Standish's reasons for her to stay in the apartment, Mary did lose something. Ms. Standish informed her that it was now against school policy for hired help to live on campus. This was a real blow for Mary. Mr. Flannigan, her guidance counselor said that he would help her locate nearby places that had live-in positions in Historical schools, or homes. His sympathy helped to make up for Ms. Standish's "cold hard facts" attitude.

Mary completed the course in Mobility. She received a card from Miss Richardson stating that she was cleared to travel anywhere independently. Toward the end of January all the seniors were made to take their S.A.T tests. The tests covered everything, and lasted for several days. Mary found some of it interesting, but some of it was very confusing, and frustrating. One morning when she was puzzling over the math section she was swinging her feet. Her desk was over in the corner. It faced a door that was never used. Her feet were hitting this door, as she swung them. It was a back entrance to Miss Futon's classroom next door. Suddenly this particular teacher rushed in to the testing room. She hollered at Mary in front of everyone. Mary was so angry that she drew a picture of herself shooting Miss Futon. The teacher looked so funny with her arms raised in the air, and a shocked look on her face, as Mary pulled the trigger. When the bell rang for lunch Mary sneaked in to the classroom next door, and left the picture on Miss Futon's desk. The next day Sue made Mary apologize for what she did. She not only felt no remorse, she found it difficult to keep a straight face as she said she was sorry. Miss Futon admitted that she was being very hard on Mary because she saw her slipping in to her shell, and didn't like it.

One evening when Mary was on her way to the gym she saw a group of people walking ahead of her. As she passed them one of them called her name. It turned out to be Diane, a staff member from The Boston Center for Blind Children. Another staff member was with her. Mary didn't recognize her. She asked how David was doing. To her surprise, Diane pulled a tall, blonde boy forward, and said "He's right here." She told him to say Hi. He mumbled a greeting. He looked just as he did seven years earlier, only he was taller then Mary. She realized that he was nearly fourteen. Along with David, there were some other familiar faces. Tommy, Kate, and Danny were there too. Kate, who was the same age as David was tall, and thin like him. She was totally blind, and still couldn't talk. Danny was quite short for a boy of thirteen. He now wore glasses, and a hearing aid. He was hyper, and couldn't stop jumping around. Tommy was the oldest. He was sixteen and wore a Boy Scout uniform. Mary wondered how he managed to fit in when he still laid on the floor every chance he got, and talked like a parrot, repeating everything that was said to him. Like Mary, they were at Perkins to go bowling. As she bowled her three strings she kept an eye on the little group from Boston. Tommy slid from his seat to lie on the floor frequently, and was made to get up. Mary observed David the most. He had always been her favorite. He was no longer as hyper as he had been when he was six. He talked now, but usually when prompted to. Diane said that he was a quiet, gentle boy, who liked to swing in the hammock at the rear of the play room. He was going to be transferred to another school soon, but Diane didn't know where. After they all bowled Mary followed them over to the snack bar. They all had something to eat. Danny hopped around the room. Tommy lay on the floor, and Kate sat looking like she was a million miles away. David kept yelling "Red Sox!" repeatedly. His speech was slightly slurred. It was Diane, who told her what he was saying. To Mary it had sounded like "Red Thox!" He obviously had a speech impediment. Mary wondered if this was why he wouldn't talk at the school when she was there. The staff claimed that he could speak a little, but refused. Diane told Mary that David was receiving speech lessons because even now he was only speaking in two or three word sentences. They departed leaving Mary to think about all she had seen, and heard that evening. She wished Beth had been around. She would have liked to see Diane, and the others.

The next morning Mary had more to think about besides David and the school. During the few minutes before Homeroom started the boys were teasing Mary about the long dresses she sometimes wore now. They also teased her about listening to classical music. When they turned to the subject of the admiral the teasing became down right perverted.. Some of them didn't even belong in the room! There was an assortment of them, some sophomores, some juniors, and of coarse seniors. She found herself answering back. As the teasing continued, becoming worse, she became violent. As she hurled Braille books at the boys she heard Lorena, and Steve imploring her to ignore them. It was too late for that. Mary was totally riled! When she ran out of books she hurled heavy braillers. One of them missed one boy's head by an inch. At this Dennis rushed over, and punched Mary. She flew at him, and beat her fists against his chest. When he grabbed her wrists she kicked him repeatedly in the groin! Suddenly a boy, named Richard announced that Miss Jackman was coming. Everyone scattered to their correct classrooms, or seats. Sometimes Mary was relieved to go home which felt strange, but she was having such bad days at school. She was worried about what she would do next. She was so angry!

Ken's warning did come true, but not to the extent that he had hoped. Ms. Standish established a system called Program Warnings. They were like demerits. If a student received three of them they were sent to detention. If they received three more they were suspended. If they continued to receive them they were eventually expelled. Because Diana had already been in a lot of trouble it didn't take her long to run out of chances. Diana was expelled from school in early February. Mary was relieved, and delighted! She supposed that other students felt this way too. However one of the teachers didn't. When she heard Mary rejoicing about Diana's expulsion she told her that if she couldn't say anything nice, she shouldn't say anything at all. Mary knew that this particular teacher had been very close to Diana, and still cared about her, but her suggestion came at a very bad time. Mary decided to take her up on her advice. She didn't feel like she could say anything nice these days. So she went on a talking strike. It was fairly easy. She simply walked around with an extra notebook. When someone talked to her she wrote "I have laryngitis "or "I lost my voice". For a few days she got away with it. Then people began to either worry about her, or become suspicious. During her talking strike the senior class was brought to a studio to get their pictures taken for the year book. The photographer couldn't get Mary to talk either, but he did get her to smile, and silently laugh at his jokes. As a result some good pictures were taken of her. She wrote him a note that said "Thank you". Back at school the teachers no longer believed that she lost her voice. Yet Mary continued to refuse to speak.

Finally after a week of this Mr. Flannigan was asked to talk to her. She wrote that she really did lose her voice. He gently informed her that he didn't believe her, and wanted her to talk about what was bothering her. She started to write her answers, but he stopped her, saying that her boss at Howe Press was having a problem with the idea of having a mute for an employee. Mary became thoughtful. She didn't want to lose her part time job. She loved working there. She felt trapped though, and this made her angry. Soon she was talking to Mr. Flannigan, and then came the tears of frustration. She told him that the boys teased her unmercifully about her choice of clothes, music, and the admiral. She told him some of the obscene things they said about her, and the admiral. She complained about Ms. Standish's uncaring attitude toward her in particular. She felt like something on an assembly line that was simply being processed, and shipped out as soon as possible. "She doesn't care if I learn anything of value! "cried Mary. "I get no History, or Science classes. Nobody wants me to come close to being a scholar. They've decided that I belong in the vocational classes. She won't let me join the hand bell ringers. I have to have Production Industries in stead!" When Diana's favorite teacher made the suggestion that she not say anything if she couldn't say anything nice it was the last straw, as far as Mary was concerned. Mr. Flannigan was sympathetic, and he agreed that Mary was intelligent enough, but he couldn't do anything about her education plan. He said he would talk to Ms. Standish, and let her know how Mary felt. Mary thanked him for his support, but didn't think he would get far with Ms. Standish.

Mary was feeling resentful about being in Production Industries came up with an idea. She had read a book during the summer. The game in the story required two teams. One team would take something from someone. Then the other team had to return it the next day. Mary couldn't come up with a team, but she thought the game could be played with two people. She took John aside, and told him about the game. He was eager to play it. Mary stole Mr. Bowdoin's pipe off his desk, and gave it to John. She told him to tell no one. He was to sneak it back to the exact same spot two days later. He left promising to play by the rules. The next morning instead of going to Howe Press Mary found herself in the office with Ms. Standish, Mr. Bowdoin, John, and another boy, named Bob. Mary knew something had gone wrong with the pipe. It turned out that John took the pipe down to the gym, and bragged to his buddies that he and Mary had taken it from Mr. Bowdoin. Ten minutes later Mr. Bowdoin came down demanding the return of his pipe. John no longer had it. He had slipped it in to Bob's coat pocket. As a result both boys and Mary were in Trouble. John had always been nice to Mary. He was sometimes like a friend. She had no idea though that he could be so dumb! Bob escaped punishment because the pipe was planted in his coat pocket. However Mary received a Program Warning and John was suspended because he had several warnings already. Mary wasn't upset about this. What bothered her was that Ms. Standish admitted to deliberately arranging the meeting in the morning so that Mary would miss an hour of work. "You will be docked for it." She said coldly. Mary wanted to rip the woman's hair out! As she left the office she slammed the door behind her, and tore some papers off the bulletin board in the hallway. On her way to Howe Press she took a saw horse, and threw it. She laughed, and ran off as one of the construction men hollered at her. At work she seethed with rage. She wanted to vandalize Ms. Standish's office, and her car. She wanted to cut a piece of her clothing to use it in a voodoo ceremony. When she started thinking about running away all her plans of rebellion went up in smoke. She realized that she couldn't run away. Those days were over. Mary and her father weren't close. They never had been, but she had never liked disappointing him. If she ran away, or got in to a lot of trouble at school she would disappoint him, and with his wife dead, Mary was all the family he had. She was trapped. As she worked she silently cried. After work Mary threw another saw horse just to hear an angry construction worker holler. The next day after a difficult time in Home Economics Mary threw several more saw horses on her way back to Elliot. She hoped this didn't become a habit. She was certain she would get in to trouble for it sooner, or later. Once in Elliot she packed her things, grabbed a pair of scissors, and headed over to the main building. Since the bus wasn't there she slipped in to the bathroom, and cut off her hair. She had come to the conclusion that if she couldn't be the kind of girl she wanted to be without being teased she might as well go back to being a Tomboy. When Mary returned to the lobby she was reprimanded for keeping the bus waiting. Mary felt so light, and free that she didn't mind. Once in Providence she had worked out a story for her father to explain her hair. She told him that she got glue in it the other day in Craft class. They went out for fish & chips like they always did on Fridays. Mr. Sullivan wasn't upset about Mary's hair. He said she looked like a little Dutch boy.

It was vacation again, the third week of February. At the start of the week Mary and her father took the ferry over to Block Island. It was a cold, windy day, but Mary was content. They bought coffees to go, and took them over to the library. They looked through many books, and Life Magazines. Some of them were very old. Just before they left Mary spotted a book about the Civil War. In it was a large picture of Abraham Lincoln sitting in a rocking chair. When her father went to get his coat she tore out the picture, and hid it in her jacket. The next day Mr. Sullivan made his daughter clean the house of an elderly couple he knew. At first it seemed the morning would never end. Mary couldn't find the cleaning supplies. When she finished the dusting the woman complained that the furniture was still dusty. Mary did it again.

The next day was Ash Wednesday. Last year Mary was excited about it because she was obsessed with Father Doyle. When other parishioners were giving things up for Lent out of love for the Lord, Mary was doing it out of love for Father Doyle. This year Lent was just another religious event that mattered to her father, not her. Mary decided to use Lent to her advantage without her father realizing it. She told him that she was giving up snacking between meals and dessert unless it was fruit. Mr. Sullivan was pleased. He thought they were good sacrifices. To Mary it was just a way to get away with trying to lose weight.

Toward the end of the week Mary knew that she was getting the "Home too long Blues." She noticed it when her father took her up the street to do the laundry. A woman started up a conversation with Mr. Sullivan. Then she turned to Mary, and exclaimed "My, how you've grown!" Before Mary could stop herself she blurted out "I HAVE NOT!! I've been Five feet since I was Twelve." She never snapped at people around her father. Luckily for her he didn't hear her. The woman walked away looking surprised. Later Mr. Sullivan dragged Mary over to the Senior School to visit people. He told Mary to take out the garbage for a woman, who still had ashes on her fore head. (You can always tell who a Catholic is when a certain Wednesday rolls around.) Mary grumbled to herself as she took out the garbage. Her father greeted everyone happily, and stayed awhile.

The following day Mary finally had some luck. Her father took her to Riverdale to roller skate. He sat, and watched as Mary, and other people of various ages skated round, and round the large room. So far this winter she had roller skated more then she had ice skated. She didn't get caught cutting in front of other skaters, but she did get caught climbing over the barrier. She got off with a warning.

It snowed on Friday, but they went out anyway. Mr. Sullivan visited the Senior School. Then he took Mary roller skating again. She also managed to get in a little bowling the following day. Mary had to admit that this vacation was better then Christmas Vacation was.

Mary continued to write about everyone around her, and to spy occasionally. One day she witnessed Shirley, Kama, and Mindy frantically looking for Pearl. They wanted to have a serious confrontation with her for spreading a rumor that they tried to burn her with a cigarette the day before. Kama was so upset she eagerly told Mary everything. When Mindy yelled from down the hall that Pearl was over in Moulton Mary rushed over there, and positioned her self in front of the bulletin board pretending to read the notices. There were no house parents around so Pearl had to face the angry girls on her own. They surrounded her, and demanded to know not only why she claimed they tried to burn her, but why she accused two boys of smoking pot. Pearl denied accusing Dave, and Steve of smoking pot. Then she said that she might have said they had pot, but didn't smoke it. After this she claimed that she had never told a lie in her life! Mary knew that she was lying at that very moment. Mary figured that Pearl would never change. She walked away, as the girls continued to holler at her, and hit her.

Mary remained close to Lorena, and Steve. They all continued to despise Senior Seminar. Miss Standish became angry one day when Lorena, who wanted to take a stand, refused to take off her hat, and coat. When the seminar ended she kept all three of them in the room. She reprimanded Lorena. Then she reprimanded Steve and Mary for refusing to pay attention. She made Mary wash all the desks because she had been drawing a group of rabbits playing baseball on her desk. When she said she would draw on it the following week Ms. Standish said she would wash them all again. "Fine you might as well put washing desks at Three O'clock on Friday afternoons on my schedule then!" Mary was afraid that if Ms. Standish got her to stop rebelling she would then get her to start participating, and acting like the other seniors. She wasn't going to do this, and she wasn't going to give up Lorena, and Steve no matter how much Ms. Standish thought they all dragged each other down. (She had heard that old song, and dance before!)

It turned out that Lorena's father was on his daughter's side. He was a tough, but caring hard working Portuguese man who looked out for his family. He thought Ms. Standish was over reacting to Lorena refusing to remove her hat, and coat during the seminar. He said that if he received a letter from her about Lorena he was going to come to the school, and have it out with Ms. Standish. Mary and Steve rejoiced with Lorena about this.

Mary still saw the students from Bennet Cottage. This year they were in May Cottage. Sometimes she peeked in the window, and saw Jimmy playing the piano. One day she saw Peter outside the back entrance of May. He had no coat on, one shoe was missing, and he was jumping up, and down in a rage! He kept screaming "Fuck you Miss Cloasey, I hate you!!" Mary was amazed. She had never seen Peter so angry before, not even when he was at the Boston School for Blind Children. Miss Cloasey must have been a very tough house parent. Mary envied the students in Secondary Services. They're day was less rigorous, and Miss Everest seemed like a warmer, more traditional person then Ms. Standish.

In Community Experience class Ms. Herman took everyone to visit their favorite radio station, WNTN. They saw how the DJ put on the records; they saw a machine that typed out the news. They stood right near the DJ while she announced the news. Then she let them make a request. They decided on an oldie from 1965. It came as a surprise to Mary that no one at the station liked oldies. She wondered if Jim Sands, another DJ liked oldies. When they left they were each given an album with" the very best oldies "on it. When they returned Mary decided to skip supper. She bought junk food, and then went to have a cigarette. Mindy flounced in to the room. She gave a loud whoop of laughter. She proudly informed Mary that she over turned the dinner table and its contents in to the laps of the boys, who were teasing her. Mindy would no doubt receive a Program warning, but she wouldn't care. She was always losing her temper, and throwing things. Mary went upstairs to play her new record.

At the end of March Mary's school review came up. She, Ms. Standish, and all her teachers were there. In spite of her occasional moodiness, and spurts of rebellion she was apparently doing very well in her classes. They made it quite clear that they thought she was capable of making it on her own after Graduation Day. If she hadn't been dreading leaving she would have been pleased with what they said. As it was she left the meeting feeling and acting as if they had insulted her. The worst thing of all was that she would not be able to continue working at Howe Press. The position she had was a student's training position. Next fall another student would work there. Mary felt like all the doors were being closed in her face, and nobody cared. They just wanted to get rid of her whether she was ready to leave, or not. She felt cheated!

One day in April Mary decided that she had enough. She wanted to make a statement. She attended the first class of the day then took off. Soon she was on the Kenmore Square bus heading in to Boston. When she arrived she rode the subway for awhile. She found it exciting. She liked hearing the conductor's voice announcing the stops. She loved how fast the train went. Afterward she wandered around looking at historical buildings, and houses. She hoped that back at school they were wondering where she was. While Mary was in McDonalds she eaves dropped on a conversation two women were having in the next booth. They were talking about their grandchildren. One of them had three. The oldest was seven. She was the darling of the family. The five year old was the brat. The youngest was a baby. She sowed her friend pictures, and said "The brat "when she held up the second one. The brat's name was Alice. Mary wondered if Alice was a brat because she was the middle child. She heard once that a middle child often felt ignored, and not at all special. Or maybe Alice wasn't a brat at all. Maybe she was just misunderstood. Mary knew this happened a lot between adults, and children. After lunch Mary went to the Boston Common. Then she decided to walk the Freedom Trail, but got lost. She never did make it to Paul Revere's house she returned to school at Four Thirty to discover that no one even knew that she had gone missing. This only added to her feeling of resentment. She had to tell Arena, the house parent on duty what she did. Arena sent her to her room. Then she talked with her after supper.

Ms. Standish did talk to Mary a few days later. She agreed that Mary needed more support in reaching her goals for the future. She didn't say how this would be done though. She also told Mary that if she wanted to give up the mean imaginary characters like the admiral, she would have to give up the good ones, like Mr. Disraeli. Mary wasn't about to do this. Ms. Standish then called a cottage meeting over in Moulton. Everyone from Elliot attended as well. Ken, and Ms. Standish reprimanded all the students for all the rule breaking, stealing, and fighting that was still going on. Dire warnings were made. After this meeting the house parents started coming down hard on students. Abigail was hollered at by Ken one morning at breakfast, and given a Program Warning for arguing with another student. She hollered at Ken, as she left the room. Mary tried to be quiet, and stay out of trouble. Unfortunately she got in to an argument with Harold because he was teasing her. It ended with Mary getting in to trouble for hurling an ash tray at him, and trying to hit him with a metal trash can. Would she ever get control of herself?

Just before Easter Vacation John, Mary's friend from Production Industries was told that he was going to a new school. They had a going away party for him. He sat right in front of the cake, and had two or three pieces of it. Mary was going to miss him. She would miss all the clowning around he did in class, and his obsession with radios. Once he traded his good radio for Mary's broken down one. He liked repairing them more then he liked listening to them. She laughed as he walked away talking excitedly to himself about all the repairs he was going to make on her radio. She couldn't even be angry at him for getting them both in to trouble over the pipe incident with Mr. Bowdoin. Why did a nice student have to leave? Why didn't they send away one of the bullies?

On Friday, April 19th everyone went home for Easter Vacation. Mary left feeling confused because she was actually wishing she could move back in to the Elliot apartment. After all, she would be in a place like this if she acquired a live-in position in another school. The main reason she resented it was because it had been forced on her, but the apartment was shut off from the big mouth students, who picked on her. Now that Jolene had moved out Mary could have her own room to decorate as she liked. The apartment was very old fashioned, and resembled an apartment from the turn of the century, with light fixtures on the walls, instead of harsh fluorescent lights over head, and a bath tub that wasn't built in to the floor. With all the changes that were being made, the apartment was beginning to seem like a small piece of the past, a refuge. Mary wondered if she should speak to Ms. Standish about this, or would she be laughed at for not being able to make up her mind?

Chapter Fifteen

Candice Returns

Mary was home for Easter Vacation. It was the middle of April in 1980. Mary had two more months before she graduated from Perkins School. The vacation started out ordinary enough. On Friday evening Mr. Sullivan's friend, Jim came over to visit. They sat out in the kitchen, talking, smoking, and drinking coffee. Because Jimmy stayed late, Mary was able to watch "The Incredible Hulk", "The Dukes of Hazard", and a movie that went on until eleven. She was worrying because she hadn't heard from Candice, a friend from Eden wood. She hadn't yet responded to two of Mary's letters, inviting her to visit her.

Saturday Mary forgot about Candice momentarily. Her dad sat her down, and told her what he knew about her real mother. He believed that her name was Nancy, and had given birth to Mary at age fourteen. With Mrs. Sullivan dead for almost a year and a half, her father felt free enough to admit that the real reason that he and her mother opposed her going to a group home in Cranston three years ago was that They suspected that relatives on Mary's Grandmother's side of the family might have still been living in the area, and he, and his wife didn't want her to meet them. Mary held in the mild resentment she felt about this. Why shouldn't she have met them? After he explained this, Mr. Sullivan showed Mary two year books from Cranston West High School. The first one was from 1959. The second one was from 1961. Mr. Sullivan thought that Mary's mother might be in the second one. They couldn't find her. He told Mary that when they adopted her at eight months, they were told that her mother's last name was Larson. However, he had reason to believe that her last name was either Reed, or Read. Mary asked him what nationalities she really was. She was told that she was English, French, and Italian. He then pointed out a girl in one of the year books. Her name was Claire Jean Fontanne. He believed that she might be related to Mary's mother's mother. Mary was more interested in her family then she wanted Mr. Sullivan to know, but she was worried about hurting him. Besides, she was afraid of trying to find them. Suppose they didn't want her? Wouldn't she only bring back bad memories for them? After all, she had been a mistake.

Mr. Sullivan showed his daughter some post cards and foreign coins. "These are from Canada." He explained. "When I retired from the state police in 1951, your mother and I took a trip to Canada." He told her about all the churches they visited. He smiled as he reminisced about the night they stood outside with a bunch of strangers. They stood in the shape of a rosary, held candles, and recited the rosary together. He made it seem like the ideal trip to take. It sounded terribly boring to Mary. However, knowing her parents the way she did, she wasn't surprised. She could picture them smiling delightedly at each other in the dark, as they prayed with all those other people.

In the afternoon Mary and her father went bowling, as they often did on Saturdays. She was on the bowling league at Perkins. This gave her an opportunity to get in some practice. Although Mr. Sullivan still missed his wife, he was developing a much more out going personality these days, and was making a lot of friends in Coventry.

Mary wasn't thrilled about going to Mass twice on Sunday, but it couldn't be helped. Aside from their regular Sunday Morning visit, there was also a memorial service in the evening for the dead who used to attend Saint John & Paul's. Before the memorial service Mr. Sullivan took Mary over to the house of an elderly couple whom he liked. They were a German couple, named Herman, and Eli. They lived in a modern home out in the woods. Mary didn't like the way they complained to her father about Jewish people. She had a crush on Benjamin Disraeli, a former prime minister of England. She carried his picture where ever she went.

Sunday evening turned out to be rather upsetting for Mary, and her father. When the names of the dead were read off, Mary's mother's name was not included. In a trembling voice, Mr. Sullivan said "and Ida Kay Sullivan". Mary felt bad for him, but was afraid to clasp his hand in hers. She had never been close to either of them. She knew that she had always been a disappointment to them. Because her father often snapped at her, and found fault with her, he might not have accepted her attempt at comforting him. When Mass ended, Mary felt nervous. She was scared that her father might take his pain out on her. When they reached their drive way, a sad, eerie feeling came over Mary. As she saw their house in the dim light, looking tired, and lonely she found herself thinking that her mother was dead, and their dog, Sandy's time was not far off. How much time did her father have? She clutched her picture of Mr. Disraeli. Once inside Mr. Sullivan cleaned up more bloody newspapers from the floor of the room where Sandy always stayed. The blood was the result of a tumor that had been growing under the dog's tail. He had it for a year now. He couldn't have an operation because of his epilepsy. All Mary, and her father could do was watch him slowly die.

On Monday a surprise birthday party was arranged at the rectory for Mary. All three priests took part in it. Mary suspected that it had been her father's idea because he knew how fond she was of Father Hoyle. Also Father Hoyle liked Mr. Sullivan because he helped the church a lot. She ate cake, opened her gifts, and happily talked to Father Hoyle every chance she got. Father Kelly took Mary's camera, and snapped a picture of her blowing out the candles on her cake. Father Davis wished her a Happy Birthday.

On Tuesday Mr. Sullivan took Mary to Providence to see her case worker from State Services for the blind. Barbara's office was in a drab, modern building with grey wall to wall carpeting, and stiff, uncomfortable chairs. The case workers all worked in their own little cubicles that to Mary resembled cages. She found Barbara in cage # 3. They discussed school, and Mary's career plans. Nothing definite came from this meeting, but at least Barbara hadn't forgotten Mary's existence.

On Wednesday Mary despaired of anything exciting happening during the remainder of her vacation. Then the phone rang. Mary's father answered it, and told her that Candice was calling to tell them that she would be arriving in Providence at ten that very evening. She would be permitted to stay until Friday night. Mr. Sullivan and his eager daughter spent the afternoon cleaning the house, moving things to the attic, and setting the kitchen table. By the time they finished, it didn't look like their house anymore. Everything was so organized, and uncluttered. Mary hoped that it wouldn't revert back to its usual untidiness too soon.

At Nine O'clock they drove to Providence to get Candice. Candice happily greeted Mary. She still looked much the same as she did at Eden wood. She wore a T-shirt and corduroy pants. On her head she wore a bandana. Mary noticed that her thick braid wasn't hanging down in back like it used to be. Candice said that she kept it pinned up in back because after Mary left Eden wood the directors used to grab her braid, and knock her to the floor when she acted up. Mary was appalled when she heard that Mark, a guy she liked, and who had stayed on as a staff member, had been one of the people who did this to her. What had gotten in to Mark? He used to be so nice! Because of this, Candice was now very protective of her hair.

During the ride home Candice had Mary, and her father laughing at her jokes, and funny tales. Eden wood didn't manage to strip her of her sense of humor. When they got home Dad went to bed. Mary thought she, and Candice would be going to bed also. However, Candice had other ideas. She wanted to go out, and explore Coventry a little. "Let's just check out Washington St, okay?" Mary reluctantly agreed. To Mary's surprise, her father said that it was okay with him, provided that they didn't stay out too late. Mary and Candice walked down South Main St and on to Washington St. She told Candice how boring the town was, but Candice wanted to see for herself. Soon they were reminiscing about Eden wood School. As they passed the Police Station Candice had an idea. She led Mary down to the rail road tracks that ran along in back of the station. She proceeded to give Mary a loud verbal reprimand, stopping to laugh from time to time. Mary stood at attention trying not to laugh, as Candice yelled at her for being silly, and having the audacity not to take Eden wood seriously. Mary thought this was funny, but she was anxious that the cops would hear, and come out to demand an explanation. She wondered if Candice was daring them to come out. Luckily, Candice tired of this, and they moved on. To Mary's dismay, Candice stopped to talk to some guys who were hanging out, and getting drunk. One of them gave her a beer. She drank it as they walked along. Then when they were approaching Mary's street she placed the bottle on someone's door step. Mary was so relieved to get home, and go to bed. She laid awake for awhile thinking. She realized suddenly that she had never given much thought to what it would be like to be friends with Candice outside of Eden wood. Drugs, drinking, dating, and going anywhere without supervision were absolutely forbidden. Without these things, Mary and Candice had the kind of friendship that two young girls would have had. They used to exchange jokes, and riddles, they read aloud to each other from scary stories. They sang silly songs, and bad mouthed directors behind their backs. Candice had a talent for writing poetry. She used to let Mary read her poems. They were full of detail, and were very moving. They got along well, and never fought. Candice fought with others though. She was abused by directors, and students alike. Mary felt bad for her, and tried to comfort her. Mary identified with Candice because she too had a temper which landed her in a lot of trouble. They both saw people in authority as corrupt, mean spirited bullies. Now Mary hoped she wasn't seeing another side of Candice. As she was drifting off to sleep, she decided to get her father to plan activities that would distract Candice from wondering off, and being too wayward.

Mary and her father woke up before Candice did. They were having Breakfast when she came out wearing only a large T-shirt that barely covered her under pants. Mr. Sullivan, and his daughter gaped at her, but she seemed oblivious to their reaction. "What are you two staring at?" she asked in a cheerful, yet petulant tone of voice. She sat down, and began to eat. Mary and her father looked at each other, but said nothing. Mary wished that her father, the adult, the parent, would speak up, and in a firm way tell Candice to put more clothes on.

When Breakfast was over Mary gave Candice a present. She had been waiting two years for this moment. It was a record with the song "Boogie Oogie Oogie" on it. This was Candice's favorite song. It used to be Mary's favorite song too, back when she still liked Disco. Candice was thrilled with the record! She played it several times, and danced to it. Then she entertained Mary and her father by doing a pantomime of a dog. She made Rover play the organ. After awhile she began to talk at length about what life was like at Eden wood. She got a tape recorder, and began making fun of the events at Eden wood, and the staff, and directors. Her silliness soon turned to hatred of the place. All the while she used the organ for sound effects. When she filled the tape on both sides she gave it to Mary. "Something to remember me by" she said. She told Mary that she was planning to make another one to mail to Eden wood.

In the afternoon Mr. Sullivan took Mary and Candice to an in door swimming pool in West Warwick. They played, and splashed around for over an hour. They had a lot of fun. Afterward they went to Burger King. They had a game there that customers could play. It consisted of a booklet with pictures of money on each page, ranging from $1.00 to $10.000. A customer would get stubs, and would try to match them with the pictures in the booklet. Candice was determined to win. In Burger King, she was more concerned with swapping stubs with people then she was with eating. This went on for about forty five minutes. When they finally did leave, Candice talked Mr. Sullivan in to stopping at another Burger King, but they were out of stubs. Mary didn't care much that they didn't win, but Candice must have been very disappointed because she convinced Mr. Sullivan that they should all go shopping, and buy each other presents. They did…with Mr. Sullivan's money. Later Candice had Mr. Sullivan drop her off at the movies. Mary didn't feel like going, so she said that she was sick from eating too much candy.

The next time Candice decided to visit, Mr. Sullivan decided that he would have to take the keys with him when he left the car because Candice tried to drive it while he was in the store. She would have driven it clear across the parking lot, but Mary talked her in to only moving it up to the next row. They sat there laughing, and wondering if Mary's father would notice what Candice did. When he returned, he did seem a little confused. When Candice told him what she did, he didn't look pleased, but he held in his anger. He even gave in to Candice's begging to be allowed to drive the car around the lot with him in it of course! The next morning Mr. Sullivan took the keys with him when he went in to the store, in spite of Candice's promise that she wouldn't move the car again. Candice wanted to get out, and push the car forward, to the next parking space, but Mary convinced her not to. Her father would be furious! When Mr. Sullivan returned he drove them to Providence. Candice was supposed to stay with Mary, and her father until evening, but she wanted to be back in New Hampshire early so that she could avoid being picked up by the van full of noisy kids from her new school, who always teased her. It was fun seeing Candice again after two years. Her visit made an otherwise dull vacation go by fast.

Three weeks later Candice called Mary at Perkins, and told her that she and her step sister were on their way to a wedding in Connecticut. She wanted to stop by, and spend the weekend with Mary, and her father. "It's okay with me," said Mary. "But you better ask Dad". Candice said that she was going to call him that very evening. Mary hung up, with an uneasy feeling about Candice, and her step sister coming to visit. Also she was very worried about Sandy. The last time she was home her father not only found blood on the dog's newspapers, he also found sores all over his body, and tiny white things which turned out to be maggots. When Mary and her father brought Sandy to the vet he explained that maggots are attracted to tumors. He was angry at Mr. Sullivan. "Don't you ever wash this dog!?" he demanded. "He's filthy! This is part of the reason he has the maggots, and sores!" The vet was totally disgusted! Mr. Sullivan could only stand there in a embarrassed silence. The vet got out a metal tub, and began to wash Sandy. Then he put him in a cage. As they left, Sandy stared after them. Mary knew the vet was right. Her parents had always been lax about Sandy's hygiene. They thought it was enough to clean up the dirty papers. They let the vet bathe him when he was brought in for check ups twice a year. In spite of this, Mary knew that her father loved Sandy, and would miss him when he died, she would too.

When Mary got off the bus in Providence on Friday afternoon her father was waiting for her. She was momentarily relieved, thinking that Candice, and her step sister had decided not to come. Then the father of one of the other students, who was getting off the bus, warned Mr. Sullivan to get those two girls away from the two African American men in a near by car. "I just got finished telling them to get away from that car!" Mr. Sullivan was furious! He swore audibly as he headed in that direction. Mary stood there with her suit case, and sighed. The two girls were Candice, and her Step sister. As they drove away from down town Providence, Candice, and Mr. Sullivan got in to an argument. He insisted that Candice, her step sister, and those guys must have been making advances at each other because the car was following them. It continued to follow them for about Twenty minutes, and then gave up.

Mary wasn't sure that her father was prejudiced. Her mother was the one who seemed to dislike African Americans, just as she disliked hippies and Asians, calling them chinks. (Her dislike of Asians stemmed from the fact that Dr. Pat was Asian, and Mrs. Sullivan believed that she and Mary bad mouthed her behind her back.) One day when Mary was ten, Mr. Sullivan was taking her to a store to select a present for her mother. Mrs. Sullivan appeared with one of the polyester vests that she always wore over her blouses. She wanted Mary to wear one of the vests because the store had air conditioning. Mary wasn't bothered by air conditioning. Besides, the vest wasn't cool looking. So she politely declined the offer. As Mrs. Sullivan was carrying the vest back inside, she called out "Would you wear it if a nigger gave it to you?" Mary stiffened, knowing that she had offended her mother, and would soon pay for it.

Oddly enough Mrs. Sullivan angrily defended an African American singer on TV a week later. Mary, who hadn't heard black gospel music before, was giggling about the way the woman was singing. Her mother had shouted at her. She didn't want Mary making fun of a woman of God. She then went Mary from the room. Mary was bewildered by her mother's unpredictable behavior. Would she have defended a hippie or an Asian person if they were of God?

Mr. Sullivan had never shown any dislike for any race of people. Mary figured that he was just afraid for Candice and Cheryl because the two men were strangers, not because they were African Americans.

As the two girls peered out the back window, Mary's father told her that Sandy died. She lowered her head, and started to cry. Her father gave her hand a squeeze. Candice sat forward, and wrapped her arms around Mary. "Oh, I'm so sorry Mary!" she exclaimed. Mr. Sullivan told her to leave Mary alone. "I don't believe in leaving people alone when their upset." Mr. Sullivan lost his temper. "YOU MIND YOUR OWN BUSINESS!" he shouted. "Just don't take over, and that's exactly what you and your step sister have been doing since you came to my house two nights ago!!" Candice sat back, and started crying. Cheryl held her, and comforted her. In spite of her own unhappiness, Mary felt sorry for Candice. Even if she wasn't being mistreated now, Mary was reminded of the times at Eden wood when Candice had been mistreated. When they arrived at the fish& chip diner Candice and Cheryl wanted to go for a walk. They wanted Mary to join them, but Mr. Sullivan said "NO!" abruptly. Candice accused him of keeping Mary to himself so that he could possess her. Mr. Sullivan became enraged! "WHAT? Listen, she is my DAUGHTER! Get your mind out of the gutter!" Candice and Cheryl walked off. While they were gone Mary's father told her that they had been treating him like a sucker. They made him buy bathing suits, clothes, and food. They left messes all over the house, and slept until Noon each day. All in all, Mr. Sullivan was treating the two of them like royalty, and they didn't appreciate it. When the Prima Donnas returned from their walk, they all went inside, and ate fish & chips.

Later Mary and her father watched TV while Candice and Cheryl went out for the evening. Mr. Sullivan said that he understood that Mary wasn't much happier with Candice then he was, and appreciated the fact that she had no desire to be like either one of them. He wasn't about to let them encourage Mary to be like them. Mary felt relieved. This feeling left her a few hours later though, when she lay in bed, pretending to be asleep. In the next room Candice was talking on a tape recorder, which she used as an oral diary. Mary was glad that she eavesdropped. She learned some important things. First of all, Cheryl wasn't Candice's step sister at all. She was a friend from school. Second of all, they weren't on their way to Connecticut for a wedding. They both ran away from the school in New Hampshire, and were merely hiding out at Mary's father's house. Mary began to realize that it was kind of odd that they showed up in the middle of the week when there were two days of school left, and Mr. Sullivan did mention to her that he hadn't received a call from Rivendell, the school they both attended, confirming that the visit was permitted. Mary rolled over, deciding that she better not tell her father until she could get the tape, and play it for him when Candice, and Cheryl went out again.

The next day Mr. Sullivan got permission to bring his daughter, and her two friends on a trip with the senior citizens. They got on a rented school bus, and went to Fen way Park, in Boston to see a Red Sox game. Mary was happy enough to go. Ever since her mother died, her father had involved himself in local activities. He was a member of The Involved Tax Payers of Coventry. He was an active participant in the church, and he was a Retired Senior Volunteer. The seniors had a lot of events to enjoy, and Mr. Sullivan had a lot to choose from. During the ride up to Boston everyone played Bingo. Candice won fifty cents. When they arrived at Fen way Park Candice asked Mr. Sullivan if she could have an additional ten cents because she wanted to buy an ice cream cone. When he asked her why she was only buying one for herself, she became angry, and asked him if he expected her to split the ice cream cone four ways. He told her that any money she received should be saved to be put toward the bus tickets they would need to get to Connecticut. "You have no right to be angry "he told Candice. "You wouldn't have won those fifty cents if I hadn't paid for you to play Bingo in the first place". Candice accused him of trying to instill guilt in to her, then she, and Cheryl went to sit some where else. Mary was quiet throughout the argument. When she and her father noticed that the girls were gone, she used her binoculars to locate them. Somehow they had managed to get front row seats! When the game ended, with Boston as the winner, Mary's father sent her to get her wayward friends. Garry the senior director was impatiently waiting for them. "Come on!" he yelled. Mary pushed her way through the crowd, trying to find the girls.

During the bus ride home, Candice, and Cheryl became rowdy. They were throwing food out the window, and shouting at the people in passing cars. Mr. Sullivan shook his head in disgust. "Thanks to them, these seniors will think all teenagers are wild". Candice even decided to give the seniors an example of an Eden wood reprimand. Mary and Candice had received many of them when they were at that school. Because of this, Candice chose Mary to be the recipient. She stood with her hands behind her back, trying to keep a straight face, as Candice proceeded to yell at her for some make-believe offense. Nobody scolded Candice for standing up on a moving bus to demonstrate a reprimand. The seniors simply looked at each other in surprise. Mr. Sullivan told both girls to sit down.

After Candice and Cheryl went out for the evening Mary approached her father, and told him that she had something to show him. She found the incriminating tape, and played it for him. They not only heard about Candice, and Cheryl not being step sisters, and being on the run, they also heard Candice complaining about not being able to get along with Mr. Sullivan. She thought he was mean, and unreasonable. She said that she and Cheryl were using his home to hide from the police until it was safe enough to go to Connecticut. "Those little STINKERS!" exclaimed Mr. Sullivan. He searched their luggage, and found the bus ticket stubs that took them from Concord, New Hampshire, to Providence, Rhode Island. They didn't lose their bus tickets to Connecticut, as they had claimed. They simply didn't buy any, probably because they didn't have enough money. They must have assumed that they would get Mary's father to buy them. He said that he had no intention of doing so, not after what they pulled. Mary wanted her father to call the police, but he said he couldn't because he could get in to trouble for letting them stay there when they didn't have permission from their school.

Mary was awakened at four thirty in the morning to find her father talking to Candice and Cheryl in the living room. He told Mary that he woke up at two thirty to find the girls trying to make a phone call. He made them go back to bed. Later he woke up, and caught them trying to sneak out of the house. Mary guessed that they discovered that the tape had been listened to, and were nervous. They thought Mr. Sullivan was going to call the police. "If you want to leave, I'll drive you to Providence, but at least wait until seven. How do you think it will look if the neighbors see two young girls leaving my house at four thirty in the morning?" Reluctantly they decided to wait. For the next two hours Candice and Cheryl told him about how awful Rivendell School was. Mary listened with her father. She didn't think it sounded nearly as bad as Eden wood had been.

Before leaving, Candice asked Mary for some money. Mary opened her shell box, where she kept her money. She had thirteen dollars in it. She took out three, and gave it to Candice. They rode to Providence. When they reached the bus station Mr. Sullivan was so eager to be rid of them that he paid their way. Later back at home, Mary checked her shell box on a hunch. As she had feared, the ten dollars was gone! Candice must have sneaked back to Mary's room when everyone was getting ready to leave. That was the last straw, as far as Mary was concerned. She never wanted to see her again. Candice might have been her friend at Eden wood, but she hadn't acted like a friend since then. "Boy, having their independence sure does strange things to some people", Mary told her father. It wasn't even necessary for him to tell his daughter that Candice was no longer welcome in his home. They both knew it already. If Candice wrote to her she would throw the letters away, and she better not even think of showing up at Mary's graduation the following month. Mary knew when she'd been had. Despite this Mary found that she had enjoyed the feeling of friendship that was developing between her and her father. Throughout the ordeal he seemed like an ally. This was a new experience for the both of them. Mary wondered if it would last.

Chapter Sixteen

Graduation approaches

When Mary returned from Easter Vacation she found the school besieged with fire drills. What made it worse was that they occurred in the middle of the night. Sunday night everyone in Elliot, and Moulton was woke up by a fire alarm, and had to stand out in the rain for nearly fifteen minutes. Several hours later the alarm went off again! Once again the students went outside. This time they were questioned because the firemen suspected that someone had been smoking upstairs. No one admitted to it. Everyone returned to their beds. The following night people were hoping for a good night's sleep. However this was not meant to be. The alarm went off a little after two in the morning. It went off again an hour later. Mary was totally fed up by this time. Instead of going outside she hid in her closet, and sulked. Still, staying inside didn't allow her to get to sleep any sooner then the other students, and this made her furious! Why couldn't the new alarm system go off during the day when they were in class, or study hall?

No sooner had the alarm system settled down then something else happened. On a Thursday morning when she was supposed to be at Howe Press Mary was called to Ms. Standish's office. She was confronted about a bunch of pranks she had pulled on April fool's Day. Mary couldn't believe the supervisor waited this long to deal with the matter. She admitted to pulling the pranks. "I admitted to those pranks back when I did them!" exclaimed Mary. "I thought the matter was dropped." Ms. Standish assured her that the matter wasn't dropped, and there was going to be a consequence. She also addressed Mary's complaints about the teasing. Ms. Standish was not sympathetic. She informed Mary that if she continued to carry pictures of her favorite men, dress differently, or listen to different music in front of the other students she better expect to be teased. "If your not willing to conform, and live up to today's standards you'll just have to suffer the consequences." said Ms. Standish in a matter of fact, cold tone of voice. Mary wanted to smack her across the face! Then she returned to the subject of the pranks. She wanted to ground Mary. She asked her if she was going home that weekend. Mary lied, and said she was. "Fine, you are to go straight to Elliot right after work, and you better not leave there until the next morning." Mary assumed a some what compliant manner, and set off to work. At four thirty she went down to the square, cashed her check, returned some books to the library, and bought some snacks for the evening. Mary wasn't confronted about arriving at the cottage an hour late. Apparently Arena hadn't been informed that Mary was grounded for the night. In fact the young, friendly house mother hung out with her for some of the evening. Mary played a silly tape that her friend, Candice made while she was visiting Mary, and her father. "It's called Candice's tribute to Eden wood" said Mary. Lorena joined them to listen to the tape. Mary explained why Candice made such a tape. Arena and Lorena were amazed that a school like Eden wood was allowed to exist. All in all Mary had a pleasant evening, and didn't feel grounded at all. She felt entitled to be sneaky after the way Ms. Standish talked to her in the office. She suspected that she was being punished for being different more then for the pranks.

Although Mary and Steve weren't members of the senior class they were allowed to go on the five day trip to Washington DC because they paid their way. They wanted Lorena to go also, but she was so disgusted with most of the seniors that she wouldn't go even though Steve and Mary promised to be with her at all times. Without Lorena; Steve and Mary had to band together because they didn't like most of the seniors either. On a Tuesday afternoon in May all the seniors packed. Mary wanted to borrow Jolene's blue sweatshirt because Jimmy often wore blue sweatshirts, and she wanted to resemble him. When Jolene said no; Mary stole the shirt, and put it on. The seniors were taken to the train station in Boston. It took about eight hours to get to Washington. Steve and Mary played a few simple card games to pass the time. When she went for a snack; Mary was complimented on the blue Old Orchid Beach shirt she was wearing. Jolene was within hearing distance. "Who's wearing–" Mary hurried back to Steve before Jolene could confront her. Later she curled up, and imagined that she was sitting on Mr. Disraeli's lap. In the morning the students and three teachers were temporarily stranded because the van that was supposed to pick them up broke down. By eleven they had checked in to the hotel, and were having breakfast. After they were unpacked Miss Jackman called everyone in to the room that she was sharing with Jolene, and Mary. A whole schedule of fun activities had been planned. An argument broke out as Mr. Brighton, Ken, the house parent from Moulton, and some of the seniors insisted on going to the Naval Academy. Miss Jackman gave in, and took the rest of the seniors to the museums. She remained firm about everyone meeting later on to see House speaker, Tip O'Neil at the Capital. Because the House speaker was in a meeting when they arrived, the students, and teachers were taken on a tour of the Capital. Mary thought the rooms were beautiful. The ceilings were high, and had chandeliers suspended from them. They each contained rich carpeting, and antique furniture. There were life sized statues of the presidents. Mary liked the one of Abraham Lincoln the best. After the tour Tip O'Neil was ready to see to them. He was an old man with white hair, who was very friendly, and talkative. Mary, who was gazing around the huge, elegant room; caught only parts of what the man was saying,. She heard phrases like "Sitting in box seats", and "A lot of red tape". She was paying attention when he said that he donated money to a hospital in Texas that was trying to help dwarfs grow from two feet to four feet. After they left the Capital building they caught the bus that would take them back to their hotel. When they got off the bus Mr. Brighton turned to Mary. "Here Mary you can guide Steve since you haven't helped anyone today, and you've been at Perkins for two years." Mary willing held out her arm for her friend, and asked Mr. Brighton why he was taking such an attitude toward her. He refused to answer. Mary hated it when someone snapped at her, then refused to be held accountable for it. She continued to confront him about this when to her amazement he turned, and yelled "SHUT UP!!". "YOU SHUT UP!" Mary was furious now. She loudly called him a bunch of names. As soon as they arrived at the hotel Mr. Brighton took off without telling anyone where he was going. He was gone for four, or five hours. When Miss Jackman heard what happened she was on Mary's side. "You don't need to justify yourself. I know that you have been guiding students who don't see as well as you do. Besides, you're here to relax, and have fun." Mary felt relieved.

The next day they had lunch at Burger King. The students were given twenty dollars a day for spending. Mary threw the contents of her tray away then left. Before they had gone a block she realized that her envelope of money was missing. Instantly she remembered leaving it on her tray with her food. When she told Miss Jackman about it Miss Jackman wouldn't let her go back for it. "You should have been more careful in the first place!" Mary was angry at herself for her stupidity, but now she was angry at Miss Jackman as well. Didn't she ever make mistakes? Back at the hotel room Mary stole five dollars out of Miss Jackman's pocketbook when she was in the bathroom.

In the afternoon they all went to the Air & Space Museum. Mary liked this, but she liked going to Ford Theatre the next day even better. They had a tour of the theatre, and saw the room where Abraham Lincoln was shot. Mary imagined herself back in 1865. She would jump on John Wilkes Booth, and prevent him from killing the president. She was shaken from her reverie as everyone made their way back downstairs to hear a man play the piano. He played songs that were known to have been favorites of Abe Lincoln. They were Jimmy Crack Corn, Gentle Annie, and The Silver Bell Waltz. Later they went to a museum that contained a lot of abstract art. Mary liked the area that contained traditional paintings. Mr. Brighton wanted to choose the restaurant where they would all have supper. He dragged them all over the city before finding one he liked.

On Friday they were half an hour late for their private tour of the White House, and had to be merged with another group as a result. Then they went on a bus tour, and saw the Lincoln, and Jefferson Memorials, and the Tomb of the Unknown Soldier. While at the tomb they saw the changing of the guards. Then they made their way back to the hotel for supper.

Everyone wanted to go to an amusement park that they heard about, but it wasn't on a bus line. People took turns calling places that might have a van to rent, but they had no success.

Saturday turned out to be fun even without the amusement park. After visiting the hotel gift shop they went to a mall where Steve and Mary got separated from the group. When they caught up with the others they received some nasty looks from Mr. Brighton. How come nothing happened to him? (Miss Jackman on the other hand had been trapped in a stall of a public bathroom twice already. The first time Mary had to crawl under the door to unlock it for her.) When they reached the Kennedy Center they split up. Ken and Mr. Brighton took some of the students to the zoo. Mary was among the students, who followed Miss Jackman in to the Kennedy Center. They decided to have lunch on the top floor. They rode the elevator with some strangers. When the strangers got off, Miss Jackman told Roger to push the button for the top floor. He accidentally hit the red button. The elevator stopped, and an alarm went off. Miss Jackman made everyone sit on the floor, and not panic. Then she proceeded to pound on the door, and scream for help. Steve and Mary were quietly laughing because she seemed to be the one who was panicking. It took ten minutes for them to discover that there was a phone in the elevator. Miss Jackman called for help. She was told to pull the "Stop "button very hard. It was a relief to find themselves moving again. They bought their lunch, and went on to the terrace. Miss Jackman proceeded to talk about the importance of manners. As she spoke Steve suddenly sneezed, spraying her arm with saliva. Then when he was trying to give her a napkin, he dropped his ice tea in her lap!

At four O'clock they left for the train station. Mr. Brighton and his group met them there. Steve and Mary showed each other their purchases. They couldn't wait to give Lorena the gift that they each picked out for her. Miss Jackman ordered them to put their souvenirs away because it didn't look mature to her for them to be engaging in such behavior. Mary groaned! Why was conformity so important?

They were three hours late when they arrived in Boston. The train broke down in New York due to engine trouble. Mary had managed to sleep part of the way. So the wait wasn't that difficult for her. They returned to Perkins at Noon on Sunday. Mary and the other seniors were pleased with their trip. All in all they had a good time.

When Lorena returned from a relaxing weekend at home Mary gave her the gift she had selected for her. It was a three dimensional picture of the White House, Capital building, and the Lincoln, and Jefferson Memorials. Lorena loved it. Mary told her about the trip. When she got to the part about Miss Jackman getting stuck in the bathroom, and Mary having to crawl under the door, Lorena laughed so hard she fell off the bed! Afterward she left Mary to collect her gift from Steve, and hear how he liked the trip.

When Mary returned from a weekend at home late in May, she mailed a resume to Crotched Mountain. This was a residential school for the disabled in New Hampshire. This seemed like an ideal job to get. Although she would be there as employee status, she would be living on a campus in school surroundings. Hopefully the school would be historical looking. If this worked out, Mary wouldn't feel that bad about leaving Perkins. With Mr. Flannigan's help Mary located a few more residential schools in the New England area. She mailed her resume to them, and waited hopefully.

Mary must have still been affected by the death of her dog. One night she had a dream that she was out in her yard at home. Thumping sounds came from beneath the ground where Sandy was buried. Terrified, Mary ran to Mr. Disraeli, who was a giant. He picked her up. They watched as Sandy, and many other dogs came up out of their graves, rejoicing over their freedom.

During the last few weeks of school Mary managed to hold her anger in, even when someone snapped at her. She devised ways of sneaking around in order to avoid the big shots, who teased her. However, holding in her feelings sometimes made her feel depressed. Fortunately there were things to take her mind off of how she was feeling. Because school was drawing to an end, there were some fun activities. A fair was held on the lawn in front of Bradley Cottage one afternoon. There were game booths and music was playing. There were balloons for everyone, and someone was painting clown faces on anyone who wanted this. Mary sat down with Jimmy. The growth hormone shots that he received were working. In less then a year he had grown nearly two inches. He still looked like a boy of about ten. While Mary talked with him he ate three or four helpings of potato salad, leaving no room for the hamburgers, and hot dogs. She learned that he was obsessed with bells, clocks, and chimes. He wanted her to ask someone in authority to play some of his favorite songs on the chimes in the tower which stood on top of the main building. She promised to try. Mary saw Madeline, the other teenager, who had growing problems. She had grown a little from the weekly shots that she had been receiving for nearly two years. She was sitting with her boy friend, Jeffery. They were acting silly, and making each other laugh.

The next day Mary's request for Jimmy was denied. She was resentful that even something like this should be off limits especially when she was asking on behalf of someone else. She got in to a heated argument about it with one of the house parents. She was told that she was illogical, and had no right to be upset. This only made Mary more antagonistic. To soften the blow for Jimmy, she ran down to the Watertown library, and borrowed a Christmas record with organ, and chime music on it. Jimmy was delighted, and said that his mother would put it on tape for him. That afternoon Mary was ordered to leave Math class by an enraged Mr. Quake because she wrote a note, claiming that she lost her voice. She went outside, and played basket ball by herself. At the end of the school day she returned with pine cones, and hurled them one by one in to Mr. Quake's classroom. He chased her down the hall, but she got away. He couldn't see well, so Mary figured that he didn't know who he was chasing. However, the next day during Math he told her that the Red Sox were looking for a new pitcher. When Mary pretended not to know what he meant, he said "You know what I mean!"

Rehearsals for graduation began after the first week in June. They had to practice walking down the aisle in Dwight Hall, and on to the stage. Mary, being the shortest, was in the lead with Steve, Lorena, and the taller seniors in the rear. Once on stage they had to practice finding their assigned seats. During the second rehearsal Mary became silly, and began walking in zig zags, and pretending not to know where her seat was. The next day they rehearsed in their caps, and gowns. Mary was serious this time. Yet something silly happened anyway. She and Lorena's caps kept falling off. When the tassel came off of Mary's cap, they were both taken away. Nobody else had trouble with their caps. Tim's remained on his head when he took a bow after practicing his solo. In the evening all the students went on a cruise down the Charles River. Before the cruise could get under way, Gene fell in to the river, taking Hedrick with him! Because it was warm out they were given towels, and allowed to be part of the event. They were all given a nice dinner before returning to school.

On Thursday most of the students went home for summer vacation. Only the chamber singers remained with the seniors because they were going to be singing at the graduation. Linda, a house parent from Elliot took Mary to an employment agency in Newton. Mary received the addresses of three residential schools in Massachusetts. She was told that they were very traditional looking. One of them was bound to hire her. Later Sue, and Pat, the janitor took Mary out to dinner. They ran in to some friction at first because Miss Jackman was taking all the seniors out to eat. She wanted Mary to join them. Mary said "No", and stood her ground. This was supposed to be a special evening for Sue, Pat, and herself.

The next day was Graduation Day. It didn't start off well for Mary. For weeks she had been begging, and bribing the house parents to let her have an old brass dinner bell from Moulton Cottage. Because of her budding friendship with Jimmy, she too was becoming interested in bells. She even promised to buy them one to replace it. The constant answer was NO! Instead of getting ready, Mary begged, and then argued with Kathy and the other house parents about the bell. They had removed it, and locked it up having anticipated a repeat performance from Mary. She was difficult, and antagonistic toward them. She was furious with them for denying her everything, even this. After giving them a piece of her mind one last time she went to get ready. Linda took her aside, and told her that the bell was very old, and was like a tradition with Moulton Cottage. "You can't buy a bell like this one any more then you can buy a statue that stands in front of a school." Mary thought she understood. She was glad that some people at Perkins cared about tradition.

Mary wearing a nautical style dress, and a big white hat, was sitting under a tree; writing when she looked up, and saw two men approaching her. They turned out to be her father, and Father Hoyle! Mary jumped up, and ran to them. They didn't recognize her at first because she was dressed up. She usually acted like a Tomboy at home.

They had a special luncheon down at the Northeast Building. Mary introduced Lorena, and Steve to Father Hoyle. Lorena clasped his hand in hers, causing him to smile. Mary took a picture of this touching scene. Mr. Sullivan took Mary down to the square to close her bank account. When they returned Graduation was just starting. Mary was rushed in to her cap, and gown, and hurried on to the stage with the others.

Father Hoyle had to get back to the rectory. So Mr. Sullivan collected Mary, and her belongings. They left Perkins late in the afternoon.

During the ride home it became clear that once all the ceremonies were over, Father Hoyle was reverting back to his old self. He ignored Mary, and only talked with her father. She leaned back, and felt sad. She wondered how much she would miss Perkins. She thought of the beautiful, historical campus. She had enjoyed more freedom there then she did at home. She thought of Lorena, and Steve. She struggled to swallow the lump in her throat. She would keep in touch with them of course. Maybe she could invite them to her house during the summer for a weekend. They wouldn't take advantage of her father like her friend, Candice had. Maybe by the end of the summer she would be working, and living at one of the schools she had applied to. She was hopeful about this.

Chapter Seventeen

Middlesex Academy

Mary's first week at home was miserable, but not so much as because she was missing Perkins, as because she hated the diner, and truck stop, small town where there was very little culture. The only kind of people she knew were senior citizens, avid church goers, and a few disabled individuals like Jimmy. Most people she saw seemed like hicks, who were content with such a life. Mary wasn't, and she suspected that her father knew this. Mr. Sullivan clearly wasn't happy with his daughter. He complained that she acted younger then she was, she embarrassed him at his friend's houses by fidgeting, he didn't like the stories she listened to, or most of the shows she watched. Mary over heard him on the phone, telling all this to her counselor from Services for the blind. Mary felt like asking him if he wanted to trade her in for another daughter. She wouldn't mind. She found him repulsive looking, and his hygiene was far from perfect.(Gone were the days of Sunday suits.) The bathtub was full of curtains, rods, stools, and mats. How did he wash up? Mary supposed he sponged bathed at the sink. She would have to do the same thing. Whenever she tried to take a shower her father yelled at her for removing the things from the tub. "Must you shower, and wash your hair every day?" he would ask in an exasperated voice. Mary, knowing not to answer back, went to her room to cry tears of frustration. Mr. Sullivan was very frugal too. He saved everything, even used napkins and paper towels. "Don't throw that away!" he would exclaim. "That's hardly been used. We can save that!" Behind his back Mary would throw the used napkins away. His attitude toward Mary was growing worse. He was going from being an ice berg, to being a tiger. One evening at supper Mr. Sullivan told her that she should try running their house for awhile. "You'll have to learn eventually!" he said grumpily. Mary reminded him that she was seeking live-in positions. "You'll get tired of a life like that. Time will tell." This made her angry, but in a cautious way, she claimed that Ms. Standish put that thought in his head. "NO ONE PUT'S THOUGHTS IN MY HEAD!" growled the tiger. Despite what he was saying, Mary knew that Ms. Standish did talk to him on Graduation Day. Lorena over heard her telling him that a live-in job wasn't right for Mary, and that she would out grow the idea in time. So why was he lying now? Mary persisted in her views about finding a live-in job. "Humph! You couldn't do the work they would require of you…Besides, you couldn't get up early. You love your sleep". He sounded so contemptuous that Mary mumbled "Some people believe in giving a person a chance". "Humph!" was his only response. Later she cried in her room. This wasn't her home. It was merely a stop-over until she could find something better.

There were a few distractions from the tension between Mary, and her father. They went to the Fourth of July parade in Bristol. They also went to the Senior Olympics because Mr. Sullivan was a participant. They went over to Jimmy's house for a few hours. Jimmy was glad to see them, but he had the runs. Kathy, his mother said that it was a side effect of the increase of growth hormone pills he was being given. She had expected Jimmy to grow five, or six inches in a year, but he had only grown two. She wanted the doctor to make her son take an extra pill a day, but because it was making him ill, the doctor recommended only increasing it to a pill and a half. Mary didn't like Kathy's pushiness about her son's growth. Why was it so important to rush him to look like others his age? Unlike his mother, Jimmy was a "Happy go lucky" sort of person, who liked the idea of growing, but wasn't worried about it. He was more interested in music, chime clocks, and weather reports which he recited like a professional. The visits weren't one sided either. Jimmy sometimes visited Mary's house. He played the organ in the back parlor, and sometimes the piano in the living room at the front of the house. Mary and her father waited on him, answered all his questions, and made him feel at home.

By the middle of August Mary was desperate to leave home. One morning she waited for her father to leave for Mass. Then she called a cab, left a note telling her father where she was going, she grabbed her suitcase, and went to the bus station in Providence. She took a bus to Boston, and made her way to Perkins. She applied for a job at Howe Press. Because she had already worked there, she thought she had a good chance of being hired right away. To her dismay, Mary was told that after filling out an application she would have to wait a few weeks to see if her name was picked. Sue drove a deflated Mary to the YWCA in Newton, Where she spent a sad, lonely night. She returned home to the little yellow house the next day a little wiser, but just as determined to get away again.

Toward the end of August, Mary received a call from Middlesex Academy, in Concord, Massachusetts. Her application had been accepted. Mr. Sullivan drove Mary to the school, and helped her move in to her small apartment in one of the buildings.

The next morning Mary was told that she would be cleaning the Theatre & Arts building, a three story structure, and the only modern building on a otherwise beautiful, historical campus. An older woman, named Gloria, who cleaned one of the boy's dorms, was assigned to work with Mary for the first three days in order to show her the ropes. Mary found the first few days difficult. She couldn't eat breakfast because her stomach was in knots, and she frequently burst in to silent tears because she was in a new environment, and realized that she had actually been starting to grow accustomed to being at home. Once Gloria was sure that Mary was adjusting well, she left her on her own, and only stopped to talk to her at the end of each afternoon before she went home. Gloria had a family, and didn't live on campus. She was a quiet, good natured, Portuguese woman in her early forties. The building that Mary lived in not only contained apartments, the school kitchen, and massive dinning room were there as well. She ate all her meals in the dinning room because the apartments didn't have kitchens in them. Mary's apartment had a small living room. Half a wall divided this room from her even smaller bedroom. The bathroom was equipped with an antique tub, which Mary blissfully soaked in each evening, and a toilet so old that she had to pull a chain to flush it. Feeling isolated, she left her door open in the evenings after her bath. Her neighbor across the hall was a teacher named, Mr. Marks. He was polite, but liked to keep to himself. Despite this it comforted her to hear someone coming in, or going out. Otherwise she would have felt so cut off that she thought the world could end, and she wouldn't know it until she stepped out of her apartment. With the door reassuringly ajar, she spent the evenings watching TV.

During the first week at Middlesex Academy Mary wandered around the campus after work. She loved the Victorian buildings, the wide spread lawns, and the trees. It looked a lot like Perkins. However, the school was three miles from a small town that contained some nice old houses, but very few stores. The library was small, and Mary had no interest in the church, even if it was old. Perkins was close by a busy, populated city, where public transportation was plentiful. Concord was dead in comparison. She missed Watertown.

Soon all the students returned from summer vacation. The campus was populated, and noisy. Mary liked this, but because of her status, she wasn't expected to mingle with anyone except the hired help, and they weren't especially friendly toward her. Still she tried to make the most of it. After all, she was on an historical campus, and had the kind of position she wanted.

Mary went home every weekend. She couldn't bear to be lonely seven days a week. What made the weekends special was that Jimmy came over on Saturdays. He wasn't aware of the positive effect he had on Mary, and her father. He actually eased the tension between them. Talkative, bubbly Jimmy caused them to act cheerfully toward each other for the next day, or two.

One night up at school Mary watched a mini series called "Backstairs at the White House "After a week, or so Franklin Roosevelt replaced Mr. Disraeli in Mary's affections. He not only intrigued her because of all he did from his wheel chair, she also liked his looks, and his blunt, but caring personality. She thought of him throughout the day as she cleaned the Theatre & Arts building. She imagined what it would be like to know him. She thought that her eye problems would draw them close together. After all, he had a disability of his own. Soon she began thinking of him as a doting grandfather. She imagined him calling her "Little girl "in the friendly voice he used when he addressed Lillian, the young maid, who walked with a crutch. He called her "Little girl "too.

Mary started teaching herself to play the piano during her breaks, and late in the afternoon when her work was finished. She was able to sound out songs that she heard Jimmy play on the weekends. She couldn't play cords yet, but she figured she would learn from watching him. She had a secret desire to be like Jimmy that had started when she was still at Perkins. She not only admired his musical ability, she also admired his easy going temperament. She wished she could brush things off the way he did. Jimmy was little, and cute. Because she still wished she was little, and cute, Mary resented the growth hormone treatments that he was receiving. Besides, he had the mind of a child. Mary didn't see why he wasn't being allowed to continue to look like one. There was one song, not in Jimmy's repertoire that she really wanted to teach herself. It was "Happy days are here again." This was Franklin Roosevelt's favorite song because it was also the name of his campaign slogan.

By the end of September Mary no longer liked it at Middlesex Academy. Nobody talked to her, and her lunch break was pushed back an hour so that she wasn't eating with the other students, and teachers anymore. This was done because people noticed her picture of Franklin Roosevelt which she carried with her everywhere. She had it at the table, and was gazing at it frequently. Someone apparently reported her to Walter, an older man, who was her supervisor. Walter told Mary that she needed to learn to hide her feelings and interests when she was in public. Because he was kind, Mary didn't get angry at him.

In the middle of October Mary left Middlesex Academy. She had told her father how lonely she was at the school. Mr. Sullivan was sympathetic, and supported her decision to give her two weeks notice. He was very nice to her when she came home on weekends, and drove her to, and from Concord. Walter; her supervisor, was very understanding when she explained why she was quitting. He said that it must have been hard for a young girl like her to be away from her home, and family.

Once at home Mary no longer felt lonely, or cut off from the world. She was in familiar surroundings, and had her possessions. However, her father no longer felt like a friend. He reverted back to snapping at her, and criticizing her. Mary found it hard to bite her tongue, and keep from crying. One day was particularly bad for her. Mr. Sullivan took her to fill out job applications at various places. He became disgusted with Mary for using her magnifier to look at the print. "You embarrass me. What will people think if they see you using that thing? Why don't you use your glasses?" She wanted to tell him that she looked just as closely at print when she used her glasses, but this would have caused an argument. "You're writing too big!" complained Mr. Sullivan. "Why can't you ever write small?" She gritted her teeth, and glared at the application. By the time they left the last factory Mr. Sullivan was on a roll! Once he started criticizing Mary, he just couldn't seem to stop. In the car Mary raged inwardly as her father rehashed the past. He commented on the special schools she had been in, and accused her of knowing nothing about the world. She wondered what Franklin Roosevelt would think of her if he heard all the things Mr. Sullivan was saying about her. She couldn't understand why he was carrying on like this. Once in the fish & chip diner in Artic, Mary sat across from her father, and listened to him continue to verbally tare her to shreds. Not being able to answer back even when she was brimming with rage, Mary lit a cigarette, and began to burn her hand under the table. She glanced down, as she burned a roundish shape on her right hand. This kept her from lashing out at her father, and helped to confirm what an undesirable person she was. By now she was angrier at herself then she was at her father. Later when she calmed down, Mary bandaged her hand. She decided that if her father asked her about it she would say that she scraped her hand. He would believe this. Clumsiness was one of the many things he criticized her about. Mary almost wished she had stayed at Middlesex Academy.

Chapter Eighteen

Living in Limbo

Meal times with her father were turning out to be the most stressful occasions for Mary. Ever since he lost all his teeth he made the most disgusting noises when he ate. They were of the chomping, smacking, slurping variety. They caused Mary painful flash backs. When she was fifteen and in a foster home, her repulsive foster father used to molest her. He made disgusting noises when kissing her. The noises were very much like the noises her father made when he ate. He too was repulsive, and he was alone now that his wife was dead. Mary sometimes feared that because she was his adopted daughter, he might resort to touching her. It had happened once. A year ago when Mary was home from school they were saying good night to each other. As if in a dream, Mr. Sullivan had turned Mary so that her back was to him. He gazed at his wife's picture which sat upon the up right piano. He groaned, and rubbed her breasts. Mary sprang away from him! He suddenly came back to himself, and said good night to her. Since then she preferred to shake hands, or wave when going to bed. Mary felt very vulnerable, and angry. She couldn't express her feelings to her father. So when he made those disgusting noises at the table she screwed up her face, twitched, punched her leg and sometimes even cried quietly as he chomped, smacked, and slurped his food. When he noticed these things, Mr. Sullivan became irritated, and said "What's wrong with you?" Mary couldn't tell him. She sometimes wished she had never been adopted. Her life would have been so different. Maybe she would have grown up at Perkins, and spent vacations with foster parents or the parents of a classmate…if only.

Mary had a part time job cleaning Saint John & Paul's school. She worked every week day from four until six. She liked cleaning all the classrooms, and the auditorium. She got the job at the end of October. Near the end of November the CETA program got her a job working in the linen room at Kent County Hospital. Mary worked there five days a week, six hours a day. She gave Father Hoyle her two week notice. In the mean time she had to continue to clean the school each day after finishing her job at the hospital. "I feel sorry for you." said Mr. Sullivan as he picked her up at the school one evening. Mary shrugged. What was a little hard work? Why didn't he feel sorry for her when someone hurt her? More importantly, why didn't he feel sorry for hurting her himself? When Mary tried to tell the friendlier people her father associated with about the way he treated her they didn't believe her because he was so nice around most people.

Mary was so glad to get the job at Kent County Hospital. Now she wouldn't have to spend her days going on errands with her father, and having to endure his irritated presence when she filled out job applications. Perhaps he would be nicer toward her now that she would be out of his way part of the day. Because the hospital wasn't on a bus line, Mr. Sullivan drove Mary to, and from work. The linen room was on the ground floor. Mary entered the rear entrance, and went down a corridor. The linen room was where all the folding of sheets, towels, blankets, johnnies, and children's pajamas were done by Mary, and an old woman, named Madeline. Their boss was a middle aged man, named Mr. Chum. He was a fairly good boss, but he was also a chain smoker with a very bad cough. Men worked in the back room. They washed, and dried all the laundry in huge washers, and dryers. When Mary and Madeline finished folding the linen they had to place it on big metal trucks. The trucks was taken upstairs, by Madeline, and distributed to all the rooms. Mary liked Madeline. She was a slim woman with short curly grey hair. She had a funny habit of saying "That's it, see?" whenever Mary was talking to her. The other workers were kind, and helpful toward Mary. Then Josephine, a heavy set, bossy old woman, returned from vacation, and things began to change. Madeline was a follower, who let Josephine take the imitative in most things. She went out of her way to agree with her on everything. Josephine on the other hand, was rather brash, and judgmental, especially toward Mary. She often criticized her. It started during break time one morning. Mary was talking about books, and movies she enjoyed. Madeline was listening politely when Josephine spoke up angrily, and said that Mary should read the Good Book instead. It was her tone of voice, more then the suggestion that rubbed Mary the wrong way. Even without the angry manner, Mary wouldn't have liked Josephine because she sounded like a religious fanatic. From then on everything Josephine did, or said got on Mary's nerves. She, and Madeline often complained in front of Mary about how selfish, and irresponsible young people were. They deliberately shut her out of their conversations. According to them, young people couldn't do anything right. Clearly they enjoyed generation gaps. Mary placed more of the blame on Josephine then on Madeline. At first she tried to ignore the portly, white haired, bitter woman. However as the weeks went by she found herself snapping at her. She tried to be careful though, because she wanted to keep her job.

In the middle of December Mary and her father went to Perkins for the first of the three Christmas concerts of the season. Jimmy, who was performing on the hand bells; invited them. Mary, who still coveted Moulton's dinner bell, hatched a plan for taking it. She took one of her bells, a bandana, and some masking tape, and stashed them in her shoulder bag, then went to help her father pack a lunch to take with them.

They arrived in Watertown around Twelve Thirty. While Mr. Sullivan was having coffee at the Northeast building, and talking to people, Mary slipped away to Moulton. No one was around. Mary quickly swapped bells. She stuffed a bandana inside of Moulton's bell to silence it, wrapped masking tape around it, and then placed it in her bag. She wondered what Franklin Roosevelt would think of the slick move she had just made. She left her own bell in its place, and met her father over at the main building. The first part of the concert always began in the rotunda, just beyond the museum. The bell ringers' performers played five or six carols. Before the bell ringers arrived, Miss Trico let Mary ring some of the bells, and play the xylophone. Mary discovered that the bells had leather handles, and the clappers were padded which was what gave them their rich sound. Because they were brass, the ringers had to wear gloves when playing them. Along with the bells, there was a harp, flute, and a mandolin. When the bell ringers arrived Mary joined the audience. She saw little Madeline among them. Mary heard her say in her high voice that her mother couldn't make it to this particular concert. Her mother? Mary knew that an older woman had been visiting Madeline for the past two years, and bringing her home on weekends. She must have adopted Madeline. She had recently celebrated her Sixteenth birthday. Despite the weekly shots she had been receiving for two years, Madeline still looked, and sounded about seven. Mary was pleased about this. She hoped Madeline wouldn't grow much more. She, like Jimmy, who was a year older, was cute. They both had round faces, and delicate features. Mary often took pictures of them, and drew pictures too. If she couldn't be little, and cute she could at least see it, and enjoy it through them.

After the hand bell concert everyone filed in to Dwight Hall for the singing. Since the bell ringers weren't going to be performing again that day, Mary, her father, Jimmy, and his parents all left together. Mary took pictures of Jimmy, and his parents, then one of him alone. He was looking sad because his parents were leaving, and he had to wait until the following Friday to see them again. Mary reluctantly left the lovely campus, made lovelier by the Christmas decorations every where. During the ride home she felt better though. The radio was playing Christmas music from the late Fifties, and early Sixties. Mary enjoyed this, as she felt her bag where she knew the Moulton dinner bell was. It had been a very successful and fun Sunday. Her father seemed to enjoy everything, and didn't snap at her once!

Christmas day was pleasant for Mary, and her father. She was glad she didn't have to get up at five in the morning like she usually did. She and her father opened their presents after Breakfast. She felt bad for her father though. He only received gifts from her, and Father Hoyle. Why couldn't her Aunt Agnes and Uncle George have remembered him during Christmas? When her mother was alive they always visited the Sullivans; or had the Sullivans visit them. Mary supposed it was because her father was only an in law, and she was only an adopted child. They seemed to have forgotten that they were her God parents. Mary had never liked the older couple very much. She thought they were a little on the cold side, but she always believed they liked her father as well as her mother. Mr. Sullivan's friend, Jim came to dinner. Afterward they stayed in the kitchen to talk. Mary went to listen to an audio novel in the living room. Novels took Mary far away from Coventry. It was as if she entered the story, and became a part of it. She felt like she knew the characters in it. When the story ended Mary would look out the window, and see the ranch style houses across the street with small lawns in front of them, and long to be far away in a place like England, or Scotland in what ever era the story had occurred in. She sometimes sewed, or worked on her Baker's Dozen comic script while listening to stories.

Mary continued to work hard in the linen room, but her relationships with her co-workers slowly deteriorated. Josephine and Madeline continued to berate teenagers in front of Mary, who at nineteen was in that category. Josephine's youngest son worked in the back room. He was eighteen, or nineteen, and was the only good teenager, as far as his doting mother was concerned. Mary didn't think he was that nice. He seemed spoiled to her. One day when work slowed down in back Roy, a big man with black hair, and Josephine's son, Stan helped fold linen with the women. Roy gave Mary a hand instead of doing his own work. She resented this. She saw it as his way of saying that she wasn't capable of working on her own. She complained about it, and asked him if he thought she was retarded or something. Roy didn't answer which made her angrier. Roy started up a conversation with Stan. Mary felt jealous of Stan. While she was ignored, or talked down to, Stan was treated like a prince just because his mother worked there. He went about looking smug, and even ignored her once when she asked him a question. When Stan left the room Mary asked Roy if they were in love because of all the joking around they did together. "You have to joke around here, or you go Bats." said Roy. "Then Josephine must want me to go Bats!" answered Mary angrily. Roy didn't respond. She assumed that Stan must be queer because he laughed like a girl, and according to his mother didn't date. Roy must have told Stan what she said. After coffee break he yelled at her. She of coarse yelled back. Mr. Chum told her to calm down, and do her work. Mary tried hard to do this. It was just that she was so disgusted with her co-workers, Josephine especially since she was the ring leader. Everything had been fine until she returned from vacation. Why did everyone follow her? Mary's case worker from CETA visited her every week at the hospital. She was a young, friendly woman, named Sue. She was sympathetic about the trouble Mary was having. She urged her not to answer back when Josephine made her angry. She was certain that one day Mr. Chum would catch Josephine being mean to Mary, and he would be forced to see her as the instigator that she was.

Mary joined The Parks & Recreation group in December. This was a group of disabled members ranging from ages five up to around Twenty One. Jimmy belonged to this group. They met every Saturday morning at the recreation center to do arts & crafts. They talked, and listened to music while they cut, pasted, or colored, and painted. Jimmy loved to ask questions. He asked about the working of lawn mowers, drills, fans, busses, and cars. He also asked about clocks, chimes, and the church organist's choice of chords at the last Mass they both attended. Most of the kids in the group were in their teens like Jimmy, and Mary. One of them, a boy named, Rodney was obsessed with turn tables. He was always making up jokes about them. The conversations that went on weren't very stimulating, but Mary was glad to get away from her father for a few hours, and she was sure that he felt the same way. Often Jimmy was allowed to spend Saturday afternoons at Mary's house. His mother, Kathy would pick him up after supper. Mary usually cooked Johnny cakes or spaghetti for supper. Jimmy and her father liked her cooking.

Mary was worried about her father's cough. Every morning she was awakened by him hacking out in the kitchen. He claimed that he switched to cigars because they weren't as bad as cigarettes. Mary saw no evidence of this. She was afraid for him. She may not have been close to him, but she didn't want him to die!

In February Mary attended Jimmy's piano recital at Perkins. His parents picked her up and drove to Watertown, Massachusetts. She loved going back to Perkins no matter what the reason was. Jimmy wasn't feeling well, but he managed to play an impressive classical piece on the great pipe organ. Many students had their turn to perform on the organ, or the piano. Later Jimmy played a song on the piano called "Armenian folk song # 7." A couple of minutes after he finished a teacher came out, and informed Jimmy's parents that their son threw up back stage. As a result he rode home with his head resting on Mary's shoulder. She was touched by this.

In March Mary and Jimmy received their confirmation along with twelve other teenagers. Sue, Mary's case worker from CETA attended it. She brought her husband. When it was over they gave her a gift. It was a record with harpsichord music on it. Mary was very grateful, not only for the gift, but for their presence at the event.

Mary celebrated her Twentieth birthday with Jimmy, and her father. It was a warm April day in 1981. She received some nice gifts, including a Victorian looking alarm clock. Her birthday cake was a Boston cream pie. It was just the right size for the three of them. Later they visited the rectory, where Father Hoyle gave her a little bell. When giving it to her he said the strangest thing. "I'm giving you this bell, but if I should ever want it back, I want to know that you still have it". Feeling puzzled, Mary nodded.

Mary attended the Hand bell festival at Perkins along with Jimmy's parents. Jimmy was one of the bell ringers. Madeline was playing them too. Later during refreshments Mary saw her with her adopted mother. She was a heavy middle aged woman of medium height. Still small, and wearing a skirt, and blouse, Mary couldn't help taking Madeline's picture until her mother looked at her suspiciously, and shielded her daughter. Jimmy's parents took her to another piano recital that their son was in. Then because they now knew, and trusted Mr. Sullivan, they allowed him, and Mary to attend the school's final assembly, and take Jimmy home with them for the afternoon. Mary was happy!

In June Mary's job under the CETA program expired. Barbara, from Services for the blind took Mary, and her father to look at Vocational Resources in Providence. It was a sheltered work shop for people with emotional, or physical disabilities, located in a modern, one story building. It was decided that she would begin working there on June 30th. Mary was given mobility lessons to acquaint her with taking public transportation. She learned that she would have to take two busses to work, and back. The first one left the top of her street at six thirty. She would return at five. Mary wasn't looking forward to such a long day, but she did want to work.

The work day at Vocational Resources went from eight thirty to three thirty. Mary managed to get out at two thirty on Tuesdays, and Thursdays by claiming to have art lessons on those days. She spent the first week in the testing unit. They wanted to know what she was capable of, and how much work she could do in an hour. At the start of her second week Mary was placed in a regular department run by two women. The workers were all paid piece work. Most of them didn't make much money, even Mary, who was fast only made about fifty dollars a week. Because it was very hot that summer they were often dismissed after Lunch. Mary liked it at Vocational Resources, but one of her supervisors was very sharp tongued. Eventually Mary got in to an argument with her, and was sent to the office.

Mary worked at Vocational Resources until the end of July, then she quit. It wasn't worth putting up with their strict ways for the small amount of pay she received. After seeing some of her pay checks, her father agreed. So she spent the month of August going on picnics, and to fairs with Jimmy, and having him over at her house. One day Mr. Sullivan took Jimmy, his sister Corrine, and Mary to Rocky Point. They all rode some of the rides. There was a new Ferris wheel. It had two wheels that rode over each other. Mr. Sullivan wanted to ride this, and called Mary "Chicken" when she hesitated. She sat silently terrified as the wheels rode over each other. Mary was scared of heights, and this was worse then a regular Ferris wheel. Mary found her hand involuntarily sliding toward her father's hand. Horrified, she pulled it back, but it continued to slide across the bar toward his hand. When the ride was over Mary feared that her father had noticed. When he dropped Jimmy and Corrine at their house Mary tensed. Would he comment on, or take advantage of her vulnerability? She kept her distance at home.

By late August Mary developed an interest in the occult. Back in early June she watched "The Exorcist", and was horrified enough to start to take an interest in God, but this soon wore off. She sent away for books about witchcraft. She began learning, and practicing spells, and incantations in secret. She hoped this would bring about changes in her life. She wanted opportunities for a happier, more fulfilling life to come her way. She also wanted to prevent her father from becoming sick, and dying. When Mary wasn't chanting over candles, and incense she engaged in her other pass time. She had read a book by Louise Fitzhugh, called "The long secret". Like the girl in the book, Mary wrote quotes from the Bible, and Bartlett's book of quotations, and delivered them to people around where she lived. Having been given some freedom, and space by her father, who was busy as a tired senior volunteer, Mary wandered around Coventry, and placed notes in mail boxes, and on windshields, tucked under the wipers. She tied notes to rocks, and threw them over fences. She also mailed notes to people. She hoped everyone would talk anxiously about it, causing it to eventually get on the news. However her father caught her doing it after a couple of months. He said that he had suspected her all along. Feeling frustrated, and deflated, Mary tried to find some other way of having adventure, but it was difficult in a small, hick town. She had a job at a factory in East Greenwich during September, but it only lasted a month. Mary had been so depressed, and afraid of the day when she would have to be on her own that she actually contemplated suicide, but she couldn't go through with it because she was afraid of what God would do to her. She continued with her magic, but found it not as satisfying as she had anticipated.

Then one day late in October Mary found an advertisement at the back of a magazine. A Psychic, calling herself Sister Theresa, claimed to have the ability to change people's lives. She lived out West. Mary dialed the long distance number. An older woman talked to her. She asked for Mary's name, and birth date. Then she told her to call back in five minutes. When Mary called back she was told of the disappointing life she had lived so far. Sister Theresa said that she knew Mary was unhappy in a small town that offered her no future. Mary was impressed! She wanted to know why her life had been so hard. "It's because someone has cursed you. I don't know who it is yet, but I intend to find out". Mary's stomach flip flopped. Sister Theresa wanted to work with her to make her life better. "But first we must remove this curse". Mary found herself going to the bank to withdraw large sums of money to send to Sister Theresa. She ran up the phone bill which made her father not only angry, but suspicious. She wouldn't be truthful about who she was calling, or why. She began to see her father as an obstacle to her happiness. Soon she was sneaking out of the house to use the pay phone to call Sister Theresa. At first when Mary wanted to back out the woman yelled at her warningly.

"If you don't let me help you, your father is going to put you back in the crazy house!" Mary wondered how Sister Theresa knew that at age twelve she had spent a few months at the RI Medical center. The hardest part was that Mary was forbidden to tell anyone about what she was involved in. "If you tell, everything I'm trying to do for you won't work out right." warned Sister Theresa. She promised Mary that she was going to meet a good man soon.

As fall turned to winter Mary remained hopeful. Once again she and her father attended the Christmas concert at Perkins. Mary thought that the school must have worked its magic on her father, as well as her because when they were there he was always nice to her. She liked the Perkins Dad better then she liked the Home Dad. This year they stayed for the whole concert because the bell ringers were featured twice. Madeline was in a gorgeous, black velvet dress with white puffed sleeves. Mary took a lot of pictures of her, and Jimmy before, and during the concert when they were in their red robes.

At the end of December Mary returned to Vocational Resources. Her father took her bank book away from her. She had to make money to send to the Sister. Mary pushed herself to earn seventy dollars a week. At the end of each month she sent the Sister two hundred dollars, and still had a little for herself. She bought her money orders down town, and used the pay phone for her weekly calls to the woman.

By early summer Mary wished desperately that she could confide in someone, but she feared that Sister Theresa's spells would lose power if she did. At work Mary often sat with an over weight, whiny girl, who was obsessed with the roller coaster at Lincoln Park. She had tantrums when rain was forecasted for the weekend. "Oh I wish the Lord would appear to me, and tell me when the next nice weekend will be!" she would exclaim. Mary felt like choking! She wished the Lord would reveal whether or not Sister Theresa was a fraud. In the mean time she had things that distracted her from her problem. She and her father went to the final assembly at Perkins to hear Jimmy play the bells. Then they brought him to Vocational Resources for a tour of the place. For months Mary had been telling everyone there that Jimmy was her brother. Now she had a chance to show him off. When the break time buzzer went off Jimmy sang out "On a key of B Flat!" in the same pitch as the buzzer. Mary smiled proudly at everyone. Then Jimmy spent the afternoon at her house.

In late June Mary met a guy at work named, Mike. (The same name of the man Sister Theresa said she would meet.) He was a tall, thin man with black hair. He was Twenty, a year younger then Mary was. He was fairly good looking, and liked Mary because she looked, and acted younger then she was. When she left Vocational Resources in July because her training program ended, they started dating. Mike lived with his mother, and father in Coventry. He had his own car though. He took Mary to the movies, and out to eat. Sometimes they hung out at each others houses. Mike liked Mr. Sullivan, but he noticed how impatient he was with his daughter. Mary liked him for noticing, and secretly sympathizing with her. Like Mary, Mike was fanciful. He wanted to build a time machine so that they both could visit scenes from history. They also made crank calls sometimes.

Mary wanted to go to Perkins for the Christmas concert. However she couldn't get a ride from anyone, and she had no money for bus tickets. Over whelmed with disappointment; Mary made a snap decision. She left a note for her father; informing him that Jimmy's parents were taking her to Perkins for the concert. Then she bundled up, and headed for the highway. She was picked up by a truck driver. He was a family man; who wasn't happy about Mary hitch hiking. He wasn't going to Massachusetts; so he let her off at the Warwick exit. Mary was just sticking her thumb out a second time when a state trooper pulled up, and ordered her to get in his cruiser. Mary was frustrated over her plans being interfered with. She refused to tell the trooper her name, or address. However she changed her mind when he threatened to take her down to the barracks. After calling her father; the trooper dropped her off at the Howard & Johnson's motor lodge in Warwick.

To Mary's complete surprise Mr. Sullivan drove her to Perkins! He said very little to her, and let her greet old friends when the concert was over. During the ride home Mr. Sullivan continued to be quiet. Mary began to notice how tired he was. He slumped in his seat as he drove, and shifted uncomfortably from time to time. Mary was suddenly ashamed of her actions. Every time she looked at her father she felt like crying. She and her father had never been very open with each other. Mary was afraid to talk to him now. Instead she turned to her imaginary father, and poured her heart out to him. She shared her longing for Perkins, her shame over hurting her father and her realization that she needed to think before she acted; with the invisible tall, blonde military man who sat beside her.

Chapter Nineteen

Trying to live for God

By February of 1983 Jimmy, who hadn't grown since summer (Could Mary's spells have been at work here?) was put on growth hormone shots. He didn't like this. He was often scolded by his mother for struggling with the visiting nurse. Mary had grown disenchanted with Mike, who always complained about how boring everything, even Christmas was. He liked to tell her all the bad things the guys at Vocational Resources were still saying about her. He sounded as if he half agreed with them. He only liked movies that featured little girls. Mary wanted a guy who liked little girls, but Mike took it to the extreme. Finally she broke up with him. He began calling at all hours to insult her. Meanwhile Mary was worried about her father. He still had a bad cough. He went to bed early because he grew tired easily now. Mary still felt compelled to call Sister Theresa, and send her money. One night Mary was watching TV by herself. She felt a sudden need to pray to God. She silently begged him to reveal the truth about the woman. She promised to act better, and help her father more. The next morning Mary called Sister Theresa from a pay phone. She wanted to know why she couldn't reach Sister Theresa for ten days. "It's because I died, and came back to life!" announced Sister Theresa. Mary heard a man laugh loudly in the back ground. "You died, and came back to life?. Now I've heard everything!" When Mary asked who was in the back ground she was told that the voice belonged to a spirit. Mary said goodbye, and hung up. God had certainly answered her prayers. She felt such relief. Suddenly life didn't seem so bad. Mary found her father, and told him everything.

After Mary was released from her secret involvement with Sister Theresa she started taking an interest in Church, not that she hadn't been involved in church activities. For the past year Mary had been playing the hand bells at a church in West Warwick. Mr. Sullivan drove his daughter to the church every Saturday morning. While she and the other girls rehearsed, he did errands. Her eye sight often got in the way causing her to have trouble seeing the music sheet. Some of the girls, who played the bells with her, were scornful of her because she couldn't always keep up. One day Mary bumped in to the table that held the Communion wine. It spilled all over the rug. The girl, who was asked to help Mary clean it up, told her that she hated her. Mary swallowed a lump in her throat, and remained silent. In spite of these hardships, Mary persevered, and tried to become a better bell ringer.

Surprisingly enough she had her father's sympathy about the girls' attitude toward her. He said that they were a bunch of little stinkers, who would get what was coming to them some day. Mary gave God very little thought. She was there to be a bell ringer, not a worshipper. Now things were different. She disposed of her magic books, candles, and incense. Although he was still impatient with her, Mr. Sullivan was pleased with the change in his daughter. What he didn't know was that despite Mary's commitment to be a good Catholic, she was very troubled. During the past few months she had seen movies about exorcisms, namely "Amityville Horror two-the possession." Mike took her to see this back in October. Mary had been haunted by it ever since. She couldn't sleep with the light off. She had trouble sleeping period. At bed time Mary went through a ritual which consisted of turning on the light in the hall before shutting off the living room light. Then she would run down the hall, turn on her bedroom light, and switch off the light in the hall. She stayed up listening to audio novels. Then when she couldn't put it off any longer, she would get in bed with the light still on, and pull the covers over her head. Her mind sent her images from that awful movie. She would see Sonny, his face contorted, as he shot his family. She could almost hear the animal voice that came out of him when talking to the priest. She saw the end when the priest became possessed in place of Sonny, who was restored to his old self. Along with this, Mary was haunted by scenes from the exorcist. She couldn't get the girl's ravaged face or animal voice out of her mind. Feeling over whelmed, Mary silently prayed to God for protection. During the day she stuck close to her father when he took her on errands, sometimes treading on his heels. He was very religious. Surely he was under God's protection. When he yelled at her, or demanded an explanation, she couldn't give him one. She was afraid of talking about her fears, believing that if she voiced them they would come true. Because Mary didn't know why people became possessed she couldn't be sure that it wouldn't happen to her.

 Along with the constant fear, Mary began to experience something else. As she thought about the Lord more, and tried to be close to him, her mind became full of blasphemies toward him. This happened most during church, or when Mary was praying. The most obscene, and violent thoughts would come unbidden in to her head. Frantically she squelched them with thoughts that rhymed. But the blasphemies always came back. Mary didn't know what to do. She feared judgment. Once the director of the senior center told her that the thoughts probably came from anger that Mary was suppressing toward God because of the difficult childhood she had experienced. Mary shook her head. "No, that can't be!" she exclaimed. God answered her prayer regarding Sister Theresa. He was good. No one was supposed to be angry at him! Mary couldn't accept what the woman told her. The blasphemies continued, often causing Mary to repeat the same prayer four, or five times. Her night terrors continued also.

When she couldn't cope any more, Mary contacted her case worker from State Services for the blind. Her case worker sent her to The Kent County mental health center for counseling. Mary found it hard to talk about her fears because if she came out, and voiced them, she was tempting fate. So she hinted, imploring the counselor with her eyes to pick up on what she was trying to say. She couldn't come out, and say what the blasphemies were either because God would surely judge her for blaspheming aloud.

Toward the end of February Mary joined the Catholic Youth Organization. (CYO) They met every Wednesday evening for prayer meetings. Sometimes they went out for pizza afterward. It was during one of these prayer meetings, followed by pizza that Mary met a girl, named Marie. She was Nineteen, and still lived at home with her mother, step father, and three brothers. She owned a car, and was in the process of trying to find where she belonged in the working world. Marie drove Mary home one Wednesday night. She made no comment about the small, cluttered house, or the three cats, one of them half balled. However, she was impressed with Mr. Sullivan. She liked his sense of humor, and thought he was very clever. Mary knew her father wasn't a bad man, but she thought that Marie was making a hasty judgment. Despite this, Mary, and Marie formed a friendship quickly. They went out for coffee on some evenings. One Saturday Marie sat in on one of Mary's hand bell rehearsals.

As February turned in to March Marie started doing landscaping for Saint John, and Paul. Mary helped her. They talked, and joked around a lot. Marie had a crush on one of the younger priests. She went out of her way to attend Masses said by him. Often she brought Mary. As Marie glanced at her and giggled in to her hand, Mary giggled with her. She knew how Marie felt. She once had a crush on a priest. The priest that Marie liked worked for Father Hoyle, Mary's fatherly heart throb. Marie's priest was young, highly intelligent, an intellectual type. Marie claimed that her real father, who died when she was very young, was highly intelligent as well. Apparently he was a lot smarter then her step father, who she felt contempt for. He was a man with average intelligence, who worked as a manager at a factory. Marie felt only a little less contempt for her mother for marrying such a man. She preferred to spend time with Mary, and her father. She thought Mr. Sullivan could do no wrong. She showed no sympathy toward Mary when she complained about him.

Still Mary continued to hang around with Marie. When they weren't talking about Mr. Sullivan, Mary found Marie to be a smart, humorous girl, who was full of energy, and adventure. They went on camping trips with some of Marie's friends. Sometimes Mary slept over at Marie's house. Marie had a nice bedroom upstairs. Yet she chose to sleep on a bed in the cellar. Her dresser, desk, and chair were down there as well. Mary used a sleeping bag, and a pillow. Marie said that she preferred to be separate from her family. Mary thought Marie's mother, and stepfather were nice, caring people, but she didn't want to challenge her friend.

Because of Marie, Mary was forced to listen to rock music, something that she had avoided since her senior year at Perkins. Eventually her resentment over this lessened, and eventually she went back to liking it.

Marie made room for the things that mattered to Mary sometimes. In May she took Mary up to Perkins for the annual hand bell festival. Jimmy, who was responding to the growth hormone shots, much to Mary's disappointment, was delighted to see them. After a little over a year of shots, he was taller then Mary and his mother sent him for permanents regularly. Mary didn't like Jimmy's new look, but she still liked him.

As Mary went out with Marie, spent time with jimmy, and battled with her fears, and blasphemies, something was happening to her father. Early in June his old ulcer, from years ago, flared up. At the same time his prostate became unbalanced. He had to go to the bathroom every ten minutes. He often complained that he couldn't urinate entirely when he went. Mary worried about him. Sometimes she thought God was making her father sick in order to punish her. This fear extended to other family members too. One day Mary tried to rouse one of the cats. The cat didn't stir. She backed away from the cat, and ran out the back door, believing that God had taken the cat's life because of her blasphemous thoughts. Seeing the cat alive, and walking around didn't lessen her belief that God would do such a thing. Still she tried to serve him, as she suppressed the unwelcome thoughts.

Like the previous summer, Mary was allowed to take part in The Parks & Recreation day camp. This camp was for young people with disabilities. Jimmy was there every day. Among the other campers was a little girl with Down syndrome. She was Eight, had straight blonde hair, and glasses. Her name was Kelly. What really interested Mary about Kelly was that she was a "Daddy's Girl". She always mentioned him, sometimes threatening to tell him when someone displeased her. Kelly not only loved her father, she loved all men. She sat on the laps of the oldest male campers, and begged them for piggy back rides. For the first week Kelly was in "Male Heaven". Then her mother told the counselors that Kelly could only act affectionately with her father. It was very hard for Mary to see Kelly so unhappy. She sympathized with her. Then during the last week of camp, one of the male counselors took pity on Kelly, and paid her some extra attention.

After a month of day camp, Mary watched her father grow worse. He was hospitalized when it was discovered that he had prostate cancer. He was promptly operated on. Once back at home, he became worse. He started getting extremely bad head aches. He frequently snapped at Mary because her ex boy friend, Mike pestered them with obscene phone calls. One day when they were visiting his friend, Tonya's house (He loaned her and her husband money to purchase the house) her little nephew was running around wildly. When he crashed in to

Mr. Sullivan's chair, he took the little boy, and spanked him! Mary stared at her father, feeling shocked, and fear. She figured he must have been in a lot of pain to react that harshly.

By the middle of September Mr. Sullivan was hospitalized again. The cancer had spread to his skeletal system. He had dime sized tumors on his head. It was decided that something had to be done about Mary. Her father's friends didn't think she should be leaving alone. Tonya, who never liked Mary, took her in for a few days, but they didn't get along. Rick, Tonya's quiet, rational husband had to defuse several arguments between them. Mary went home. Marie stayed with her most of the time.

Mary suffered a head injury one day when the lid of her cedar chest came down on her. The sudden shock of pain enraged her! Believing that God was responsible, she slammed the lid on her head several more times, all the while silently asking God if he was now satisfied. Because Coventry had free ambulance service, Mary not only rode to the hospital in an ambulance, she also rode home in one. During the ride home Mary found herself engaged in a friendly conversation with a handsome paramedic. Mary was in love. She thought about the paramedic all the time. She visited the fire station, leaving drawings with the man's name on them. At first she was welcomed. Then he grew tired of her. All the same, Mary thought she could win him over. She started dressing, and trying to act like a woman, and wearing make up. When this got her no where with the tall, handsome paramedic, Mary hoped to meet someone like him.

Before the cancer that was now rampant inside of Mr. Sullivan, ruined his vocal chords, Mary over heard him telling a nurse that his wife died of colon cancer. Mary did a double take! Five years ago he had told her that Mrs. Sullivan died of a heart condition. All this time Mary had thought herself responsible for her mother's illness because she was such a "Problem Child". After the nurse left Mary timidly asked her father about what she over heard. He told her that he lied about her mother's illness because he thought the other students at Perkins would have shunned her if they knew that her mother died of cancer. Mary accepted his explanation, but wondered if the students really would have thought that cancer was contagious.

In October of 1983 Mary's father died at Kent County Hospital. Mary was painting the living room when the doctor called, and gave her the news in a mechanical tone of voice. Two women, selected by Mr. Sullivan stepped in to help Mary. They were Pauline, and Joan. Mary had known Pauline for almost five years. She and her husband were members of the Involved tax payers of Coventry. They had been good friends of Mary's father. Joan's husband was an electrician, who did a lot of work for the Senior citizens center. Pauline and Joan took care of Mary's finances. In December they moved her out of the little, yellow house that was in disrepair. The main beam was rotted through because of termites. With some influence from the right people, Mary was placed in Woodland Manor, an apartment complex in rural Coventry. It was a few miles down the road from Pauline, and Joan, who lived near each other. Although they helped her, the two women wanted Mary to be independent of them for the most part.

The apartment building where Mary lived was at the back of the property. The apartment was gorgeous, and subsidized. But Mary wasn't happy there. For the first time in her life she had to walk everywhere, or take the bus. Woodland Manor was off the beaten track. It was a three mile hike to the nearest bus stop. Mary continued to go to church, and to her counseling sessions. She also went to bars, and often drank too much. She had been doing this since September. She started going to the bars with Marie, and some of her friends. Soon she was going without Marie sometimes. Now Marie was married. So Mary didn't see her as much. She was very lonely in the apartment.

In order to improve herself, Mary signed up for a course in writing at The community college of RI in January. She spent many days doing her home work at McDonalds. She bought food and coffee periodically. As a result nobody bothered her. She still fantasized about the paramedic until one evening she saw him at McDonalds, and was introduced to his girl friend, a tall blonde woman, who found Mary amusing. Mary wasn't trying to be amusing. She not only disliked the woman for having the man of her dreams, but for looking down on her as well.

In February Mary called the Catholic Diocese in Providence, and found out where Sister Jane was living. She was given an address in Kentucky. With some trepidation, Mary called the convent. How would the nun react to Mary looking her up after so many years? The first nun she spoke to put her fears to rest. "Oh Mary, she never forgot about you~" exclaimed the woman. She put Sister Jane on the phone. Sister Jane was so happy to hear from Mary. Mary felt happy as well, and relieved. They reminisced about the times Mary stayed at Saint Vincent's infant home in Providence. Mary learned that Sister Jane, and the other sisters had been sent back to Kentucky in 1970. Mary had been nine, and happily embracing life at Bradley Hospital, unaware that the woman, who had been like a mother to her was no longer living in RI.

Mary wrote to, and called Sister Jane frequently over the months. Sister Jane was always receptive to her. Pauline and Joan were pleased that Mary was in contact with the nun. They were also pleased that Mary was participating in a minstrel show, organized by The Hope Jackson Ladies Auxiliary of which Mary was a member. Mary practiced with the chorus, and was planning to do a solo as well. The show was scheduled to take place early in June.

In April of 1984 when Mary was turning twenty-three, her case worker placed her in the Blind Venders Association. Every day Mary had to take the bus to Providence where she and some other visually impaired people were trained to run snack bars in government buildings. After a few weeks Mary realized that she would rather work for a vender, instead of becoming one. She was a good worker, but was frequently criticized for not smiling. This made her more shy and self conscience.

There was a young man in the training program named Roy. He had curly, dark blonde hair, and glasses. He liked Mary. He was about the same age as she was. He joked with her, and told her a little about himself. He lived with his parents in Olneyville. He had two sisters, and three brothers. One of his sisters, and her son lived there with them. In May Roy invited Mary to his house for Sunday dinner. Because there was no bus service to Coventry on Sundays Roy had his cousin pick Mary up.

Roy, and his family lived on the first floor of a n apartment house on the corner of Delaine St. Roy's home was cluttered, but was filled with friendly, social able people. They all welcomed Mary.

Chapter Twenty

Life in the fast lane

Roy and Mary started dating right after her first visit to his home. During the week Mary worked at one of the snack bars for a woman named Ella. Her snack bar was in the city hall. Roy was working hard at another snack bar. He wanted one of his own eventually.

Mary began spending weekends at Mama Sara's house in Olneyville. She lived there with her husband, Roy SR, their son, Roy, and their grandson Little Roy. Roy's young nephew's parents were divorced. His mother Diane lived there sometimes. She was a young, friendly, woman, who liked to party with her friends. Mary liked her. Roy had another sister. Her name was Carla. She was a single mother with a two year old daughter named Shannon. They lived in Cranston. Carla had a room mate named Jean. They often visited the house in Olneyville. Roy also had two brothers. One of them lived out of state. They were both married, and had kids. Roy had friends, and cousins. The house was usually noisy, and crowded. As with most big families, arguments often erupted in the house, but Mary didn't mind. She loved staying there. It was so different from her lonely existence back in Coventry. She found her busy life in the city to be a welcome diversion from her phobia about possession, and the blasphemies that plagued her mind. Mary still had commitments back home. She did Aerobics at a gym down the road from where she lived. She was still practicing for the Hope Jackson Minstrel Show.

In June the show was put on. Mary sang with the chorus, and did a solo. The show was a hit! Everyone performed without any disasters. Pauline and Joan came to watch. As if this wasn't enough, Mary prepared to go visit Sister Jane in Kentucky right after the show. She packed the new summer clothes she had just taken off of lay away. Her hair had recently been dyed blonde, and she now wore glasses. She brought a bottle of coffee syrup to give to Sister Jane to remind her of the twelve years she lived in RI. When Sister Jane met her at the airport in Cincinnati, she was wearing a new white dress. The nun recognized her right away. Apparently Mary still resembled the five year old that Sister Jane remembered. She found this reassuring some how. It was Sister Jane's pleasant voice, and southern accent that Mary recognized because she, like so many other nuns, no longer wore a habit. In her early fifties, Sister Jane now wore her brown hair in a perm. She dressed comfortably, but conservatively.

The old convent was in a city called Covington. Because of the crime in the area, an alarm was used at night. Mary was as happy to see Sister Jane as she was to see her. The other nuns welcomed her too.

During her first night there Mary was home sick for Roy, and his family. She had her picture of her latest heart throb to make things easier. Thomas Jefferson had been a part of Mary's life when she was fifteen. Now he was back.

Sister Jane had to work during some of the week that Mary was with her. She worked as a nurse at a home for unwed mothers. Outside of work they went to visit Sister Jane's elderly mother, who lived in a small, modern house just outside of Covington. Sister Jane swept through the house like a whirl wind, cleaning everything, and doing the laundry. Mary was eager to help her. While they worked, they talked. Sister Jane told Mary that it was she who weaned her off the bottle. "When you were about a year and a half your mother readmitted you because she couldn't wean you. So I had to go through that with you". She told Mary that she helped her through most of the mile stones that babies and toddlers go through. They went to amusement parks, to restaurants, and to a special dinner for all of The Sisters of Divine Providence. Some of them remembered Mary when she was a baby, and a little girl. She frequently stayed at the infant home in Providence where they once worked, back in the sixties. A lot of reminiscing went on with Mary listening, and asking questions. She discovered that one of the things her mother yelled at her about throughout her childhood didn't happen the way she said it did. Mary expressed regret about having spread German measles around the infant home when she wasn't quite three. The nuns didn't remember this. "I was told that the babies had the measles, and I went in to visit them after being told not to. As a result, I caught the measles, and caused an epidemic!" Sister Jane and the other nuns were puzzled. Then Sister Jane explained that she used to be in charge of the isolation wing at the home. "I received all the new arrivals, and kept them with me for a few weeks, just to make sure that they had no contagious illnesses. Then they were placed with the other babies, and small children. Now that I think of it, you did have German measles as a toddler, and some of the babies did too, but it wasn't an epidemic!" Mary felt some what relieved. Sister Jane told her that she was always in the isolation wing when she was at Saint Vincent's because she was a special case, on account of her poor eye sight, and Sister Jane was in charge of her. "Did I like it there?" asked Mary. "You liked it enough not to want to go home!" answered the nun abruptly. Mary feared that this was a rebuke, but Sister Jane went on to say that Mary always put up a fight when she had to leave. "I remember what a hard time we had getting you in to your parent's car. But you were little, and didn't understand things." Mary nodded, adding that she had been very attached to Sister Jane. "Yes, and you knew who to run to for protection when you were in trouble too." Sister Jane laughed as she said this. She recalled how Mary used to burst in to the chapel every morning with an angry child care worker hot on her heels because she wanted Sister Jane to save her from being smacked for not eating her breakfast. Something else happened that her mother didn't tell her about. Sister Jane met Mary's real mother. "It was on the day you were brought to us. Your mother was a young girl about five feet tall with medium length, light brown hair. She reluctantly handed you to me." In spite of Mary's questions, Sister Jane could only recall one other thing. "You started out as Joanne. That was the name she chose.

Many of the other things Mary's adopted mother talked about did happen, but they had been exaggerated in some cases. Although she had been high spirited; and mischievous, she wasn't quite the little monster that her mother had made her out to be. Sister Jane wasn't the dizzy, irresponsible, selfish person that Mary grew up believing she was either. In fact, everyone around her respected Sister Jane, and said that if someone needed a friend, they should look for this particular nun. Mary remembered this to be the case even though her mother had tried to cloud her memories with her jealous remarks.

All too soon the visit ended. When Mary arrived at Green Airport Pauline and Joan were waiting to take her home. Pauline had hoped that the visit might lead to Sister Jane inviting Mary to live near her, but this didn't happen. Mary was mildly disappointed as she told Pauline that nothing like that developed. She and Sister Jane continued to write, and call each other though.

Mary and Roy continued to see each other until the end of July. She was the one who backed out of the relationship because she wasn't attracted to Roy, and she could see that he was crazy about her. She stayed in Coventry, and went to the gym. She kept up with the Hope Jackson Ladies Auxiliary meetings. They were preparing to start rehearsals for another show in December. Even with these activities Mary still had plenty of time on her hands because she no longer worked at the snack bar on a regular basis. She was made substitute status, and only worked occasionally. Her friend, Marie, and her husband had a baby. His name was Jeremiah. He was only a few months old. Marie's husband, Larry was a warm, loving person, but he had a demanding, ill tempered side to him as well. Mary didn't feel comfortable around him. Once Marie told her that Larry found an old love letter that she wrote to the priest she was fond of. Larry screamed, swore, and smashed his guitar against the wall. Then he threw himself down, and cried in her lap, apologizing repeatedly for his performance. Marie tried not to laugh as she smoothed his hair, and said comforting things to him. She wanted to say "It was your guitar you broke. Why should I care?." Like before, they got along fine when Marie didn't talk about Mary's father. Once in Burger King Marie said that she had treated Mr. Sullivan like a jerk. Mary's temper flared! "Oh yeah Well you treated your mother like a jerk!" Marie shrugged. "Well my mother is a jerk. So that doesn't count."

One day late in September Mary was doing aerobics at the gym. A song that she and Roy loved came on. It was "Let's hear it for the boy." This had been their song. She found that although she didn't love Roy, she missed him. She figured that maybe she could grow to love him if she tried. She called him. They talked for an hour, or so. They decided to try again. She went back to staying on the weekends.

Mary tried to grow close to Roy, and find him attractive. They took bathes together; she trimmed, and used a blow dryer on his curly, dark blonde hair. They made out on the floor in front of the TV when the visitors went home. They stayed up late watching their favorite science fiction shows. They slept with the stereo on throughout the night. Sometimes Roy's sister Diane's friends would show up at two in the morning, honking their horns, and wanting to know if she was home. Some of her friends were nice to Roy, and Mary. They gave them rides to restaurants, and doctors' appointments.

When Mary finally did make love she was surprised that there was no blood. Then she remembered that she hadn't been a virgin since she was Seven. An older boy had penetrated her then stopped out of fear when she struggled, and cried out. Then of coarse she had been molested in a foster home when she was fifteen. Because of these experiences, Mary hadn't had much of a sex life since then, unless you counted the brief flirtations back in the Coventry taverns the previous winter soon after her father died.

By Thanksgiving Mary still wasn't in love with Roy. Instead she had a major crush on Captain Kirk, from Star Trek. However she was hopeful that something would develop if she stayed with Roy long enough. Besides, she liked his family, friends, and the location of their home. Mary knew that the neighborhood was run down, and had a lot of crime. But she was impressed. She felt like she had "hit the big times", as some would say.

The first time she told Roy that she loved him was when he was in the hospital. Because he needed to have a cyst removed. She spent the evening visiting him. As she was leaving he told her that he loved her. She looked at him lying in the hospital bed, and said that she loved him too. He smiled at her warmly. Back at the house Mary was dismayed to discover that she didn't feel the same way. She felt relieved to be at the house without Roy. She began to realize that she had confused concern with love.

In the spring of 1985 Roy asked Mary if she wanted to get engaged. By now she knew that she didn't, and probably never would love Roy. It was one thing to live with a guy, and his parents, but she couldn't get engaged to, or marry someone she didn't love.

Mary was working at the snack bar in the courthouse. This was her part time job. She was there from nine until Three, Monday through Friday. She worked for an elderly, blind woman named Ruth. The snack bar sold cigarettes, coffee, sandwiches, juice, soda, candy, pastry and newspapers to the lawyers, cops, judges and criminals that occupied the building. Once a young woman with long, blonde hair selected a candy bar, and handed Mary a one dollar bill. As Mary gave her the 60 cents change, the woman insisted that she had handed her a twenty. "No you didn't!" exclaimed an outraged Mary. "You gave me one dollar" She pulled open the drawer and lifted out the cash box. "See? There are no twenties" At this, the woman turned away and sat down at one of the tables. Mary supposed that this happened a lot at these snack bars, seeing as how they were operated by the Blind venders association. She was grateful to be partially sighted. She felt triumphant, having caught a dishonest person in a lie. a feeling that she didn't often experience around people. It was the spring of 1985, and Mary had been working for various venders for the past year.

One afternoon when Mary was having her coffee break, a tall, woman with shoulder length dark brown hair entered the snack bar. "Mary?" she asked tentatively. Mary turned in her seat. "Yes?" "Hi it's Patricia Davies, Warren's wife. Remember? I talked to you at your bus stop and you said you worked here part time" Mary groaned inwardly. So the gung ho religious woman didn't forget her or where she worked, what a shame. It was just her luck!! Now she was going to have to sit here and hear more about how she was going to go to hell if she didn't accept Jesus as her lord and Savior. Patricia told Mary about her mixed up, sinful, past and that of her husband's" But that doesn't matter to Jesus. He loves us unconditionally. We just have to turn our lives over to him, and ask him in to our hearts". In spite of the woman's pushiness, something nagged at Mary and she found herself agreeing to go to church with her the following evening.

The next afternoon at four thirty, Mary said goodbye to Mama Sara and her daughter Diane, who had recently moved back home. Unwilling to tell them that she was doing some thing so not cool as visiting a church, she said that she would be out shopping. She was careful to get out of the house without Mama Sara's son's dog Berretta following her. He often did this. The big, black dog had a mind of his own and went where he wanted; whenever he wanted. He was seen by many raiding the garbage cans, looking for food to enjoy. Mary was afraid to actually stand up to the large dog. So she slipped out of the house. She hurried down Audrey St and waited by Almacs .Fifteen minutes later Patricia Davies picked Mary up and headed up to Greenville where the church was. In the car were two of the three daughters that Warren and his wife had. Mary saw their third daughter, a little girl named Nora when they arrived at the church. She had been injured several months earlier. The pastor and his wife got in to trouble with the law for refusing to let the little girl receive medical attention, because they thought that God would heal her. Mary saw Nora moving quickly around the one story church with its wall to wall carpeting and paneled walls. She was on crutches and her head was covered by a bandana. Her light brown hair was in braids. She was cheerful and talked animatedly to everyone. At one point she happily but innocently said something inappropriate and was gently corrected by one of her older sisters. Mary noticed that Nora and all the other small children were wearing pajamas with feet in them. They looked ready to be put down to sleep soon after the service started. When it did, Mary was totally unprepared for what she saw.

No sooner had the music started, then everyone, children and adults alike, even Nora got to their feet and began jumping and clapping! Mary who had been brought up as a Catholic, looked around at these peculiar people and wondered what planet they were from! She felt like crying. She struggled hard to swallow the lump in her throat and wished heartily that Father Hoyle, a priest she much admired, was with her. Surely he would rescue her and comfort her. However, Father Hoyle was out in Coventry, and couldn't help her. Oh why had she got herself in to this mess? After about five or six songs, Pastor Warren got up to give his sermon. He talked about the usual things, everyone being a sinner, Jesus loving them in spite of it, how they must love others as well. He told them that when he was in downtown Providence one day, a handful of people jumped him and beat him up badly. "But in spite of what they were doing to me, I was praying for them and asking God to forgive them." Mary found this hard to believe. She figured that he had to say this because he was a minister. Nobody could be so forgiving. She wondered if he received the beating because he and his wife wanted to let God heal their youngest daughter's head injury instead of taking her to a doctor. Mary remembered hearing about this on the news. The couple temporarily lost custody of the little girl but were allowed supervised visits with her at the hospital. And seeing her at church this evening, Mary couldn't find much wrong with her.

Pastor Warren's sermon changed coarse. He began to belittle the Catholic Church. It became apparent to Mary at least, that he had a deep hatred of Catholics. Then she remembered hearing a rumor that he had once tried to become a priest but was rejected for some reason. Still, as a minister, it didn't seem right for him to be so full of anger. There were a lot of young people in the congregation, some regulars and some visitors like Mary. Pastor Warren turned his attention to them. "I hate to tell you this, but if your parents are Catholics, they're going to hell!" He paced back and forth, gesturing wildly. "It doesn't matter if they lead good lives. They will go to hell unless they are converted. So you better go home and start converting them!" Mary gaped at this boisterous man. "Her father, a devout Catholic, was dead…did that mean that he was in hell?

Afraid that she was going to start balling right then and there, Mary got up, asked where the bathroom was, and hurried there. Once inside, she cried her eyes out! She and her father had never been close. It had always been clear right from the start that most of his love, devotion, moral support, and sympathy was for his wife, not Mary. However, he had always provided for her and tried to make sure that no harm came to her. And all the good things he did for other people and the church itself. That had to count for something in God's eyes. If it didn't, she didn't want God!! Mary splashed a lot of cold water on her face as she tried to get her emotions under control. All she wanted to do now was go home to Mama Sue's house. But she was up in Greenville with no way of getting home until the service ended. So Mary went back out in to the sanctuary and tried to keep up a brave front.

When Mary got home she sat down to watch TV. Roy, her boy friend, would have laughed if he knew about where she had been, and so would his nephew, Little Roy. The only person in the house who paid any mind to church was Roy SR., who was visited by a priest, and given communion once a week because he couldn't walk.

Mary sat there, and thought about the ride back to Olneyville with Patricia. She wanted to know what Mary thought of her husband's church and his sermon. It seemed best to take the "polite but not too eager" approach. And this was exactly what Mary did. She had no intention of taking such a reckless wade through a strange gathering of people again, with such a reckless man such as Pastor Warren appeared to

As spring turned in to summer, Mary continued to live with Roy, and go on outings with his friends. However, Roy was starting to become cold, and antagonistic toward her. He often made fun of her in front of everyone for drinking too much. When they all played card, or board games Roy would make fun of her if she made a mistake. Mary retaliated. They both were spending a lot of time with a couple, who lived in the projects. Paul and Corrine was a mixed couple. Paul was African American, and Corrine was white. They had three small children. As time went on Mary found herself spending more, and more time with the little girl, and her two brothers. Kenny, the oldest, was hyperactive, and very sensitive. He was always in trouble with his father, and Roy because of this. Mary made a point of being extra nice to him.

Finally Mary realized that the relationship with Roy was going no where. Toward the end of August she broke up with him, and moved back to Coventry. She continued to visit Roy's mother, Mama Sara, and her husband.

Mary got off the bus in Olneyville Square. She was wearing her new Reeboks and listening to her radio. She stopped at the bank to get some money. While in line, she noticed an old woman with a skinny girl who was about eleven or twelve. She kept hopping from one foot to the other and trying to twist out of the woman's tight grip. "Grandma, let go of me. I won't run away, I promise!" She had to plead several times before the woman would even consider it. Finally she said "Are you sure you will stay in line with me if I let you go?" the girl eagerly promised. The woman released her hold. With lightning speed, the girl broke in to a run! But the old woman was prepared for this. She grabbed the girl's skinny wrist before she got more then ten feet away. Mary stared wide eyed at this performance. What was wrong with the girl anyway? With a little extra money in her pocket, Mary set off for the house on the corner of Cypress and Audrey.

When Mary walked in to the house, she heard a familiar sound. Mama Sara's raspy voice was raised in fury. "Roy!! Get your fuckin dog off this bed! I just changed the sheets and he came in from swimming in that dirty river and is lying on the bed!" As she shouted at her son, she beat at the big black dog with a broom. There was a much polluted river that ran along in back of the houses on the right side of Audrey St. Roy's dog, Beretta, who was part sheep and part Doberman and all trouble, was always leading the other dogs of the neighborhood on pillaging expeditions. Eventually Beretta got tired of being hit with the broom and slowly got up and ambled in to the kitchen just as Ray entered from the parlor. "What are you doing now? he asked peevishly. "Stay out of trouble, you got it?" Mary could almost hear Beretta saying "Whatever" His attitude was so readable. Roy said "Hi" to Mary before flopping down in front of the TV. Mama Sara and her husband, Ray SR were a bit more hospitable. They offered her coffee and asked her how she was doing back in Coventry.

An hour later, Mary walked down to Almacs supermarket. Before she was even halfway there, she realized that Beretta was following her. "Oh no! " she exclaimed determinedly. "You're not following me in to the market again!" He had done this three or four time in the past. And Mary had to admit that it was funny to see a dog in the market a few times. But after being warned by the security guard, she no longer found it funny. Mary took ten or fifteen minutes to lose Beretta before entering the store. However, she had only been shopping for five minutes when the security guard, a burly, grey haired man with a bad attitude came up to her. "Come with me!" he said. "Why?" she asked. "That dog was in the market again" He reached out to grab her arm. "But it's not my dog!" exclaimed Mary indignantly. "Well, you're receiving a summons this time. That dog has been in here too many times" He led her to an office on the second floor where he proceeded to make a phone call. "Hello, this is Pete Sawyer at the Almacs in Olney Ville. I need the dog catcher down here immediately!" When he hung up Mary said "The dog belongs to-" before she could finish the old security guard said "Shut the fuck up, you idiot!" Mary swore back at him. At this, he strode across the room and grabbed her by her face, his rough fingertips digging in to her cheeks. "Let go of me you monster!" yelled Mary. He let go, saying "hu, I'll give you a monster!" But he left her alone until the dog catcher arrived. By this time, Mary was sitting in a chair, trying to feel as fierce as she looked.

The dog catcher was a slightly over weight, middle-aged man with a nicer disposition then Pete, who proceeded to explain that the dog had gotten away before he could grab him and hold him upstairs with Mary. The dog catcher turned to her and asked her where she lived. "Coventry, RI." Mary promptly replied. "Now listen here you fucking idiot!" Pete yelled.

"I LIVE IN COVENTRY, RI!!" hollered Mary, pushed past endurance by this storm trooper. The dog catcher held up a hand. "That's enough you two" he said. He looked at Mary. "If you agree to go with me and call the dog, I might be able to convince Pete here to give you a break" Mary eagerly agreed. Pete reluctantly agreed.

The man and Mary walked all over Olneyville calling for Beretta and asking people if they had seen a large black dog. Some people had seen him but didn't know where he was at the moment. Finally the dog catcher and Mary returned to Mama Sara's house, hoping that Beretta would show up there. While they waited, Mama Sara told the man about what a pest the dog was and how her son was at the end of his rope because he just couldn't train him properly. "He won't listen to anyone!" exclaimed Mama Sara, at which point, her husband backed her up, in a voice slurred by too many beers. "You know, every day my wife goes to the Nickerson House for lunch. And that damn dog insists on following her" He stopped, hiccupped, then continued. "No matter how much she shouts and swears at him he still follows her. When he gets in there he steals food off peoples plates and my wife gets in to trouble." Mary suppressed a giggle, remembering how she used to hear Mama Sara threatening to "fork" Beretta if he didn't stop following her.

After half an hour the dog catcher gave up and left, leaving a phone number for the family to use when and if the dog came home. As if Beretta knew what was going on, he stayed away for nearly forty minutes before coming home. Everyone shook their heads and rolled their eyes in exasperation as the big dog lumbered through the door, trying to look innocent. However, nobody called the dog catcher because they didn't want to hurt Roy.

Eight months later, Beretta's carefree days came to an end. The Providence police took custody of him and trained him to be one of their best police dogs.

One day when Mary told Mama Sara that she put an application in a high rise down town, Mama Sara invited her to move back in to her house as a boarder. She would only have to pay her a hundred dollars a month until an opening was available at the high rise. Mary took Mama Sue up on the offer. Having quit working for an older blind woman in the family court building back in July, She had recently been hired to work as an assistant at the snack bar in one of the other court buildings down town. Now she would be close to her job. Mary moved back in with Roy's family at the end of September. She tried to stay out of Roy's way as much as possible. When Pauline and Joan found out what she was doing they made her give up her apartment in Coventry. Mary did so gladly. She continued to go there to have lunch with them every other week. They paid her bills out of her government check. What was left over was given to her as an allowance.

Mary lived as a boarder at Roy's parent's house throughout the winter. She waited hopefully for her own apartment down town. In the mean time she was expected to wait on family members, and the constant visitors that came to the house. Along with cleaning up the ash trays, and empty beer cans, she had to serve beer, and give up her seat when someone arrived. Roy SR sent her to the liquor store for him regularly. She also helped Mama Sara with the laundry, and dishes. When kids were brought over Mary was sometimes expected to act as the baby sitter, especially when Roy's sister Carla brought Shannon over. Mary quietly accepted what was expected of her even when it made her angry. She supposed it was a small price to pay for being allowed to live there.

Mary got off the bus downtown. It was 3:00 on A Friday afternoon in January of 1986. She was in no hurry to return to Mama Sara's house. In fact, she couldn't wait until her name came up on the waiting list at the high rise downtown. Then she would be out on her own and not have to put up with loud, intoxicated people ordering her around. Mary often wondered why the adults treated her like a servant and the kids who lived there made fun of her. Was it because she was visually impaired, or because she often came across as being more naive then she actually was? If so, it certainly wasn't intentional. One evening Mama Sara's oldest daughter had refused to let her hang out with her. "Your too fragile" she had said "You couldn't take hanging with me and my friends" This had made Mary furious! "I'm not fragile!!" she screamed. This was something she hardly ever did anymore. Mary usually tolerated people's abuse. After all, she didn't want to remain in this home. She had been in other homes as well as special schools because she used to act up or run away. Now she just wanted to avoid trouble and not cause any waves. It wasn't easy though. People made her so angry sometimes.

So instead of heading home she turned down a dingy, narrow street because she knew there were a few shops that sold trendy clothes. With the money she made at her part time job she could sometimes afford to add a pair of designer jeans or a sweater or even a pair of cool looking boots to her wardrobe. So enthused was she over this idea that she ignored the feeling that was telling her to turn around and go back out on to the main street. Mary went in the store on the left side of the street. The place was packed with rows and rows of clothes, plus rows of shoes and boots on the floor. Mary pushed through the crowd of shoppers, hardly noticing any of them, and found a pair of bell bottomed jeans in two different colors the upper half were pink and the lower half were dark purple. She quickly grabbed them and paid for them. Then because she was in no particular hurry, she decided to stick around and browse some more. About ten minutes later she noticed two women admiring themselves in a full length mirror. They were both young, in their twenties, One was an African American, short, slightly overweight, with hair that stuck straight up in back. The other woman was mulotto looking with short black hair combed back from her forehead. She was a lot taller and thinner then her friend. She carried a toddler in a pink snow- suit. As the two women passed Mary, the toddler reached out and grabbed the bag that held Mary's jeans. The bag tore. Mary pulled the bag against her chest, smiled nervously and said "ooh, excuse me." The tall woman, who was carrying the toddler, said "she looked so scared, grab it again Lisa grab it again!" Something about the way the tall woman said this really rubbed Mary the wrong way. She followed them to the door and as they stepped on to the street, she put out her tongue and gave them a raspberry. The woman who was carrying the toddler in the pink snowsuit turned and yelled "I'll punch you in the face!" Mary didn't take this seriously until the woman reentered the store. There was nothing Mary could do on such short notice except run back to the nearest clothes rack. "Look at her run!" she heard the woman say to her friend. Not good Mary had time to tell herself. They'll really think you're a wimp now! Ashamed, she stood facing the first of the clothes racks, wondering what was going to happen to her. The woman with the toddler stood behind her. "You can grab her bag anytime you want to, hu Lisa?" "Yeah" the toddler said in a high, but determined, voice. "You started it" Mary said. The woman laughed scornfully. "Oh, I started it, you hear her?" she said to her friend. Before Mary could totally realize just what a foolish statement she had made, she felt someone's knee ram itself in to her backside. Fleetingly, she thought of a tough guy that she greatly admired, would he think her a wimp if she didn't retaliate? She shoved the woman with the toddler because she knew that she was the one who had rammed her knee in to her backside. A large hand suddenly covered Mary's face. She felt herself spun around and pushed down on to a pile of shoes! Feeling defeated and extremely frustrated, she looked up at the woman with the toddler and said "You fucking whore!!" At this, everyone in the store said "OOOOHHHH!!!" Mary realized that she had just made some kind of major mistake. The woman with the toddler turned to her shorter, darker friend and said "OOHH this fucking white bitch!!" To Mary's surprise, they left the store. That couldn't be the end of the matter, could it? It wasn't. A few minutes later the two women returned without the toddler. Unreasonably, Mary found herself wondering what they had done with little Lisa. She knew she was in trouble, yet she found herself thinking of the possible places they might leave a two year old. She couldn't escape the fact that they obviously would leave her almost anywhere in order to deal with Mary. Sure enough, the taller of the two women called out to her "Hey you, come outside with us!" Mary knowing why they wanted her to go outside refused. "I want that bag!" the tall, mulatto woman announced. "NO!" Mary replied with more defiance then she actually felt. A slim, middle-aged, black woman smiled kindly at Mary and said "You better give her the bag, she's just going to get it from you anyway" But Mary wasn't sure if the woman's smile was kind or mocking. She turned away from the woman, clutching the torn bag that held her new jeans. By this time the two women minus the toddler, were in the store, watching Mary like a hawk. They followed her up one isle and down another. As if this wasn't bad enough, Mary noticed for the first time that she was the only white girl in the place. The other shoppers were either African American or Hispanic, and the people who ran the store were Asian. How could she have failed to notice this before?? How could she have been so totally stupid?? She felt like she had just waked up from some trance. Now what was she supposed to do?

It was all too clear that the woman wasn't going to leave her alone. Mary not only found this scary, she also found it extremely embarrassing! As the blood hungry woman and her amused, smiling, friend followed her around the store, Mary tried to look like some disinterested shopper who had nothing to do with what was going on. It worked until she was cornered by the woman who demanded the bag once again. Before Mary could refuse once again, a short African American woman in a white jacket squeezed past her and yelled "Would You get the fuck out of my way!" Feeling trapped and stupid, Mary tried to comply. The tall woman who was out for blood brushed Mary's long brown hair out of her face and said" She's just in everyone's way today!" Mary, sickened by the woman touching her, jerked her head away. Desperately trying to keep up the pretense that this was not happening to her, Mary inched her way around the rows of shoes. Suddenly the woman reached out and grabbed Mary's bag. She took out the jeans and examined them. "They're too small for me" she told her friend," but I can give them to my boyfriend and he can sell them for me". The woman's big hand came out again, this time to grasp Mary's purse. But Mary was ready. She hung on tightly and yanked her purse away from the woman. It wasn't over though. The woman and her friend continued to follow her around the store, sometimes urging her to go outside with them or loudly telling each other that she had better buy herself a good pair of running shoes. Mary Continued to pretend to shop, all the while feeling scared, ashamed, stupid and just plain helpless. Who could she turn to? About forty five minutes in to the ordeal the woman came up to Mary and made a deal with her. She told her that if she bought some clothes for her and her friend that she would leave Mary alone. Mary was so eager for the whole thing to be over that she decided to comply. Mutely she nodded and took out the correct amount of money. The saleswoman looked puzzled and asked Mary if the two women were friends of hers. Before the petrified girl could respond, the taller of the two women leaned menacingly toward her. Mary had no choice but to nod her head yes. Before leaving the store the woman once again turned to Mary and said "Oh, I'M from Boston. I need bus fare to get home. Just give me the rest of your money." As Mary reluctantly handed over the last of her pay she heard an elderly, heavy set African American woman say sarcastically "Oh yeah, she's from Boston, uh hu! "There were no reprisals for her though. After the two women left the store Mary stayed there for around fifteen minutes, still pretending to be an innocent shopper who had nothing to do with what had just happened in there. One thing was for sure, they had not succeeded in making her cry...they never would either. No, she would NEVER cry about what happened to her that day. As she finally left the store she also knew that she would not be informing the police about what happened. The last thing she needed was to be told that the incident was her fault and that she got what she deserved.

Mary saw those same two men several months later. She had just moved in to Dexter Manor. They were strutting down Broad St. Mary noticed that they had a third woman with them. They were wearing brightly colored spring clothes, and were talking loudly. Mary wanted to run across the street, but instead she made herself walk toward them. When the tallest, the one who had robbed her, saw her, she said "Hey! Remember that lady?" The one in the middle remembered. As Mary was passing them, the tall one yelled "YEAH MANNNN! " right in her ear. Mary, feeling enraged, kept walking, but she did stick out her tongue at their backs.

Mary saw them a few more times down town in the coming months. Always her tormentor was with one, or more of her "Home Girls", acting like she owned the city. Did she ever go anywhere alone? Once on a bus she heard her tormentor in the back, bragging about how she got the upper hand on a little punk, who dared to mouth off at her in a store. Mary, who was sitting up front, rolled her eyes. The incident had occurred over a year ago, and the woman was still bragging about it.

In spite of feeling angry, and helpless, Mary was finally able to come to the conclusion that the woman was a total coward, and an idiot! Mary had friends, but she was able to go around on her own a lot of the time. She wasn't afraid like that bully apparently was. This made her believe that perhaps she was the braver one, in spite of what she got herself in to in that store.

Chapter Twenty One

Mary on her own

Mary couldn't believe it. She was finally getting away from that family in Olneyville.

She was almost twenty five years old. Although she didn't feel grown up, she was glad to have the privacy and freedom her own apartment would give her. Her social worker from Services for the blind helped her get on the waiting list for an apartment in Dexter Manor, a high rise in down town Providence. Now here she was, in her new apartment. Mary didn't care that it was an efficiency apartment,- other wise known as a studio apartment, consisting of one large room and a small bathroom. She had her privacy, the place was clean, and there was no one there to yell at her and order her to clean up after them. It was March of 1986, and she had finally come to terms with living on her own.

She already had two friends in the building. They lived on the third floor, right across the hall from each other, a thirty five year old blind man and his retired father. They were Arcady and Joe Ruiz. They moved to Dexter Manor after Joe's mother died. Joe was born in New York City. His father, a Catholic, from Puerto Rico, was a musician. He immigrated to America with his orchestra in 1938. They performed in night clubs in New York. He met, and married a woman, named Irene. She came from a Russian, Jewish family from Boston. They had their honeymoon in New Orleans. Then Arcady was called up to serve in World War Two. Their son, Joe was born late in 1951. Because he received too much oxygen in the incubator, he became blind. His parents were devastated, especially his mother. She became very over protective.. She refused to let Joe go to Perkins School for the blind when he was old enough. As a result, Arcady, who got a steady job playing at a night club in Providence, could only see his wife and son on Sundays. Finally when Joe was fifteen, his mother took him, and moved to Providence. Joe attended the special program at Nathaniel Greene Middle School before going on to Central High School. Upon graduating, he joined The Blind Vendors Association.

Arcady and his son knew Mary and liked her. Several times during the previous year Mary helped Joe at his snack bar. One day in July he took the week off and allowed her to come in each day and run the place for him. The job wasn't very challenging, she had to make coffee, set out the pastry, fill the refrigerator and soda machines clean the counters and floors and of course, wait on people. There were no tables or chairs in the small room. The customers had to take their coffee, sandwiches, soup back to their offices. The snack bar was located on the second floor of the post office which was in downtown Providence. The post office was not responsible for the snack bar though. It was run by The blind venders association. They had snack bars in many other government buildings all over the state. Mary had worked in four or five of them already. She liked Joe's best. Not only because of the warmth and friendliness of Arcady and his son, Mary was able to take time to draw or write in her journal. And because the snack bar was in an isolated part of the second floor, she could not only listen to her favorite top 40 station, she could even turn the radio up sometimes. This however, did not interfere with her work. As a result, Arcady and his son put in a good word for Mary with the management at Dexter Manor.

So, here she was, all ready to go up to Joe's apartment and have a few drinks with him and his father and remind them of how grateful she was to them. From the few times she had visited, she was able to see that Joe's apartment was always used for company. She also saw that Joe, friendly as he was, could be very demanding, temperamental, self centered and just plain spoiled. It was clear that his parents had overprotected him and given in to his every whim. Still she liked Joe and his father. They were very hospitable and always treated her like she mattered. This was a new experience for Mary.

Mary left her apartment; feeling satisfied with the way her life was going. Halfway down the corridor her newest friend in Dexter Manor called out to her. Mary paused, and then entered the musty smelling efficiency room. It hadn't taken long for her to figure out why the door was always left open. Big Bob was a very social man who received visitors on a regular basis. He lived at Dexter manor, in one room with his obese brother, John. They both drank a lot. John, when he was at home, suffered from extreme gas, which was the other reason that their door was always kept open. Neither of them worked, which meant that they were free to spend their entire day at the bar. It didn't occur to Mary to wonder how they qualified for disability or subsidized housing when they were only in their fifties. Were they disabled in some way? She supposed so, but it didn't really matter to her. It also didn't matter to her that Bob was a heavy consumer of alcohol. In fact, she had felt compelled for years to align herself with people who were street wise and just plain BAD! However, she had little success until now. Maybe she could make up for lost time and finally put behind her all of the times the kids had laughed at her. "Hi Mary, do you want some pot?" Bob asked. Mary did want some pot but she was on her way up to see Joe and his father. "How about later" she answered eagerly. Joe always went to bed early on week nights. "I'll be back by nine thirty." She left her good natured friend, lying on his bed, watching the country western videos.

Joe was waiting eagerly for Mary. Because he was blind, she not only drew pictures, she also scratched in the lines that made up the pictures so that Joe could feel the pictures as she described them to him. His father was always ready to pour them more scotch and soda or fill their plates with cold cuts, pickles and low salt chips. Although Mary enjoyed these visits, she was anxious to go back downstairs. Every night at Nine thirty she would politely dismiss herself and rush down to the first floor. Sometimes Bob was there with his sleeping brother, other times; one of his teenaged sons was with him. Geordie was Mary's favorite. He was just about fourteen. He only looked twelve. There was something in his personality, not only a need for friendship, but a vulnerability that made the shy, timid, Mary feel comfortable around him. She was able to let her guard down around him and even joke around and just be herself. It often escaped her that Geordie was a little more then Ten years younger then she was. He taught her to smoke pot in an interesting way. He would inhale on the joint, and then exhale in to her mouth. She would then inhale, wait, then exhale. Mary had been smoking pot for several years, but she had never smoked it the way Geordie showed her. Because of his patient guidance, he seemed older then her. She wasn't attracted to him, as much as she liked him, she still craved the attention of an older man, one she could look up to, be turned on by, and depend on.

Bob was lying on his twin sized, unmade bed. He was staring at the TV. The country channel was on. Two of his sons were visiting. Bob JR was sixteen. He was tall, slim and had dark, wavy hair like his father. He worked part time at a donut shop. Bob SR always told both boys to spend whatever money they made because if they died, the state would get their money, not their family. Geordie would soon be working and would soon be subjected to the same catechism.

Feeling relieved that she had done her duty, Mary entered Bob's friendly abode and quickly purchased a bag of pot and a number of valume. She then proceeded to help herself to a mixed drink that she and Bob really liked. Several weeks earlier Bob JR had informed her that people who sat and waited for their drinks and food to be served to them were not welcome. Mary had quickly made a mental note of this and proceeded to act accordingly. Geordie was drinking and in a very silly mood. When his father made a remark about Geordie's bare feet, the boy suggested that his father put his bare feet in his mouth and suck on them. This sent the already intoxicated Mary in to peels of laughter! Geordie, knowing that he had an audience, continued to be funny and obnoxious

Everything would have been fine if only Bob hadn't started lusting after Mary. He destroyed her sense of security when he let her know that he wanted to go to bed with her! She actually felt as though her heart had leapt up in to her throat the first time he mentioned it. Why couldn't he see her as simply a talkative, friendly drinking partner, instead of a whore? These were the times when Mary was not so sure that she wanted to belong to the adult world. Was it filled with fun and opportunity, or was it filled with fear and trauma? Mary was reminded of the unpleasant sexual encounters from her past. In all that time, Mary had never learned to say "No". In fact, she was afraid to say "No". Why was that?

Now here she was, faced with the same problem "When did you first realize that you were attracted to me?" Mary asked Bob one night. He thought a minute, and then said "It was on Easter Sunday. I saw you walking down the hall in that short, denim skirt with those tights." Mary inwardly groaned and thought, note to self; never wear short denim skirts again. However, she knew that it was already too late. Bob, through words, gestures, dope and alcohol gradually broke down Mary's excuses and defenses. Soon he had her right where he wanted her. But he knew that she was not happy about it. More and more often he became verbally abusive toward her; she retaliated, once by throwing her phone out the window. She was so tired of his jealousy toward Joe and his father. Bob made it clear that he did not believe that Mary went upstairs to draw pictures and describe them to Joe while his hospitable father served them food and drinks. "You go up there and get it on with them both, don't you?" Bob often yelled. Nothing Mary said made any difference. Worse still was the fact that she had been too loose with her tong, telling Bob which car in the parking lot belonged to Joe and his father, what apartments they lived in. She even blurted out the fact that they did not like Bob and had warned her to stay away from him because he had bad connections. This was true, not only was he a drug dealer, he was also a loan shark. Mary did not care about this. She liked Bob because he seemed to accept her just as she was. He didn't care that she still liked dolls or had a hard time fitting in with people. He sounded sympathetic, often saying "Me too buddy, me too" when Mary or any one else confided their troubles to him. And other people did visit his room, to joke with him, complain to him, even to cry about their problems. This impressed Mary. But there was a hostile, spiteful, sly side to Bob. Once, just to remind her who was in charge, he showed up at the snack bar in the superior court building where Mary had been called in to work at. He walked in, unshaven, smiled wickedly at Mary, and ordered a lunch. He took his time eating it, never taking his eyes off Mary. She tried to do her job but she was shaking badly. What would he do? Would he loudly brag about their sex life to anyone who would listen? She knew she would die if he did.

Finally one evening the relationship fell to pieces. Bob and Mary spent the afternoon at the safari lounge. After a number of drinks, they decided to head back to the high rise. Although they were a bit tipsy, Mary thought that the afternoon had been lots of fun and they both were in a great mood… until Bob started talking about Arcady and Joe. "They're just friends!" Mary told Bob for what must have been the hundredth time. But Bob would have none of it. He became very hostile! He yelled at Mary, swore at her, told her that she was a no good, filthy, lying, double crossing whore! When they reached Dexter Manor, Mary was so frustrated and hurt that she attacked the dumpster with fast and furious kicks! Bob stood there and laughed his head off. Mary was not only surprised, she was also enraged!! How dare he laugh when he was the reason she was kicking the dumpster in the first place! She screamed obscenities at him, which only made him laugh more. Finally, with her fists clenched, Mary marched toward the building, shouting over her shoulder at her laughing tormenter. Upstairs things became even more explosive! As Bob continued to verbally rip her to pieces, Mary found that yelling back was not satisfying enough. She was so upset and intoxicated in fact that she did something that she would not have done under normal circumstances. She ran to the bathroom and grabbed a razor. Through her tears, she frantically hacked at her wrist. As the blood dripped in to the sink, Bob suddenly appeared behind her. He became remorseful and tearful. "NO Buddy! Don't do that!" he cried. He led Mary back in to the bedroom. They both fell on to the bed and sobbed openly. What am I doing here? Mary wondered. As her twisted boyfriend cried on, she wondered if he was play acting. Or was he really as upset as she was? He didn't sound Sincere as much as he sounded just plain crazy? Mary looked up at the ceiling, and wondered about God. Was he looking down at them and rolling his eyes with a combination of disgust and disbelief? She would have been will at he would have reacted in such a way. She hoped that he would not give up on her or even Bob. Was he a forgiving God?

After Bob went down the hall to his room, Mary pulled herself together and went upstairs to Joe's apartment. Instead of acting like everything was alright like she did every other night, Mary told Joe and Arcady all that had happened since she had moved to Dexter Manor. Arcady washed and treated Mary's cut wrist. He and Joe listened to her account of everything that had happened to her at Dexter Manor since she got involved with Bob and his sons. They listened attentively, even when she told them about the time that the fire alarm had been pulled on a Sunday night. "It was me" Mary confessed. "Bob made me so provoked that night that I ran down the hall and pulled the fire alarm, and then I got scared and hid on the backstairs." Arcady listened patiently until she mentioned the incident that led to her throwing her phone out the window. "Now do you see what a liar you are?" he asked teasingly." You told me that the crazy lady next door made you throw that phone out the window" Mary felt ashamed and embarrassed, but she also realized that she was developing a crush on this clean, tidy, multitalented, careful, well mannered man who was the father of a friendly but self centered blind man. However, this evening it didn't matter that Joe was demanding and self centered, or that Arcady was regarding her with gentle disapproval. The apartment felt like a safe haven from all the insanity and abuse that existed beyond the door.

To prevent another confrontation with Bob, Arcady told Mary to spend the night on Joe's couch. He also warned her to stay away from Bob. "But what if he won't stay away from me?" asked a anxious Mary. "Walk away from him and keep walking." advised Arcady "Tell him firmly that your busy and don't have time to talk" If only it was that easy thought Mary. Bob was the type of person who didn't put up with being ignored. As Arcady put sheets and a blanket on the couch, he told her that the woman who he had recently been going out with wouldn't have liked him making up the couch for her. She resented being fussed over and complained whenever he did this. She said she didn't like to be treated like a baby. Mary thought the woman was totally stupid and maybe a little crazy as well. She felt such gratitude toward Arcady for helping her. As far as she was concerned, that woman could go take a flying leap! Mary would love to take her place in Arcady's life. If only she could prove that she was worthy. She would start by avoiding Bob from now on. It wouldn't be easy but she had to try.

Early the next morning Arcady came over and hurried Joe and Mary out of bed. He wouldn't

explain what was going on. He said that he and Joe had to go somewhere that day and that Mary must go downstairs. A long, lonely and stressful day awaited Mary. She was correct about Bob's reaction to being dumped. He refused to accept it when Mary told him that it was over. He began to stalk her. He not only followed her everywhere, he also cornered her and told her that he was going to torch Arcady's car and beat up Joe. "I won't even have to do it myself" he belligerently informed her. "I can be sitting in the safari lounge drinking. And someone who has been paid will burn that fucking car and beat up that old man and his blind son!" No matter how firm Mary tried to be, her resolve melted once Bob started talking like this. How did he know that she would give in when he threatened her friends instead of her?...why did he have to know this?? With these threats, he was able to get in to Mary's room, day or night. While he satisfied himself at her expense, Mary worried that Arcady would be able to see in her window. Dexter Manor was L shaped, with the new wing in back. Because of this, Arcady, who had a bird's eye view of Mary's room, could possibly see what was going on. She hoped, even   prayed that he would not! She really wanted to earn his trust. She just needed to give Bob time to wean himself off of her. The question was, how much time did he need?

Sometimes to avoid Bob, Mary would hang around the Brick mall. She either shopped in Woolworth, or sat out in front of it. Every morning Warren Davies stood out there, loudly preaching the Word of God. His wife and another woman from his church stood on either side of him, facing each other. They stood stiffly at attention, both holding bibles. Mary knew them. She had visited their church not long ago. She didn't find it to her liking. However, she was somewhat drawn to the Word of God, though she hardly ever admitted to it. Once a homeless man became over come at what Warren was saying. He burst in to tears. Warren knelt before him, and tried to lead him to Christ. The man seemed some what receptive. The incident left Mary a little impressed. At the other end of the mall was another preacher. He was even more boisterous, and energetic then Wade. He was a real Hell, Fire, and Brimstone kind of preacher. He had this habit of ending every statement with "LOOK OUT!" He seemed to really enjoy shouting this. Joe's father, Arcady liked to refer to him as the "Preacher with the high ass!" This always made Mary laugh. He did kind of have a high rear end. She wondered if anyone ever told him this.

One evening Mary, Joe and Arcady sat down to supper. Mary was in a very good mood. Arcady told her that the reason he and Joe left so quickly the previous week was because they had to go to Block Island. The hotel-restaurant combo burned to the ground. Arcady and Joe had been playing in a band there for years! The place was called Ballard's, and like much of the property on Block Island, it was owned by a tough, shrewd middle aged businessman named, Paul Philippi. Arcady and Joe were hoping that Paul would decide to rebuild Ballard's. It looked promising. Mary listened eagerly to her two friends as they reminisced about the good and bad times that they had on Block Island since the early sixties. All in all there seemed to be more good times then bad. Suddenly there was a loud knock at Joe's door, followed by several louder knocks! Arcady looked through the peep hole. He turned to Mary in total disbelief and in a loud whisper informed her that it was Bob. "Quick get in to the bathroom and close the door!" Mary obeyed, but could not resist the temptation to open the door a crack and listen. It was clear that Bob was very angry. He shouted at Arcady, claiming that Mary had been making a pest of herself, slipping love letters under his door and following him around. "You better make her stop it or I'll punch her in the face and I'll punch you in the face!" All the while, Arcady told Bob repeatedly that he didn't want to hear anymore of what Bob had to say. "It's none of my business. Please go away and leave us alone" After Bob left, Mary came out of the bathroom feeling terrible! Arcady was right, it was none of his or Joe's business and Bob had no right to involve them!! Arcady was visibly shaken by his encounter with Bob. He pointed to a couple of crumpled pieces of paper in the waste basket. "Your love letters to him, apparently." Mary shook her head. "No" she managed to say hoarsely. She would have grabbed those papers and unfolded them for Arcady to see except that she remembered that on two different occasions she had wrote to Bob, telling him how much she appreciated their friendship. They were by no means, love letters, but she was afraid that they would still count against her with Arcady.

So she sat there and looked longingly at those papers, but didn't touch them. This was a choice that she regretted for a long time. Joe was upset too. But he soon recovered and suggested that he and Mary try out the kazoos they recently bought at the music store. "I am in no mood to hear ka- zoos!" exclaimed Arcady as he cleaned up the kitchen. He went on to say that he didn't want Mary around anymore. Joe began to whine, and then sob like a five year old. "Shut the fuck up!" yelled his exasperated father. "Look what you got me in to, insisting that we move to Providence! We could have stayed in North Providence after your mother died. But you had to live here. And it's caused us nothing but trouble!" Joe didn't seem to care about what his father was saying. He continued to cry and protest. "No more coming up here, Mary" he said firmly. Mary was feel- too guilty to argue with him. She willingly left the apartment, and taking his advice, used the backstairs to return to her apartment. She felt abandoned, but she also felt that she deserved to be abandoned. So, there was no resentment on her part. But what would she do with her life now? Should she just give in to Bob and his "low life" friends and family? Bob must have been thinking along similar lines because he sent Geordie, his youngest son, over to her apartment to coax her in to sharing a bag of pot with him and confiding in him… and maybe returning to Bob's room afterward. Mary almost said yes. Indeed, when she saw Geordie at her door, looking disappointedly at her, it took all the willpower she had to tell him no. The boy's father knew her too well. He knew that she had some rapport with him even if she wasn't attracted to him. Later Joe called sounding upset. Apparently Arcady had managed to get through to him and make him realize just how serious the situation was. He gave Mary quite a tongue lashing. Feeling like she lost her only ally, Mary nevertheless, listened and agreed with everything Joe angrily said to her. It had been decided that he and his father would give her one more chance to be in their lives, provided that she stayed away from Bob and his friends and family. Mary agreed eagerly then hung up. As she sat there, she realized that she was at a turning point in her life. If she listened to Bob she would have many years of trouble and heartache. If she listened to Arcadio and Joe life would be a lot easier and a lot more secure. As Mary sat at the table, staring at the wall, she thought of her adopted father, dead only a few years. Unlike her adopted mother, she had felt some rapport with him and had cared, to a degree what he thought of her. She was sure that he would be proud of her right now and of the decision she was making.

Bob continued to stalk and harass her throughout the summer. As difficult as this time was for her, she did learn to be much more cautious around people and to be more tightly lipped with her and other people's information. She felt proud of these accomplishments.

Chapter Twenty Two

Making it up to Arcady

Arcady and his son decided to give Mary another chance, in spite of what she had done. This didn't mean that they were quick to forget, or stop being afraid. This was especially true of Arcady. He was a kind, generous man, but he was also very cautious and suspicious.

Arcady told Mary to use the back stairs in the high rise whenever she went to and from his son's apartment. "Don't ever take the elevator alone either. You might run in to Bob." Mary, who felt guilty and ashamed of the mistake she made by going out with a man like bob, was eager to please Arcady, and prove herself worthy of the second chance she was being given.

Mary found herself in a dilemma. She was not only grateful to Joe and his father for not giving up on her; she found that she was developing a crush on Arcady. The little, Hispanic man was always well dressed, clean, and very tidy. His thin hair was black, and his face was relatively unlined; despite the fact that he was in his late sixties. He spoke English as well as he spoke Spanish. He was polite and soft spoken generally.. Mary was impressed with his abilities too. Arcady not only played the trumpet; he cooked, and cut hair as well. He did the entire book keeping for the snack bar that his son worked at. Arcady had a lot of stamina. He brought Joe to work at six thirty in the morning where they had a quick breakfast. Once he had the snack bar ready with Joe behind the counter to serve the customers; Arcady left to do errands. He had a little time to himself to do what he wanted. By two thirty he returned to the snack bar to help Joe close up for the day. Back at the high rise they had an early supper. Mary was always invited. For two hours Arcady returned to his apartment to rest and take a shower. Then like Mary, he went back to Joe's apartment until bed time. Mary wondered why everything occurred in Joe's place rather then his father's.

What amazed Mary was that even as she found herself falling for Arcady; she noticed that he seemed to share her feelings. He no longer went out with the Hispanic woman who lived down the hall from him and his son. He called her a "Gold digging Bitch", who argued with him and eventually dumped him; calling him an old man with contempt in her voice. Mary was more then willing to take her place. He flirted with her, and said flattering things to her. He made casual suggestions about how she could improve her wardrobe; suggestions which she hastened to follow. Arcady started calling her "Sweet Heart". He often put an arm around her. Mary had felt drawn to various people over the years, but no one she sought out had ever returned her affections…no one except Sister Jane that is.

Having someone reciprocate was exhilarating to Mary. Arcady kissed her, hugged her, and quietly made out with her on the couch while Joe talked animatedly about his day. What made the situation a dilemma was that the relationship was a secret from Joe. Arcady said that it had to be because his son was attracted to Mary as much as he was. He felt guilty deceiving Joe; who was blind, and accustomed to getting his own way. Mary on the other hand didn't care! She was finally getting love from a real person after so many years of having to depend on dolls, and pictures of men. She wanted to stomp her foot, and say "I don't care if Joe gets upset! Why can't he learn that he can't have everything his way?" She felt that this was her chance for happiness, but she didn't want to hurt, or betray Arcady. So she reluctantly agreed to be discreet. In her mind's eye she could picture Joe having a tantrum, and yelling "She's my girl Dad!" Mary felt like laughing, but she didn't find the idea of Joe being mean to, or even harming his father funny at all, and she feared that it might happen. As friendly, and comical as Joe could be; he had quite a temper. Mary contented herself with snuggling with Arcady on the couch periodically in the evenings, and having sex with him when Joe went to perform his nightly ritual of using the bathroom, and flossing and brushing his teeth. Arcady was so connected to his son's well being, and unexpected needs that he couldn't visit Mary's apartment, or invite her to his. Sometimes he called her to talk for a few minutes, but he wasn't a big believer in discussing feelings. He often said "Talk and talk and talk don't mean nothing" He always said "nothing" in a sing song voice. Mary tried to accept this most of the time because she wanted to please him. However there were times when things needed to be discussed,. Yet Arcady usually blew her and her concerns off.

In September Mary got a job in a work shop for the blind. It was located in Pawtucket. She was excited about having a steady job. Joe was happy for Mary, but his father wasn't do happy. He liked having Mary help out at his son's snack bar and occasionally go on errands with him. It was during the errands that Mary could talk openly with Arcady. He was more receptive at these times. He told her that he was sometimes taken for an Italian rather then a Latino because he was light complexioned. "I would love you whether you were Latino or Italian" Mary told him sincerely. He smiled happily, and thanked her enthusiastically. This was one of their special moments. It was possible that he was getting over his distrust of Mary on account of her previous relationship with Bob; the unstable, alcoholic who lived on her floor. Arcady's suspicious attitude toward Mary had wounded her even though she knew he had a right to feel that way. She strove to earn back Arcady and Joe's trust. She made herself constantly available to them. They always knew where she was even when she wasn't with them. Because her inability to maintain eye contact with people made Arcady more suspicious of her; she tried to over come it. It wasn't easy for her. Establishing eye contact with anyone involved a certain degree of intimacy; which Mary had never felt comfortable with. For the sake of her relationship with Arcady; Mary decided to work on it.(Most people never commented on her lack of eye contact. They simply chalked it up to the fact that she couldn't see well). Now though Mary wanted to get a job; make some money of her own instead of taking their hand outs, and get away from Joe's temper tantrums. There was another reason she wanted to go to work though. She was certain that if she was never around during the day Bob would finally stop stalking her.

Mary went to the work shop on a Monday morning in mid September. The first person she met was a middle aged chain smoker who was nearly blind. Her name was Frances. She was pleasant, and talkative. She brought Mary to the cafeteria because it wasn't time to start work yet. Frances was well dressed, and her dark grey hair was impeccably neat.

The building was wide with only one floor. There were other organizations in it as well as the work shop. Mary noticed that in the center of the building was a big auditorium. She was too nervous to notice much besides the place where she would be working. About twenty blind or legally blind people of various ages were sitting at long tables doing assembly work. There were a few foot presses at the back of the room. A couple of Asian women were working on these, and talking happily to each other. Mary was placed at the second table and told to pack pen refills in cylinder shaped cardboard containers. Twelve of these were placed in a thin box. Twelve boxes made up a gross. She would be paid according to how many gross she did. Many other workers were doing this job. A few were packing little erasers in tubes and boxing them. One of the supervisors was a tall old man with white hair named Ben. He was nice, but strict. He frequently had to correct, and even reprimand a young woman with long hair and glasses because she talked, made obnoxious noises, and joked around all day. She had a side kick; an African American man in his forties who kept up a constant commentary with her. He didn't get corrected much. This was because he managed to get a lot of work done. Some of the workers were moderately mentally challenged, as well as visually impaired. One of them was a young man, named Billy. He talked with a slight speech impediment, and had a habit of burping constantly. Many times he leaned over and burped in the ear of an older blind man who fell asleep a lot while working.

On her first day at work Mary suffered with home sickness. She missed Joe and Arcady immensely. She thought of all the outings they had together over the summer, going on errands with Arcady, helping Joe at work. She missed the customers who joked around with Joe when they came in to buy things. Some of the funniest customers were FBI agents. This surprised Mary, who thought they were supposed to be so serious. As Mary worked she kept her head lowered so that the supervisors wouldn't see her crying. She felt like a five year old who was starting her first day of kindergarten.

As fall turned in to winter Mary and Arcady continued their secret relationship. It was starting to become strained though. Mary became frustrated with the lack of communication between them. In the evenings she looked forward to sitting beside Arcady on the couch; whether they always cuddled, kissed, made out, or not. To her dismay Arcady didn't invite her over all the time. Sometimes he would whisper, or gesture in passing that it wasn't safe because Joe might get suspicious about why she was on the couch with him regularly. When Mary used the excuse that the wooden kitchen chair was hard to sit on; he bought a cushion for the chair. Mary reluctantly sat on it, and looked over at him periodically with a pleading expression on her face. Eventually Arcady would gesture for her to join him. One evening he made her wait longer then usual. She began to sulk; then to cry quietly. Why was he being this way? She dressed up in a skirt, blouse, nylons, and high heels every evening when she went upstairs. She wore nail polish and a little make up. She only put on a small amount of perfume because she didn't want Joe to ask questions. Mary was learning a lot about discretion and this made her feel proud, and confident, but she couldn't understand Arcady's attitude toward her sometimes. The reactions Mary received for her tears were quite unexpected. Arcady became angry with her! He came over and took her drink away from her, and dumped it out. "I don't want you up here if you're going to act that way!" he exclaimed loudly. Joe became alarmed, and wanted to know what was going on. "If you're doing drugs again go downstairs with your friend, Bob." Stricken; Mary gaped at him! "I haven't touched drugs since the start of the summer!" she cried. Arcady told Joe that she was crying when there was no reason to cry. Joe questioned Mary. She couldn't tell him the truth. So she made up a story about having had a stressful day at work. This was enough to satisfy him, but his father wasn't satisfied. He sat back on the couch and gazed at Mary with his chin thrust out self righteously. Mary's sadness turned to anger. She glared at him. "I'm watching you, Mary" he told her. "Oh yeah well I'm watching you too!!" she retorted. She knew she sounded childish, but she couldn't help it. She hated it when he looked at her that way! When Arcady thrust out his chin and acted angry and suspicious of her he reminded her of her mother. And how could he think she still bothered with Bob? She did everything she could to reassure Arcady and Joe that she was totally faithful to them. She actually tolerated Joe expecting her to call him during her coffee break, and again when she got home from work. She put up with him scolding her when she was late. What more could she do?! "If you're going to treat me like this I'll go!" Mary finally said in frustration. To her surprise Arcady said "Well go! I don't want that drug use up here!" He wouldn't listen when she tried to convince him that she only drank alcohol now. Joe tried to calm Mary down, but she kept saying "He doesn't give a damn about me!" "Yes he does. He's just worried" said Joe.

That night Mary hardly slept at all. She tossed, turned, and cried intermittently. She was trying so hard to gain back her friends trust and respect. Of the two of them; Joe seemed more willing to give her the benefit of the doubt. Yet it was his father who she desperately wanted to win over. Why was it that the person she felt Luke warm toward was willing to accept her while the person she was drawn to rejected her? It always happened to her. In spite of the love she sometimes received from Arcady; the over all feeling for her was of being used, then tossed in a corner until the next time. As Mary lay in bed crying she summoned all her imaginary friends from the past, and called on them one by one for comfort. They didn't fail her.

The next morning Mary had the shakes. She tried to conceal it from Joe and Arcady as they walked her to the bus station. She actually turned, and vomited, but they didn't notice because they were in front of her. She was going to visit Pat and his family up in Massachusetts for the weekend. Pat still worked as a janitor at Perkins School for the Blind. Mary was grateful that he continued to want to keep in touch with her. She visited his home twice a year.

When she returned from a relaxing weekend with a warm family Mary decided to give Arcady another chance. Things went smoothly for a while. Then one night when they were watching a comedian on TV Arcady laughed at an obscene joke made about The Holy Ghost. He even touched his crotch to emphasize the meaning of the joke. Mary didn't turn to the Lord as often as she should have, but she knew blasphemy when she heard it. "That's wrong!!" she cried. Arcady laughed. Joe said "That's your opinion Mary." "But it's not just an opinion! What he said is blasphemy. I swear, and laugh at dirty jokes like others, but that guy went too far." She was brushed off by both men. They didn't want to hear it.

Mary began to worry about Arcady after that. She knew that sooner or later she was going to have to get right with God. Did such things ever cross Arcady's mind? She knew that he scoffed at the church. He didn't want to go and hear Mary play the hand bells at a church in down town Providence. He chose to do the book keeping with his son instead. Mary had been angry, and hurt by this. He sometimes talked about how his father and the village priest used to beat him for not going to church. He told her that he hated it when someone tried to convert him. So persuading him to try a different church was out of the question. From time to time Mary had dreams in which Arcady rejected God. In one dream he was laying on a bed with her. Suddenly he reached up, and turned the crucifix on the wall up side down.

By the spring of 1987 Mary celebrated her twenty sixth birthday. She went out to Coventry and had a birthday party with Pauline and Joan; her faithful payees. Although she dressed casually nobody seemed to mind. They ate cake, and enjoyed each other's company. Mary was happy with the gifts she received. However things were different in the evening. When she came upstairs to have champagne and cake; followed by the usual several glasses of scotch and soda that they drank every evening; Arcady asked Mary why she wasn't dressed up. Mary shrugged, and said "I don't know. We're not going out, are we?" In recent months Mary had lost some of her affection for Arcady. As a result she became lax about what she wore. Arcady wasn't happy, and he made that very clear. He scolded her, and told her she wasn't grateful for all he did for her. "I'm sorry." said Mary imploringly. "Look I'll go down and change right now." Arcady wouldn't hear of it. "Forget it. It's too late for that! You should have dressed up in the first place." For the remainder of the evening Arcady carried out his duties as a host, but he was sullen and spoke to Mary as little as possible. Joe on the other hand sang to Mary, joked around with her, exclaimed enthusiastically over each gift she opened, and all in all made her feel at ease. This was typical. Would the person whose approval she sought ever be the one who didn't let her down? Mary still liked Arcady; and had fun with him, but she had already replaced him in her heart with an actor from the movies, who appealed to her.

Oddly enough as Mary became some what indifferent toward Arcady he became more consistent in his attempts to be close to her, and have sex with her when Joe lingered in the bathroom. It was no longer desirable for Mary now. She merely tolerated it as she had with other men in the past.

Despite the deterioration of her relationship with Arcady; Mary had a lot of fun during that summer. She made several friends at work. Her favorites were Frances; the chain smoker, who showed her to the cafeteria on her first day, and an over weight blind man, named Bob. They went everywhere on the weekends. They took trips to Newport, Rocky Point Park, the movies, and sometimes they went on picnics. They were able to do this because Joe and Arcady were playing with their small orchestra at the newly restored Ballard's over on Block Island. They were there every weekend during July and August. On Sundays Mary took the ferry from Providence and arrived in time to watch Arcady and his band do the matinee. They played from one until five. Mary sat at the bar drinking, smoking, and applauding for the men in her life. She sometimes got up and danced when a song that called for group dancing was called for. Afterward Arcady and Joe joined Mary for fish & chips before taking the ferry back to Galilee where the car was. In the middle of August Mary went on a Penn Dutch tour. Along with seeing the Amish; they learned about the battle of Gettysburg, and visited The Hershey factory. Mary returned home with souvenirs for friends and a crush on Abraham Lincoln.

Toward the end of 1987 Mary was trying to gradually pull away from Arcady and his often temperamental son. She decided to take an art course at the RI School Of Design. This kept her out on Thursday evenings. Next she started going bowling with the Summit Association on Monday nights. This club consisted of disabled adults; most of whom were in wheel chairs. There were volunteers who came each week to help them bowl, get to nearby restaurants afterward, and with whatever evening activity was planned. One of the participants was a tall thin man with handsome features. He had brown hair and side burns. He lost his sight to Diabetes, and was slowly losing his ability to walk because of neuropathy; a complication of the disease. His name was Barry. He was very intelligent. Before he went blind he taught toxicology at a university. He liked folk music, and often played his guitar. Mary had known him for several months. They both belonged to some of the same clubs. One evening at a banquet put on by The Federation of the Blind Mary greeted Barry, and talked with him for a few minutes. When she said she was returning to her table he grabbed her hand and kissed it! Mary was besotted! Suddenly this tall gangly man with the sometimes corny sense of humor was the most attractive man on the face of the earth.

Mary began thinking of Barry all the time. This of course meant that she drew pictures of him and carried one with her wherever she went. Monday became her favorite day of the week because she knew that she would see Barry at the bowling alley. Barry talked to Mary whenever she approached him. He helped her obtain an application to become a member of the club. He sometimes let her go out to eat with him and his side kick; a short heavy set man, named Robbie. Robbie had trouble walking, but he had good eye sight. He owned a car. He hung around with Barry a lot. Mary didn't like him as much as she liked Barry. Robbie liked to tease her. He loved saying things that he knew would make her steamed! His favorite way of getting to her was to call her a little girl. In spite of his teasing; Robbie seemed to like Mary. He sometimes played catch with her, or asked her how she was doing. He smiled when he saw her whether he was about to tease her or not. Yet Mary had eyes only for Barry. The problem was; Barry acted just as indifferent toward Mary as she did to his buddy, Robbie. Mary remembered how she had been swindled by a phone psychic back in the early eighties. It had been so easy to believe Sister Theresa when she told Mary that someone had cursed her. Even though this woman had turned out to be a fraud; Mary wondered if she might have been right after all.

Arcady and Joe had an argument with Mary right before Christmas. They were upset about her indifference toward them. They must have picked up on the fact that she was gradually distancing herself from them. They had grown accustomed to Mary being at their beckoning call. Mary allowed it to go on since the summer of the previous year. Now it no longer seemed important, or worth while. She wanted to find people who would appreciate her. She was hoping that Barry would be one of them Joe was so verbally abusive that she seized on it as an excuse to stop seeing them. Joe had shouted at her too many times. If she had been feeling more charitable toward Arcady; she would have acknowledged the times that Joe shouted at him too.

Mary went through a lot in 1988. Although she didn't bother with Arcady, or his son; she had her friends from work. Some of them were in the recreation groups with Mary. Outside of these groups she and her close friends went on many day trips. They even attended Perkins Alumni weekend. It was fun being back on the Perkins campus again. Mary had ceased to think of it as a gateway in to the Victorian Era. Late in July They spent a week up in New Hampshire at a Christian camp. This was the first time Mary tried to get saved outside of the Catholic Church and let the Lord in to her life; if not her heart.

Barry continued to play a big part in Mary's life, and mind. She saw him every weekend, and talked to him on the phone. Although he didn't feel the same way as Mary did; he decided to accept her as a casual friend. Mary tried to be content with this, but it wasn't what she longed for. Her payees told her over lunch one day that she wanted too much. This statement really stung Mary. It also made her angry. She felt like lashing out at someone; mainly Barry. She mailed him an insulting letter; knowing that he had someone who read his mail to him weekly. She called him up from time to time, and insulted him; disguising her voice each time.

By the fall Mary had become disillusioned with the adult world. She began reverting back to how she had been when her father was alive. She dressed like a little girl, and started buying dolls again. She carried a childish looking back pack, and became defensive when anyone criticized her about it. She tried to block out the psychological knowledge she had gained from counseling, TV, and books. Knowing that God would not approve of this; Mary shut him out too. She was in fact trying to become less self aware. It was quite a struggle. She often felt exhausted. Her consumption of alcohol increased until she was drinking every night. It was a wonder that she was able to get up, and go to work in the mornings. It was as if Mary was running away without actually being in motion.

By January of 1989 Mary was an emotional wreck! So when Arcadio and Joe approached her, and invited her for supper she eagerly accepted. In retrospect; it didn't seem to Mary that they had been that bad to be around. Maybe a lot of it had been her fault. Arcady was as hospitable as he was two and a half years ago when she first moved to the high rise. Joe was very good natured, and cooperative. He apologized for being angry, and demanding in the past. Mary felt surrounded by warmth and security. Joe's apartment felt like a refuge from the turmoil that was always in her head. It wasn't surprising that Mary was soon going up there every evening like she used to. She became once again at his beckoning call. Arcadio resumed his amorous relationship with her. Perhaps sensing that Mary no longer shared his feelings; he reached for one of her dolls. "Hold this while we do it. I don't mind. I'm very understanding." He whispered. And to Mary he did seem understanding. So she quietly submitted to him.

Chapter Twenty Three

Blind betrayal

It was possible to be so angry at a person that you not only couldn't stand to look at them, but you actually couldn't stand to be in the same room with them!

This was exactly how Mary felt right now. She glared over at the thin, gray haired woman in the next row. The woman was bent over her work and talking animatedly to a short, chubby, woman with black hair. "Don't be fooled by her friendliness, Laura!" Mary longed to shout "She'll stab you in the back the first chance she gets "But she kept her mouth closed and continued to pack the pen refills for AT Cross. A lot of the people in the large room were doing this job. Some of them were packing merchandise for other companies, and a few were working at sewing machines. The place where they worked was a sheltered work shop for the blind. There were also a couple of deaf employees as well. The workshop was in Pawtucket. Mary had been working there for almost four years. Tossing her long, brown hair back over her shoulder, she bared her teeth at the skinny, gray haired woman. "I'm not giving her back the ten dollars she loaned me" murmured Mary to herself, "it was my own money she loan-ed me in the first place, damn thief!"

When the bell rang for morning break every-one headed to the cafeteria. Mary could hear her name being called. She didn't answer. Finally one of the cafeteria staff caught up with her. "Mary, didn't you hear me calling you? Your friend, Frances wants to talk to you" Mary almost choked! Her friend!? She no longer thought of the gray haired woman as her friend, not after what she had been doing to her. Frances continued to call out to Mary. So, she had no choice but to answer the summons. It came as no surprise to Mary when Frances asked for the ten dollars. Mary tried to stall by saying that she didn't have the money. .Finally though, she told Frances that she suspected her of stealing her wallet. "It's been going on for over two years now" said Mary. Every time you're around, my money disappears!" Frances became indignant! Soon they were both arguing. When Mary accused her of being a phony Catholic Frances jumped up, grabbed her white cane and headed out of the cafeteria. "You want to make fun of my religion? We'll see what the supervisor has to say about this! "exclaimed Frances loudly over her shoulder.

A few minutes later Mary was called in to the office. Pete, the supervisor informed her that Frances was making quite a fuss about the ten dollars. After Mary told her side of the story, Pete said that it would be best if she paid Frances. After all, she had loaned her the money and Mary couldn't prove that Frances was a thief. She didn't actually see her take the wallet. Fuming, Mary agreed to do as Pete asked. Because there was so much resentment between them, Pete thought it would be wise that she give him the money, and he would give it to Frances.

All day as Mary worked, she fumed inwardly. She also planned; the plans involved making her ex friend Frances pay. Mary knew she was guilty, even if she hadn't actually caught her in the act. And she was going to punish her!

It was September of 1990. Mary and Frances had been close friends for almost four years. Together with a couple of other blind friends, they took many day trips. Aside from going to Newport, Block Island, Martha's Vineyard, they also liked to go out to eat and go to flea markets. Because Mary was partially sighted, she would sit in a movie theatre and quietly describe the movie to Frances who was almost totally blind. Sometimes they just sat and talked. Frances who was twenty years older then Mary, was somewhat isolated. Mary had to tell her about sex, drugs, child abuse etc. These were all things that Mary had experienced on one level or another, especially child abuse. She wondered where Frances had been keeping herself. Frances talked about her upbringing. She had an older sister and a younger brother. They were raised Catholic, all three of them attending Catholic schools. Their father was a likable, out going man, who enjoyed company. His wife was a stern, reserved woman who didn't want company around. Frances got along better with her father then her mother. Although she loved her brother and sister, she was jealous of them, particularly her brother, who received more of her father's attention, and was doted on by their mother. Frances developed an eating disorder as a little girl. She used to gorge herself with all kinds of food, then run outside and throw it all up. This problem continued well in to her adult years, after which she became almost anorexic. When Frances was thirteen, her parents sent her away to a Catholic boarding school. Because she was legally blind, she was finding it hard to make friends and keep up with her studies in day school. Frances, eager to make friends, eagerly went to the catholic academy that her parents selected for her. She chose to remain on weekends.

However, Frances didn't make many friends. Most of the girls were mean to her. Every morning she got up early, showered, dressed, and attended Mass. This was not required. The other girls chose to remain in bed until seven. Frances was at Mass with all the nuns, who she totally admired and wanted the approval of. Frances liked one nun in particular. Her name was Sister Ann Marie. She was stern, but fair, and had a dry sense of humor. Although she liked Frances, she often said "I can stand a boy crazy girl, but I can't stand a nun crazy girl". One afternoon, when classes were over for the day, Sister Ann Marie heard a noise in the cloak room. "Whose there?" she called out. "No one" answered Frances, "it's just us cloak bottles". Mary, listening intently, laughed at the pun, but she didn't laugh at the rest of the story. The other girls resented Frances for one reason or another. Soon they started getting up early just so that they could hamper Frances' attempts to get ready for Mass. They hid her clothes, smeared peanut butter and jelly in her hair, and slapped her around. Out raged, Mary demanded to know why they were so mean to Frances. "I don't know" replied Frances. "But they were, and the mother superior knew about it. She asked me why I didn't tell her what was going on" Mary gasped! "If she knew, why didn't she do something?" Frances just shook her head despairingly. "She wanted me to tell her before she stepped in and took action". Mary couldn't understand this. As far as she was concerned, what the mother superior did was criminal!! She was glad that she was friends with Frances. Surely she realized that she had a caring, loyal, morally supportive friend in Mary.

Frances talked about going to Mass every day, even now. "Well you're very religious" said Mary. "No, I'm not, really" replied Frances. "But I sure try to be" She has such humility! thought Mary.

It was about two years ago that Mary began to notice that some of her money was disappearing. One night Frances stayed over at Mary's apartment. The next day ten dollars was missing from her wallet. Frustrated and puzzled, she complained to Frances about it. Frances seemed just as puzzled. About six weeks later Mary took Frances to a class reunion at the Perkins school for the blind, in Massachusetts. They went up there with two other blind friends, two middle aged men, named Bob and Al. Mary and Frances shared a room in Bridgman Cottage. They did a lot of talking when they weren't at a scheduled activity. It was on the afternoon of their second day at the reunion, when Frances got upset with Al because he didn't want to attend Mass later on. The disagreement turned in to a full blown argument. Frances was screaming at Al and accusing him of being selfish. Bob, who hated conflicts among his friends, became upset with Frances. Leaving an agitated Frances in the room they shared, Mary decided to go watch a sporting event. Frances wanted to be left alone for awhile.

In the end, Al agreed to go to Mass. Bob, who was angry about the performance Frances put on, refused to go. Frances tended to go easier on Bob for some reason. She said nothing about his refusal. Instead She Mary and a humbled, repentant Al set off to St. Patrick's Church in Watertown Square. It was toward the end of Saturday evening mass, that Mary opened her wallet to give a dollar to the church. She discovered that she only had a dollar! What happened to the sixty dollars she knew her wallet should contain? As they were leaving church, she told Frances about the missing money. "What I don't get is why the thief left me with a dollar! "Maybe the thief has a conscience" said Frances. "They night have figured you'd need the dollar to call home or something" "All I know is that I left my pocketbook in our room when I went to watch the ballgame. Were you in the room the whole time I was out?" asked a frantic Mary. Frances thought for a moment. "Well, I did go take a bath at around three O'clock; But I didn't hear anyone walk by"

A month later Mary, Frances and three or four of their other friends spent a week at a camp up in New Hampshire, along with many other blind and visually impaired adults. That first night Mary and some of the other campers wanted to go swimming in the Olympic sized pool. Frances declined. "I think I'll just sit outside" Not knowing what else to do with her pocket- book, Mary asked Frances to keep it with her. Frances readily agreed, and Mary went away feeling secure about her best friend.

Mary and Frances weren't put in the same cabin. So at bedtime, Mary followed some girls she didn't even know. After her shower, Mary checked her wallet and to her horror, found that her money was gone! She told a tall, woman with short, blonde hair, who seemed to be in charge, about the missing money. An announcement was made but nobody knew anything about it. Mary went to bed angry. And the next morning she got up and put a note on the bedroom wall that said "GIVE ME BACK MY $40.00. YOU BAPTIST THIEVES!!" When Frances found out about the note she found it very amusing indeed. She kept laughing, shaking her head, and repeating what she heard the note said. Mary put aside her anger and resentment long enough to laugh with her.

Then one day when Frances was visiting, Mary left her alone in the room momentarily. When she returned Frances quickly turned away from the couch with a tense look on her face. She popped a piece of candy in to her mouth. But what had she been doing a minute ago? Mary looked at her pocketbook which was sitting next to Frances' pocketbook and for the first time began to suspect that her friend was the one who had been stealing from her. "Is everything alright, Frances?" she asked, wishing she had the nerve to come right out and ask her if she was a thief. Frances quickly assured her that everything was fine. Mary fingered the twenty dollar bill in her pocket. She had earned it by cleaning her friend Joe's apartment and doing his father's laundry. She was immensely happy that she hadn't gotten around to transferring it to her wallet yet.

Finally Mary received some interesting advice from her counselor, who she met with twice a month. She told her that the next time she was going to be with Frances she should take most of her money out of her wallet and hide it. Then leave the wallet where Frances will find it. Make sure that no one else is around. Then if the money disappears, Mary will know that Frances is a thief.

Soon after this, Mary and Frances took a trip to Amish country, together with a bunch of other people on a tour bus. The trip lasted four days. Mary and Frances enjoyed everything.

On their last night in the hotel Mary decided to put her plan in to action. She hoped she would be proven wrong as she carefully packed her suitcase, hid most of her money under her pillow, and placed her wallet containing four dollars at the foot of her bed, along with a book, a brush, and the clothes she would wear next day.

The next morning when Mary woke up she noticed that someone had gone through her suitcase. It's contents were spilled out on to the rug, but nothing was missing. However, when she opened her wallet she found that the four dollars was gone! Mary felt like she had been hit in the stomach! "That dirty, sneaky, weasel!" mumbled Mary "It was her all along, I can't believe this!" But she had to believe it. There was no getting around it. After they ate breakfast and left their luggage outside their door to be loaded on to the bus, Mary confronted Frances about the missing money. After a pause, Frances did answer her, but only to claim that she knew nothing about the theft. Yeah right thought Mary grumpily. During the bus ride back to RI she quietly cried as she stared out the window. Some friend Frances turned out to be! When they got home Mary stopped bothering with Frances entirely. They didn't speak to each other for a few months.

Eventually though, Mary grew tired of her silly, immature, self absorbed, friends. She began to miss Frances's company. Along with her knowledge and loyalty to the Catholic Church, Frances was also in to politics and human interest stories. She felt strongly about abortion, gay rights and child abuse. As a result, she spent a lot of time listening to, and calling the local talk radio stations. She enjoyed listening to autobiographies, biographies, mysteries, and novels on tape. With all this, Frances was an interesting person to talk to. And Mary was for the most part, a very forgiving person. So when Frances approached her work bench and said that she wanted to apologize for everything, Mary accepted the apology. She didn't ask her friend to specify what she was apologizing for. She decided that Frances was referring to the stealing, but was too embarrassed to say it.

One day when there was no work, Mary took the bus over to Frances' house. They were going out shopping together. While Frances cleaned up the kitchen and got the garbage ready to be taken out, Mary asked to use the phone. "Use the one in the bedroom, will you?" said Frances "The one in the kitchen isn't working right" Mary dropped her bag on the chair and hurried in to the bedroom. A few minutes later they set out for the store. Mary helped Frances pick out some clothes. Then she looked for some clothes for herself. It was when they were getting ready to pay that she discovered that her wallet was missing! She felt like she had been punched in the stomach. How could she have let this happen again?! For a blind person, Frances was very crafty. If only Mary could say that she had seen her take the wallet. But she had been busy on the phone. She couldn't honestly say for sure that her wallet didn't drop out of her bag on the way to Frances' house. However, she was much more careful about her things then she was a few years earlier.

When she frantically informed Frances that her wallet was gone, Frances loaned her ten dollars. Feeling confused, frustrated, ashamed, Mary went home. She called her friend, Joe, who lived in the same building as her. He invited her up to his apartment. His father was there when she arrived. They were both sympathetic. Because they were both generous people who happened to like Mary a lot, they each gave her ten dollars and told her to keep the money. Mary was so grateful to them. But she was still going to have to buy another wallet and replace the cards that were in the old one. After talking to Joe and Arcady, it was decided that Mary should call Frances and inform her that she was going to tell the police about the missing wallet. Frances wasn't home. So Mary left a message on the answering machine. Then she stretched out on Joe's couch and wondered aloud where Frances was. "Out spending your money!" replied Joe abruptly.

Now here she was two days later, sitting at work, fuming and planning. She would punish Frances, oh yes she would!

The following morning, a Saturday, Mary left early and took the bus to Frances' neighborhood. She knew that her ex friend attended Mass daily. She snickered to herself about this. a holy thief?, HA! Feeling like her heart was trying to pound its way through her chest, she stood in the shadows and waited. Soon a tall, thin, figure with curly gray hair appeared. She was using a white cane to guide herself to the side entrance of the huge, old church. Mary darted forward, and in almost the same instant, opened the jar of paint and splattered Frances' coat with it. Knowing how Frances felt about clothes, Mary smiled as she imagined how upset she would be when she found out her coat was ruined.

Mary proceeded to France's house, which was down the street from the church. She took Frances' mail, tore it up and dumped it in the bushes. Then she filled the small, black mailbox with mud. Making sure that there was no one in the immediate area, Mary took out another jar of paint and and a brush. Working quickly, she put up a message that said "The blind woman who lives in this house is a thief!!" Feeling pleased with herself, Mary gathered up her things and hurried to the bus stop. She was pretty sure she hadn't been seen, but even if she had, they would n't be able to identify her. She was wearing a baggy sweatshirt under a pair of overalls. Her long, brown hair was tucked up inside of a baseball cap.

Once home, Mary typed a phony love letter to a man who used to be a supervisor at Work shop. Frances was secretly in love with him. She used to tell Mary how much she wished she could have him. After finishing a somewhat embarrassing but not too graphic a love letter, no one who knew Frances, would believe that she was capable of anything graphic). Mary typed the man's address on the envelope. Her handwriting wouldn't be an issue at all.

The following week Mary was called in to the office of the workshop director. Besides the boss, there was a detective from Pawtucket sit- ting there waiting to talk to her. He was a stern looking man of about thirty five, with brown hair and a mustache. He informed Mary that he was there to talk to her about an assault that had happened to a middle aged, blind woman in Pawtucket. He made it clear that she had been seen in the area and that even though no one saw her do anything; he was convinced of her guilt. Mary insisted that she didn't do anything. Without looking up from the papers on his lap, the detective said that the woman claimed that Mary threw paint on her, destroyed her mail, filled her mailbox with mud, painted her front door, and hit her over the head with a blunt object. Mary gaped! She was guilty of everything but the last charge. It looked as if Frances was a liar as well as a thief! Because the grim faced detective couldn't get anything on Mary, he left saying that if he did get proof that she was involved, he would personally make sure that she was prosecuted to the fullest extent of the law. As Mary returned to work, She hoped that Frances would be caught stealing some day.

Chapter Twenty Four

The Forbidden Climb

At the foot of Mount Onancock there was a large campsite. It was owned by an organization known as The Onancock bible conference. It was located in Jaffrey Center, New Hampshire. It had been   in operation for many years. Every week activities were held for various groups of people. Even in the winter months people stayed up there for weekend retreats. It was a time to not only do some skiing, hiking, swimming or mountain climbing, it was also a time to attend church services, read the bible or be counseled by the visiting minister.   Each year, during the last week of July Onancock opened its doors to blind Christians.

This year Mary joined her friends at the camp. It was a hot summer in 1995 and she had nothing planned outside of work. Despite her overly religious adoptive parents, she had never embraced religion. She in fact had rebelled against it most of the time. Choosing to get high, steal, and mouth off at authority. She had a deep mistrust and hatred of most authority, believing that people who were in charge were dishonest bullies who didn't care about anyone but themselves. So what was she doing going to a Christian camp? She already knew that Christians believed in submitting to authority more then anyone else. They seemed to spend a lot of time submitting, to God first and foremost. They thought this was more important then anything else. Mary supposed that some of what her parents and other Christians had been drilling in to her must of had a lasting effect on her. Whether she liked it or not, she did believe in God, the devil, heaven and hell. And she didn't want to go to hell when she died. Besides, some of her friends were Christians and they wanted her to accompany them to camp this year, just to see if she liked it. Mary had been to this camp on three other occasions though. On the first occasion back in "88" she brought a blind woman with her, who was stealing money from her. Not realizing that her friend was the thief, Mary had accused her roommates of taking her money. The two other times she attended the camp, in "92", and "93", nothing major happened to her. She just bided her time, and tried not to be bored. Now, two years later, she had decided to give the camp another chance. One of the reasons that Mary agreed to this was because she knew that they took campers up Mount Onancock each year. And not just the children in the nearby day camp either. Guides took blind and visually impaired campers up the mountain too. Mary had always wanted to go mountain climbing. She longed for adventure. Unfortunately, Camp Onancock didn't seem to be known for giving the blind much adventure. Aside from the two religious services that were held each day and were mandatory, there wasn't much for the blind campers to do except sit on the porch and rock while talking or listening to music or stories on tape... unless you counted the shopping trip to Caldor's and the service at the cathedral of the pines. Whoopee thought Mary contemptuously. When does the real fun begin? The previous evening she received her first real disappointment at the camp. Aside from the mountain climb that was scheduled for Thursday, Mary was looking forward to the weekly hayride. The rain didn't upset her because she heard that it would stop before evening. And it did, yet the hayride was cancelled! When she asked why she was told that the wagon was all wet and the ground was too muddy. Mary threw up her hands in disgust!! Did they really think that blind people were totally helpless and needed to be treated like old people? In rebellion, Mary sat backwards during the evening service and refused to stop chewing her gum. She even blew a few bubbles and snapped her gum. She knew that she was being immature. This was not the way a woman should act. But was her behavior creating a more absurd picture then a group of blind adults sitting in rocking chairs, being talked down to by guides who in some cases, were half their ages? Why didn't the authorities at this camp think that blind and visually impaired adults could cope with outdoor life?

One evening after the service had ended, and everyone was having a snack over at the main building, Earl, a middle aged camp counselor sat Mary, and her friend, David down, and asked them if they had accepted the Lord as their savior yet. He must have noticed David nodding off during the services, and Mary chewing gum, and writing in her journal instead of paying attention. Mary wasn't that worried about the well meaning interrogation issued by Earl. She had been through this before, but she was concerned about David, who was sensitive, and tended to hold in feelings of frustration. Would Earl push him past his limit? Mary glanced at David frequently, as Earl gently chided them on their lack of enthusiasm, and urged them to accept Jesus in to their hearts. He told them to admit to being sinners. They both acknowledged this. When he asked them if they wanted to be saved they said that they did. Then he helped them pray the Sinners Prayer, where they said that they were sinners, and were sorry for it, and wanted Jesus to be their Lord, and Savior." You're saved!" Earl happily said. To Mary's surprise, David held up his hands, and said "Hurray! We're saved!" She detected a note of sarcasm in his voice, and hoped that Earl didn't notice this. Joe, who got saved back in 1991, was sitting at their table stuffing himself with ice cream bars, chips, soda, and a big pretzel. "Hurray, David, and Mary accepted the Lord!....Ah, I need a napkin".

Finally Thursday morning arrived, the big day that Mary had been waiting for. Soon she would be able to do something really adventurous! She and her friend, David went to the blue room at 9am to wait for the local tour guide, who was an expert mountain climber. Twenty minutes later he arrived, along with two other guides from the camp. They were Tom and Brad. She didn't find out the name of the local guide, and she didn't really care, as long as he took them up the mountain. As they set out, Mary latched on to Tom because she didn't find Brad to be very friendly toward her. And Tom was in to Star Trek like she was. It was a hot and humid sunny day. This did not dull Mary's spirits; she was determined to make the climb. However, David was not so fortunate. He being overweight became overcome by the heat and had to stop. The guides being over protective used his misfortune as an opportunity to cancel the climb "Someone up there hates me!" growled Mary through clenched teeth. Ten minutes later two men arrived with a stretcher to carry David back to camp. But he was made of stronger stuff then they could have imagined. He walked back, supported by a guide on each side of him. As they walked back, Mary felt disappointed and angry...not at her friend, David couldn't help getting sick and she knew it. She was angry at the overprotective guides. He could eat less and exercise more thought Mary angrily. She found that .she was frustrated with the lack of adventure she and her friends really had. They never did anything very exciting. Mary realized suddenly. No wonder I crave adventure so much! Of all her friends, Joe was the one she spent the most time with. They had grown close; almost like brother and sister. He was her drinking partner, and confidant. He usually supported her when she had a conflict with someone. But his dependence on her drove her crazy sometimes! When could she ever go off and do what she wanted to do when she had to play nursemaid to him? If only his father's mind hadn't gone senile. Sometimes Mary wished that the three of them were still living at Dexter Manor. Arcady's mind started to go a few years back. He couldn't take care of Joe, or himself anymore. This resulted in him being placed in a nursing home the previous year. After living with a roommate that he didn't get along with; Joe moved in to the building where Mary now lived. With her resentment of her situation burning inside of her, Mary allowed herself to be led back to camp

. As far as everyone else was concerned, the climb was over. But Mary had other ideas. By the time they returned to camp, she had a plan. Putting her plan in to action, she approached David, who had decided to sit in one of the rocking chairs on the porch. "Tell everyone that I went to take a shower, and that Im going to take a nap afterward." David assured her that he would tell everyone concerned what she had said. Suspecting that she was being watched, Mary went to her cabin. Then, as if she had been shot from a cannon, she burst through the back door and made her way over to the park entrance where she would pay yet another three dollars to climb the mountain

. It was as hot as ever and more difficult then she would have expected, but she struggled up the mountain. She was glad that she had been able to hang on to the food she had been given that morning and koolade. .At first; the climb was easy because she was on a dirt path. But as she continued up, it became necessary to climb over some rough terrain. As hard as it became, Mary imagined that the people at the place where she worked would be proud of her if they could see her now. This kept her going.

She was three quarters of the way up the mountain when she decided to take a break. Mary sat down and noticed how picturesque everything was She also noticed how much cooler it was up on the mountain. She didn't want to go back down to that hot, humid, demanding world down there. She wanted to finish the climb, then take a long, refreshing nap before going back down to camp. However, she knew that this could not be. Not with a self centered, neurotic, friend like Joe. He would be sure to make a fuss and draw everyone's attention to the fact that Mary was not at lunch. He would have half the camp out looking for her. Sometimes she desperately wanted to yell at him! Reluctantly, Mary started back down the mountain. Before she had gone very far, she ran in to some kids from the day camp nearby. They pointed out the white dots that were painted on almost every other rock. If only she had known about this from the start, her climb up would not have been as treacherous. With the White dots guiding her, Mary quickly descended the mountain, stopping to fill her canteen at a stream.

Once again she was experiencing the heat. When she reached the park at the foot of the mountain Mary found one of the head counselors waiting for her. "That was a definite no no, Mary" he announced. He hurried her in to the police car that his son usually drove. Mary was tempted to ask him to turn on the siren as he drove her back to camp. But somehow she managed not to. When they returned to the camp, Mary looked around at the people on the porch. She wondered if her nervous, worry wart friend Joe was there. He wasn't, but Bob and David were. Her friend Laurie was sitting outside too. She was listening to her organ music on her tape player. Laurie loved the camp, and looked forward to going every year. However she didn't have a strong urge to climb mountains like Mary did. As the head counselor led her across the porch, Mary noticed Kathy, a young totally blind Christian girl from Connecticut, who loved to listen to Jewish music. Fleetingly, she felt a surge of envy for both Laurie and Kathy. They weren't in trouble like she was. Still, Mary had been craving adventure, and she just finished having one. She didn't care what was going to happen now. Let them forbid her to come the following year.

Mary was led in to the blue room, where Pat, one of the camp nurses, was waiting. She gave Mary the tongue lashing that was probably deserved. "Do you always act so selfishly?" Pat demanded. "No!" Mary responded angrily and truthfully. "As a matter of fact, I usually think of other people" Her friends certainly could vouch for that. "But you didn't think of other people today, did you?" asked an unimpressed Pat. "No not today "Answered Mary emphatically and unashamedly. She had wanted to climb that mountain so badly and experiences a real adventure that there was little room for regret over the people who she made worry and look for her. Soon afterward she did feel shame and regret though. But not because someone yelled at her and told her how selfish she was. Russell, the camp director was a middle aged man with grey hair, a clean shaven, kind face with a calm, friendly disposition. He stopped by the blue room where Mary was finishing up the lunch that she had taken on her climb. She could tell by the look on his face that she had disappointed him. "I'm- sorry Russ" she said tentatively. He nodded slowly. "I believe you Mary. But you must understand that you had a lot of people worried." Mary nodded and tried to be patient as he quietly lectured her like a concerned father would. She really was sorry that she had let him down. But she was also frustrated because she now had to check in with her counselor before she did anything. This was going to be humiliating! Still, Mary felt that Russ handled the situation better then Pat did.

Mary wondered if she would ever get a chance to climb Mount Onancock again. She knew that now was not the time to ask if she could try again next year. Would she be allowed back next year? Did she even want to come back next year? One thing she did know was that if she wanted a more interesting, adventurous life, she was going to have to reserve a little more time for herself now and then.

Chapter Twenty Five

Paul, a friend indeed

Paul moved in to Hilltop Apartment's in August of 2002. This was his second time there. Paul had moved many times. One could say that he was a connoisseur of apartments in the Providence/Pawtucket area because he had lived in so many of them.

Paul was born in Boston, in 1945. He never knew his father. His mother didn't take good care of him, or his half brother, Peter. She loved to party with various men. Paul must have felt his mother's neglect. At age six he had a crush on a popular singer of that time. Her name was Kate Smith. When she was singing on TV he used to crawl over, and kiss her face on the screen.

By the time Paul was eight, his mother gave him, and his half brother to his Grandfather. His Grandfather said that he couldn't afford to adopt both boys. So he kept Paul, and gave up Peter for adoption. Paul was so hurt and angry over his Grandfather's decision that he set his bedroom on fire! As a result, he was put in The Myles Standish State School for boys. (In 1959 it was renamed The Paul A Dever School.) The school was in Taunton. It consisted of thirteen L shaped buildings that had originally housed German POWs during World War Two. The school was under funded. The staff was often abusive toward the patients, and the school system there was so poorly run that Paul, and many other boys never got past grammar school. When Paul was about ten he was sexually assaulted by an older boy. Because of the poor conditions there, he never received any counseling about the incident.

As bad as the school was, the boys were taken on outings sometimes. Paul loved to go to the movies. He was fascinated by the MGM lion that roared on the screen before a movie began. His Grandfather, and occasionally his mother visited him.

Paul remained at the state school until he was twenty. His mother had died due to an exploding pancreas, when Paul was in his teens. Upon leaving, he went home to his Grandfather, took care of him until he died. His Grandfather taught him how to cook. Because they were Jewish, they couldn't eat pork. One night a cousin brought over a dish that he had prepared. He claimed that the meat wasn't pork. Afterward he laughed, and admitted that it was pork. Paul's Grandfather was so angry that he didn't speak to the cousin for several years.

In 1972, when Paul was going on Twenty Seven his Grandfather died. He moved to Providence, RI. Although he had had a little work experience in Boston, he found himself in a sheltered work shop, called The Community Work shop. (It was later called Vocational Resources.) It was while he was working there that he met a tall, thin man with a mustache. He was an Eighteen year old High School drop out, named Tom. He was kind of shy, and was close to his mother, who he still lived with. He had three other brothers. Paul and Tom took to each other right away. They liked many of the same TV shows, and enjoyed going to the same kind of places. They both hated sports. Paul had a particular reason for hating sports. Many times American Band Stand, his favorite show, was canceled, or postponed because of a ball game.

Paul's Grandfather had left him an inheritance. Every weekend Paul and Tom went to New York City, and lived it up. Several other friends joined them. However, when the money ran out, Tom was the only friend who stayed at Paul's side.

With the help of Traveler's aid, Paul was able to locate his long lost half brother, Peter. Initially they were happy to be reunited with each other, but they soon discovered that they had little in common. Eventually they drifted apart.

Tom took Paul to his mother's house, and before long he was like one of the family. Tom, like Paul never knew his father. He and his brothers grew up on the water, fishing, swimming, and core hogging with their Grandfather. His mother was an out going, hospitable woman, who threw many parties. She also loved dolls. Later when she was dying of cancer she was surrounded by her beloved dolls, and sons. Tom was the most devastated by her death, but he had Paul to lean on. Every night after work he ate supper, and watched TV with Paul before going home. Paul could no longer work because he was developing a bad case of arthritis. It affected his back, and his knees.

In 1978, when Paul was going on Thirty Three he became a Born Again Christian. He credited this to the influence of TV Evangelist, Jimmy Swaggert. (Later when the evangelist fell, Paul staunchly defended him, and refused to lose faith in him.) Paul started attending Four Square Pentecostal Church, in Providence. Tom, who went everywhere with him, attended the church as well. Tom wasn't saved though, and sometimes acted immature around the other parishioners, who had become Paul's friends. Paul always defended Tom. The church was an inner city church that ran a soup kitchen. Paul often helped out after the service. He met, and made friends with a middle aged couple, named Fred and Marge. Like Paul, Fred was a Jew, who had embraced Christianity. He was a quiet, good natured man. Marge was an out going, humorous woman with a high infectious laugh. They both remained life long friends of Paul and Tom.

The Pastor and his wife, also a pastor, were good people, but they were strict, and had very definite ideas. When they criticized Jimmy Swaggert and Paul's friendship with Tom,

Paul changed churches. They attended many churches before settling down at an Assembly of God church, in Providence.

It was in August of 2002 that Mary came in to Paul, and Tom's lives. She had been living at Hilltop for nine and a half years. The tan, six story building was well named. It sat upon a hill. There were two ways that a tenant could reach the building. They could walk up the steep grassy hill, or they could go up Ridgeway, which was steep as well. For Paul, who was now in a scooter, Ridgeway was the only way for him. Mary had met Tom and Paul a couple of times on the bus over the past few years. They had always greeted each other happily. Now with Paul living down the hall from her, it became possible for Mary to develop a friendship with Paul, and of coarse Tom, who visited every evening, and on weekends.

The first thing Paul did for Mary was to hook up two VCRs to her TV so that she could duplicate videos of her favorite show, Gene Roddenberry's Andromeda. For the past year she had been quite taken with one of the characters on this show. His name was Reverend Behemial Far Traveler. He was an alien, from a race of savages, who found God, and became a monk. Because he was brilliant, and multitalented, Rev served as not only the ship's spiritual adviser, he also manned the sensors, refusing only to fire missiles because this went against his religious beliefs. He worked as a medic in sick bay, and helped out in hydroponics.

Mary became a born again Christian back in 1998. She was adjusting well to her beliefs, and the church she attended regularly: Faith & Hope Baptist Church. She supposed that this was what made someone like Rev Bem so fascinating, and endearing to her.

Paul made it clear right from the start that he accepted Mary as she was. He had no problem with the dolls she painted, stuffed, and sewed of her favorite TV characters. Tom, his best friend, followed suit. However, he unlike Paul, had a crush on Mary, and made it clear that he wanted more then friendship with her. Mary wasn't interested in anything more then friendship from either one of them.

Every Wednesday, and Saturday Mary spent the evening with Paul and Tom. They had supper together. Then they watched one of Paul's movies, followed by a short feature. Paul liked action, horror, and Disney movies. Mary liked it that many of his movies featured kids. (They were usually boys.) His short features were shows like Super Man, Roy Rogers, Bonanza, Dragnet, Hawaii Five-O, and 7th Heaven. He also liked Jimmy Swaggert, and Pat Boone. Mary liked Pat Boone in The Cross and the switch blade, a movie about street gangs in New York City, in the early 70's.

Often while they watched movies Tom would get down on the floor with Mary, and brush her hair, or rub her back. She accepted his attention up to a point because it felt good, but when he began to grope her she pulled away. Paul, sitting in his recliner, never commented on this. At Nine Thirty Tom took the bus home, and Mary returned to her apartment four doors down from Paul's. They both had to get up early to go to work. Tom worked at a box factory that had hired him nearly twenty years earlier. Mary worked at a jewelry factory, where she had been employed for the past four yeas. In spite of the tight security she enjoyed working there, and had had very few conflicts with people. The only thing she didn't like was the way most of the women talked down to her there. They were nice, but they seemed to think she was very naive, and clueless. She had managed to make two friends at work. One of them, a woman, ten years her senior, saw Mary outside of work. She was a Catholic, named Marie, who still lived with her mother. She had a habit of talking loudly, and rapidly. Mary found it over whelming at times. But she liked the fact that Marie wore her dyed hair long, and dressed in trendy clothes in order to look younger. She listened to up to date music, and had little tolerance for oldies. Marie and Mary went out to eat every Friday night. Sometimes they took trips to places like Newport, and Martha's Vineyard on Saturdays. Soon Mary was including some of her other friends on these outings. Marie didn't like this at first. "Mary why do you have to bring all these people?" she would exclaim, as if ten instead of only three other people were being included. However, she soon got used to it. Most of Mary's other friends were blind, or legally blind like she was. She had once worked with them at a place called Insight. They seemed to like Marie, so she grew to like them as well.

By late September Mary hired Paul to DJ her parties. He had expressed a longing to be a DJ. "It's been a dream of mine for years." Mary knew how important unfulfilled dreams were. She paid him Twenty dollars for each party. All of Mary's friends came, including Marie. Paul sat in his recliner with his stereo, CDs, and microphone. He played music from the fifties, sixties, and seventies. He periodically threw in some old time gospel music. He liked to ask trivia questions about music, and old TV shows. People often got up to dance. In the early days of her friendship with Paul, she had the pleasure of seeing him get up, and do the twist. Paul was a heavy man, who had trouble with his knees, and back. So he couldn't dance for a long length of time. A lot of time Mary danced with Tom, alternating with David, a short, good natured Italian, who had sight in only one eye. There was always alcohol at the parties. Mary, Tom, Bob, and Joe, Mary's long time, blind friend, were the only ones who drank it though.

Tom was used to Paul giving him his way in just about everything. When he swore, and griped about the kind of music Paul was playing, Paul would immediately switch over to Tony Orlando and Dawn. Tom would dance with a big smile on his face, no trace of embarrassment over the tantrum he had recently thrown. Mary quietly marveled at this, as she danced with him. All too often Tom's cheerful mood would turn to anger, and jealousy. He didn't like Mary dancing, and joking around with David. He acted as if she was his girl friend. He sometimes yelled, and swore at David, who was mildly mentally challenged, and didn't know how to handle such a conflict. Once Tom shoved him as he stormed from the apartment! Paul's way was to just go on with the party, and talk to Tom later. He made excuses for his friend, but could usually get him to apologize to David before he went home. Clearly Paul wanted to keep peace between everyone, but he wasn't good at being firm with those he cared most about. One major concern of Paul's was that John, one of the guests, used to sit beside an elderly woman, who was mildly mentally challenged. John was half her age, but was attracted to her. He often put his arm around her, and touched her inappropriately in front of everyone. Paul, as a Christian, was shocked by this, especially since John was a Christian as well! Paul, Tom, and some of the others confronted John, and warned him that he wouldn't be invited to the parties anymore if he continued to act this way. John promised to behave. Yet one evening at a Halloween party when he was dancing with a blind woman, named Laurie, he kissed her and touched her breasts several times. As a result, he was banned from the parties for a few months.

Mary celebrated Christmas with her payees, Pauline, and Joan, and their husbands on the last Sunday before the actual holiday. They always went out to eat at Ribs & Co, in Johnston. They did this every year. They also took Mary out for her birthday, which was in April. Normally she saw Pauline and Joan every other Friday. They had lunch, and took care of her bills. Afterward she went shopping with what was left over from her government check. Pauline and Joan liked Paul and Tom. They were happy that her friends were multiplying.

Mary sang in the church Christmas pageant. She invited Paul and Tom. She was in the choir, and appeared too shy to Paul. He told her so later. She spent Christmas Day with them. Paul invited one of his other friends over, an older woman, named Barbara, who wore her hair short, refused to wear a bra, and dressed like a man, but was pleasant enough. They ate a big turkey dinner, and watched some of Paul's old American band Stand videos.

In early February of 2003 a space shuttle crashed, killing the astronauts on board. Jim, one of Mary's friends, who was a Christian, and an artist, was very upset by this. Together with Paul, Tom, Joe, Mike, and Frances, Mary went over to Jim's apartment one Saturday to hang out with him, and comfort him. Jim, a former veteran, was very patriotic. He had a giant American flag on his parlor wall. But what really impressed everyone was the huge poster he made in honor of the dead astronauts.

At the end of May Mary, Marie, and most of the other women in their department were laid off for the summer. At the same time Frances found that she was homeless. Her land lord decided to throw everyone out of the tenement house, renovate it, and charge higher rents to the new tenants. Frances had a brother and a sister. They couldn't, or wouldn't take her in. She also had two friends, elderly women, who had known her for years. They couldn't, or wouldn't take her in either. Finally Mary got permission from the office to let Frances stay with her for a couple of weeks. Because of the stealing Frances had done in the past, Mary Frances Proofed her apartment. She hid her money, and valuables in a closet which she kept locked. Not only had Mary forgiven (though not forgotten), she just couldn't live with herself if she allowed an elderly, blind woman to be put on the street. Besides, she was a Christian now. It was her duty to help people, even those who were not worthy of trust.

When Mary wasn't out with Paul, (Tom worked during the day.) or trying to find apartments for Frances, she spent her days lying on her bedroom floor rewriting old journals, or drawing pictures of George Washington, her new heart throb. She always had her stereo on, and would record from the local top 40 station. In the next room Frances sat with the shade pulled down against the heat of the summer. While chain smoking, and drinking numerous cups of coffee, she listened to Talk Radio on her transistor.

Even though she attended the parties, and accompanied Paul and Tom on outings, Frances didn't always like them. She was in fact jealous of them. Before they came along Mary spent most of her time with Frances, Bob, David, Joe, Mike, and Marie. Mary still did this, but often Paul and Tom were with them too, and Paul liked to plan where they were all going to go. Sometimes Frances tried to make Mary see that Tom was a trouble maker, and Paul was selfish, and demanding. (Paul sometimes saw Frances as the selfish, demanding one, and had said as much) Mary felt stressed by trying to appease Frances, please Paul and Tom, and trying to fit everyone in to her life at all the right times. She often drank too much. Tom got a kick out of it sometimes because she acted funny, and danced a lot, but Paul worried about her, and said so.

In the middle of June Mary, David, and Bob left to attend Alumni Weekend at Perkins school for the blind. A close friend of theirs, a blind woman, named Laurie had recently been abandoned by her husband, also blind. She was very upset, and cried on, and off over the weekend. David, who had always liked her stayed at her side, and comforted her regularly. Bob and Mary were friendly, and supportive toward Laurie, but Mary couldn't help worrying about her apartment. She had been afraid to leave Frances alone there for the weekend, less because she might steal, and more because she might set the place on fire! A blind chain smoker was dangerous. So Mary asked Jody, another friend of hers, to spend the weekend with Frances. Jody though was legally blind, and didn't always get along with Frances. Paul and Tom had promised to look in on them from time to time. Mary was only some what relieved.

When she returned home Sunday afternoon her apartment was still in tact. But sparks were flying! Apparently Frances and Jody had spent much of the weekend bickering. Frances was a staunch, old time Catholic, and Jody, a young, born again Christian. They were both very opinionated. Tom, who had listened outside the door several times over the weekend heard them arguing about religion. Paul had stopped in to talk to them, and had invited them over for supper. Frances refused the invitation. Mary was pounced on by each woman, as they both aired their complaints about each other. Later when Jody went home, Paul sat down with Frances and Mary. Frances couldn't stop talking about how loud, silly, and inconsiderate she thought Jody was. Paul listened, and was sympathetic, but he did say that having grown up with all sorts of people in the state school for boys, he had learned to be tolerant of people with all kinds of problems. Mary knew this to be true. While Tom, in his drunken moments expressed jealousy over Mary's friends, and even her dolls, Paul not only accepted Mary's differences, he sometimes held Rev Bem, her favorite doll when they were watching movies.

As the weeks went by it was obvious that finding Frances an apartment was going to be harder then Mary thought. She called a nun, who knew Frances well. The nun urged her to get Frances in to an assisted living facility. "I know she has the money" she said with a laugh. Mary now knew that Frances had money too. Not long before she talked to the nun Frances admitted that her aunt had left her a trust fund, making it impossible to get in to Subsidized Housing. Mary wondered why Frances lived like a pauper, and stole people's money.

Paul and Tom tried to help Frances find an apartment, but she only wanted one in the Pawtucket area because she had lived there for years, and it was familiar to her. In July a nun from a soup kitchen in Providence found Frances a home in the Edgewood section of Cranston. She would be living with another older woman. However, Frances only lasted one night with her. The next day the woman told her to find another place to live. Frances told Mary that all she had been doing was wandering around the house, lost in the middle of the night. The woman wouldn't tell Mary anything.

Tom was able to get Frances a room in the tenement where he lived, but after one night there, she was on the verge of a nervous break down. She claimed that she couldn't find her way to and from the communal bathroom, and that no one would help her. Paul and Tom came to get her while Mary was at church.

Finally late in July Frances moved in with a young Mulotto woman, who lived in Pawtucket. She was strict, but Frances smoking. She didn't want her doing it in the house. She often had friends over, some of them were men. Frances slept on the couch in the living room. She hated it there almost immediately. As a result, she spent the weekends with Mary. She constantly complained about Corrine, her roommate. Corrine had some complaints of her own mainly that she had caught Frances on two different occasions stealing money from her purse. Still she let her stay there.

Mary, Paul, and Tom continued to go out a lot. Because Paul used a scooter, and needed the chair lift, they always sat at the back of the bus. Sometimes Joe, Bob, and others accompanied them. Whenever there was a free concert at the dog track in Lincoln, They would take the

Ride van to and from it because the concerts ended late. Mary and Tom always drank a lot, and danced to most of the songs, usually oldies. They also took a ride on the Bay Queen one day. Joe, Bob, and Paul's other friends, Dickey and Kathy joined them. The couple went to festivals with Paul, Tom, and Mary as well.

In 2004 the outings and parties continued. Paul was still only plagued by diabetes, and bad knees. He could still walk short distances with only the aid of a cane. By this time He and Tom were attending Mary's church because Four Square Pentecostal church was closed. Although they had stopped going to this church years ago, they learned that Fred and Marge, close friends of Paul's in particular, were attending Mary's church now. Because Faith & Hope was a Baptist Church, Marge laughingly referred to herself as a Bapticostal! She and Fred were happy to see Paul and Tom there, as was Mary. Soon after Tom confessed to the church elders; and later to Mary, that he had put a substance in her coffee to make her want to have sex. It hadn't worked though because she poured it out when she noticed that it tasted sweet. The five of them always sat together. Often Paul, who loved to sing, would get up in front of the congregation, and do a solo. Tom loved to sing too, but he was too shy to sing in front of people. Mary was now working in a factory over in Riverside. The jewelry factory was where she used to work was folding up, and preparing to move over seas.

In the fall of that year Mary visited Sister Jane in Kentucky for a week. (Mary visited her back in 1999.). When Sister Jane wasn't taking care of the elderly nuns she took Mary on outings. The convent was no longer located in Covington. They were now out in a rural section of Melbourne. They talked a lot, and watched TV together in the evenings. Mary was sorry when the visit ended. She had a pleasant surprise when she landed in RI though. Paul and Tom were waiting for her when she got off the plane. They treated her to dinner at an All you can eat buffet.

In June of 2005 Paul had his right knee replaced. It was a risky operation simply because he was a diabetic. He had to remain in the hospital for a few weeks before being transferred to a rehabilitation facility. Many people visited Paul, but he was home sick. He was happiest in his living room surrounded by his large collection of videos, and DVDs. His knee continued to bother him possibly because he didn't exercise it enough. It would be a while before the other knee was operated on.

As summer turned in to fall, Mary continued to get together with her friends. For years her apartment was filled with people sleeping on couches, and mattresses on the floor during weekends. Bob, Joe, and Frances were the most constant weekend guests, with David running at a close second. Mary jokingly called the apartment "Mary's bed and breakfast". Paul sometimes told her to give herself a break, but once she started this tradition it was hard to stop. Everyone wanted to go out on weekends, and they couldn't always get transportation.

Drinking often went on. Paul visited, but abstained. Tom however, drank with Mary, Bob, and Joe. One evening after Paul went to bed Tom started giving Bob one beer after another. Mary was worried. "Don't do that! "she whispered frantically. "If he get's sick, I'll be held responsible." Tom stopped after admitting that he resented Bob because he thought he was showing off. After Tom left Joe couldn't find his slippers. As Joe began to whine then yell, Mary searched for the slippers. She knocked on Paul's door, and asked Tom if he had seen them. Tom said he hadn't. Back in Mary's apartment Joe was becoming hysterical! Mary searched again, and then ran to Paul's apartment where Tom was waiting with a big grin on his face. He handed over the slippers which he had worn, unnoticed by Mary when he left. Tom often did things like this. But just when she found herself thinking that he was devious, and selfish, he would suddenly do something nice for her. She usually found that she had mixed feelings about him. Once during a party she caught him looking around in her bedroom closet. He abruptly claimed that he was just admiring her dolls. Two of Paul's criticisms were appreciated by Mary. The first was her smoking. He told her that if she could quit for six months he would treat her to dinner. She did quit, and was treated to dinner. (Paul always kept his word). The other criticism came when she lost her wallet, and couldn't go on a trip with Marie. It was a coach trip to the cape. Marie still could have gone, but she resentfully backed out, and blamed Mary. "I think you owe me the twenty six dollars that I lost by not going." She said on the phone one day. "But you still could have gone. You would have been with other people, and a tour guide!" insisted Mary. "No, I don't like to travel alone, even if I'm on a guided tour" Marie answered in a whinny voice. Paul was in the room during the phone call. He was out raged! "If you give her that money, I'll never speak to you again!" Mary strengthened by his support, refused to pay Marie. A few weeks' later Frances talked Marie in to making up with Mary, and the matter of the money was dropped. Mary was grateful to Frances. She supposed that she was trying to make amends for the stealing. She no longer lived with Corrine. She now had her own apartment in Pawtucket, but she never got all of her belongings back from Corrine. This was because when she was moving out Corrine told her that she owed back rent. Frances had reluctantly agreed to give her a check for the amount she owed. However when Corrine took the check to the bank, making Frances wait outside until she returned, she discovered that Frances had called the bank, and canceled the check. "You're a slick, old lady, Frances!" announced Corrine. Mary had warned her other friends to watch their money when Frances was around and they did, but every now and then they were careless, and Frances was able to strike!

Paul and Mary loved to sing duets in the church's occasional talent shows. For weeks they would rehearse in his room while Tom watched TV. When they did perform, it went off without a hitch! Mary always invited her other friends to the event.

Like the year before, Mary, Joe, Paul, and Tom celebrated Christmas Day over at Paul's friend, Frank's apartment. He and his girl friend, Philomena, lived in a high rise off of Cranston St. Tom, Joe, and Mary drank, and danced a lot. Paul sat, talked with Frank and his girl friend, and played with their cats. Frank was a good host. He enjoyed waiting on his guests, and cooked a terrific dinner.

In 2006 Paul was tired of living at Hilltop. He moved to a high rise just down the street in late June. Mary was disappointed, but she knew she would see just as much of him as before. Despite this, she missed the convenience of having him down the hall instead of down the street.

Fred and Marge came over for the day on July 4th. They all watched TV, and ate pasta and meatballs.

In the fall Paul became very ill, and had to be hospitalized. He was in intensive care for a couple of weeks. He was eventually transferred to a regular room, but took a turn for the worse, and was put back in intensive care. Tom and Mary visited him every day. The doctors informed Paul that he had a serious infection, caused by a bug. Paul believed that the doctor meant this literally because while he was practicing a song for church, he swallowed a bug. River edge was next to a rather polluted river. It attracted many bugs. Paul suspected that the bug he swallowed might have carried an infection. He had Mary get him an application from Hilltop. She helped him fill it out. Soon he was on the waiting list to move back to Hilltop. She was thrilled about this! However, more was wrong with Paul besides an infection. His kidneys and liver began to malfunction. The hospital started giving him dialysis. Fortunately after only a few treatments, his kidneys began working on their own again. He still wasn't out of danger yet. One day when Tom and Mary were visiting him, Tom commented on how yellow Paul's skin and eye balls were. Mary took a closer look, and discovered that Tom was right. She was scared! Paul's doctor took him off of one of the pain medications because it was damaging his liver. After this Paul's complexion began to return to its usual ruddiness.

After a month Paul was transferred to a nursing home for physical therapy. He wasn't happy about this. Once when Tom and Mary were there he started crying, as he talked to the nurse. Paul was normally a loud man, who could be a bit bossy at times, but he had a sensitive side. He was given to tears more then the average man was. The nurse was sympathetic, but firm. She informed him that he wouldn't be allowed to go home until he could walk for at least five minutes with a walker, unassisted. Tom and Mary tried to comfort, and encourage him.

In early November Paul was at last able to come home. He had to avoid dark soda, even if it was sugar free. He had to cut back on food containing potassium, and protein, and of coarse sugar because of his diabetes. For a few weeks a nurse and a physical therapist came to assist

Paul. In spite of this, he never regained the ability to walk with only a cane. He claimed that it was just too painful. In the mean time his doctor continued to prescribe various kinds of pain pills. Some of them were so strong that they had a high street value. If an addict had known what Paul was carrying they would have mugged him. As it was, the pills sometimes made Paul sluggish. Once, or twice his scooter hit a bump in the street, and the scooter toppled over. It was fortunate that Tom was with him on both occasions.

Paul continued to DJ parties for Mary and her other friends. In December he hosted a Christmas party. Everyone came, including Fred and Marge. Mary had given up drinking, and smoking by this time, but Tom and Joe were enjoying the alcohol, which Tom bought. When it came time to distribute the gifts Tom found that one of his gifts from Mary had been wrapped with newspaper. She had done so much wrapping that she ran out of wrapping paper. Tom was insulted. He was also drunk! He screamed, and swore at Mary in front of everyone, then angrily stormed out. While he was gone they had an anxious meeting about him. It was decided that when he returned, Fred would tell him to get his gifts, and leave. Tom did as he was told, stopping only long enough to criticize Paul for not taking his side.

Later when Mary was taking Laurie, Bob, Joe, and David downstairs to get rides home, she discovered that someone had smashed the up and down buttons that were between the two elevators. No one could use them. Mary, and her friends suspected Tom, but nobody had seen him do it, so they couldn't accuse him.

Mary helped Paul pack up his Cds, and equipment. They took the Ride van back to Riveredge. Tom, who had a key, was at the apartment when they returned. He sat in an angry silence, as Mary helped Paul take off his coat, and get his walker. Then Tom exploded once again. He accused Mary of trying to take over. He believed she wanted to steal Paul away from him. He said that she only liked blind people, and her dolls. He accused her of being a lesbian. He was red in the face, partly from the gin he was drinking, and partly from his rage! Mary screamed back, and swore at him. She wanted to know why he was still single if he was supposed to be such a desirable man. Paul began to cry, as he begged them to stop shouting. "You two are my best friends. Why do you have to fight?" He cried too because he was in a lot of pain. Mary felt sorry for Paul, but she was furious with Tom for the way he had acted all afternoon. He had scared her blind friends, who had done nothing to him. She was also furious with him for wanting her so much. If this was what love did to someone, she didn't want it! Because she knew she couldn't sit in the same room with Tom, she told Paul she was going home. It was hard though to resist his cries for her to remain. He made excuses for Tom, and reminded her that Tom was drunk, and didn't mean it.

She called Pastor John, from Faith & Hope. He told her not to go back there that night. He said that Tom needed to learn that there were consequences for his actions. He thought too that Paul needed to learn to stand up to Tom if he wanted to have other friends. Frances called Mary soon after. She told her that she shouldn't be too quick to let Tom off the hook. "A drunken man's words are a sober man's thoughts" she pointed out sagely. Mary felt strengthened by the two phone conversations. The next day Tom apologized. "You didn't hurt me, I hurt you" he said with his face averted. Mary accepted his apology, but later told Paul privately that if Tom ever abused her again she would only bother with him when Tom wasn't around.

In March of 2007 Tom lost his job at the factory. He decided that he needed to get away for a while. He took a three day trip to Atlantic City. Mary loaned him her camera. Tom returned saying that he won over two hundred dollars. Unfortunately while he went to collect it he left his coat on the back of his chair. Someone stole it. In the pockets were his false teeth, and Mary's camera. He bought her a new camera, but couldn't afford new false teeth.

Paul had his other knee replaced the following month. He had to spend several weeks in the hospital, and several more in a habilitation center for physical therapy. It was hard for him even though Tom, Mary, Fred, Marge, and even the pastor visited him. He wanted to be home playing his DVDs, and going out to eat.

Paul returned home at the start of summer. Together with Tom, Mary, and her other friends, Paul went to places such as Newport, Galilee, Oakland Beach, and Mayor's Day at the park. This was a annual event. They also attended an international ceremony at The Providence Assembly of God church.

Chapter Twenty Six

Finding family

Since last December Mary had slowly become consumed with a desire to find her birth mother, and relatives. It was now the summer of 2007. The desire was so strong that she could put it off no longer. Over the years she had tried occasionally to locate her mother, but she had little to go on, the adoption records had been closed, and she had no idea what her mother's married name might be…if she was in fact married, and Mary supposed she was.

One day in July Mary called the Diocese of Providence, and discovered that the adoption records were now open. They put her in touch with a woman from records, named Leona. She told Mary to call back the following day, and she would have the adoption record ready to read to her. "You can't take the records out of the office" she explained. Mary's boss, a considerate, caring man, named Bob told her to use the phone. He put a pad, and pen in front of her, and told her to take as long as she needed.

Mary's mother's name was Nancy. (No last names were given). Her mother's name was Ruth. Her mother was English, and her father was Italian. Nancy's father's name was Andrew. His Father was Scottish, and his mother was Irish. They had four other children besides Nancy. The three sons were Andrew, Joe, and Charles (Norman). Nancy had a little sister, named Ruth (Robyn). At the time that Nancy was pregnant with Mary she was going on sixteen, her older brothers were 21, 19, and 17. Robyn was only 4. Nancy's father had been suffering from congestive heart failure since the previous summer. During that time Nancy was going with a young man, named Kenneth. He was employed at the jewelry factory in Attleboro where her father and one of her brothers worked. Her father was the plant manager. Kenneth was a quiet man, four years older then Nancy. He lived near her home in Cranston. He was tall, slim, and had black hair, and brown eyes. He was French. Nancy was short with light brown hair, brown eyes and a slight build. She liked people, music, dancing, and sewing. She didn't like school very much.

The nurse who took care of Nancy's father was a close friend of her mother. When he showed signs of recovering he returned to work, only to die on the job late in February of 1961. Nancy, who had been pregnant since late August, had somehow managed to conceal her growing stomach from everyone. Two weeks after her father's death she told her mother about her pregnancy. Together with the nurse who was Ruth's friend, they went to the diocese to fill out an adoption application. Kenneth was no longer in the picture, and Ruth wouldn't let Nancy keep her baby. In the office Nancy and the nurse did most of the talking. Ruth had little to say, and was leaning on her friend to get her through this difficult time. The nurse took Nancy in until Mary was born. It had been estimated by the doctor that Mary wouldn't be born until May. However, Mary came in to the world on April 21st.

Nancy was urged not to hold her baby after she was born, since she couldn't keep her. But Nancy insisted on doing so. She expressed concern about the marks on Mary's forehead which had been caused by the doctor's forceps. "It's just homeostasis" explained a nurse. Nancy held her baby as she accompanied her mother and the nurse to Saint Vincent's infant home. She was the one to hand her baby over to the waiting nun, Sister Jane Frances, who was in charge of all new arrivals.

After a few weeks Mary was placed with the babies outside of the isolation wing. When she was Four months old it was discovered that she had poor vision. It was decided that she would be put back with Sister Jane for some individual attention. Somehow during this time Nancy was able to visit Mary at Saint Vincent's. It wasn't known how many times she did this. It was clear however that Nancy cared about Mary and wasn't enthused about giving her up.

In order to ensure that Mary would find a good home, an article, and a photo of her with Sister Jane were placed in the newspaper. She was referred to as Baby Joanne. Apparently the article received sixteen responses! Many couples were interviewed. Among the applicants were a middle aged couple; who were financially secure, and had no other children. They claimed that they wanted to adopt on religious principles. The other couples wanted to take Mary on a trial basis. The older couple wanted to adopt immediately. This couple turned out to be Mr. and Mrs. Sullivan.

Her father had once read an obituary about her Grandfather to her shortly before he died. Mary had tried to locate the obituary, but because she thought her Grandfather's first name was Joseph instead of Andrew, and assumed the last name her father had also given her was Read. Now she went on the microfilm, and found what she was looking for. In 1961 Andrew Reed (Read) died suddenly at the factory where he worked. The names of his wife and children all matched what was in the adoption records. She even found the name of the street in Cranston where they had lived. Unfortunately a freeway was put through part of it a few years after she was born. Mary found this last bit of news on the computer, not the micro film.

Early in August Mary got up the courage to call her oldest uncle, who lived in Warwick. Assuming that her mother was married, and might not want the family to know about Mary, she quickly concocted a plan. She called Andrew Reed JR and claimed to be an old friend of Nancy's from school. She wanted to put together a reunion, and needed Nancy's number. To her complete shock, and dismay, her uncle informed her that Nancy died of a heart attack back in 2004. "Like her father?" asked Mary "Exactly "confirmed Andrew Reed. Mary was so baffled, and deflated that she simply said Goodbye, and hung up. The next day she sent a letter to the Reed residence requesting a picture of Nancy. She received no response. She felt angry, and confused. Finally her friend Frances offered to call the Reeds, and explain Mary's situation to them. Mary was grateful for the offer, and eagerly accepted. She supposed that this was one of Frances's ways of trying to make amends for stealing in the past.

The following evening Frances called Mary and told her to call the Reeds again. "You must call them Mary. They want to talk to you!" she excitedly announced. Mary took a deep breath, and dialed the number. A woman answered. She said her name was Ann. Mary apologized for the deception, and proceeded to tell Ann everything she had learned from the adoption records. As she spoke, Ann responded with "Yes" to all of it, sounding more, and more convinced. Finally she told Mary that she was her Aunt. She had married Mary's Uncle back in of 1960. "Your mother didn't attend the wedding. She chose to stay at the hospital with her father, who was recovering from a heart attack" explained Aunt Ann. Apparently Ann and Nancy were pretty close because she later told her about having a baby girl with eye sight problems, who she was made to give up. Ann was a friendly, open sort of person, but she was very trust worthy, and was good at keeping secrets. When Mary's Uncle Andy was brought to the phone he was baffled. This was the first he had heard about Mary's secret birth. He was a little hurt that Ann had concealed it even from him! But as far as Ann was concerned, a secret was a secret. Once over the initial hurt, Andy began to talk openly with his new niece. He talked about his Grandfather, Andrew SR, who was born in Scotland. He married a young woman, named Bridget O'Malley, whose family was from Boston, Massachusetts. Her family was against her marrying a Scots man, but they eventually forgave her for it. Andrew and Bridget had six children. Andrew JR married Ruth Fontanne. Her mother's maiden name was Lee. She was supposed to have been distantly related to the Lees of Virginia. Her husband was Benjamin Fontanne. Together they had seven children. Ruth was one of the middle ones. After having five children with Andrew JR (The first was still born) he was called up to fight in World War Two. However it was early February of 1945. So he didn't see much fighting. He was stationed in the Philippines. He was a cook in the army. After the war Andrew eventually got a job as a plant manager at a jewelry factory. He was well liked by everyone. Outside of work he coached little league, belonged to several clubs, and enjoyed ball room dancing. Although he believed in rules, and discipline, he was the favorite of the two parents. He doted on Nancy, and later her little sister, Robyn. Ruth on the other hand, was a good house keeper, but she was somewhat domineering, and could be rather unpleasant at times. In later years she became eccentric. She used to put powder on the floor so that she could measure the foot prints. Since she knew the shoe sizes of all her family, she could tell if they were bringing other people in to the house. Ruth didn't welcome company as a rule.

Nancy and her older brothers grew up in Providence, right across the street from the Catholic school they attended. A year after Robyn was born the family moved to Cranston. They moved in to a house that was owned by Andrew's parents. They were dead. Both of them suffered from diabetes.

Uncle Andy remembered Kenneth, Mary's father as a timid, quiet man, who used to sneak around corners when visiting Nancy because he was afraid of her mother. He lived near the Reeds in a big house with four other siblings. No one knew what happened to his father, but his mother was a nice woman. Uncle Andy was rarely around at the time. He was in the army in the late fifties. He was stationed in Germany. He never met Elvis Presley, who served at the same time, but he did get to deploy him back to the United States. He said that he heard that Elvis was well liked by the other men.

After Mary told her aunt and uncle a little about her upbringing they arranged a date to come to her apartment for supper. Mary decided that Frances should be there too, seeing as how she had made it all possible.

On a Tuesday evening late in August her new relatives arrived. Leaving Frances in the kitchen, Mary ran to wait by the elevator. When the door slid open she saw a tall, rather heavy, middle aged man with grey hair, and a ruddy complexion. He walked with a cane. Mary remembered being told that he had suffered a stroke recently. Beside him was a slim woman a little over five feet. She had reddish, brown hair. A smaller woman with short, dark blonde hair, of about fifty accompanied them. As they followed Mary to her apartment, they introduced the small woman as Elaine. She was a cousin of Uncle Andy.

Mary had made spaghetti, and meat balls. She served Italian bread with it. She served sugar free Jello for dessert. This pleased Uncle Andy because he was a diabetic. "You better watch out" he told her. "Diabetes runs in our family. Not only did my father's parents have it, my mother, and one of my brothers has it too." Heart problems apparently ran in the family as well, but Diabetes was more predominant. As they ate, they reminisced about the past. This was the best way to learn more about her family Mary realized. All three of her uncles, and her aunt had children. Uncle Andy had six, Uncle Norman had three, Uncle Joe had four, and Aunt Robyn had three. Mary had sixteen cousins! Uncle Andy and Aunt Ann raised their brood in Warwick. Uncle Joe and his wife Beatrice raised their children in Providence. Uncle Norman and his wife, Sandy raised their three in Providence, and then moved out to Greenville. Aunt Robyn and her husband, Jim had lived out in Seekonk, Massachusetts with their three sons for years. Mary's mother, Nancy married a man named Joe Richitelli soon after Mary was born. Their first, a boy, was still born. Then they had four more children Joe JR, Steve, Cara, and Mark. They lived in Providence until the mid 70s. Then they moved to Warwick. Soon after this, Nancy and Joe got divorced. She went back to school, and got her G.E.D. She became a nursing assistant, working in several different nursing homes before eventually being promoted to office work in the nursing homes. Later she worked in a bank as a mortgage lender. Nancy was a smart woman, who had come a long way from the ninth grade drop out that she was at the time of Mary's birth. She could do anything she set her mind to. She sewed all her children's Halloween costumes every year. She loved interior decorating, and even taught herself how to use a computer. She enjoyed comedies, plays, and musicals. The Phantom of the opera was her favorite. She also loved to see the Nutcracker Suite every December. In spite of all her attributes, Nancy had a few faults. She tended to hold her anger in, and brood a lot. She avoided confrontations when it might have been better to face them, and she hated going to the doctor. As she got older her health declined. She had always been a heavy smoker, and her blood pressure, and cholesterol were out of control. Mary learned some things about her father that evening. He married a woman, who gave him six sons. Mary was amazed that she had one half sister, and nine half brothers! They lived out in West Warwick. The Reeds rarely saw them. They occasionally were in contact with one of Kenneth's brothers.

Three of Nancy's children were parents themselves. Cara had a one and a half year old daughter, named Lisa. Steve had a son nearly three named Steven (Stevie) he had two older step sons as well. Mark the youngest, had a son a little over a year. His name was Andrew. Joe, only two years younger then Mary was childless, and unmarried like she was. He had a girl friend though. Cara, Joe, and Mark looked like their father, a full blooded Italian. Steve on the other hand, looked like the Reed side of the family, like Mary did.

Ruth, Mary's Grandmother died in the early 200's, having out lived her husband by nearly forty years. She had been seeing a very good psychiatrist, who seemed to be helping her. He was impressed with how normal her children had turned out. Mary's uncles had laughed at this. "You don't know us Reeds. We can survive anything!"

Mary showed her company her photo albums. She was pleased with their surprised reactions as they looked at her baby, and childhood photos. They commented on her resemblance to various family members. She resembled her mother a lot. She was of the same height and build, their features were very similar, but Nancy's face had been longer then Mary's was.

When the visit was nearly over Aunt Ann looked at her husband, then asked Mary how she felt about meeting the rest of the family. Mary hadn't expected this. She thought she was lucky just to meet her oldest aunt and uncle, and their cousin. She said that she would love to meet everyone else. No definite date was given because they wanted to talk to Aunt Robyn first. She was going to college, and studying hard. When her work load slowed up a bit they would have a meeting with her.

After her company left Mary was so excited she didn't know what to do with herself. She paced the kitchen floor, talking animatedly to Frances about all that she had learned. Then she called Paul, who would soon be moving back to Hillcrest, and told him all about her evening. She felt bad that he hadn't felt well enough to visit that evening.

In September Paul moved back in to Hilltop. Mary was delighted that he was given an apartment directly across the hall from her! The new management was remodeling the building. One of the things they wanted to do was fill the first floor with tenants who had physical disabilities. Mary visited Paul, and Tom, who had lost his job, quite often. Paul had not regained his strength, and it looked as though he would always need his walker to get around.

In late October Uncle Andy and Aunt Ann picked up Mary, and brought her to their modest little home in Warwick. It had been decided that she would meet her aunt, and other uncles. Mary was nervous, but happy, and very curious. Uncle Joe was a short, slim man with grey hair, and a mustache, and beard. He welcomed Mary with a hug which surprised her. Uncle Norman was tall, of medium build. He was a quiet man with light grey hair, and a mustache. His wife, Aunt Sandy was short, with closely cropped white hair. She wore a Patriot sweatshirt, and claimed to be a big fan. Mary supposed that this made her a big fan of Uncle Norman. Most men would love to have a wife, who cares about the things they care about. Aunt Robyn was a little over five feet. She was only fifty. She looked a lot like Mary. Uncle Jim was a polite, good natured doctor, who liked to play tennis. He didn't stay long because he had a game scheduled for that afternoon. Uncle Norman gave Mary a list of who was who in the family. He had printed it from his computer. A huge plastic bin full of old photos was presented to Mary. She was allowed to select some of them. She was most fascinated with the pictures of her mother. Once again Mary gained knowledge by listening to everyone reminiscing about the past. She learned that her Grandfather was a likable, but stubborn man. After his heart attack, he was put in a medically induced coma to allow his heart to get strong again. When he came out of it he was told by his doctor that he could live a couple of years if he didn't return to work. Andrew, who had always been an independent, hard working man, was out raged! He argued with his doctor, and went back to work. This was his undoing. The family believed that if he had lived he would have let Mary's mother keep her. He, unlike his wife, didn't worry about what people thought. "He would have doted on you, like he doted on all little girls" Uncle Joe told Mary. This made Mary feel both bad, and good. She was glad that her Grandfather was like this, but she was angry that he died.

This information was added to the list of reasons she was angry at God. She was angry with him for not letting her mother live long enough to meet her, and she was angry at him for not making her friend, Paul better. How could a loving God allow Paul, a humble, Christian to suffer so? Despite her family's acceptance of her, Mary wasn't grateful toward God. She didn't credit Him with any of it! Indeed she no longer felt like a Christian. She lost that feeling over a year ago. Half the time she skipped church. When she did go, her heart wasn't in it anymore. She saw her mother's death as a slap in the face from God. Hadn't he taken enough from her over the years? Also there was the fact that though they had been trying, none of her siblings had given birth until after Nancy died, and she had wanted Grandchildren so badly!

Soon after the visit with her aunt, and uncles, Mary, and her older, but trendy, friend, Marie took a trip to Salem, Massachusetts. Mary's friend, Ralph accompanied them. Because she was angry at God, Mary delved in to the occult. She even visited a psychic fare, hoping to make Him just as angry as she was. When she returned home Paul was still growing weaker, but Tom had found a job in a factory out in West Warwick. He claimed to have met a girl in the bakery across from the factory. They were apparently dating, but so far, Paul and Mary hadn't met her.

In November Mary was taken over to her sister, Cara's house in Warwick. Cara was eight years younger then Mary. She was a little over five feet, and slim. She had straight black hair, and sometimes wore glasses. Her husband, Tony, a burly, likable man with wavy black hair, did all the cooking. Aunt Robyn and her brothers were there with their spouses. Mary's brothers, Mark and Joe were there also. Joe was a heavy set man with very short black hair. He was rather quiet, but friendly. Mark, the youngest was thin with a crew cut. He spent much of the time playing with his one year old son, Andrew. (Drew). Mary had been told not to expect Steve and his wife to be there. They were away for the weekend. The gathering at Cara's was a lot of fun. She met her little niece, and nephew. Though only two months apart in age, Lisa was considerably bigger then her cousin Drew. One and a half year old Lisa was extremely fond of her little cousin, who was rather shy.

Soon after this event Cara came to visit Mary. She brought along a DVD of Mark's wedding, which had occurred just two months before Nancy's death. Mary invited Paul over to watch it with them. She enjoyed watching the wedding. Mark married a pretty young woman with blonde hair, named Denyse. However, what interested Mary most was getting to not only see her mother at the wedding, then dancing with Mark, but getting to hear her talk a little during the reception. She congratulated Mark on his choice of a wife. Later at her table she spoke again, this time to urge them to have lots of babies.

Late in November Steve and his wife, Julie picked her up, and brought her to visit their home. Julie, a slim woman with short, straight, dark hair; cried when she first saw Mary because of the resemblance to Nancy, who had been close to Julie. At their home in Cumberland, Mary met Anthony, who was going on sixteen, Greg, who was ten and little Stevie, who was almost three. The two older boys returned to their rooms after the introductions. Stevie, who was very much a Daddy's boy, remained downstairs. As he climbed all over his father, and rough housed with him, Steve and Julie talked about what a great mother and woman Nancy had been. They showed Mary a photo album that contained pictures of their wedding back in the summer of 2003. Nancy was there with her boy friend. She was wearing a sleeveless, pink dress, and had dyed her shoulder length hair blonde.

Mary, who had been suffering from cataracts on top of the eye sight problem she was born with, under went cataract surgery in November. Right after this Uncle Norman and his wife, Sandy began inviting her out to dinner at a tavern near their home every Tuesday evening. Uncle Joe picked her up, and later brought her home. He in fact became a regular visitor to Paul's apartment every Saturday evening. Paul, assisted by Tom, would prepare supper. Afterward they watched a movie. Uncle Joe always left around nine because he bowled on Sundays, and had to get up early. Steve and sometimes Julie visited Paul on Saturday evenings frequently. They brought Stevie, and occasionally Anthony and Greg. Paul was very hospitable. Tom was too.

In December Paul, Tom, and Mary took part in a Christmas party down in the community room at Hillcrest. Karaoke was made available to everyone. In between songs Mary asked Tom about his girl friend. "Oh, I made that whole thing up "Tom abruptly replied. In the same exact instant Paul could be heard saying "Oh, he made that whole thing up" in just as an abrupt tone as Tom had used. Mary shook her head, and laughed. The three of them joined the church choir that had been formed just for the Christmas season. They all sang at the Christmas service. Nobody begrudged Paul's sitting while he sang. They knew he could barely stand, let alone walk unassisted.

In January Paul became very ill, and had to be hospitalized again. His liver and kidneys were rapidly losing their ability to function. Fred and Marge were with Tom and Mary at the hospital when the doctor announced that if Paul didn't go on dialysis immediately, he would die. Paul was in such a fog that he couldn't sign the consent forms. Fred had to do it. A catheter was placed in the upper part of his chest. He would be receiving the dialysis through this. Mary, who had never visited friends in the hospital regularly, was there for Paul almost every day. Because she knew he accepted her just as she was, she felt a bond between them both. This made going to the hospital a lot less of a chore then had been with her father! It was hard for Paul to remain in the hospital so long. Once or twice he spent a whole evening crying, yelling, and begging to be signed out. At one point Tom, who couldn't take it anymore, hollered at Paul, and threatened to stop visiting him if he continued to protest his confinement. Paul stared at Tom for a minute. Mary thought she could read his mind at that moment. Did Tom really mean it? Paul quieted right down after a minute or so. Along with Fred and Marge, Pastor John, and a few others, Mary's Uncle Joe and her Uncle Andy's wife, Aunt Ann visited Paul. When Paul had to recuperate at a nursing home in Warwick, she was there almost every day. She brought him sugar free candy, and talked with him for an hour or so. When he first arrived there, he was in such a fog that he couldn't even feed himself. Mary watched, as Aunt Ann picked up the fork, and proceeded to feed Paul. Mary was grateful to her. Aunt Ann liked Paul, not just because of his friendly disposition, but because she had had a brother, who was on dialysis. Paul grew to like her as much as she liked him.

Early in March Paul was finally allowed to go home. Uncle Andy and Aunt Ann drove him back to Hilltop where he found a surprise waiting for him. Mary had made a poster of Mr. Ed, the talking horse. On it she wrote WELCOME HOME, BUDDY! Paul loved it. This was one of his favorite TV shows.

Throughout the spring Uncle Joe, and sometimes Steve and Julie continued to visit Paul, Tom, and Mary. In January Cara had given Mary a computer. Mary was trying to learn all she could about it. Her siblings were very skilled with the computer, and she wanted to catch up with them. Often on Saturday evenings Uncle Joe or Steve would accompany her to her apartment to teach her what they knew. It was a slow process, especially since Mary was usually somewhat intoxicated. Paul accepted the half hour interruption, but Tom was not so tolerant. He complained, and accused Mary and her brother of being rude, and ignorant. Mary tried to apologize to Steve for Tom's attitude, but Steve didn't seem bothered by it.

In April Paul played music at a birthday party for everyone who had a birthday in that month. Steve was included in this. Paul's two friends from River edge came as well. They were middle aged twin sisters, who relied on scooters like Paul. They were Cheryl and Betsy. Cheryl was more out going, and was very fond of Paul. Mary also went out to dinner with Pauline and Joan like she always did for her birthday. She went to Cara's house for Lisa's second birthday party. Her birthday was the day after Mary's. Then the family threw a surprise party for her at the tavern near Uncle Norman's house. Mary truly felt like one of the family. It was a shame that Cara, Joe, and Mark weren't there though. Steve, Julie, and their sons came, and had fun with everyone.

On Mother's Day Steve, Julie, and Stevie came to get Mary. The older boys were with their father for the day. After looking for a beach house that they hoped to rent in July, they went out to dinner. Mary had a great time! Then when she got home she discovered that Paul had been rushed to the hospital again. It was a sad ending to a fun filled day. This time Paul was placed in a hospital room by himself. A sign was hung on the door. It said ISOLATION ROOM. Anyone who entered had to wear a gown, mask, and gloves, whether they were a visitor, or a hospital employee. Paul had somehow picked up a nasty, contagious infection. It was believed to have started because of the catheter he wore. The doctor wanted to have Paul receive a needle for the dialysis, but his veins weren't strong enough. After a couple of weeks in the hospital he was transferred to a nursing home for physical therapy. Mary and Tom visited him regularly. Paul wasn't looking good. His skin had a yellowish hue to it, and he was losing a lot of weight. Because only ten percent of his liver still functioned, his stomach became filled with fluid, which had to be pumped out every week. They took out as much as five gallons. Immediately afterward Paul felt better, and could eat a decent sized meal. Yet all too soon the fluid came back. He was told to avoid salt, but this did little to keep the fluid away. With the weight loss, he was also losing more of his strength. Mary now knew that he wouldn't be well in time to participate in the church's talent show which was scheduled for the end of May. She was very disappointed because they had been planning to sing a duet together. Now she would only be doing her solo. Paul had been planning a solo as well.

Steve, Julie, Stevie, and Uncle Joe came to Talent Night. Mary, who was a little intoxicated, sang a song by Taylor Swift. She dedicated it to Paul because he couldn't be there. A lot of people from the church participated. There was even a hot dog eating contest. Pastor John, Mary's friend, Joe, and a few others took part in this. The amorous young man, who used to touch women inappropriately at Paul's parties won.

By the end of June Paul was back home. Normally he was committed to his dialysis treatments. But he foolishly decided to skip dialysis on July 4th to go to a cook out. Mary had tried to talk him out of it, even getting Julie to talk to him, but his mind was made up.

By August Paul was so weak he needed Tom, who was once again unemployed, to help him out of bed, or his recliner, and in to his scooter. He could no longer walk unassisted on a walker. Mary often came over to help Tom when she was finished with work for the day. Tom was becoming bitter. He hated being out of work. He resented having to take care of Paul constantly. Sometimes Mary heard him yelling at Paul for not going in to an assisted living program. He took his anger out on Mary and her friend, Ralph, who often stopped by. One night Tom screamed at him for coming over just to eat. This wasn't true, but Tom was too angry to listen. Poor Ralph screamed "I'M SORRY, OKAY?" Mary was afraid of Tom when he acted like this. Later she found Ralph, and comforted him.

One day Paul fell off the toilet. Tom called Mary over to help get him off the floor. Paul was wearing diapers by now. He needed to be cleaned up. The next morning the visiting nurse couldn't wake Paul. He was rushed back to the hospital. He had gone in to a coma, but came out of it hours later. They kept him there because he had another infection, one that was so rare, there had only been one other case like it in RI. He was once again placed in an isolation room. Everyone had to wear gowns and gloves when they were in his room. Paul was very discouraged by this time. He had taken to using foul language, and questioning his faith. Mary found that she couldn't blame him. A nurse was made to sit by his bed to prevent him from pulling out the tubes that were in his arms. He begged Tom and Mary to sign him out. He said he just wanted to go home, and die. The hospital couldn't allow him to do this because his infection was so contagious.

Mary's Uncle Andy and Aunt Ann moved to Florida in September. She called them to tell them about Paul. She had a hard time holding back her tears, as she heard their sympathetic responses. Uncle Joe hadn't been around for a while. Once the summer arrived he spent as much time as possible outside. Steve and Julie asked about Paul regularly. Cara expressed her sympathy for Paul, and Mary, who she knew would miss him.

By the middle of September Paul had to breathe through a hose that went down in to his throat. They kept him sedated most of the time. One day the nurse, who usually took care of Paul, asked Mary if he was a drinker. "No, why?" she asked, puzzled. "Because his asophacas is completely rotted through" Shocked, Mary pointed at the shrunken, yellowish, form on the bed. "That man doesn't drink!" she said emphatically. "Tom and I are the drinkers, not Paul". The nurse couldn't understand the state of Paul's body, neither could Mary.

When Mary wasn't visiting Paul, she was working. She was having a difficult time at work. Bob, the well liked boss had retired a year earlier. He was replaced by a tall middle aged woman named Megan. She was very strict. She was friendly to some extent, but she clearly put rules ahead of people's needs. Everyone in the department tried to adjust to having her as their new boss. Sometimes she hollered at people unjustly, and sent them home for minor offenses. One of the workers, a tall man named Donald, who had a mild case of aspergers syndrome, developed a real dislike for the boss. He chose to show it by provoking Mary. He did this by constantly scraping his chair when ever he got up. He knew how much this noise got on her nerves. They engaged in petty games of Tit for Tat. This along with a religious fanatic, who joined the department in August, made life at work almost unbearable for Mary. She was already struggling with her growing anger toward God for taking people away from her. She had recently lost a friend from her department back in April. He was a likable, funny man named David. He died in his sleep one night. Between confused, angry thoughts about God, (she didn't realize at the time what a toll her nightly drinking was having on her over all well being), Donald's chair scraping, and Joy's talk of hell fire, Mary just couldn't cope. Every day she found it harder to contain her emotions.

Tom knew that Paul wasn't going to make it. He began empting out his friend's apartment. He gave away Paul's compact discs and videos. He sold some of the DVDs, but allowed Mary and her friends to have some of them as well. He threw out bags of things that belonged to

Paul. This caused people in the high rise to criticize him, and talk about him behind his back, because Paul, though gravely ill, wasn't dead yet.

Tom wasn't as callous as people thought he was. At the hospital he sometimes burst in to loud sobs, as he told Mary that he had been with Paul for thirty five years, and didn't know what he was going to do without him. He truly felt lost, and scared. Mary felt the same way, but to a lesser degree because she had only known Paul for six years, and had other people to turn to.

On the twenty fifth of September of 2008 Tom told Paul's doctor to go ahead, and pull the plug on the respirator. Paul died two hours later, released from his pain ridden, malfunctioning body. He had managed to live just four days after his sixty third birthday.

Mary was at work, quite unaware that her friend had just died. She was sneering at Joy, the boisterous, prideful, Born Again Christian. Tom met her down town, and gave her the news. She wasn't surprised, but she felt both sad, and angry.

At the start of summer Mary had made contact with Dr. Pat, the psychiatrist who saw her when she was at Bradley Hospital. They emailed each other regularly now. Mary had thought of this doctor a lot over the years, but it wasn't until she began writing about her past that she felt a desire to look her up.

The Saturday following Paul's death Mary and Dr. Pat went out to breakfast together. They talked about their pasts as they ate. Dr. Pat remembered Mary's mother, and had always believed that the woman was unfit to be a parent. Mary appreciated hearing this. Although she had emailed pictures of her siblings, uncles, and aunts, she told Dr. Pat more about them. Dr. Pat, a small, soft spoken, Asian woman was now in her seventies, but she could have passed for sixty. Her face had few lines, her hair was still black, and she dressed with style. She was married to a Jewish writer who did a lot for the community. He was a warm hearted, friendly man. They had raised two boys and a girl. Unfortunately one of their sons had died back in the spring. Dr. Pat still cried when she spoke of him.

Mary returned to counseling in an attempt to pull herself together. Alas it wasn't soon enough to save her job. In December she was fired over an altercation with the instigating Donald. She didn't feel much regret about leaving the place. She had been planning to quit and take a computer course anyway. However, she took the argument with Donald to be a sign that she really was out of control. A few weeks later Mary gave up drinking. She had been warned continually about this, by her doctor. Then she had a long talk with her favorite pastor. He was able to convince her that God really did care about how she felt. He addressed her anger about people who hurt others, herself included. "In the end nobody gets away with anything" After their talk she began to feel some inner peace, and returned to church on a regular basis. The anger she felt toward God diminished as she talked to her counselor and her bible study teacher. She now knew that half the battle had been getting free of the alcohol. She was certain that with time, the rest would sort itself out. She had a lot to be hopeful about.

About the author

Susan Kelly lives in Providence, RI. She is visually impaired. She enjoys writing, drawing, and learning about the computer. Currently out of work, she pursues her hobbies, attends counseling, and participates in the Baptist church, where she is a member, and is involved in the lives of her siblings, an aunt, three uncles, and many cousins. Sue hopes to work with computers soon. After all, it's never too late to learn something new.